REVOLUTION WITHIN THE REVOLUTION

ENVISIONING CUBA

LOUIS A. PÉREZ JR., EDITOR

Envisioning Cuba publishes outstanding, innovative works in Cuban studies, drawn from diverse subjects and disciplines in the humanities and social sciences, from the colonial period through the post–Cold War era. Featuring innovative scholarship engaged with theoretical approaches and interpretive frameworks informed by social, cultural, and intellectual perspectives, the series highlights the exploration of historical and cultural circumstances and conditions related to the development of Cuban self-definition and national identity.

REVOLUTION
WITHIN THE **REVOLUTION**

Women and Gender Politics in Cuba, 1952–1962

MICHELLE CHASE

The University of North Carolina Press | Chapel Hill

This book was published with the assistance of the Anniversary Fund of the University of North Carolina Press.

Set in Utopia and Univers
by Westchester Publishing Services
Manufactured in the United States of America

Chapter 3 appeared previously in somewhat different form as Michelle Chase, "Women's Organizations and the Politics of Gender in Cuba's Urban Insurrection (1952–58)," *Bulletin of Latin American Research* 29, no. 4 (October 2010): 440–58.

The paper in this book meets the guidelines for permanence and durability of the Committee on Production Guidelines for Book Longevity of the Council on Library Resources.

The University of North Carolina Press has been a member of the Green Press Initiative since 2003.

Cover illustration: Deena Stryker, "Presidential Grandstand, Military Parade" (ca. 1963), Deena Stryker Photographs, Archive of Documentary Arts, Duke University

Library of Congress Cataloging-in-Publication Data
Chase, Michelle, author.
  Revolution within the revolution : women and gender politics in Cuba, 1952–1962 / Michelle Chase.
      pages cm.—(Envisioning Cuba)
   ISBN 978-1-4696-2500-3 (pbk : alk. paper)—ISBN 978-1-4696-2501-0 (ebook)
1. Women—Cuba—History—20th century.   2. Cuba—History—Revolution, 1959—Participation, Female.   3. Women—Cuba—Social conditions—20th century.   4. Women's rights—Cuba.   I. Title.   II. Series: Envisioning Cuba.
   HQ1507.C43 2015
   305.42097291—dc23
                                                                    2015010505

For Vinod, Rishi, and Rohan

CONTENTS

ILLUSTRATIONS

ACKNOWLEDGMENTS

This book has been many years in the making and has led me to incur many debts in the process. At New York University, where this project began its life, I was lucky to work with a group of truly generous and engaging faculty. I am especially grateful to Ada Ferrer, whose passion for Cuban history is infectious and whose professional guidance is extraordinary. Greg Grandin's seminar on revolution and counterrevolution raised the initial questions that eventually led me to write this book. Sinclair Thomson, Barbara Weinstein, and Linda Gordon provided invaluable feedback that greatly enriched this project through their multiple careful readings of early drafts of the manuscript.

I have benefited from the support of various institutions for the research and writing of this book. New York University supported me with multiple internal grants and fellowships over the years, including the MacCracken Fellowship and the Warren Dean Memorial Fellowship. I am grateful for the writing fellowship provided by the American Association of University Women and a library research grant provided by the Friends of the Princeton Library. The Instituto de Historia de Cuba provided invaluable institutional backing, which made island research possible. The New York Public Library's Wertheim Study provided a quiet place to read and write and gave me access to the library's unparalleled collections. I would also like to acknowledge the very professional archival staff at the Cuban Heritage Collection at the University of Miami, the National Archives and Records Administration in Washington, D.C., and the Smathers Library at the University of Florida, Gainesville. I am also particularly grateful to Series Editor Louis Pérez Jr. and Senior Executive Editor Elaine Maisner at the University of North Carolina Press for their professional guidance and their enthusiasm for the project.

A large number of friends and colleagues provided insightful feedback on portions of the manuscript. For their companionship and encouragement as well as their scholarly insight, I thank Jennifer Adair, Devyn Spence Benson, Joaquín Chávez, Marcela Echeverri, Anne Eller, Anasa Hicks, Tristan Kirvin, Aldo Marchesi, Yuko Miki, Rachel Price, Sarah Sarzynsky, Rainer Schultz, Ernesto Semán, Carmen Solíz, Federico Sor, Cristina Soriano, Franny

Sullivan, and Tamara Walker. Sam Farber deserves particular thanks for contributing to this project with both his scholarly acumen and his detailed personal memories. Similarly, Gladys Marel García has shown great commitment to this project both as interviewee and as mentor. I would also like to thank several of the masters' students who took the seminar on the Cuban Revolution I taught at NYU and who influenced my thinking on Cuba greatly, especially Yesenia Selier, Kate Bedecarré, and Roque Planas. Others who have contributed to this project directly or indirectly, by sharing documents, giving professional advice, or simply providing encouragement, include Laura Isabel Serna, Sarah Teitler, Monica Campbell, Danny Schechter, Albert Manke, Ilan Erlich, Matilde Zimmermann, Lexi Baldacci, and Jean Weissman.

I am indebted to Bloomfield College for the collegial atmosphere in which this book took its final shape. In particular I would like to thank Laura Warren Hill, for her exemplary passion for both teaching and scholarship, and Danilo Figueredo, for always being willing to talk about Cuba. I would also like to thank my colleagues in the Humanities Division and beyond who make Bloomfield College such a warm and supportive community, especially Yuichiro Nishizawa, Ada McKenzie, Martha LaBare, Angela Conrad, Paul Puccio, Brandon Fralix, and Paula Craig.

In Havana, I am eternally grateful to the many people who made me feel welcome in that luminous, decaying city, especially Virgen and Octavio, Cachita and her family, Sidiam and her family, and Nilka and her neighbors. I am also particularly grateful to the many Cubans who shared their life stories with me; to several young historians, especially Maikel Fariñas and Ricardo Quiza, for their warmth and professional advice; and finally, to the late Emilio Hernández, who seemed to subsist entirely on coffee, cigarettes, and long conversations about Cuban cultural history. Havana is a lesser place without him.

Last but not least, my family has provided a seemingly infinite amount of encouragement, patience, and support through these long years of research and writing. Vinod Menon has endured many early mornings, a few late nights, and various bouts of crankiness. No one will be gladder than he to finally see this book in print. Rishi and Rohan Menon arrived as this book was in its final stages, bringing much joy, and always reminding me of what is truly important.

ABBREVIATIONS AND ACRONYMS

CDR   Committee for the Defense of the Revolution (Comité para la Defensa de la Revolución)

CIA   Central Intelligence Agency

DR   Revolutionary Directorate (Directorio Revolucionario)

FCMM   José Martí Women's Civic Front (Frente Cívico de Mujeres Martianas)

FDMC   Democratic Federation of Cuban Women (Federación Democrática de Mujeres Cubanas)

FEU   Federation of University Students (Federación Estudiantíl Universitaria)

FMC   Federation of Cuban Women (Federación de Mujeres Cubanas)

MOU   Opposition Women United (Mujeres Oposicionistas Unidas)

MRC   Civic Resistance Movement (Movimiento de Resistencia Cívica)

PSP   Communist Party (Partido Socialista Popular)

UFR   Revolutionary Women's Unity (Unidad Femenina Revolucionaria)

USIA   United States Information Agency

WIDF   Women's International Democratic Federation

REVOLUTION WITHIN THE REVOLUTION

INTRODUCTION

On January 1, 1959, events in a small Caribbean nation captured international headlines. The ragtag revolutionary forces that had been engaged in a guerrilla war to oust a strongman named Fulgencio Batista had suddenly triumphed. The leader of these rebels was Fidel Castro, a man scarcely over thirty, who promised to implement true democracy and social justice. Within four years, this unexpected revolution had embraced socialism and the Soviet Union, confronted and defeated a U.S.-backed invasion, stood at the brink of nuclear war, and seen some 10 percent of its population—including an enormous proportion of its professionals—decamp for exile. The fact that these massive changes took place on an island that was once best known as America's sugar bowl, and which was fast becoming the vacation playground of the American middle class, was even more astounding.

Still, the revolution was most astonishing not for its radical redistribution of wealth and resources, its abolition of most forms of private property, or its successful confrontation with the empire at its very doorstep. Its deepest ambition went further: to completely reform the individual. Thus the Cuban Revolution promised nothing less than the reinvention of humankind. The revolutionary leadership envisioned the creation of a "new man," one tirelessly dedicated to the collective rather than driven by individual self-interest. Less explicitly stated, the revolution also intended to create new women, and here again its ambitions were immense: to transform society to such an extent that women would be liberated from oppression, exclusion, and prejudice. In less than a decade, the revolutionary leaders pronounced these enormous goals accomplished. As Fidel Castro announced triumphantly, women's emancipation was a "revolution within the revolution."[1]

This book tells a different, more complicated story about that process. It asks how women themselves participated in the revolution, what impact their participation had, and how gender relations were challenged—or not—by one of the twentieth century's most radical social experiments. Rather than viewing women as the passive beneficiaries of the revolution, mobilized and liberated by an enlightened leadership, this book argues that women were crucial actors in the revolutionary process. Women did not necessarily drive the revolution forward by imposing a more radical vision on the revolutionary leadership, although in some cases this did happen; more often they contributed in myriad ways to the conditions under which a certain revolutionary vision congealed and spread. By mobilizing and protesting, by mourning and denouncing, by joining revolutionary or counterrevolutionary groups, even by decamping for exile, women changed the course of the revolutionary process.

This book focuses on women, but in doing so it also sheds light on men's political participation. It illuminates distinctions in how men and women conceptualized their own political roles and how each was incorporated into the revolutionary project. While it argues that women played a major role in the revolution, it also explores the way certain celebrated men came to embody it. More broadly, this book explores how ideas about gender—that is, the hierarchies that govern relations between women and men and bind institutions such as the family and marriage—propelled the political process. It suggests that the insurrection was driven not merely by anger over the usurpation of formal democracy but also by images of state infringement upon the sanctity of the family and by dominant notions of masculinity and femininity. Likewise, it shows that the conflict sparked by revolutionary victory after 1959 not only was a struggle over property rights, political democracy, or international relations; it also tested and redefined constructions of femininity and masculinity, of motherhood and childhood, of marriage and the family.

Placing women and gender at the center of the story opens new windows onto the revolution and tempers the seductive nature of the "official" narrative. That familiar narrative, transmitted through the Cuban media and echoed abroad, views the revolution through the prism of the rise of Fidel Castro and his cohort, from their stunningly bold 1953 attack on the Moncada military barracks, to the formation of a rebel army in the Sierra Maestra, and finally to their triumph over Batista's army.[2] This theater of war was predominantly a man's world, as was the inner circle of revolutionary leadership that emerged after the 1959 triumph.[3] But if we shift our gaze away from the histories of individual leaders and the main revolutionary organizations, and if we move from the mountains of Oriente Province to the streets of Havana, different patterns emerge. This book recovers those untold stories.

Toward a Gendered History of the Cuban Revolution

Revolutions are those few times in human history when it seems that anything is possible. For a brief, stunning moment, the world can be made anew. The ability of human action to turn the tide of history is confirmed. Traditions that had seemed as fixed as the landscape are suddenly swept away. When the Cuban Revolution came to power on January 1, 1959, its many supporters sensed they were witnessing a moment of historic proportions. As one Cuban wrote rapturously: "We are living . . . the upsurge of a new Cuba, such as was dreamed by our eminent philosopher José Martí. . . . We are witnessing the rebirth of a Cuba worthy of its people and of its glorious destiny, facing its future fearlessly."[4] The upheavals of the next few years soon marked the Cuban Revolution as one of the most radical social experiments of the twentieth century. Its impact quickly radiated outward, prompting the ill-fated 1961 Bay of Pigs invasion and then nearly bringing the two Cold War superpowers to nuclear war in 1962. It served as inspiration, safe haven, and training ground for the insurgent groups that arose throughout Latin America in its wake. Globally, the revolution also inspired an entire generation, helping give rise to a New Left that sought to emulate and defend Cuba's triumph.

This unexpected revolution also sparked a flood of international scholarship on Cuba and, indeed, on the whole region.[5] Beginning in the early 1970s, the first wave of nuanced academic studies offered serious assessments of Cuba's deep social, political, and cultural changes and the functioning of its new centralized state.[6] The 1970s also saw the rise of feminist scholarship in the American academy. For feminists seeking to challenge entrenched inequality and patriarchy, Cuba provided a seductive alternative. While the revolution preceded the rise of global second-wave feminism by a decade, it seemed to have achieved—and even surpassed—many feminists' goals. Cuban socialism appeared to have established full social equality. And although for years the Federation of Cuban Women—founded in 1960—had resolutely denounced feminism as bourgeois, by the mid-1970s it was softening its antifeminist rhetoric somewhat.[7] In 1974 the influential book *Cuban Women Now*, published by the American activist Margaret Randall, who resided on the island, conveyed an inspiring image of Cuban women swept up in the revolution's efforts to construct a new society. The following year, a new Family Code mandated equality between men and women within marriage and in divorce, going so far as to decree that even housework must be shouldered equally. Dazzled by the revolution's audacity, an early generation of feminist researchers from outside Cuba often implicitly endorsed the official narrative of women's liberation in Cuba. While duly critical of the persistence of a gendered division of labor and other entrenched forms of gender inequality, for the most part they balanced their criticism with optimism.[8]

But over the past several decades, a new consensus has been taking shape, far less celebratory, far more critical. Several factors contributed to this shift. The collapse of the Soviet Union in 1989 spurred critiques of the grand narratives offered by Marxism and raised sharper questions about the ability of socialist states to alleviate historical grievances surrounding race and gender. The fall of the Soviet Union also left Cuba in dire financial straits. In the difficult period that followed, social inequalities resurfaced, creating skepticism about the revolution's legacy.[9] And slightly relaxed state control over scholarship, prompted by the crisis of the 1990s and then accelerated by new trends in communications in the 2000s, has facilitated the elaboration of subtle historical reinterpretations published by island scholars as well as more openly critical fictional accounts by novelists.[10]

In the American academy, scholars turned away from models that emphasized women as fixed historical subjects and toward studies that saw gender relations as broadly constitutive of power.[11] By the mid-1990s, younger scholars had begun to rephrase old questions. They shifted their focus from assessing the Cuban Revolution's impact on women or on gender inequality—as measured by statistics indicating women's integration into the workforce, levels of education, or maternal mortality rates—to asking more broadly how gender ideals were reconstituted by the revolution.[12] Particularly in sociology, anthropology, and literature, scholars began to examine the ways patriarchy was reconstituted after 1959 by studying the discourse of the Cuban leadership, the way state discourse was engaged by authors and intellectuals, and the way state policy was experienced in daily life.[13]

At roughly the same time, new research emerged on women and revolution that put Cuba in a broader regional perspective. Scholarship on the revolutionary movements in Central America and elsewhere noted the prevalence of women in guerrilla warfare and the subsequent development of "revolutionary feminism" among those former insurgents.[14] From this vantage point, Cuba seemed to be lacking. A more authentic and autonomous revolutionary feminism had been precluded, some scholars argued, by socialism's economic redistribution—that is, by the resolution of the daily burdens that helped prompt feminist critique elsewhere. Autonomous expressions of feminism were discouraged by the revolutionary state's centralized decision-making power and by the large state-run Federation of Cuban Women, which brooked no competition.[15]

Despite the evolution of scholarship over the years, a more grassroots perspective on the role of women and transformations to gender in the Cuban Revolution has remained elusive. It has proved easier to critique state discourse and policy than to uncover women's active agency in these historical processes.[16] While we have insightful studies of the leadership, of diplomatic relations, and of "high politics" on the one hand, and nuanced studies of gender and everyday life in the postrevolutionary period on the other, no existing account yet offers a fine-grained historical analysis of the Cuban insurrection and revolution that focuses on women, gender, masculinity, or sexuality. A reassessment of the insurrection and the earliest years of the revolution is crucial: the period is slowly fading from living memory but has not yet been illuminated by detailed historical scholarship. Important questions remain. To what extent did women participate in the anti-Batista movement? How did the "woman question" first emerge and then evolve toward a deeper notion of women's liberation? To what extent were relations within the private sphere, such as marriage, sexuality, and the family, transformed? How much were they credited for?

This book broaches those questions by providing a narrative social history that centers women and the politics of gender. It draws from recent approaches of both women's and gender history, which I see as complementary, not antithetical or contradictory. That is, while I am invested in recovering histories of women as agents, I hope to avoid a heroic, teleological reinsertion of women into the historical narrative.[17] I also want to interrogate the ways both femininity and masculinity were constructed by historical actors. As various historians have argued, it is important to treat "men as well as women as gendered historical subjects," and to show how masculinity and femininity were configured in relation to one another.[18] This study is also mindful of the fact that gender is implicated in other categories of social difference, particularly race and class. As the historian Kathleen Brown has argued, class, race, and gender are "categories produced by relationships rather than things in themselves."[19] This book thus explores the linked histories of gender, race, and class in the Cuban Revolution.

In its social history approach, this study adheres to methods established long ago in Latin American historiography, but which have barely penetrated the vast literature on Cuba. Most accounts of the revolution, whether penned by supporters or detractors, focus overwhelmingly on leaders such as Fidel Castro and Che Guevara, reflecting a shared view of "great men" as the motors of history.[20] Echoing the intense focus on the Castro brothers and Che Guevara found in policy circles and the mass media, this paradigm has established a lasting framework of interpretation that distills the broad and complex forces of a social revolution into the figure of one man.[21] This study provides a different approach, excavating the many other forgotten actors who shaped the Cuban Revolution. It does so partly through its choice of period. Rather than focusing on Cuba's consolidated socialism after 1962, it examines the messy phase in between, as one order was dismantled and another erected in its place, a period I have broadly construed here as the "revolutionary moment." This period provided a tumultuous political opening in which many voices were raised and contested. Going back to its origins reminds us that the revolution was never simply synonymous with its leadership. Or, as historian Lillian Guerra notes, "1959 gave birth to many revolutions."[22]

THIS BOOK ADVANCES several arguments that challenge our understanding of the Cuban Revolution in fundamental ways. First, it shows that, contrary to popular assumptions, women participated in great numbers in the mass movement to oust Batista in the late 1950s, especially in the urban centers. Whether collaborating with the urban underground, joining one of a handful of all-women's opposition groups, or staging mass public demonstrations, many urban women participated *as women*, often mobilizing under notions of maternalism or moral authority. Focusing on women also gives us a glimpse into the broader world of the urban insurrection, nearly always overshadowed by the popular romance with the rebel army. Here we find that the women and men who joined that revolutionary movement came from many walks of life—young and old, longtime militants and political novices, Catholics and Marxists, people of all social strata. By restoring these forgotten actors to the frame, this book reveals that the Cuban revolutionary process was broader in social composition and political ideology than official discourse and much previous scholarship have recognized. But the increasing focus on the rebel army and the romantic figure of the guerrilla after 1959 narrowed the way "revolutionary" was defined, and the urban women and others who did not fit this new revolutionary ideal were obscured in both history and memory.

Most importantly, this book posits an alternative to the top-down version of women's emancipation after the revolution's triumph in 1959. Popular accounts often credit the new leadership with a visionary will to dismantle gender inequality.[23] As the revolution radicalized, it is often assumed, leaders naturally broadened their scope to include women in the quest for true human dignity and freedom. This book challenges those dominant accounts, arguing that the rise of the "woman question" was due to several other factors. The first and most crucial factor was the vast but forgotten women's mobilization in Cuba's urban centers that followed the 1959 victory. In the tumultuous revolutionary moment, activist women of different political stripes pushed the leadership to address problems within the private sphere, such as food provisioning, domestic labor, and child rearing. In so doing, they raised more transformative notions of women's liberation and gender reform. Thus, in many important ways, women led rather than followed.

A second factor that contributed to the emergence of a more transformative vision of women's emancipation in the revolutionary moment was the rise of anticommunism and anti-Castroism. Opposition to the revolution is usually told as a military story culminating in the Bay of Pigs invasion. But it was also a war of ideas, including ideas about the family, and those clashing visions influenced internal Cuban politics. As the new revolutionary policies restructured education, confronted the church, and intruded into the private sphere, the growing political opposition denounced these measures and specifically appealed to women and mothers to protect their families from the state. Thus in the turbulent context of 1960 and 1961, the revolutionary state was partly *forced* to appeal to women in order to compete for their political loyalties in the face of mounting opposition. In other words, the leadership sought to mobilize women due to anxiety over women's purported social isolation and susceptibility to counterrevolutionary sentiment as much as by a desire to end gender inequality.[24]

Finally, alterations to gender and family dynamics were often the unintended consequences of political changes. New volunteer campaigns and the formation of the new mass organizations increasingly drew women and adolescents from the confines of the family home, sometimes in opposition to family patriarchs. These new mass campaigns not only disrupted traditional family patterns; they also increased movement between city and country. In a desire to redeem and uplift the countryside, city dwellers were called to serve in rural areas, and many served with zeal. This trend was most evident in the island-wide literacy campaign of 1961, when children as young as twelve struck out into the countryside to reside with and instruct peasant families, especially in the impoverished east. At the same time, young people—including young women—from rural areas were brought to urban centers for education and training. Whether Cubans embraced or recoiled from these changes, the boundaries of gender, generation, class, and region that had defined the Cuban Republic were permanently unsettled.

SEVERAL BROAD THEMES emerge throughout this book that invite us to rethink the history of the Cuban Revolution and, by extension, revolutionary movements and the Left throughout Latin America. The first is the dynamic between leadership and "the masses," or the question of whether revolutions are driven forward by pressure from above or from below. Unlike the Mexican, Chilean, and Nicaraguan revolutions, Cuba is frequently interpreted as a case in which a radicalized leadership imposed its politics on a more moderate populace and always retained the political initiative. This book questions this view, using women and gender as a prism through which to incorporate a ground-up analysis of this complex period. Rather than cast women's emancipation as the natural and inevitable extension of revolutionary deliverance, I highlight the way in which many actors struggled to define how women and men would be incorporated into the new revolutionary project. Careful reconstruction of events suggests that the revolutionary leadership could be reactive rather than proactive, pushed into appealing to women by women's own grassroots organization and participation in the fast-paced changes of the period. The leadership was thus only gradually drawn toward more transformative ideas about gender, influenced by women's demands from below and by the growing opposition.

A second main theme deals with the roles of the so-called Old and New Lefts in raising the banners of gender and racial equality. The New Left emerged globally in the late 1950s and early 1960s, seeking alternatives to the rigidity of orthodox communism and the repressive legacy of Stalinism.[25] A broad "movement of movements," it encompassed everything from student radicals, to the civil rights movement, to second-wave feminism.[26] The New Left is sometimes favorably contrasted to the "Old," Marxist Left, rooted in labor movements and Communist parties, which was presumably disinterested in social categories other than class.[27] This critique of the Old Left is compounded by the histories of socialist states, which prioritized bringing women into paid, "productive" labor without enforcing an equal distribution of domestic labor within the home. More generally, they viewed gender inequality as the by-product of more foundational forms of economic exploitation and hoped it would automatically disappear with the eradication of capitalism.[28] In Cuban historiography, in particular, the prerevolutionary Communist Party (known as the Popular Socialist Party, or PSP) has been vilified for its "conservative" visions of the family and the leading role some PSP militants took in moralization campaigns after 1959.[29]

This book rethinks the interplay of the Old and New Lefts in the rise of more transformative visions of gender reform. It shows that in practice PSP militants played a complex role in the early revolutionary period. The PSP had developed a clear postwar program for women's equality, and women affiliated with the Marxist Left pushed that agenda onto the table after the revolutionary triumph. Although the PSP did not support the insurrectionary movement until 1958, women of the Marxist Left swiftly brought their decades of organizing experience to bear in 1959 and 1960. While they and the younger women of the revolutionary movement usually saw each other as rivals, activists of the Marxist Left were indispensable in helping to raise the banner of women's inclusion and equality. Thus this book argues that if the revolutionary movement overthrew the old order, the "Old" Marxist Left helped give content to the new order that emerged.

A third interpretive theme raised here is the role of the cities in revolution. There is a tendency in Latin American historiography to focus on rural settings and the peasantry as revolutionary actors. In a region with a predominantly rural population until the 1950s, and where peasants took a leading role in twentieth-century revolutions and civil wars, that approach makes sense. But it has also left the cities to our imagination.[30] This book concurs with other scholars who have argued that in many ways the Cuban insurrection was primarily an urban phenomenon.[31] It thus focuses on the urban resistance, broadly conceived—a mass movement encompassing civic and armed wings, including but extending far beyond the famous Twenty-Sixth of July Movement. Contemporaries rightly viewed the urban centers as cauldrons of revolutionary activity. But in the years following revolutionary victory, the city was reimagined as the site of political apathy and counterrevolution.

A social history of the city in revolution raises a series of new questions about revolutionary processes, including the different political expressions of the urban insurrection, the dramatic changes to urban consumption after the revolution, and the political role of the urban middle class. From the perspective of a history that centers women and gender, this shift in perspective is particularly revealing. If women were important but exceptional actors in the Sierra Maestra, where a small but influential group of women formed part of Fidel and Raúl's inner circle, women's participation in the urban anti-Batista struggle was the norm. And the radical post-1959 changes to urban consumption and everyday life suggest ways that revolutionary transformations could affect men and women differently, as women, traditionally tasked with household provisioning, often bore the brunt of daily shortages.

Finally, and most broadly, this book insists that ideas about gender were central, not marginal, to revolutionary politics. In fact, I argue that it is impossible to fully understand the major political processes of the period—including insurrectionary alliances, political radicalization and polarization, mass emigration, and the rise of an internal opposition—without seeing how these were linked to gender relations. As this book documents, the political transformations of this period were suffused with references to masculinity, maternalism, sexuality, and the family. These tropes often provided unifying narratives around which various political alliances could congeal, subsuming deeper conflicts over policy.

At the same time, a focus on gender politics provides fresh analytical insights. For example, the Cuban leadership is often portrayed as radical, even reckless, obliterating capitalism, defying the United States, promoting revolution throughout the hemisphere, and bringing the world to the brink of nuclear war. But from the perspective of changes to race or gender, the leadership seems cautious, perhaps consensus-seeking. And while changes to public policy could be declared by decree, changing private practices was more complicated. For example, studies of private practices of sexuality challenge narratives of extreme rupture from the pre- to postrevolutionary period, suggesting instead that in some realms revolutionary Cuba exhibited surprising continuity with republican Cuba.[32] And in Cuba and beyond, with regard to policies on homosexuality, Latin America's revolutionary Left has been characterized as conservative or even reactionary.[33] Thus one of the most interesting aspects about studying the gender politics of revolution is that it does not map out neatly onto Left-Right binaries. Centering women, gender, and sexuality, and studying changes to both the private and public spheres, allows historians to reevaluate the actors and dynamics of social revolution.

Overview of the Book

This book begins with the much-mythologized but still poorly understood struggle to oust the dictator Fulgencio Batista. Chapter 1 explores the birth of that movement, drawing on the earliest recorded protests and ephemera to shed light on a relatively unknown period. These first years of the anti-Batista movement, from 1952 to 1955, are typically treated as mere precursors to the rise of the rebel army in 1956. But I argue that an embryonic form of urban popular insurrection was taking shape, one that drew on demonstrations, petitions, boycotts, and other creative civic actions. This movement to unseat Batista was initially broader than previously recognized and, while somewhat amorphous in organization, was inclusive in practice. In particular, it pioneered forms of political protest that were accessible to many urban women. Women who wished to act upon their opposition to Batista were not necessarily required to move "from the house to the street." Rather, these early protest actions straddled the public and private spheres, utilizing and politicizing spaces that were semipublic but often implicitly designated as female, such as movie theaters, department stores, churches, and the family home. Such actions have been overlooked by historians and belittled by the leadership, but I argue that they were crucial acts in the campaign to discredit Batista. The chapter thus shows that women—too often cast merely as the revolution's beneficiaries—were present at its origins.

But as state violence increased, the anti-Batista movement changed. The rise of armed insurrection and state violence, paired with the revolutionary leadership's tendency to reproduce the dominant gender ideologies of the 1950s, contributed to a new gendered division of labor within the movement. Chapter 2 explores the new ideals of revolutionary manhood that emerged with the armed movement, in both the cities and the Sierra. It explores the wide variety of references to proper manhood found in the insurrectionary movement from the mid- to late 1950s, influenced by ideas of family, religion, and sexuality. It argues that the rise of the image and myth of the *barbudo*, the bearded guerrilla rebel, mobilized Cuban oppositionists and the public at large, and galvanized an entire generation throughout Latin America, but also increasingly tied notions of political action to a hypermasculine, militarist vision, eclipsing other possible forms of political action and identity. It did so partly by drawing on familiar ideas about honor, propriety, and paternalism. As such, if the triumphant rebel army helped usher in the radical 1960s, it also reflected the family ideals of the 1950s.

Women did not retreat from oppositional activities as their male counterparts took up arms. But after 1955, as the political center of gravity shifted to armed opposition, anti-Batista women more often expressed their protests in maternalist terms—that is, they linked their political activism to their moral authority as mothers. Chapter 3 asks how we should understand these expressions of political maternalism. Examining women's activism in public protests and clandestine networks, the chapter shows that many activists strategically referred to their moral authority as women and mothers in order to construct a unifying identity for oppositional women. While maternalist discourse could replicate familiar terms of patriarchy, involvement in oppositional activities could also push women to challenge patriarchy in practice. These maternal expressions also complemented a view that stressed the revolutionary movement's protection of the Cuban family and the *barbudo*'s embodiment of traditional values of masculine honor, bravery, and decency. Women's utilization of their presumably inherent moral authority as women and mothers was thus instrumental in establishing a narrative that helped legitimize the use of political violence to oust Batista.

Chapter 4 charts the untold story of how activist women mobilized in the revolutionary moment. Many women who had participated in the insurrection continued and even increased their activism after 1959, now aiming to transform society rather than to oust a dictator. Others who had not participated now joined, inspired by the euphoria ushered in by revolutionary victory. Women did not wait for the male leadership to establish organizations on their behalf; they formed their own new political groups. In the process, they inspired many other women to enter the revolutionary process for the first time. Women's activism in this period largely moved from a language of moral authority and maternalism toward a clearer articulation of women's rights as citizens, workers, and revolutionaries. In so doing, women activists pushed the revolutionary leadership beyond vague and infrequent remarks about the need for women's "redemption," and spurred the formation of a mass organization for women.

However, this process was not without conflict. Women from Fidel Castro's Twenty-Sixth of July Movement and women from the Communist Party expressed different political visions and mobilized through different organizations. Throughout 1959 and 1960, women from the Communist Party rose to prominence in the new state-sponsored revolutionary organizations, although most had not actively taken part in the insurrection. They often sidelined the younger militants of the Twenty-Sixth of July Movement in the process. Cuba's "revolution within the revolution"—Fidel Castro's famous phrase for women's post-1959 liberation—was therefore not born in a vacuum. It emerged during a period of intense mobilization and conflict involving various actors, rather than merely being a top-down imposition from the leadership.

The final chapters turn toward thematic analyses of two pivotal issues during the period of the revolution's radicalization from 1959 to 1962: consumption and family reform. Chapter 5 chronicles the growing food shortages in the urban centers, set in motion by structural changes in the countryside and then vastly aggravated by U.S. economic hostility. Those shortages disproportionately affected women, traditionally tasked with household labor. As long lines stretched outside food markets and the black market spread throughout Havana, women pushed the revolutionary leaders to take action on these issues. The government, too, recognized women as important protagonists in this daily economic battle. Leaders called on women, as the city's primary shoppers, to improvise cooking solutions and denounce hoarders and black marketers. Yet the leadership, on the whole, also belittled the increasingly difficult task of domestic reproduction as secondary to the real, military battle.

Detailed attention to these episodes challenges the commonly held notion that the revolutionary government immediately emphasized incorporating women into paid labor, seeing this as the path to true liberation. Contrary to these common assertions, I suggest that the revolutionary government early on appealed to women more often as consumers than as potential laborers. The leadership thereby reinscribed traditional gendered divisions of labor that assigned men to roles in production and national defense, and women to the less important realms of consumption and neighborhood-based vigilance. If the revolution eventually introduced radical changes to Cuban society, it also relied on familiar gendered imagery, especially in this early period.

Chapter 6 begins by sketching out some of the government's earliest attempts to reform the family. These initial programs were not radical; they were moderate liberal reforms designed to improve and uplift the working-class family. Nonetheless, increasing numbers of Cubans began to decry government interventions into the private sphere. These warnings eventually culminated in the Patria Potestad rumor campaign, an intentional disinformation campaign that claimed that the government would abrogate parents' custodial rights to their own children. Despite an apocalyptic tone and patently unrealistic claims, the rumors had widespread uptake. How can we explain such extreme reactions and fears on the part of many urban parents? This chapter argues that the Patria Potestad rumor campaign catalyzed diffuse but widespread anxieties caused by transformations to the private sphere. These changes were perceived as deliberate attempts to alter the balance of power within families, although they were most often indirectly and unintentionally generated by other major revolutionary transformations, such as educational reform.

As these tensions were mapped onto Cuba's polarizing political landscape, the image of the beleaguered family became a lynchpin that helped unify the burgeoning anti-Castro movement. The threatened disruption of the family seemed to encapsulate everything that was most fearful about the revolution. For liberals, state encroachment on the family was part of the foundation of an authoritarian regime. For Catholic anticommunists, the state control of children posed a threat to the very soul. Thus a focus on the family helped various segments of the poorly unified opposition articulate their opposition to the regime. It helped forge a moral anticommunism that appealed beyond the propertied, calling on women and mothers to do their duty by opposing the revolution. It also pushed the revolutionary leadership to respond with a more radical vision of its own, promising female liberation through waged labor and political participation, and defending the working-class "right" to motherhood. As the broad prorevolutionary coalition splintered, the revolutionary leadership and the growing opposition each rooted their political authority in claims that they best protected the family.

By examining these forgotten episodes of the revolution, this book seeks to offer a new perspective on one of the most radical social upheavals in the modern world. If the Cuban Revolution might now seem exhausted or discredited, we must remember that the revolution challenged the very premises of global power relations in 1959. At that time vast swaths of the world were still colonial possessions; the first tremors of national liberation had scarcely begun in Asia and had yet to reach Africa. Latin America seemed eternally burdened by entrenched poverty and inequality, impervious to reform. In that context, the Cuban Revolution raised and acted upon the promise that small, underdeveloped, former colonial countries could become truly sovereign and that impoverished and hierarchical societies could become truly equal. This book contends that, however unevenly or conflictingly, the revolution also raised the notion that both men and women could be fully liberated and fully equal. These were and are powerful propositions. Understanding the Cuban Revolution's promises, triumphs, and failures thus gives us insight into fundamental questions about human liberation and national sovereignty during the Cold War. To that end, this book offers a new story about the revolution—one that helps us rethink the meaning and legacy of this world-historical event.

A Few Words on Sources

Rarely have the events of history so thoroughly shaped a country's historiography. Of scant interest to academics prior to 1959, Cuba sparked a flood of polemics and analysis after the revolution, generating a surge of interest in the history and contemporary politics of the entire region. The radical changes introduced by the revolution encouraged certain types of documentation and suppressed others. From Che Guevara's destruction of the archives of the Bureau for the Repression of Communist Activities in the cleansing euphoria of the first few days of the revolution, to the careful preservation of the Communist Party's twentieth-century newspapers by the historical branch of the Cuban Communist Party in the 1970s, the revolutionary leadership's policy decisions have shaped and will shape for some time to come the way the history of the island is written.[34]

These policy decisions have included the restriction of public access to documents deemed of national security interest, and this unfortunately includes the majority of the government documents generated during the period examined in this book. This lack of access has long discouraged scholars seeking to reassess the revolution. Still, the wealth of information available both within Cuba and elsewhere gives historians various materials from which to reconstruct the insurrection and the revolution. With some creativity and patience, we may yet arrive at a detailed understanding of this complex period.

Cuba's particular historical development as the wealthiest of the sugar-exporting Caribbean islands, long under the informal dominion of the United States, had generated a relatively sophisticated postwar media apparatus—including press, radio, and television—renowned throughout the region. Havana in particular, with its relatively large urban middle class, supported numerous dailies and weeklies of high caliber. By the same token, the insurrectionary groups of the 1950s, whose leaders were mostly drawn from the urban middle class, also made savvy use of the media, both print and broadcast. Indeed, more than a few young members of the insurrectionary groups worked for print publications and radio stations, or staffed the growing ranks of Havana's advertising industry. For this project I have drawn liberally on both the mainstream and clandestine pre-1960 press, conserved in repositories in Cuba and in the United States.[35]

As the revolution began to radicalize and confront the United States, this conflict also manifested itself in a struggle between the revolutionary government and the private-sector press. Some newspapers shut their doors of their own accord in mid-1960. The government intervened and nationalized many others. In the highly polarized environment of the period, the state-run periodicals now shifted toward the primary goal of reader orientation rather than the transmission of news. Partly as a result of those same processes, many editors, publishers, and journalists flooded into exile. Some resurrected their former publications in their adopted cities of New York, Miami, or Caracas, occasionally with the financial support of the CIA.[36] Established in the heat of revolution and openly dedicated to the overthrow of Fidel Castro, the exile press tended toward heavy-handed polemical denunciations of the revolution. Yet its proponents also saw it as part of their mission to release information censored on the island, which was crucial to the construction of public opinion around their political platforms. Before ties between the United States and Cuba were more decisively severed, first by the Bay of Pigs invasion and then by the missile crisis, the exile press gathered information through clandestine correspondents, frequent direct communication with the island by phone and mail, and fresh news brought by recent arrivals. Thus the press of the period 1960–62, both in Cuba and in exile, can be an excellent source when used carefully.[37]

Another principal source used here are the declassified State Department documents, which primarily capture the correspondence sent from the U.S. embassy in Havana to the Department of State in Washington, as well as some correspondence between the provincial U.S. consulates and the American embassy in Havana. After 1959, these documents became increasingly focused on the question of Fidel Castro's relationship with communism and with the attempts of the U.S. government to cobble together various fragmented, competing opposition groups into a unified counterrevolutionary front. With the end of U.S.-Cuban diplomatic relations on December 30, 1960, the American embassy was relocated to Miami, where it dedicated itself to monitoring Cuban radio broadcasts and conveying news and rumor brought from Cuba by recent exiles. If the utility of these documents for a social history of the revolution therefore declined precipitously after 1960, the State Department dispatches from the insurrectionary period are invaluable. Although Eisenhower's political appointee to the Havana embassy was famously pro-Batista, many of his subordinates had different views, and some openly sympathized with the Sierra rebels. The consulate in Santiago, in particular, was staffed by perceptive career diplomats who met frequently with opposition leaders and carefully documented the increasing violence of security forces and the corresponding anger and militancy of the city's populace.

Like other world-historical events, the triumphant Cuban Revolution drew enthusiastic intellectuals, journalists, academics, and other sympathizers, anxious to see the new revolution with their own eyes in the 1960s. Many left published accounts of their visits. While mostly descriptive and anecdotal, these publications capture some of the details of daily life in revolutionary Cuba.[38] Also in the 1960s, some scholars conducted important and rigorous academic studies with unrestricted access to archives and interviews, something that would become much more difficult with the onset of the so-called Gray Period (Quinquenio Gris) in 1970.[39]

The Gray Period ushered in a far more restrictive spectrum of permissible expression, but also saw the institutionalization of certain processes. For example, the historical branch of the Communist Party was formed in 1974. Initially dedicated to studying and preserving the history of the party, it soon evolved into a more general research organization and repository.[40] It was also in the 1970s that some Cuban government organizations began to undertake what I suspect are very complete oral history projects with the participants of the insurrection, though these have not been opened to the public.[41] Additionally, some Cuban scholars and former participants of the insurrection began their own meticulous studies of the urban underground in this period. True labors of love, these research projects often did not see publication until the late 1980s or the 1990s, but they remain some of the most important studies of the urban opposition movements of the 1950s.[42]

One of these books proved particularly influential during my research. Called *La lección del maestro*, it documented the experiences of an all-women's anti-Batista organization. When I stumbled upon it in a Cuban library, it struck me as the most compelling source I had yet read about the urban anti-Batista movement. It told a story so different from that of the rebel army in the Sierra Maestra that it was almost unrecognizable as the same conflict. Some time later I found myself commenting on the book to an older man affiliated with one of Havana's research institutions. He was acquainted with some of those women, he responded enthusiastically. Perhaps some of them would even be willing to meet with me to share their stories. That encounter gave me the sense, for the first time, that there were groups of former participants within Cuba actively attempting to spread their own version of the insurrection, one that usually complemented but occasionally contradicted officialist narratives. Since then I have come across many Cubans of various political persuasions, on the island and in the diaspora, willing to share their versions of events, inscribing their own complex personal histories onto the impersonal and often simplistic narratives that have come to dominate our understanding of the revolution. I eventually conducted interviews with dozens of people in Havana, Miami, New York, New Jersey, and Washington, D.C., including multiple interviews with some individuals.[43]

Oral histories are not transparent records of the past. As innumerable scholars have recognized, they must be treated carefully, especially under conditions of political polarization. Certainly, personal narratives on both sides of the Florida straits have been heavily shaped by the official histories emanating from Havana and Miami. But when weighed against those official narratives and evaluated with an eye toward their intended interventions, oral history interviews open remarkable windows onto the everyday experience of the revolutionary process. This work would not have been possible without them.

I love
you

1 | DEAD CITIES AND OTHER FORMS OF PROTEST, 1952–1955

Nineteen fifty-five was a busy year for some women in Havana. It began with months of pounding the pavement, collecting signatures for the campaign to grant amnesty to political prisoners. It was marked by a series of inspiring public rallies and heartrending funerals. It ended with a series of arrests during a rowdy women's protest against police violence on the downtown streets of Galiano and San Rafael. These actions—rarely mentioned in histories of the Cuban Revolution—reflected several years of mobilization and organization sparked by Fulgencio Batista's 1952 coup d'état, which unleashed a variety of protest actions that continued for the next few years. In retrospect, we can see 1955 as a year of transition, as civic protest began to give way to armed opposition, a shift that would have implications for both women's and men's roles in the anti-Batista movement. This chapter seeks to recover and analyze these largely forgotten events in order to establish a richer and more complex historical narrative of the revolution, and also to suggest some explanations for their having been forgotten in the first place.

This chapter focuses on the early years of the anti-Batista opposition movement, from 1952 to 1955, a poorly understood period that is often seen retroactively and teleologically as the period that gave birth to the rebel movement eventually led by Fidel Castro. Thus the earliest protest actions, and the earliest anti-Batista organizations that formed, tend to be viewed as "precursors" to the Twenty-Sixth of July Movement rather than being examined in their own right.[1] To some extent this narrow focus is testament to the strength of the official revolutionary narrative that emerged after 1959, which privileges the role of the cohort around Fidel Castro in the Sierra Maestra.[2] It also reflects challenges with regard to sources, as most easily available documentation of the period focuses on the leadership and on the guerrilla war. But by examining the surviving ephemera, carefully combing State Department reports, and drawing on interviews, we can sketch out the contours of the early opposition to reveal something of its assumptions, aims, and constituency. Methodologically, attention to the geography of protest suggests interesting patterns, raising questions not prompted by the scrutiny of speeches, manifestos, or other forms of written or spoken discourse. What emerges is a portrait of a vibrant, varied mass movement in the making, which disrupts standard narratives of the anti-Batista resistance.

Most strikingly, women were often important actors, contrary to popular assumptions. The presence of women in this early period of anti-Batista opposition reflects several characteristics of the movement. First, early anti-Batista protesters forged a creative repertoire of dissent that included many actions that were relatively accessible to women as well as men. Urban protesters undertook an array of actions, including public demonstrations, phone chains and rumor campaigns, collective "stay-at-home" days, "flash" protests, patriotic street theater, boycotts, and other consumer actions. Early anti-Batista protesters also adopted a creative and flexible use of space, pioneering forms of civic activism that either never required public protest or redefined how public protest might be imagined, blurring the gendered boundaries between house and street. Thus the earliest years of the Cuban anti-Batista movement were characterized by what we might call gender-inclusive protest strategies, in which urban women and men together forged a compelling range of protest actions. It was the rise of the armed movements from 1955 onward that introduced sharper distinctions between women's and men's roles in the anti-Batista opposition.

A second important factor in explaining the prevalence of women in the early anti-Batista movement is the importance of urban consumer culture. As this chapter suggests, the anti-Batista protest movement of 1952 through 1955 was primarily—perhaps exclusively—an urban movement. As such, it was shaped by the concerns of its urban constituency and the urban space in which it emerged. Since early in the century, Havana had developed a lively commercial center and modern, American-influenced consumption practices. The earliest protest actions often focused on disrupting these patterns of consumption through boycotts or other consumer-oriented actions. Protesters targeted department stores, movie theaters, and other sites of consumption and leisure, or they called for some combination of not buying, not paying taxes, and withdrawing from society entirely for a day. Women, who were implicitly imagined as consumers par excellence in Cuba and elsewhere, were therefore particularly implicated in these types of protests. If these early calls to action sometimes relied on limiting and prescriptive language regarding women's implication in consumer culture, or implicitly saw their field of action as confined within the family home, they nonetheless opened channels for women to participate politically in the incipient anti-Batista resistance.

Finally, early anti-Batista protesters seem to have often been drawn from the ranks of Ortodoxo Party sympathizers, which may also help explain the presence of women that we find here. The Ortodoxo Party—a reformist political party that was growing in strength in this period, as will be discussed further subsequently—seems to have enjoyed widespread support from urban women, although the phenomenon has yet to be explained in the scholarship.[3] A 1949 survey that polled greater Havana residents on whether they preferred the Ortodoxo leader Eduardo Chibás or Fulgencio Batista showed that Chibás owed his narrow lead to disproportionate support among the women polled. (Among men, Chibás and Batista came in neck and neck.)[4] And the Ortodoxos had been so successful at mobilizing women in Santiago for public protests in the early 1950s that contemporary sources occasionally claimed that the majority of participants in Ortodoxo rallies were women.[5] The life histories of individual militants also suggest that many of the women who eventually rose to leadership positions within the revolutionary movement had first been members of the Ortodoxo Party, like their male counterparts. For example, Celia Sánchez Manduley, now best known as Fidel's loyal right-hand woman in the Sierra, had been an organizer for her local chapter of the Ortodoxo Party in the late 1940s.[6] Similarly, Gloria Cuadras de la Cruz, one of the pillars of Santiago's anti-Batista underground, had been head of the women's section of the Ortodoxo Party in Santiago.[7] In Havana, Pastorita Núñez who became a Twenty-Sixth of July leader and a founder of the group José Martí Civic Front for Women, had been a leader of the women's section of the Ortodoxo Party in Havana.[8] These and other women brought their previous organizing experience to bear on their new political activities.

The antidictatorial movement that ultimately led to one of the twentieth century's most radical revolutions has too often been narrated as a straight line from the spectacular armed attack on the Moncada barracks led by Fidel Castro in 1953 to the rebel army's triumph against the regular army in December 1958. Rethinking the earliest period of anti-Batista protest gives us another perspective on that storied turn to guerrilla warfare. Of course, the growing guerrilla struggle was increasingly important, and by late 1958 a sizable part of the Cuban public supported the rebel army. But that was never the whole story. Broadening the scope of our inquiry suggests an incipient mass civic protest movement, spanning both house and street, involving both women and men. Importantly, many of the creative forms of public protest described here persisted throughout the entire insurrectionary period, institutionalized after 1955 through the growth of the Civic Resistance Movement (Movimiento de Resistencia Cívica, MRC), a civilian opposition movement affiliated with the Twenty-Sixth of July Movement. Although a deep reappraisal of the MRC falls beyond the scope of this chapter, further historical work will surely reveal the full extent of its influence and particularly the role of women activists within it. However, even a brief reassessment of the MRC's actions after its formation shows that it drew heavily and successfully from the repertoire of protest pioneered between 1952 and 1955 by anti-Batista activists.[9] Thus this early period of opposition activity was foundational, establishing patterns of mass activism that endured alongside the rise of arms, albeit often belittled as the rear guard. Exploring these other stories sheds light on little-known chapters of the urban resistance and raises questions about how the revolution was made.

Fulgencio Batista and His Adversaries

Fulgencio Batista burst back on to the Cuban political scene with a remarkably fast coup d'état executed on March 10, 1952. Batista has been so vilified in Cuban officialist historiography and in popular memory that in retrospect it can be hard to fully understand what his return to power meant. We know that Cuba's elite groups and institutions at least formally supported Batista's coup.[10] He also apparently still enjoyed some popular support.[11] Although Batista is often depicted as a bloodthirsty right-wing dictator, such caricatures rely on his final few years in power, by which time he relied overwhelmingly on the military for his support and used force to repress the revolutionary movement that opposed him. But a longer focus on Batista's entire political trajectory suggests that he was a military reformer, not unlike the other populists who rose to power in the circum-Caribbean region in the same period. Men like Rafael Trujillo of the Dominican Republic and Anastasio Somoza of Nicaragua began their ascent in the turbulent 1930s with significant popular support. Their long careers ended several decades later in the polarizing atmosphere of the Cold War, when they ruled as far more repressive dictators. They owed their powerful early appeal to policies that genuinely, if unevenly, benefitted the urban or rural popular classes. Perhaps more importantly, they were often the first national leaders to describe the popular classes—at least popular-class men—as crucial citizens of the modernizing nation.[12] Batista fits within this general panorama. Never a truly right-wing or even politically conservative dictator, he embraced a corporatist and militarist vision of modernity and reform.

Batista originally rose to political prominence in the tumultuous aftermath of the 1933 revolution, which ousted Gerardo Machado. As a sergeant in the army, Batista became a member of an unstable five-man group of leaders referred to as the pentarchy, which disintegrated when the U.S. government supported Batista over more democratic reformers such as Ramón Grau San Martín and radical nationalists such as Tony Guiteras. Over the next few years his power grew. Batista repressed the revolutionary Left led by Guiteras, but by the late 1930s, firmly in power, he had incorporated many of the 1933 revolution's proposed reforms. In 1940, his administration presided over the drafting of a remarkably progressive constitution, a "tropical version of the Rooseveltian New Deal," in the words of the historian Jesús Arboleya.[13]

As president, Batista undertook some progressive initiatives, such as promises for agrarian reform and the abolition of large estates, the extension of rural education under a quasi-militarized rubric, and increased state regulation of the sugar sector. He struck a tactical alliance with the Communist Party, seeking to widen his popular base of support, and implemented some concessions to labor, such as the eight-hour day, social security, maternity leave, and paid vacation.[14] Batista cast himself as being "for the working man," and he was still remembered that way in some interviews conducted fifty years after his overthrow.[15] He won the 1940 presidential elections, apparently without resort to fraud, and yielded office in 1944 to his old rival, president-elect Grau San Martín of the Auténtico Party.[16]

In the eight years during which Batista was absent from national politics—from 1944 to 1952—the institutionalized forces of political reform were fragmented and weakened. While the Auténtico Party's 1944 rise to national power was initially greeted with widespread optimism, by 1952 the party's corruption in office and violent suppression of some labor activists had largely discredited it. In the same period, the dynamic Ortodoxo Party, founded as a splinter group from the Auténticos, became immensely popular in the urban centers. Its fiery leader, Eduardo Chibás, helped to discredit the Auténticos through frequent public allegations of corruption. But after Chibás's "martyrdom" (he committed suicide in 1951), the Ortodoxo Party never regained its institutional strength. Subsequent party leaders lacked his charisma and unifying power, and internally, party militants unofficially splintered into several groupings based around rival leaders.[17] Still, Chibás's legacy remained strong.[18] Some of the earliest anti-Batista groups directly referenced Chibás as an inspiration, while others indirectly referenced his famous slogan, "Honor against corruption" (*Vergüenza contra dinero*). Indeed, many of the early anti-Batista groups were likely derived from disillusioned factions from the ranks of the declining Auténtico and Ortodoxo parties.[19]

If Cubans grappled with how to respond to the abrupt end of constitutional rule after March 1952, they were not alone. Throughout the region, leaders such as Rafael Trujillo in the Dominican Republic and Marcos Pérez Jiménez in Venezuela increasingly ruled with an iron fist. The short-lived postwar optimism toward the possibility of social democracy and development soon waned, as the postwar democratic consensus gave way to the polarization of the Cold War. Organized labor and the leftist parties that had flourished in the immediate postwar period were curbed by national elites with the backing of the United States.[20] The strains of the period were perhaps particularly acutely felt by the small countries of the Caribbean, which had little industry and declining agriculture, whose sovereignty was compromised by the immense weight of U.S. influence, and whose urban political sphere was rife with struggles over government spoils and sinecures.[21]

The combination of the external transformations associated with the rise of the Cold War and Cuba's own internal political flux explains the strong sense of political crisis that emerged among contemporaries. Cuban politics was already in a crisis of sorts even before Batista's 1952 coup. These developments also help explain why protest in response to the coup was initially rather limited, as it came at a time of political fragmentation and cynicism for mainstream political parties. At the same time, as we have seen, Batista was a man with a history of popular support, and his return to power was thus met with some ambivalence by labor and the Left, who recalled their recent histories of expansion under Batista's watch.[22] Yet once back in power, Batista eventually alienated his earlier bases of support and increasingly used violence to maintain himself in power. Thus an opposition movement grew gradually over the course of the next few years.

Most popular historical narratives focus on the 1953 attack on the Moncada barracks led by Fidel Castro as the opening salvo of an insurrection that would culminate with the toppling of Batista and Fidel's triumphant entry into Havana in January 1959. But the early response to Batista's coup was complicated, involving many actors. Fidel Castro and his cohort were not the only group who planned an armed uprising. Various small groups who favored an armed ousting of Batista emerged across the island. Some drew on a previous generation of men who had opposed the Machado dictatorship of the 1930s, while others drew on the youth section of the Ortodoxo Party. For example, the Movimiento Nacional Revolucionario, led by Rafael García Bárcena, an older intellectual who had participated in revolutionary movements in the 1930s, had planned a similar conspiracy, but they were arrested before their uprising.[23] Meanwhile, there were other expressions of civic protest, usually described as centered in the university, but also moving beyond the university, as we shall see.

The Moncada attack was easily put down, and the surviving attackers—including Fidel Castro—were imprisoned for the next two years. Upon their amnesty in 1955, they sought exile in Mexico, the base from which they plotted and eventually staged an armed invasion of the island by boat, the now-legendary Granma. The Granma expeditionaries landed in the remote terrain near the Sierra Maestra and, from there, gradually built a guerrilla army rooted in the local peasantry. This story has come to overshadow the other initiatives that took place on the island in the meantime. While some scholarship has traced the arc of the professional and civic associations that sought direct dialogue with Batista in this period, there were also more grass-roots, civic protest initiatives, which are the focus of this chapter.[24]

"Dead Cities" and Other Forms of Protest

Historians have long recognized that many of the initial expressions of anti-Batista protest occurred within the university ambit.[25] Still, the types of protest actions employed by students have not been sufficiently analyzed, nor is it often noted that such actions often included both women and men. The earliest bursts of anger over Batista's unconstitutional return to power through a coup often mobilized young women, a pattern that would continue through 1955. U.S. State Department analysts noted the presence of young women beginning with the very first demonstrations. For example, in one of several small-scale demonstrations pitting youths against police, "a group of agitators including two women bearing an anti-Government slogan on a large strip of cloth caused some commotion before being dispersed or arrested."[26] And an alternative 1953 Labor Day event held at the University of Havana to counter official celebrations contained "mostly women" by some estimates.[27]

The very earliest protests carried out in response to Batista's coup frequently drew on political symbolism and sought to dramatize political opposition through spectacle. This performance aspect of protest is usually overlooked in histories of the period, but it seems to have formed an important ritual for contemporaries, and may have provided an avenue for women's participation, especially when related to themes of death and mourning. For example, on the first anniversary of Batista's coup, groups of young women students stood at major intersections in downtown Havana to offer black ribbons to passers-by that could be tied around the arm to symbolize bereavement.[28] A group of women might form an honor guard at the head of a mock funeral procession, or on occasion appear at a protest dressed as the Cuban Republic, with a flag-adorned dress. Other early spectacles referenced or mimicked some aspect of formal republican politics. For example, young men and women at the University of Havana laid out large tables in front of the university entrance, calling on other students to sign an oath of loyalty to the 1940 constitution.[29] And the Federation of University Students (FEU) announced a daylong burning of electoral identification cards, a theatrical and visually striking manifestation of discontent.[30]

Early protesters frequently dramatized their patriotic sentiment by referencing Cuba's founding fathers or anticolonial heroes, especially José Martí, Cuba's revered independence leader, philosopher, and poet. They did so through the use of public monuments, narrative performances, and other cultural expressions. Anniversaries often provided the opportunity to hold public ceremonies, especially nationalist "martyrdoms."[31] Two all-women's anti-Batista groups—both of which are discussed further in chapter 3—proposed cultural activities such as performances of Martí's plays or art exhibits to raise broad public awareness about the coup.[32] Lest we assume these performances were merely docile theatrical rehearsals, it should be noted that during a May 1952 performance on a sugar plantation near Camagüey, a seventeen-year-old playing the part of Martí "expressed some of Martí's thoughts against dictatorships" and was subsequently killed by a soldier in attendance who took offense.[33]

Existing scholarship often places emphasis on students' activities in this period, but an exclusive focus on the university is too narrow. Other anti-Batista groups were forming in 1952 and 1953. And even when protests took place on the centrally located campus of the University of Havana, they increasingly attracted sympathizers from beyond the student body. As Havana embassy officials noted after protest activities on the anniversary of Batista's coup in March 1953, university police were unable to prevent "outside elements" such as "non-students, hangers-on and secondary school pupils" from entering to join the students. In fact, a relatively greater number of non-students took part in the first anniversary protests as compared to similar events held on the university campus several months prior.[34] At the same time, students and other anti-Batista groups increasingly sought each other out for collaborative protests that spilled beyond university borders. For example, students and members of the José Martí Women's Civic Front joined forces to ceremonially lay a wreath at the statue of Martí in Havana's Central Park. Thus protests did not long remain confined to the university ambit; they quickly spread beyond it.

Although many early demonstrations drew their power from their visibility and their performance-oriented public nature, protests against Batista in this period were decidedly not limited to public space. Indeed, one interesting aspect of protest actions from 1952 to 1955 was their attempt to utilize the home, and in fact to see actions carried out within the home as crucial to opposition activity. The gendered division of "house" and "street" was a bastion of midcentury Cuban popular culture, as it was elsewhere in Latin America. According to this logic, the home was a woman's proper domain.[35] We can thus surmise that opposition calls to use the home as a symbolic protest vehicle were imagined to include women, or perhaps even to specifically target women. Early anti-Batista groups often admonished opposition sympathizers to stay at home for some particular action, such as the Day of National Sorrow in May 1953, in which sympathizers were told, "Do not leave your house that day and keep it closed and with the lights out."[36] Similar exhortations were made in a 1952 protest chain letter that explained to readers, "You can do much to combat tyranny and demonstrate that the people of Cuba do not surrender or submit. *Without leaving your house* you can contribute to civil resistance" by buying only indispensable items, delaying payment of taxes, boycotting newspapers that sympathized with the regime, and refraining from attending parties or other forms of public entertainment, as would befit a country "in mourning."[37]

In retrospect, these forms of protest—which essentially counseled a simultaneous physical withdrawal from economy, society, and politics—may feel strange to us. They were simultaneously deeply ambitious and yet nonconfrontational. The earliest anti-Batista actions often reveal a sweeping conceptualization of politics and political action, taking broad aim at Cuban society, economy, and urban life. The forms of action some early protesters engaged in were distinctly *not* physically aggressive, yet they nevertheless encompassed a deep sense of civic activism. They were individual actions that were designed to have a collective impact, interweaving an emphasis on urban space, consumer culture, and economic activity.

Contemporaries imagined creative tactics such as stay-at-home days as collective protest actions that would radiate outward from the shuttered family home to engulf the entire urban center and, ultimately, the nation. For example, some opposition groups called for something like a combined symbolic performance of mourning with a brief withdrawal from participation in the economy and society. The groups themselves referred to this strategy as passive resistance, a concept that would come to seem a contradiction in terms after the triumph of the revolution. In retrospect the concept stands in stark contrast to the ideas about "action" and "virility" that would characterize the revolutionary movement by the late 1950s. It also challenged the association of the physical space of the home with the domestic, the private, and the apolitical. "Passive resistance" described something like a general boycott and other consumer actions, and it also encompassed at least the threat of a general strike, including work stoppages lasting from a few minutes to an hour. This passive resistance could theoretically culminate in the shutting down of the whole city—what contemporaries called *ciudad muerta* ("dead city"), a tactic derived from the labor movement.[38]

The dead city demonstrations—as well as other forms of civic activism—could have an important impact. Like the *cacerolazos* that became famous throughout Latin America in the 1970s, in which protesters banged pots and pans while leaning out windows at an appointed time, protests like these drew their power from the visual or aural conquest of the city, mobilizing the home as both site and medium of protest. They also sent a collective message of opprobrium in a way that was relatively safe for individuals—or families—to undertake. The idea of a symbolic protest using the home later became a mainstay of civic opposition demonstrations when it was formalized by the Twenty-Sixth of July Movement's civic wing, the MRC. The MRC tried to institute a weekly shutdown of the principal cities, which they referred to as "dead cities" or days of "absolute resistance." The mere fact that the MRC purposefully continued or institutionalized many of the early protest forms described here suggests their impact.[39] The degree to which urban residents complied with these revolutionary calls, or *consignas*, varied over time, as the anti-Batista resistance waxed and waned between 1952 and 1958. But at their peak, such demonstrations served as a point of pride for the urban opposition and as inspiration for subsequent mobilization attempts. For example, in 1957 the MRC praised the results of a dead city demonstration in Oriente Province, noting, "It has been beautiful to see the city sad and empty, the houses dark and shuttered as a sign of rebellion before such dishonor [*ante tanta desvergüenza*]."[40]

From a logistical perspective, individual activists could also utilize the private home in multiple ways. For example, it was often a private home that served as the site for the reproduction, storage, and distribution of propaganda. Opposition news and instructions circulated by chain letter: citizens were exhorted to make five copies of a letter they received by mail, and then send the copies to people they knew who sympathized with the opposition movement. Here we have abundant evidence that women predominated in these forms of collaboration and strategizing. We know from multiple sources that many women undertook such tasks, and that women tended to have higher rates of participation in the circulation of propaganda than men.[41]

Opposition sympathizers also used the telephone as a vehicle of propaganda. These tactics, too, pioneered in the early years of Batista's dictatorship, persisted throughout the duration of the insurrection and were eventually adopted by the MRC. For example, in one handbill printed by the MRC in 1957, readers were exhorted to call at least ten people, "and when they answer your call, say only the following slogan: Cuba free and sovereign without Batista; Resist and we will triumph!"[42] Phone chains could be useful in disseminating information in the climate of strict press censorship that eventually evolved, especially before the establishment of clandestine radio stations. As Vilma Espín later recalled of the Santiago underground, *consignas* for phone chains included instructions such as "Call ten other people . . . and say that Fidel is in the Sierra [that is, in order to counter false reports of his death], that there was a combat in such-and-such a place, and that there were this many deaths in the army."[43] Phone chains could also be used to intentionally spread rumors. In fact, rumors became so powerful during the insurrection that government officials sometimes had to publicly discount them, and the Batista cabinet eventually passed an emergency decree specifying draconian punishments for the spreading of rumors.[44] For those who had access to a personal phone and sufficient free time—that is, mostly middle-class activists, perhaps especially middle-class women—these forms of intelligence gathering and propaganda allowed one to engage in activism without leaving the home.

As violence mounted from 1956 onward, the home also took on additional significance as a clandestine shelter, as it was increasingly necessary to provide safe houses for movement militants identified by police. The most famous safe houses were often run by women. For example, one Havana widow's house and photo studio in the lower-middle-class neighborhood of Lawton offered the perfect cover: the studio's business explained the constant foot traffic, and the absence of any adult males shielded the family from suspicion of political involvement.[45] Movement propaganda increasingly appealed to the general populace to provide shelter, often at a moment's notice. For example, a 1957 bulletin exhorted its readership, "Facilitate the entrance of your house to give shelter to someone. You can save a revolutionary."[46] And Radio Rebelde broadcasts, on the eve of the attempted general strike of April 1958, called specifically on Cuban women both to take to the streets in protest and to open their homes to revolutionaries fleeing police violence: "Cuban woman: leave the door to your house ajar so that it may serve as a refuge if necessary to the Cuban revolutionaries."[47]

Unlike the dead city demonstrations, which purposely drew attention to the dark and shuttered home as a visible political statement, support activities such as these were effective only when invisible. The predominance of women in these unsung, behind-the-scenes forms of activism based in the home gave rise to the common assertion—rarely substantiated or discussed in detail, however—that "housewives" played a very active role in the urban underground.[48] Indeed, interviews with former urban militants offer insight into the underground's reliance on the organized participation of women as messengers, "spies," and providers of safe houses.[49] In particular, women not employed outside the home could be valuable collaborators because of the flexibility and geographic mobility they enjoyed throughout the day. Additionally, women activists used their "apolitical" image and association with the home as cover for their actions, as they did in antidictatorial movements elsewhere.[50]

Beyond the family home, anti-Batista activists also mobilized other spaces typically characterized by contemporaries as "feminine." For example, churches were occasionally used as sites of protest and denunciation in this period, especially by women. Cuban church attendance was overwhelmingly female, urban, and middle class in this period, and the use of churches as political sites had historically opened space for women's public participation throughout Latin America.[51] Gloria Cuadras, head of the women's section of the Ortodoxo Party in Santiago and later an important figure in Santiago's anti-Batista underground, recalled a 1954 church service held to mark the first anniversary of the Moncada attack, during which she and other women handed out small cards that interwove passages from the Bible with quotes from the patriotic writings of José Martí "that fit [their] revolutionary objectives to a T."[52] The Catholic-infused ideals of morality and honor, and the use of the church as a protest venue, suggest that the early anti-Batista movement may have had special appeal for several overlapping groups: Ortodoxo Party sympathizers, urban women, the middle class, and active lay Catholics.

All-women's anti-Batista groups or all-women's protests in particular might use the exterior of a church as their staging ground for a public protest, as we will see further in chapter 3. Angela Alonso, who eventually became a member of the José Martí Women's Civic Front, recalled her first sighting of the women's group in October 1956. She came upon a tumult between a group of women and police in front of a centrally located Havana church, outside of which the women had tried to place a wreath to protest the dictatorship and honor José Martí. A crowd of people had formed, shouting in support of the women. "The argument was heated," she remembered; "the nucleus of the group was formed by a group of women dressed in black . . . trying desperately to save a floral wreath" from destruction by the police.[53]

Public demonstrations like these might also radiate outward from Havana to surrounding towns. In the first months of the dictatorship, some protesters—groups of young men and women—traveled from town to town. They planted themselves in public plazas, often outside churches, hoping to inspire small-scale public rallies, calling on people to reject the coup and sign a petition asking for the restoration of the 1940 constitution and handing out copies of the manifesto they had written. One member of the Juventud Obrera Católica, a lay Catholic youth group with a political bent, recalled the group's earliest itinerant acts in the main plazas and in front of churches in various small towns in Pinar del Rio Province, a short drive from Havana:[54] "We would stop in front of churches with little handouts [and say,] 'Hey, everyone come over here,' with a bullhorn. 'Come sign [a statement against] the coup.' We would say that the constitution had been broken; that the institutions had been dissolved. Now everything was in the hands of the military. . . . [We would say] that congress no longer existed, that [Batista] was a dictator. That the patriots hadn't fought the War of Independence for this!"[55]

Attention to the geography of protest during the first few years of Batista's regime thus reveals several salient characteristics of the opposition movement. The earliest protests unfolded in the home and the church, along major street corners and commercial thoroughfares, and, as we shall see, in department stores and movie theaters—all spaces that were frequently coded as feminine.[56] Women's participation was further encouraged by an imagined continuum of house and street: rather than viewing the private home as a closed-off space permitting a retreat from politics, protest actions were intended to radiate outward from the home to confront and destabilize the regime. Cuban protesters of the early 1950s creatively repurposed "apolitical" space and traced political claims onto the city in ways that were similar to other, subsequent urban antidictatorial movements in twentieth-century Latin America.[57] Early opposition efforts also tended to include inventive tactics drawing on performance and symbolism, such as the use of rites of mourning, commemorative dates, and republican symbolism. Finally, the sites described here suggest that opposition activity, even in the early period of 1952 to 1955, was not restricted to the university ambit, as much existing scholarship implies. Even if many of the early protesters were students or other youths, they clearly sought to move beyond that milieu to a broader public.

Although by the spring of 1958 the mountain-based rebel army viewed the civic opposition and even the armed underground as mere support groups for the guerrilla struggle, there is evidence that some urban-based militants thought differently, continuing to see the urban struggle as fundamental, rather than as rearguard.[58] In February 1957, just as the growing rebel army was beginning to garner international attention and popularity, the MRC still occasionally held up Gandhi as a model of civic resistance that could complement the armed struggle in the Sierra Maestra.[59] And another clandestine periodical promised in July 1958, "You will see . . . that collective action [acción conjunta] of an entire people can be more powerful than the most powerful army."[60] If existing historiography acknowledges the starring role awarded to guerrilla warfare by mid-1958, we may also surmise that some segments of the urban anti-Batista resistance embraced diverse strategies, continuing to raise the banner of mass civic struggle even while supporting the growing rebel army.

These stories help us recapture the richness and diversity of the anti-Batista struggle. If the development of guerrilla warfare rooted in the countryside proved to be the more lasting and powerful legacy of the Cuban insurrection, we must note that the urban protest movement also pioneered creative tactics of gender-inclusive protest and consciousness raising that helped discredit the dictatorship. As we shall see, the turn to arms soon transformed both men's and women's roles in the opposition. Yet it is important to remember that women were present in the very earliest expressions of protest, and would remain important actors as the insurrection grew.

Gender, Morality, and Consumer Culture

As we have seen, anti-Batista protests from 1952 through 1955 often involved organized disruptions of urban life. One subset of these actions explicitly targeted urban patterns of consumption and leisure, demanding that oppositionists refrain from purchasing certain goods or partaking in nightlife. Beyond their stated demands, it is also noticeable that early anti-Batista protesters often targeted the physical sites of leisure and consumption, such as department stores and movie theaters, rather than strictly "political" sites such as government buildings. Our point is not merely to explain why some urban Cubans opposed Batista, for to many contemporaries his betrayal of constitutional rule was obvious. Rather, we need to understand why anti-Batista expression took certain particular forms and occurred in particular sites. Understanding these early anti-Batista expressions therefore requires a contextualization in the previous decades of Cuban history, particularly the rise and decline of the appeal of U.S.-influenced urban consumer culture, as well as its gendered expressions.

Cuba had been firmly embedded within a U.S. sphere of influence since the mid-nineteenth century, accelerating with the U.S. military occupation of 1898 to 1902, following the Spanish-American War. For the next several decades the newly independent island took shape in the heavy political and economic shadow of its northern neighbor.[61] By the 1920s, North American mass-market production had flooded the Caribbean, coinciding with the sugar boom of 1919–20. As Louis Pérez has shown, this onslaught of U.S. commercial culture transformed everyday life as U.S.-made products, some affordable even to working-class Cubans, gave new meaning and tangible form to upward mobility, "progress," and "civilization."[62] There was a widespread belief that U.S. forms of consumption promised a better life, and these goods and habits were viewed "not as instruments of oppression, but as material goods eagerly adopted to improve daily life."[63] These everyday forms of consumption and their related performance of upward mobility depended on public displays in urban spaces such as the hotels, department stores, and cafés that had proliferated in early twentieth-century Havana, particularly in the neighborhoods of Centro Habana and El Vedado.[64] The earliest anti-Batista protests often occurred in these same areas.

Although all Cubans felt the influence of U.S. consumer culture to some degree, urban women were affected in particular ways. Some new practices and products, combined with expanding employment and education opportunities, granted women a new sense of freedom. Those women with disposable income enjoyed affordable mass-produced fashions, greater physical movement, new forms of leisure, and access to a world beyond family tradition from the 1920s onward. These changes were often experienced most keenly by middle-class women, who had traditionally been subjected to a greater degree of family sheltering. "Women of 'respectable' families [now] went out unaccompanied to shops, to movie theaters, to nightclubs," Pérez notes. Men occasionally resented these transformations, seeing women as emboldened and empowered by urban consumer culture. Women's new physical freedoms of movement, and their new mannerisms and comportment, such as smoking, were correspondingly denounced by some men as evidence of sexual promiscuity or superficiality.[65] This male backlash suggests the way gender informed these conflicting associations with American modernity, which threatened older forms of male privilege while also offering new opportunities. As Lauren Derby argues in the case of the Dominican Republic, "women became scapegoats for all the evils of the creeping 'Americanization' of the country."[66]

By the 1950s, the tropical pursuit of the American dream was seen as increasingly untenable. Buffeted by the declining economy, the appeal of American consumer culture had begun to wane, and one now heard the first mainstream calls to "buy national."[67] Similarly, the first serious and sustained critiques of U.S. tourism emerged in this period, decrying Cuba's reputation as the Las Vegas of Latin America. Calls to clean up Havana and reject the "immorality" fostered by foreign tourists were accompanied by assertions of the "decency" of Cuban women, who were portrayed in tourism brochures as sultry bombshells easily available to foreigners.[68] If an openly articulated condemnation of U.S. neo-imperialism remained rare, as Louis Pérez notes, a new and more critical sensibility was slowly beginning to emerge.[69]

The prevalence of modern consumer culture and the ambivalence it was beginning to provoke helps us contextualize the first bursts of anti-Batista protest. Opposition strategies reflected midcentury urban culture and were often centered on disrupting urban daily life. These strategies reveal conflicted contemporary associations with consumer culture and urban entertainment, which represented modernity for many Cubans, but could, in the context of a political crisis, also represent superficiality and lack of political consciousness. Consumer culture was both the terrain and the target of much early anti-Batista action. Early protest actions evoking consumption practices also seemed to critique women's insertion into the consumer culture of the postwar period, explicitly admonishing women not to purchase makeup, perfume, or dresses.[70] These somewhat narrow appeals to women, in which their participation would be defined by not purchasing, nevertheless opened avenues for their participation.

We find many of these themes addressed by the group Acción Cívica Cubana, which in January 1953 exhorted Cubans to avoid entertainment venues such as theaters and cabarets, and to undertake a kind of symbolic performance of mourning. The group suggested a boycott of imported products specifically, particularly those that might be characterized as luxury items: "Do not buy any more than what is strictly indispensable for consumption in daily life; do not buy imported articles: perfumes, textiles, automobiles, televisions, preserved foods [alimentos en conserva], American cigarettes, etc.; do not pay taxes; do not pay utilities, [do not pay] rent for either urban or rural properties, etc.; do not buy lottery tickets; do not attend social parties or frivolous shows: theaters, cabarets, bars. Think of the country as in mourning."[71] The group did not address women directly, but its calls to abstain from purchasing perfume and other luxury articles, such as imported foods, were likely implicitly directed to women.

The group Movimiento de Resistencia Popular, probably comprising mostly Ortodoxo sympathizers, similarly exhorted the public to avoid certain purchases in the immediate aftermath of the coup. In a flyer distributed in movie theaters in March 1952, the group admonished those who owned cars to buy only the minimal amount of gasoline necessary and warned them not to attend live shows (espectáculos), a prohibition that could have referred either to club acts in Havana's many nightclubs or to the music and dance performances that often preceded films in upscale movie theaters. It warned Cubans in general to "not buy any more than what is necessary to live," including not consuming any more electricity than necessary. Cubans were warned not to pay taxes or purchase lottery tickets—both abstentions that could be assumed to hurt state coffers, as the lottery was run by the state. And the group explicitly addressed women as shoppers and consumers: "Cuban woman, do not buy any more than what is necessary, no makeup, powders, lipsticks, and so on; don't buy dresses; take care of the ones you have, set an example of citizenship with your actions [ejemplariza con tu gesto la ciudadanía]."[72] The group thus called upon sympathizers to engage in politics ("citizenship") largely through consumer abstentions. These calls reflect a view of women as particularly embedded in consumerism, coveting luxury items such as fashionable dresses and makeup. Such appeals to women welcomed them to political opposition actions while also positioning them primarily as consumers.

How should we interpret the widely varied targets described in these early handbills, including government and the private sector, both foreign and national products and companies, and entertainment venues? They seem to suggest that these early actions were not predominantly instrumental in character, unlike the far more specific calls emitted by the Twenty-Sixth of

July Movement several years later to save one's money in order to donate it to the movement. We might assume, then, that these early measures had primarily symbolic importance. They were not predominantly programmatic or policy-oriented, but they were revealing in what they eschewed. They essentially requested a full withdrawal from existing commercial and social activities, suggesting a sense of decadence in Cuban public life that went beyond formal politics. The repeated entreaties to avoid luxury items and musical acts, and to "think of the country as in mourning," reveal a deep sense of unease not merely with the unconstitutionality of Batista's coup, but also more generally with the way Cuban urban culture had developed, with its strong emphasis on entertainment and consumer culture. At the same time, they might imply a worldview that saw many strands of the polity and economy entwined—that is, they seemed to simultaneously decry Batista's place at the political helm and the skewed development of Cuba, particularly its unequal dependence on U.S. trade.

In addition to explicit references to consumer behavior, attention to the geography of protest again suggests interesting patterns. In retrospect it is surprising how infrequently anti-Batista protests in this early period took place in spaces and sites typically thought of as "political," such as the area around the National Palace or the newly constructed Plaza Cívica. Rather, protest actions often seemed clustered in the commercial heart of the city, designed to disrupt major thoroughfares, moving from the hotels and department stores of central Havana to the movie theaters of La Rampa.[73] These areas were not entirely middle class, but had strong middle-class resonances. The choice of these sites suggests that early protesters—perhaps out of habit or familiarity of the protesters themselves—undertook actions in spaces primarily frequented by other middle-class publics.[74] Protesters targeted commercial districts, such as central streets lined with stores and offices, for staged interventions, propaganda distribution, and petition drives.[75] Young activists undertook "lightning interventions" in major department stores, suddenly leaping onto countertops to shout slogans against the dictatorship, to the surprise of shoppers.[76] Thus, during the first few years of the anti-Batista movement, protesters not only decried consumer culture but also intentionally disrupted and repurposed sites of modern consumer culture.

Movie theaters too were frequently the sites of spontaneous or planned political expressions and disruptions, such as when, in the weeks following Batista's coup, theatergoers jeered at Batista's image in newsreels, while former president Prio received "applause unknown to him since the first days of his administration."[77] As the American Embassy noted, just two weeks after Batista's coup, copies of a flyer entitled "Cubans, take your place of honor!" were dropped from balconies onto the crowds below in some Havana movie theaters, "taking advantage of the large crowds usually in attendance on Saturday nights."[78]

As we know from later antidictatorial protest movements throughout Latin America, the visible disruption of the city and of everyday life was an important method of communicating with the public under conditions of censorship or repression of public protest.[79] Yet the choice of department stores and movie theaters as sites of intervention requires some explanation beyond their merely pragmatic utility as centrally located, well-attended locales. Movie theaters, like department stores, still represented modern forms of consumer culture that many *habaneros* would have associated with progress, urban life, and, to some extent, American mass culture.[80] In addition, movie theaters were still the site of explicit political discussion, since this was where audiences were exposed to nightly newsreels, which had not yet been displaced by television. Interventions in cinemas and department stores were not, then, merely pragmatic attempts to hijack a captive audience. They evoked broader questions of politics, consumption, and modernity. And given the disapproval of frivolous consumption and leisure that we find in the opposition worldview, protesters may have specifically intended to snap unwary publics into political consciousness, liberating them from the depoliticizing distractions of shopping or moviegoing.

Early anti-Batista opposition statements not only explicitly called for the disruption of consumer activity. They also seemed to posit the continuation of consumption and leisure practices under conditions of political dictatorship as an ethical problem. That is, beyond accusations of superficiality or mere absence of proper political consciousness, indulging in shopping or partaking of nightlife posed a peculiar affront to the nation's "honor." Associations of consumption or vacuous leisure with political apathy or reaction would persist and even sharpen throughout the course of the insurrection, suggesting the strength of that correlation for contemporaries. For example, one of the Twenty-Sixth of July's most famous propaganda campaigns was known as "o-3-C," which stood for "zero club, zero cine, zero cabaret."[81] A flyer advertising the 1958 campaign printed by the MRC juxtaposed drawings of young socialites engaged in shopping and other leisure activities with members of the rebel army dying in battle. The flyer's accompanying text, written in the form of a traditional *décima*, juxtaposes revolutionary honor with apathetic vanity and excessive consumption:

Due to some vain caprice
You buy things in excess
And while you spend your money
Another Cuban is dying!

You give your money to the tyrant
And contribute to his evil.
Leave off with your vanity . . . !
Your honor has a date with destiny.
What Cuba really needs to buy
Is her liberty![82]

As the flyer's illustrations suggest, women were imagined as central to these activities. Women were thus specially implicated in calls to substitute frivolous entertainment with revolutionary sacrifice—a pattern that would continue after 1959.

Yet women could also manipulate these associations. For example, on the occasion of Richard Nixon's ill-fated tour of Latin America in 1958, the young activist Selina Bernal, affiliated with the university-based armed anti-Batista group the Revolutionary Directorate (DR), fashioned a long open letter to the American vice president. The letter criticizes the warped moral values and political obliviousness of American youth, who are blamed for indirectly enabling the U.S. government's support for dictators in the region. It suggests that Cuban youth have been forced to transcend apolitical distractions such as movies and football games, and posits young Cuban women as heroic, suffering figures who have been forced to make personal sacrifices in their struggle for liberty, in striking contrast to their U.S. counterparts: "Latin America is a broken artery, through which escape torrents of incredibly young blood, that of adolescents different from yours, who drink Coke in drugstores and cheer at football games. . . . Irresponsible, carefree girls who eat popcorn and cry in the movies next to their boyfriend of the moment can't conceive that, a little farther south, girls their age forget about the theater . . . to try to gain the strength [to undertake] a secret mission. It's hard to believe from the diving board of a swimming pool. But it's horribly true. Young Cuban women don't see their boyfriends next to a jukebox, but behind bars, or below marble."[83]

While the letter reinforces the notion that young women in particular may be guilty of frivolity and consumerism, it shifts the burden from Cuban to American women, while also indirectly linking Cuba's moral poverty

CERO COMPRAS

Por cualquier capricho vano
vas a comprar con exceso...
¡ Y cuando gastas un peso
está cayendo un cubano !

Le das tu peso al tirano
y ayudas a su maldad.
Deja ya tu vanidad !...
que tu honor tiene una cita:
¡ lo que Cuba necesita
es comprar su Libertad !

CERO CABARET

Cuando por placer mundano
vas una noche de fiesta
en nuestra gloriosa gesta
está muriendo un cubano

Cae la sangre de tu hermano
derramada por su fe.
¡ Ayuda tú... ponte en pie !
No traiciones a tu tierra..
Si toda Cuba está en guerra
¡ no vayas tú al cabaret !!

A clandestine flyer published by the Civic Resistance Movement juxtaposes leisure activities with revolutionary martyrdom: young men and women shop and dine against backdrops of a falling barbudo and chained hands. (Ernesto Chávez Collection, Special and Area Studies Collections, George A. Smathers Libraries, University of Florida, Gainesville, Florida)

with the influence of the United States. We see here a tendency within the urban anti-Batista movement, as it escalated from a civic protest movement into an armed insurrection, to increasingly suggest a linkage between ideas of superficiality, urban entertainment, and consumption and those of dictatorship, capitalism, and even U.S. imperialism, and to view young women as particularly implicated in these processes.[84] A critical vision of Cuba as corrupted and debased by U.S. commercial culture, tourism, political interference, and organized crime had been slowly emerging in the 1950s. This discourse may have been strongest in Havana, the hub of Cuba's emerging tourist economy, and it drew on the moralizing rhetoric so successfully mobilized by the Ortodoxo Party. It now found sharp expression in the anti-Batista movement. This incipient anti-imperialism, filtered through the lens of urban decadence and consumer apathy, suggests different roots for Cuba's post-1959 radicalism. Cuba's postrevolutionary stress on anti-imperialism and the necessity of austerity and sacrifice drew not only from the socialist political imaginary or the idealized "New Man" who reflected the ascetic communalism rebels found in the Sierra Maestra. It also emerged from the disillusioned heart of urban commercial culture itself. The culmination of these elements in the "great bordello" of Batista's

Cuba became part of the official narrative after 1959, and helps explain the purifying moralist pretensions of the young revolutionaries.

The Rise of "Action" and the Gendered Division of Labor

By 1955, angered by Batista's seeming intransigence and provoked by increasingly violent police tactics, many oppositionists began to turn toward direct action in protests. Over the course of the next few years, some took up arms. Although a few oppositionists had advocated armed struggle from the very beginning, such as the Moncada attackers led by Fidel Castro, the widespread acceptance of armed resistance was a longer process. In retrospect the rise of the Cuban guerrilla movement feels inevitable; yet its emergence was certainly not a given at the time. Young people in high schools and universities and in other student groups fiercely debated whether to form a militia or some other kind of clandestine political movement.[85] The rise in state violence was central to these changes of heart. Throughout 1955, street fighting between police and protesters had been on the rise. The police had viciously attacked several large student marches in the spring and summer. In December, when protesters interrupted a baseball game by running onto the field with banners denouncing Batista, the police beat them savagely, captured in footage that was transmitted live on national television. Such rampant displays of state violence had a deep impact on many Cubans, especially youths, who were greatly moved by acts of participation and witnessing.

This, then, was the context in which some Cubans initially decided to move toward action. What exactly was the meaning of "action"? It did not at the time refer exclusively to the use of arms; it was primarily defined as something that involved the use of the body, which implied physical risk.[86] Valeria Espinoza, a former member of the Twenty-Sixth of July Movement, explained the concept of direct action as it applied to public protest as having a consciousness-raising or pedagogical aspect: it was a way "to teach the people to combat Batista with their bodies on the line [*de cuerpo presente*]."[87] That physicality, that direct use of the body, was understood in juxtaposition to "thought" or "talking." As another former Twenty-Sixth of July Movement member recalled in an interview conducted in Havana, she and others attempted to convince other young people of the need for action. "Why *action*? Why do we have to go to *action*?" she would ask them. "Because we can't just be talking, talking, talking. That doesn't work any more," she would explain.[88] Espinoza similarly explained that action was "a way to be *doing*, not just *hoping* Batista would stop being dictator."[89] Young activists saw engaging in action as an important turning point. As one young member of the Twenty-Sixth of July's Youth Brigades recalled, her first attempt to explode a Molotov cocktail was highly ineffective, yet she felt elated "for having moved from 'thought' to 'action.' "[90]

The concept of action was broad: it included armed attacks on security forces in both city and country and sabotage such as bombings and arson. It could also include the rowdy, "combative" street protest, in which protesters clashed physically with police. It was the very antithesis of efforts at dialogue and reconciliation, such as those attempted by some civic associations in 1955. As the guerrilla war grew after 1956, such activities were seen as increasingly central to the definition of revolution: "Revolution is action," declared one clandestine publication in 1958.[91] As another former member of the Twenty-Sixth of July Movement explained, a "man of action" was one who was "capable of giving his life for a cause."[92] Action thus implied the ultimate commitment, that of "martyrdom."

This change in strategy, and its attendant implications for the use of the body, accentuated differences between men's and women's roles in the anti-Batista protest movement. Until 1955, protests often had a sober, stately quality, using performative or symbolic elements such as mock funeral processions or ceremonies that swore loyalty to the 1940 constitution. But throughout 1955, the character of protests changed, becoming more violent physical confrontations with security forces. At first some protesters tried to adapt by leading with a contingent of women, under the assumption that this would discourage police from launching a violent frontal attack on the march.[93] Others placed women in the middle of a march, flanked by men on either side to protect them from police assault.[94]

But in general, as the protests became increasingly violent, the protesters became increasingly male. Indeed, young men themselves counseled their female counterparts not to undertake the risk the protests now entailed. As one woman activist and leader of the university's student federation recalled, "Women also went [to violent protests]. They did. But the majority were men. The men themselves [encouraged us not to go]. I remember [the student leader] José Antonio Echeverría would say to me, 'Don't go . . . look at all the police down there.' But I wouldn't leave. I would just stand a little bit behind the others."[95] The anecdote reveals both the way men counseled women, casting themselves as their protectors, and the way young women navigated such advice. Thus the transition to "action" changed both the literal demographic composition of protests and the relations between men and women committed to the anti-Batista movement.

As we have seen, women had taken a substantial part in the organized disruptions of urban daily life that characterized the earliest years of the anti-Batista resistance. But women tended not to physically take up arms. Thus, after 1955, the growth of the armed opposition groups resulted in an increasingly gendered division of labor within the anti-Batista movement. Many young men joined the new, armed groups of the urban underground and the rebel army in the Sierra Maestra. Many women henceforth operated more as a support network, taking over the practically important but less glamorous work of organizing, strategizing, fund-raising, and distributing propaganda, as well as the symbolically and materially important duties of publicly protesting and attending to the wounded, the dead, and the incarcerated.

The issue here is not simply about the literal predominance of men over women in the urban underground and in the rebel army. "Real" revolutionary participation was also understood as being linked to traditional notions about physical strength. For example, as Espinoza explained, "a kind of natural division of labor emerged [because] a man can carry a weapon better than a woman. A woman can transport a weapon . . . but when it comes to shooting . . . a woman's strength—with some exceptions—isn't the same [as a man's]. It's like a natural division of the struggle. Each person does what they can do best. . . . Men concentrated more on physical violence, and the women . . . concentrated on organizing, relaying messages, taking information to the press."[96]

This explanation seems disjointed, relying on the counterintuitive notion that shouldering and firing a weapon require a different level of strength than merely transporting one. In theory at least, the use of automated weaponry could equalize differential strengths in battle. Then again, the notion of physical strength does not seem particularly apt for the urban underground, whose militants rarely had access to rifles, instead using mostly small pistols or flammable material for bombs. Instead, this seems a purely ideological explanation for the division of labor that emerged. Thus movement activists, including women, reified socially constructed views about who was fit to undertake physical violence by resorting to "natural" or biological explanations.

Contemporaries occasionally remarked on the transition in women's activities in positive tones. For example, Dysis Guira, an organizer for the DR, described in 1959 how her contributions to the anti-Batista movement had changed over time: "Of course I attended all the rallies and all kinds of public protests. But later another kind of work began, less notable but perhaps more efficient. We transported and handed out revolutionary pamphlets and arms; we . . . helped hide *compañeros*; sold bonds; accompanied the *compañeros* when they needed a female companion to look less suspicious."[97]

Yet that experience of feeling sidelined within a movement may have left a bitter aftertaste for some women. In a recently published memoir we find this same transition described with a more critical inflection. As former Twenty-Sixth of July member Sonnia Moro writes, "in this type of organization [that is, a militia], we girls were at a disadvantage." As her male counterparts joined underground militias, they henceforth enjoyed the solidarity, leadership, and formal structure of an organization with various hierarchies of rank and belonging, not to mention postrevolutionary honors as veterans. They came to represent the vanguard of the revolutionary struggle. "And we girls? The collaborators, the assistants, the rearguard, we took on apparently secondary roles," Moro writes, "overprotected [and] undervalued . . . by our male *compañeros*."[98]

The urban protest movement that had developed during the first few years after Batista's coup included both men and women, and pioneered protest actions that ranged from stay-at-home days, to boycotts, to marches laden with nationalist symbolism. But as we shall see in subsequent chapters, the changes of the next few years tasked men with being brave enough to take up arms, while women increasingly turned to other outlets, including all-women's public protests or the hidden work of propaganda distribution and strategizing. The outlines of a mass protest movement visible between 1952 and 1955 now shifted. Opposition energy was channeled underground, and an attendant division of labor emerged between men and women, as well as between men who took up arms and those who did not—a distinction also understood in gendered terms, as we shall see. But these complex histories have been overlaid with a simpler story.

On the twentieth anniversary of the Moncada attack, Fidel Castro pronounced in a speech, "If yesterday we were just a handful of men, today we are a whole people conquering the future."[99] The phrase—subsequently circulated on posters—well encapsulates how the insurrectionary struggle has been memorialized in Cuba: a "handful" of brave men took the initiative in sparking a revolution, eventually mobilizing and then liberating the masses. The implicit danger of such stories is to reify a class of untouchable male political leaders who suffered and sacrificed and who are therefore entitled to lead. Yet, as we have seen, the first few years of the opposition movement suggest a far more complicated picture, encompassing various actors and different strategies, and taking numerous urban locales as its terrain.

2 | THE DOMESTICATION OF VIOLENCE, 1955–1958

"I was an employee of a company based in Cuba, married with two lovely kids; I had my car, my TV, and in the summer we spent a month at the beach." Thus read an open letter written by a middle-class urban professional who had joined the rebel army. The letter, which circulated throughout Havana as a clandestine flyer in the summer of 1958, explained how the author had overcome his initial reluctance to join the movement. Although he had been inspired by the valiant young men who attacked the Moncada military barracks in 1953, he was moved to take action himself only several years later when his young daughter reported that a classmate's father had died in the struggle. That death opened the letter writer's eyes; he decided that he too must fight. The letter thereafter describes his decision to join the insurrection as stemming from a combination of masculine honor, patriarchal duty, and Christian faith.[1] While historians have long recognized the importance of the Cuban revolutionaries as political actors and cultural icons, the flyer's references to religion, class, and family suggest that the appeal and meaning of the rebel army to Cuban contemporaries may have been more complex than we have recognized.

When the triumphant rebel army descended from the Sierra Maestra and entered Havana in January 1959, it inaugurated both a new historical era and a new revolutionary subject. The inspiring image of the *barbudo*—the bearded guerrilla warrior—would reverberate enduringly in Cuba and beyond. It is difficult to overstate the impact this unexpected victory of guerrilla warfare had beyond Cuba's borders, especially among youths and the Latin American Left. For one thing, it signaled a bold new strategy: guerrilla warfare drawing on the peasantry as its primary social base, built up through small groups or *focos*. Furthermore, the idea that a dictator could be overthrown after a mere two years of guerrilla warfare was a seductive lesson for the many Latin Americans who despaired at the region's entrenched poverty and inequality. The Cuban victory proved that there was no need to wait for propitious conditions for revolution; those conditions could be created through sheer force of will.[2]

Beyond its implications for political strategy, the image of the "heroic guerrilla" also had an enormous cultural impact. In particular, it conjured up a specific set of associations regarding manhood. Rebel victory fostered an idealized image of revolutionary masculinity that subsequently inspired young men throughout the Latin American Left, who strove to live up to this new example of bravery and self-sacrifice.[3] As the historian Florencia Mallon notes in the case of Chile, the "multifaceted image of the dedicated young *barbudo*, who risked everything in the name of revolutionary justice and emerged untouched and empowered on the other side, was heady stuff indeed." It exercised "extraordinary power over people's imagination and morality, inspiring them to action."[4] Among U.S. youths, the Cuban rebels were seen as a third worldist rejoinder to conformity and the "company man." According to the historian Van Gosse, "the ragged *barbudos* led by Fidel Castro, chomping their cigars and darting down green mountain slopes to ambush Batista's garrisons, were every teenage boy's dream of gunfighting, personal heroism and nose-thumbing at received authority."[5] The Cuban *barbudos* thus simultaneously seemed to rejuvenate the international Left and flagging midcentury masculinity.

The rebel commander Che Guevara, in particular, came to epitomize the figure of the heroic guerrilla. Scarcely known to most Cubans during the anti-Batista insurgency, he soon became the prototype of the revolutionary "new man," held up as a standard to be emulated in Cuba and beyond. In Che's moving autobiographical account, which was read voraciously by Latin American youths, he and other rebel combatants were reborn in the crucible of battle, gradually developing a collective consciousness that allowed them to transcend their social differences and overcome their own inner weaknesses and lack of discipline. In his telling, the rebel army represented the mystical communion of uprooted urban militants and the dispossessed peasantry of the Sierra. After Che's death in Bolivia in 1967 at the hands of security forces, his image acquired even more poignancy. Throughout the 1960s, Che's iconic photograph seemed to be everywhere, representing both revolution and a particular brand of masculinity. "In student spaces, apartments, offices, even occupied buildings— the ubiquitous image of Latin American revolutionary Che Guevara portrayed a bearded, young, brash, gun-toting, self-confident image of the masculine rebel."[6] Through the media images and publications of both Che and Fidel, the *barbudo* came to represent anti-imperialism, third world revolution, and a brashly confident hypermasculinity manifested in the will to act.

This chapter examines the way masculinity was construed in the anti-Batista resistance in the late 1950s in order to illuminate the contemporary meanings of gender, political violence, and revolutionary will. The particular brand of warrior masculinity that we have come to associate with the Sierra leaders—such as risk taking, physical bravery, military prowess, and triumphalism—grew in importance over time. Yet as this chapter shows, the constructions of revolutionary masculinity found in the anti-Batista resistance also went beyond these traits. This becomes especially clear if we look at the anti-Batista resistance movement as a whole, encompassing both city and country, and if we move beyond the writings and speeches of the Sierra leadership to examine other sources, such as the memoirs of rank-and-file participants, the clandestine press, and other forms of contemporary ephemera. Men involved in insurrectionary activity referenced male honor and martyrdom, fatherhood and paternal duty, Christianity and defense of the Catholic Church, and sexual discipline. This chapter argues that the repurposing of these traditional tropes of masculinity allowed the anti-Batista resistance to ground and domesticate potentially radical politics in familiar notions of masculine honor, paternal responsibility, and sexual propriety. Thus, while many Cubans supported significant—even radical—reform by 1959, part of the attraction of the revolutionary movement was simultaneously its self-projection as a sexually disciplined, morally correct, white, middle-class, Catholic group of men.

Recovering the varied contemporary meanings associated with revolutionary masculinity in both the rebel army and the urban underground suggests new explanations for the way the anti-Batista resistance movement legitimized the use of violence and why it eventually came to enjoy wide public support. It also begs the question of how these diverse constructions were telescoped into the rough-and-tumble image of the gun-toting, cigar-chomping, bearded rebel that became so emblematic of the 1960s. To that end, this chapter explores the making of the "heroic guerrilla" icon that eventually enjoyed such power. It emerged at a specific time, when the Twenty-Sixth of July Movement changed strategies, deemphasizing the broad urban struggle that was initially so important, betting instead on a purely military victory led by the small rebel army ensconced in the Sierra Maestra. Thus the famous *barbudo* icon was not merely the natural and organic expression of the growth of the guerrilla army; it was the self-constructed image of the winning faction of the Twenty-Sixth of July Movement, disseminated after the failure of other strategies and alliances. Other imagined agents of revolution—such as the urban martyr or the militant worker—faded into historical oblivion as the *barbudo* gained prominence in the social imaginary by late 1958. As this chapter shows, the *barbudo*'s appeal to Cuban contemporaries was somewhat distinct from subsequent interpretations. For example, the Sierra Maestra rebels stressed their sexual discipline and moral purity, characteristics that are now usually overlooked. But as the *barbudo* icon swept the globe after 1959 it took on a life of its own, becoming "a central trope of the radical component of the New Left," as historian Eric Zolov notes.[7]

The Rise of Arms in the Sierra and *el Llano*

Nineteen fifty-five was a pivotal year. It witnessed a growing break between those who sought to unseat Batista through civic means, such as negotiation and early elections, and those who adopted the "insurrectionary line," as it was referred to then. While in retrospect the turn to arms may seem inevitable, it sparked significant dispute among contemporaries. Political parties, university associations, and even high school organizations splintered after intense internal debates that put members on opposing sides of the issue. The insurrectionary line had been championed as early as 1952 by a minority of oppositionists, including Fidel Castro and his collaborators in the Moncada barracks attack of 1953. But by 1955, in the face of Batista's intransigence, the failure of calls for civic dialogue, and growing police violence, the insurrectionary tendency began to gain wider support. The same year witnessed the formation of various armed anti-Batista groups based in the urban centers.[8] The cohort around Fidel Castro, recently amnestied from prison and exiled in Mexico, forged a more formal, durable organization named for the date of their spectacular attack on the Moncada barracks: the Twenty-Sixth of July Movement. The Twenty-Sixth of July subsequently became the best-known and most powerful of the armed opposition groups, but it was not the only one. In Havana, the Revolutionary Directorate (Directorio Revolucionario, DR), a university-centered group that was initially an offshoot of the Federation of University Students, enjoyed significant respect and support, perhaps exceeding that of the Twenty-Sixth of July Movement, at least until 1957.

In our tendency to equate the rise of arms with the rebel army, we often forget that the period from 1956 through early 1958 marked the peak of the urban underground, also known as *el llano*, which comprised the urban sectors of the Twenty-Sixth of July Movement, the DR, and other smaller armed groups such as the Triple A and Organización Auténtica. While both the DR and Twenty-Sixth of July Movement eventually formed guerrilla armies in rural areas, it must be remembered that they began as urban clandestine organizations and always retained an urban wing. In other ways, too, one could argue that the urban theater was the true epicenter of conflict until early 1958. The cities bore the brunt of state repression. Batista at first concentrated army troops around Havana and Santiago, sending only a few thousand soldiers to the mountains of Oriente to contest the growing rebel army.[9] The cities were also disproportionately important as centers of public protest, public opinion, and political plurality. Havana in particular was characterized by a number of opposition groups with varying strategies, and was thus the site of some political conflict among the various anti-Batista groups. For example, until mid-1958 the Communist Party denounced the use of arms, arguing instead for a grassroots mass movement. Unlike in the Sierra, then, in Havana, the Twenty-Sixth of July Movement never exercised uncontested hegemony.

How large was the urban underground? Ramón Bonachea and Marta San Martín estimate its membership—that is, the total number of dues-paying individuals associated with the clandestine groups named above—to have been about 10,000 in mid-1958, swelling to 30,000 by the end of the year. Within that, they estimate that there may have been 1,000 "hard-core fighters" in early 1958 and perhaps as many as 5,000 or 6,000 by the end of the year.[10] (The rebel army, on the other hand, probably never counted more than 3,000 members at its peak in 1958, and until then numbered only in the hundreds.)[11] Yet the concept of "membership" risks exaggerating the extent to which participation in oppositional activity was formalized. In practice, the boundaries of each group could be porous, and many militants belonged to more than one group either simultaneously or sequentially. Political affiliations were often driven by personal loyalties, and members might flow from one group to another as leaders were imprisoned or killed. Furthermore, militant activities took place within a broader context of urban opposition sentiment, and many underground militants also took part in public protests or other civic actions, at least until 1958. Scholarly and popular focus on the principal rebel groups has tended to obscure this fluid and informal atmosphere. But particularly outside the small nuclei of group leaders, the experience of many participants was not merely of collaborating with a particular anti-Batista organization, but of belonging more generally to a militant, action-oriented political culture with a high degree of cooperation among groups and a continuum of actions, from legal to extralegal, from spontaneous to tightly coordinated.[12]

The French intellectual Régis Debray and others popularized the notion in the 1960s that *el llano* was more politically moderate than the Sierra, reflecting the presumably more middle-class background of *llano* militants. But as the political scientist Samuel Farber has noted, that distinction cannot hold. *El llano* contained most of the Communist Party militants, who were ideologically farther to the Left than the Twenty-Sixth of July Movement. There were also many moderates in the Sierra, some of whom turned against the Castro government in the early 1960s.[13] And many militants who joined the rebel army had initially formed part of the urban underground. Rather, both the Sierra and *el llano* contained militants whose politics ranged from moderate to radical.[14] This de facto Center-Left alliance explains why programmatic statements released periodically by the leadership of the Twenty-Sixth of July Movement were often imprecise or intentionally vague, intended to garner the widest possible support, or reflecting evolving political alliances.[15] At any rate, the anti-Batista resistance was often not explicitly ideological. The clandestine press of the period was characterized by amorphous and emotional prose, with broad demands such as the restoration of national dignity. Much movement ephemera also focused on strategy, such as on the importance of immediate action and the removal of Batista.[16]

We can gain a sense of this sensibility—emphasizing action and militaristic nationalism—from the following poem, which circulated widely through the University of Havana as the student body debated the use of force. It was a passionate, quasi-spiritual call to arms that inspired many youths:

The dawn will be tinted red with the blood of your children
But the green morning will come, like a call of hope . . .
Fatherland [*patria*], give me a signal to enter into combat
For the restless phalanxes of our dead
Who smash the earth to return to life
And liberate the nation.
Fatherland, give me your blessing and signal [*tu santo y seña*] to enter
    into combat.[17]

The frequent emphasis on action over clear policy demands could make it hard for Cubans to perceive what a particular group or leader stood for, beyond the will to act. Enrique Oltuski, who eventually joined the Twenty-Sixth of July Movement, remembered trying to decipher Fidel Castro's politics as the movement took shape. "Fidel was the total revolutionary. . . . He lived for revolution twenty-four hours a day. But . . . what exactly did he believe in? That [was not] so clear. Fidel spoke only of the next landing in

Cuba, of the uprising that would take place, of the fight, of arms."[18] This concrete focus on action, as well as the more abstract references to morality, honor, and dignity, shifted the terms of the insurrection toward sentiment, often subsuming more serious ideological debate.

Negotiating Masculinity in the Anti-Batista Insurrection

Certain presumptions about manhood and its proper characteristics were central to how urban militants conceptualized their participation. For example, there was a genuine sense among "men of action" that the entire strategy of armed urban opposition was literally premised on bravery and virility. They believed that the inequality in weaponry and resources between security and insurgent forces could be overcome only by the almost superhuman bravery of the insurgents. Miguel Guillén, a former Twenty-Sixth of July member in the Havana underground, explained in an interview, "As we used to say, 'A weapon is only worth as much as the man who wields it.'"[19] That is, only a man's bravery could compensate for the flagrant disparity in arms. Some men of action correspondingly disdained men they viewed as lacking the "virility" to use arms, characterizing any criticism of the use of political violence as "weakness" or "cowardice." While the gendered division of insurrectionary labor between men and women seemed to obey "natural" laws about physical strength, as discussed in chapter 1, men were divided between those who sufficiently possessed idealized masculine characteristics such as bravery and those who did not. Indeed, manliness, as John Tosh reminds us in his study of nineteenth-century Britain, "was fundamentally a set of values by which men judged other men," constructed not only—perhaps not even principally—in relation to women.[20]

Leaders of the action-oriented opposition publicly manipulated allegations of cowardice to foreclose the possibility of any legitimate alternative to political violence. This was especially true at important political junctures, as the growing anti-Batista organizations sought to gain allies and thwart competitors. Thus in 1955, as the Twenty-Sixth of July Movement was in its early stages of formation, Fidel Castro wrote, "This is the hour where one proves the real combatants; this is the crucial hour [*hora útil*] in which the weak, the indecisive, the mediocre and the poor in spirit will be left behind."[21] After the disastrous landing of the *Granma* in December 1956, Fidel publicly denounced the Revolutionary Directorate as "cowards" for not having joined the urban uprising timed to coincide with the landing.[22] Similarly, in their

1957 manifesto, the armed group Organización Auténtica explained the difference in "character" between the men who engaged in civil versus armed protest. They praised "the integrity [*entereza*] and spirit of [personal] sacrifice that must animate the men of action to confront the . . . tyranny that oppresses us."[23] Thus men publicly imputed each other's masculinity during crucial stages as the revolutionary struggle became more violent. Some young men internalized this fear of censure, using it to press themselves onward when they felt paralyzed by fear. As Oltuski told himself, "I had to keep fighting. If I quit, I would be a coward."[24]

Allegations of cowardice were not mere blustery pamphleteering. In the everyday interactions of the anti-Batista underground, young men negotiated the messy reality of divergent political strategies and different expressions of masculinity. We can glean a better sense of how these masculine codes of behavior operated in practice through two brief biographical sketches. The case of the conflict between Marcos Rodríguez ("Marquitos") and the Revolutionary Directorate shows that, on occasion, disagreements over the use of arms could provoke near-violent confrontations and elicit searing allegations of improper masculinity. The oral traditions surrounding the urban underground leader Gerardo Abreu ("Fontán") illuminate what revolutionaries and police viewed as the *antithesis* of proper revolutionary masculinity, involving transgressive racial or sexual identities.

Marquitos had been a philosophy student at the University of Havana.[25] He was a member of the Socialist Youth, an affiliate group of the Communist Party (PSP), and worked with a cultural organization supported by the PSP, Nuestro Tiempo. During his time at the university, Marquitos apparently cut something of a bohemian character. He wore leather sandals, footwear understood by contemporaries to indicate homosexuality.[26] He was small and thin and usually carried a book beneath his arm. He embodied the image of the university-based, sexually suspect intellectual.[27] Following the PSP's line, Marquitos was outspoken in student discussions about the necessity to organize the masses into a broad opposition movement rather than rely on what he called "aggressive"—namely, militaristic—methods of opposition to the Batista dictatorship. Marquitos's criticisms were directed particularly at the Revolutionary Directorate's strategy to "strike at the top"—that is, their attempt to assassinate Batista in order to bring an immediate end to the country's political crisis.[28]

The 1964 trial in which Marquitos was convicted of relaying the whereabouts of DR militants to police is now infamous for publicly pitting the Twenty-Sixth of July Movement, DR, and PSP against one another. But it also showed that even when conflicts were largely political and strategic, they could be expressed through allegations of improper sexuality or insufficient masculinity. As the highly publicized trial exposed, Marquitos had several altercations with men belonging to the DR over questions of strategy. In one incident, probably from 1957, Marquitos was speaking against U.S. imperialism on the University of Havana's public address system. One of the leaders of the DR cut him off, saying, "Our problem is not with the Yankees but with Batista."[29] DR members' verbal attacks on Marquitos focused on his lack of manhood. For example, they "expressed scorn for the Communists . . . and told [Marquitos] they 'had no courage to carry a revolver.' "[30] In another altercation, men belonging to the DR chided Marquitos for being a "chicken" (*gallina*) and a homosexual: "They said, what was a faggot doing in the affairs of men [*qué hacía un maricón en cosa de hombres*]."[31]

As various authors have noted, the allegation of homosexuality had strong meanings in Cuban political culture. It was the culmination of allegations of effeminacy and lack of machismo, a quick way to politically discredit an opponent.[32] As Lourdes Casal noted: "To launch an accusation of homosexuality against a political enemy was one of the most terrible insults. . . . It was a way of calling him weak and unworthy of holding power."[33] Marquitos's story reveals the seeds of normative revolutionary masculine codes and conflict over the contours of men's appropriate behavior. These attributes reinforced views of masculinity and revolutionary action that not all men embraced. Revolutionary understandings of manhood emerged in dialogue with notions of family duty, religion, or self-sacrifice, as we shall see, but they were also constructed against "cowards" such as homosexuals and Communists.

As the epicenter of the opposition shifted to the armed groups, leaders correspondingly put an increasing emphasis on the ideal of masculine bravery, militarism, and the willingness to engage in or support direct action. Nevertheless, it is important to note that constructions of masculinity were not static or monolithic. There was a tension between different masculine ideals, such as discipline or self-control, on the one hand, and bravery or recklessness, on the other.[34] Famed leaders of the urban underground such as Frank País, killed by police in July 1957, were known by contemporaries less for their bravado than for their excellent strategic and organizational capacities, which relied on planning, control, and discretion as well as on physical bravery. The case of Fontán, killed by police in February 1958, sheds light on these dynamics.

Born in 1931 to a working-class Afro-Cuban family, Fontán held various odd jobs until he was hired as an announcer by a pharmaceutical company that sent cars with loudspeakers through the streets of Havana to advertise its products. From there he became known as a spoken word performer (*locutor*), recording short interludes on the radio or reciting poetry and performing in nightclubs.[35] Fontán joined the youth section of the Ortodoxo Party, and like many young Ortodoxo militants in Havana, he became involved in the Twenty-Sixth of July Movement, becoming one of the movement's few black urban underground leaders. He seems to have been interested in organization and in consciousness raising rather than simply in military action; for example, he was initially opposed to the formation of the urban militias, although he eventually became one of seven captains of the movement's action and sabotage sections in Havana and oversaw their reorganization.[36]

Memories of Fontán reveal the divergent leadership qualities that existed at the time between "men of action," who were presumably more spontaneous, passionate, and demonstrative, and "men of ideas" or organizers, who were more calculated and reserved. Oral sources make it clear that, unlike many of the young men in the movement, Fontán was able to control his temper, was careful not to be overcome with passion, and thought carefully before taking action. One former comrade recalled, "We saw him in the most dangerous moments stop to analyze the right measures, the consequences, and . . . the risk that the other *compañeros* might run."[37] As another Twenty-Sixth of July member who worked with Fontán at a radio station recalled, Fontán carefully measured his words while at work. "Once . . . I had an argument with a singer who was criticizing the [*Granma*] expeditionaries. I responded [angrily] and the argument [accidentally] went out over the air. Fontán told me to be careful not to expose myself that way."[38] Perhaps this careful, measured quality is what prompted one former comrade to say that Fontán "didn't seem like a man of action. He spoke slowly, he didn't have a strong personality. He was very delicate in his dealings. He was a great organizer."[39] And of course, these recollections—recorded decades after revolutionary victory—have inevitably been filtered through the sheer enormity of the figure of Fidel Castro, an inspirational and charismatic persona, hot tempered and gifted in oratory. Fontán, a serious, introverted man, cut a rather different figure.

Two related stories about Fontán capture something of the way "correct" revolutionary masculinity was understood by contemporaries. The first anecdote, documented by a former revolutionary participant, explains that Fontán was captured in late 1957 with two other Twenty-Sixth of July members. They were taken to the Bureau of Investigations to be interrogated and perhaps tortured, but upon seeing the detainees, the bureau chief said of Fontán, "Not him, this delinquent-looking black guy can't be a revolutionary."[40] The second anecdote, captured in an interview with a former Twenty-Sixth of July member, is so similar that it is evidently a different version of the same incident, with one revealing difference. According to this version, Fontán was arrested and taken to the Bureau of Investigations. "And he enters . . . passing himself off as a homosexual. But totally! With all the [right] gestures. And the chief of the Bureau . . . said, 'Hey, bring me the [real] revolutionary, not this guy!' And they threw him out. And he was the most wanted man [in Havana] at the time!"[41]

Stories like this form a corpus of oral traditions in which clever insurrectionaries outwitted police, often under the guise of some other social identity.[42] Although superficially similar, the morals of the two stories are different. In the first, the security forces are duped by their own assumption that the revolutionaries are exclusively white, and thus they mistakenly overlook the leader under their very noses.[43] The second story, likely a corruption of the first, attributes agency to Fontán, who cleverly manipulates police assumptions. But the implied absurdity of the situation suggests that police and insurrectionists shared a normative notion of revolutionary masculinity that was fundamentally incompatible with homosexuality, perhaps particularly black homosexuality.[44]

As these stories of Marquitos and Fontán suggest, the turn to arms drew new distinctions among men as well as between men and women. But the revolutionary masculinity that emerged was never a monolith. It evolved over time, delineated through practices and tensions in the urban underground and in the guerrilla army.[45] Men negotiated different models of revolutionary masculinity, praising different kinds of behavior depending on the context. The warrior masculinity we have come to associate with the Sierra rebels coexisted with other constructions, only gradually overshadowing them. Alongside the growing emphasis on bravery, physical strength, and the willingness to fight and kill, we also find references to masculine honor garnered through political martyrdom, and of the duty to join the revolution as an extension of familial or even religious duty. These references to masculine honor, paternal responsibility, and Christian duty served to "domesticate" the use of violence, which had been discredited since the late 1930s in Cuban politics, by infusing it with a sense of righteousness and linking it to the enactment of familiar gender roles.

Honor and Martyrdom in the Urban Underground

The concept of revolutionary martyrdom was important for galvanizing support for the opposition during the anti-Batista insurrection. An analysis of political martyrdom helps illustrate the intertwined logic of how revolutionary masculinity and male honor were imagined and the way in which revolutionary violence was justified as defensive. The construction and celebration of martyrdom were particularly important in the highly dangerous urban underground. The fabled battles between the rebel army and the demoralized and conscript-staffed regular army in the Sierra Maestra have become the stuff of legend. The much grittier and more punishing conflict between Havana's highly efficient police force and the poorly armed urban underground is a less familiar story.[46] Throughout 1957 and 1958, police units—sometimes accompanied by federal troops—detained, tortured, and killed hundreds of members of the various revolutionary groups located in the capital. The psychological stress of urban clandestinity was significant; underground militants were "always shut in, waiting tensely, with the prospect of an unequal battle with the repressive forces" looming before them.[47] Young men of the urban underground feared police torture in particular, and contemplated suicide should they be captured. They noted the way imprisonment and torture changed men's personalities, hardening some, causing severe anxiety or memory loss in others.[48] As one man wrote of a *compañero*, "prison and torture had made him a different man, what you would call 'a good revolutionary.' "[49] In this context, the concept of political martyrdom helped militants negotiate the extreme vulnerability and danger they faced by combining the ideals of personal honor and self-sacrifice that were so central to the construction of revolutionary masculinity in the urban underground. Beyond militants' personal experience, the concept of martyrdom also helps explain why and in what terms the anti-Batista organizations garnered popular support.

The idea of martyrdom was also powerful in the Sierra, but the rebel soldiers' deaths in battle fit cultural definitions of a "good" death. As Ramón Bonachea and Marta San Martín have written, Cubans shared certain assumptions about how a revolutionary leader should die. Most Cubans who supported Fidel Castro in the 1950s scarcely believed he would really come to power. But Fidel "would know how to die, fighting to the last minute. . . . One day, Fidel, out of ammunition, would be encircled with his fighters. Fighting against the superiorly equipped army, they would fall one by one, and Fidel would then die with 'valor and with dignity,' two very important elements of the mystique."[50] The idea of a good death was also tied to idealized notions of masculinity. It was said that Che Guevara had declared his intention to "die like a man at the head of his troops" should the insurrection fail.[51] As members of the urban underground frequently noted, this kind of death would be vastly preferable to an unarmed death at the mercy of security forces. Death in combat was dignified; death in a detention cell was not.[52] The concept of political martyrdom helped resolve this disparity, posthumously elevating victims of police violence to political and quasi-religious glory.

The "political" funerals that punctuated the revolutionary conflict in Havana and Santiago became important sites for enacting these ideals. These mass funerals, presided over by fellow militants, derived their importance from the rites they contained for establishing the honor of the young men killed in the urban underground. They were important rituals for asserting and rehearsing a certain kind of masculinity. Examining these public rituals helps us understand both how violence was framed as defensive and necessary and how insurgent political identity was framed as masculine.

In order to understand the passionate nature of these funerals, we must first note the widespread anguish within insurrectionary circles over the sheer physicality of police repression. For example, what emerges most clearly from the various surviving handbills and clandestine publications is a sense of outrage over state violence, conveyed through general denunciation as well as detailed descriptions of the extrajudicial killings of militants and innocents. In interviews, most members of a clandestine organization explained that they initially joined upon hearing about the torture or killing of a friend or acquaintance; thus each death had wide repercussions, prompting others to assume greater risks. As a handbill printed by the Civic Resistance Movement (MRC) said bluntly: "Look around you. Think of . . . the families you know. Is there [even] one that hasn't had at least one member suffer humiliation, abuse, illegal detention, torture, or assassination?"[53] Moreover, movement militants understood police brutality as intentionally emasculating; interviews and contemporary accounts make frequent reference to police practices such as disrobing and genital mutilation.[54]

In this context, the commemoration of martyrs became an important force in driving the movement forward. Mass funerals of "martyred" insurgents became important public acts throughout the urban insurrection, loaded with political and emotional weight.[55] When well-known activists were killed during protests, their funerals could draw up to thousands of people, including delegations sent by the major opposition groups to important funerals outside Havana.[56] The atmosphere of these mass funerals and burials was rowdy; attendees shouted out revolutionary slogans and waved their respective organizations' banners. They often sparked violent conflict with the police, and thereby set off a new cycle of funerals and protests.[57] Mass funerals were also the site of rousing oratory given by both political and religious figures who used the platform to denounce the violence of Batista's regime. They were one of the few public sites where such sentiments could be expressed after press censorship was imposed regularly in late 1956 and public protests became increasingly dangerous. Yet funerals, too, soon became risky. In at least two cases, police opened fire on funeral corteges, most famously in Pinar del Rio, when one attendee reportedly unfurled a Twenty-Sixth of July flag, and police in response opened fire, killing four and sparking a riot.[58] And an aerial strafing of a Manzanillo funeral resulted in some forty-five deaths.[59]

The concept of martyrdom is often central to revolutionary struggle. It is important for understanding death as a necessary way of furthering the struggle, a meaningful rather than a useless sacrifice. Martyrs prepare the ground for future triumph, often metaphorically "seeding" or "watering" the nation's soil. This idea is captured eloquently in an Ernesto Cardenal poem:

They thought they were killing you . . .
They thought they were burying you
And what they were doing was planting a seed.[60]

The symbolic "survival" of martyrs depends on their loved ones continuing the revolution. Thus the concept of martyrdom implied the present and future duty of others to carry on the struggle.[61]

As the anthropologist Katherine Verdery has argued, burials and other death rituals can be a particularly rich site for the construction of political, national, or ethnic community, as the tangible presence of the dead serves to concretize more abstract notions of belonging and imbues the secular political order with the power of the sacred. Funerals make the usually abstract domain of politics tangible and real, imbuing dry concepts such as "the nation" with emotion.[62] Cuba in particular had long antecedents for the importance of revolutionary martyrdom. The Wars of Independence placed great emphasis on individual sacrifice and masculine valor, visible, for example, in the influential essays of José Martí.[63] As Louis Pérez argues, the liberation struggles of the late nineteenth century framed how armed struggles were understood in the republican period. The armed movements against Machado in the 1930s and against Batista in the 1950s "drew explicitly upon nineteenth-century formulations of sacrifice and self-immolation: the necessity to submit to death as duty and destiny as binding and inescapable." Self-immolation served as a "propaganda of the dead," calling others to the cause.[64]

The political funerals of the late 1950s were thus an important ritual for imbuing violent death with meaning. The way young revolutionaries viewed these funerals gives us insight into the internal dilemmas experienced by those in the urban underground. For the young men overwhelmed by the risks they faced, the idea of an honorable martyrdom invigorated them. They feared torture by security forces but often accepted death as inevitable. They comforted themselves with the idea of a "useful death" and a "combative" funeral. As one participant recalled, the Twenty-Sixth of July leader Arístides Viera "was sure he would die in the struggle. He liked to talk about how his burial would be. He assigned himself a funeral that would be an act of combat for his *compañeros*. He would describe the shouts of the crowd, the revolutionary chants [*consignas*]."[65] While containing some elements of fatalism, such as an acceptance of inevitable self-destruction, the concept of martyrdom posited victory as a long-term and collective goal to which each individual death contributed. Thus young men reassured themselves that their deaths would be politically generative and that they would be posthumously honored.

Movement militants viewed attending funerals as an important act. As Dolores Nieves Rivera, a member of the Twenty-Sixth of July Movement, later recalled, "Whenever I could, I attended the funerals of dead comrades [*compañeros*]"—that is, other members of the Twenty-Sixth of July— even those she had not known personally; "I did it as an act of protest."[66] And militants who could not risk attending funerals because they had been identified by police requested full descriptions from others. Nieves recalled a fellow member of the Twenty-Sixth of July Movement asking her to describe a *companero*'s funeral repeatedly, with full details. He "asked if I had seen any acquaintances [there], if I had seen Enrique dead, and I explained everything: that the casket had been closed, that I hadn't been able to see him."[67] After another funeral, she and others explained to a friend "how the funeral cortege had reached the town; that everyone had come out to watch it pass, in silence. And that the buses had mourning ribbons on their windshields."[68] The clandestine press also served this narrative function, providing extensive description of the funeral procession of important militants with accompanying photos, or recounting in detail the martyrdom of *compañeros*, emphasizing their bravery in action and promising postmortem glory.[69]

Funerals formed part of a series of public mourning rituals, such as collective prayer conducted on the spot of a militant's death or the decoration of sites of killings with funerary flower wreaths, which were then often destroyed by police in their own counterefforts to erase memorialization.[70] Marking, reclaiming, and politicizing sites of death were important aspects of the struggle at the time, insistently making visible an otherwise hidden geography of physical persecution. Temporal markers were also important: the urban opposition planned actions for yearly and even monthly anniversaries of militants' deaths, as well as for historically important martyrdoms from the anticolonial struggle, thus inscribing the deaths of anti-Batista activists within a longer narrative of nationalist struggle. For example, the DR planned citywide protests on the first monthly anniversary of the killing of its leader José Antonio Echeverría. And when the Twenty-Sixth of July Movement in Santiago torched a local candle factory on the anniversary of Josué País's death, it was wistfully remarked in the streets that rebels were "lighting a candle" for Josué.[71] Indeed, reading over memoirs and clandestine ephemera from the insurrectionary period gives one the sense of constant agitation around graveyards, sites of notorious killings, and historical commemorative statues. The imagery and discourse outlined here helped construct a passionate cult of masculine honor, shaped by the context of rising state violence. It was strongly linked to ideas of political "martyrdom" and defense of self, family, and nation.

The concept of martyrdom was implicitly gendered. It was almost always young men who died, leaving women to mourn.[72] As the anthropologist Begoña Aretxaga argued in her study of the Irish Republican movement, men's and women's suffering are understood differently. "Men encounter suffering in the violent death generated by an unjust social order," and although martyrs are cast as the passive victims of state violence, their image serves to justify the rise of other young men who will purposefully engage in violent resistance: "We have the right to take up arms."[73] The suffering of women, on the other hand, is indirect, experienced through the loss of their menfolk. Thus "men's suffering is inscribed in their own bodies through their fighting; women's [suffering] is inscribed in the bodies of others; fathers, sons, brothers, husbands, or friends."[74]

That gendered dynamic was performed and reified at political funerals, as women relatives and women militants in Cuba's revolutionary movement enacted mourning rituals to honor the dead. In fact, there was often a literal predominance of women at funerals, either because police tried to prevent men from attending or because men involved in the urban underground feared exposing themselves.[75] Thus funerals could have the feel of a women's protest, and women were often both the predominant actors and "audience" members of a funeral, so to speak.[76] Women led funeral processions, made emotional graveside speeches, and assisted a victim's family members.[77]

Women members of the urban clandestine organizations played an important role in claiming the bodies of recently killed militants, because police sometimes tried to have bodies buried quickly, without being identified, fearing the repercussions of a mass funeral occasioned by the death of a particularly well-known insurgent.[78] Militants interpreted this practice as not merely a pragmatic attempt to prevent a political rally but also as the purposeful profanation of a cadaver. These ritual commemorations of revolutionary martyrdom and battles with police over custody of a cadaver stoked the insurrection by legitimizing opposition violence as defensive and invoking the masculine honor of the revolutionaries. These somber body politics, or "wars of the cemetery," were common in other twentieth-century conflicts, but scholars have not always noted the largely female labors of mourning and remembrance necessary to produce male martyrdom and heroic masculine agency.[79]

Women also engaged in performative strategies to restore the compromised masculinity of their fallen men. On a few occasions when the "martyred" militant had been married, young widows attended their husbands' funerals wearing their wedding dresses.[80] Or they presided over the funeral visibly pregnant, in moving acts of political pathos that were remembered sharply by their peers half a century later.[81] Women affiliated with the Twenty-Sixth of July Movement also went to great lengths to procure rebel army uniforms, for there was great symbolic importance in burying men in the uniform, even if they had never worn the uniform in combat.[82] In other cases men were buried with the trappings of an alternative revolutionary masculinity. The mother of DR member Joe Westbrook, killed by Havana police in March 1957, noted in a letter that Joe "had a black suit in which his fiancée would say of him, 'You look like [José] Martí.' He . . . always warned us: 'If I should fall some day, I want you to bury me in this suit of Martí and with his "Selected Works" in the coffin.' That is what we did."[83] Through acts such as these, women bestowed masculine honor, virility, and warrior status upon the defeated men whose bodies had been so unceremoniously abused and disposed of by security forces.[84] Martyrdom thus gave positive meaning to the patent vulnerability, weakness, and defeat of the urban underground. And it was female labor in particular that helped make meaning out of death, converting it into the useful sacrifice of martyrdom.

Revolution as Paternal Duty

If revolutionary masculine honor could be derived from bravery in action or publicly established posthumously through death rituals, it could also be related to the performance of paternal duty. We find various references in clandestine ephemera to incidents of men being prodded toward political engagement and taking strength from the idea of being an honorable husband or father. In some cases young militants seemed to feel pressure to live up to these standards, as women and children were indirectly made honorable by the actions of their men, and thus an entire family's honor might be premised on one man's correct masculine comportment.[85] In the vulnerable conditions of the urban underground, men also relied on their sense of being an honorable father to withstand imprisonment, torture, or an unarmed and "undignified" death. This discourse about the enactment of proper patriarchal obligations during the insurrection may come as a surprise to us now. Yet the articulation of this "revolutionary paternalism" provides a useful counterpoint to the more common scholarly focus on maternalism (which will be discussed extensively in chapter 3): men too occasionally posited their political engagement in familial terms.

Clandestine ephemera from the urban underground frequently included references to the idea of being an honorable husband or father, or in the rejection of being cowardly or weak. For example, as one detained Twenty-Sixth of July member was undergoing a severe beating by police during detention, he was gripped with a fear of dying and leaving behind a widow and young daughter. But he was also loath to give the police the information they demanded, both from fear of debilitating the movement and from concern over his manly reputation. He thought to himself, "Would his wife be happy with an informant husband? And the shame of his daughter faced with a weak father!"[86] Similarly, the captain of an action and sabotage brigade for the Twenty-Sixth of July Movement in Havana wrote a letter to his twelve-year-old son in which he tried to prepare the boy mentally for his father's death: "If I were to die for this cause you would feel proud of me; but if, due to cowardice, I betrayed it, when you grew up you would feel shame to say you were my son."[87] Some women echoed the sentiment that a brave, honorable death was preferable to cowardice in men, including a group of women who audaciously proclaimed that they would "rather be widows of brave men than wives of cowards."[88]

Paternalist discourse could also be used to explain and justify why men felt compelled to join the movement in the first place. The open letter quoted earlier, which was circulated as a handbill by the MRC affiliated with the Twenty-Sixth of July Movement, illustrates this political paternalist discourse by exposing the internal dilemma of a man who strives to be an honorable father and husband. In the letter "a rebel" describes his transformation from a comfortable middle-class professional, husband, and father into a revolutionary. After his young daughter tells him that a classmate's father had died in the struggle, he spends a sleepless night wracked by guilt for not having responded sooner to forces "that were destroying what are, after God, the greatest values of the human being: the nation [*patria*] and the family." Having made the decision to join the rebel army, the letter's author breathes easier with "the satisfaction of a duty fulfilled and the admiration of my friends and family [*los míos*] and of my wife, who today in addition to knowing that she is a woman, wife and mother, knows she is a Cuban." The letter ends by exhorting his fellow Cubans to join the cause: "You will feel a little more manly [*un poco más hombre*] and a little more dignified . . . and when your grandson asks if you fought the dictatorship . . . you'll sit him on your lap and tell him your story."[89] Even if this letter was a well-crafted piece of propaganda rather than a description of one individual's authentic experience, it gestures toward a widespread view that revolutionary participation would ensure honor and masculinity to men and bestow unity and dignity upon their families for generations to come.

It is instructive to compare this letter to the widely-cited public letter Che Guevara wrote to Fidel Castro in 1965 upon his departure for Bolivia, in which Che noted matter-of-factly that upon his death he would entrust the care of his wife and children to the state.[90] The implication of Che's letter was that revolutionary men would be called to serve and their families would correspondingly accept their sacrifice, receiving material support from the state. Yet the letter cited earlier employs a different logic. Its author chronicles a transition from one form of masculine duty to another, assuring his readers that these two models are not incompatible. Being a rebel is imagined as an extension of his duty as a family patriarch, not the shirking or sacrificing of his family duty. Perhaps this assertion was made more important by evidence that revolutionary participation could, in practice, have dire family consequences.[91] Unlike Che, who posited family life as a distraction from politics, some movement militants evidently saw the two realms as closely related.[92]

The open letter explicitly raises the idea of a man's Christian duty. Clearly troubled by the use of violence, the letter's author struggled to reconcile his faith with his duty as a revolutionary, reminding himself that "even Jesus had taken up the whip to expel the impious merchants from his Father's temple." The role of religion has often been overlooked in discussions of the Cuban insurrection, not only in terms of the literal presence of active Catholics in the insurrection but also as an important rhetorical justification. Yet Catholicism too could be used to sanction political violence. And for some men, defense of "innocents" and of sacrosanct institutions such as church and family were strong motivating factors for taking up arms.

Direct attacks on churchmen in particular served to anger and mobilize many Cubans, and some men felt "shamed" into joining the movement by the example of unlikely revolutionaries such as priests and women, as well as the example of other men.[93] Police beatings of priests or ministers were rare, but when they did occur they were described in detail by oppositionist propaganda.[94] For example, clandestine publications such as *Aldabonazo* and *Acción* featured drawings of priests being abused by security forces on their covers, perhaps intending to galvanize opposition among Catholics in particular.[95] In an interview published in an exile periodical, a sister of the Castro brothers similarly sought to appeal to readers' sense of outrage over security forces' targeting of innocents, including priests: "What sustains the despot in power . . . is terror, the repressive action of the regime, which has led it to torture 15-year-old children, priests, women."[96] Some men were motivated by the idea that "innocents" were under attack, and that even women and priests were being drawn into the struggle. A 1957 flyer printed by the MRC appealed to these sentiments directly: "Every day the problems confronting Cuba are more serious. You know that *peaceful* and honorable *men* of all social classes, including priests, are joining the struggle, abandoning work, family and social position to risk their lives to benefit Cuba. . . . You know that *women*, unconcerned with their own comfort, but only in leaving their children an honorable country . . . are being persecuted, imprisoned, and beaten [*vejadas*] by the repressive forces."[97] Thus the logic of paternal duty toward one's actual family could also be extended to protection of other innocents. This rhetoric regarding the protecting of innocents helps explain why many Cubans came to support or at least accept political violence by 1958. Armed opposition was cast as necessary, defensive violence against the rampant abuse by the security forces.

With its prominent reference to the sacrifice of middle-class trappings—the renouncing of worldly things—its open references to formal Catholicism, and its overall framing as a kind of conversion experience, the open letter discussed earlier raises questions about militants' class background and identity. The perceived state violation of family sanctity and church authority as presented in movement ephemera may have had cross-class resonance, but church and home were certainly pillars of middle-class Havana society. The 1957 flyer's special mention of "men of all social classes," some of whom are sacrificing their "social position," raises this question further. And studies of contemporary antidictatorial upheavals in Venezuela and the Dominican Republic uncover similarly class-inflected justifications for political opposition.[98] For example, an anti–Pérez Jiménez flyer in Venezuela employed language and sentiment similar to that in the MRC flyer noted earlier: "Defenseless ladies [*damas indefensas*] have been jailed and thrown into prison cells, in outrageous proximity to criminals, and, afterwards, forced into exile." As the political scientist Elisabeth Friedman notes, this outrage over the persecution of women applied only to certain women—namely, middle-class women.[99] Thus class and gender were closely intertwined in some appeals to political mobilization.

The "class character" of the anti-Batista insurrection has long been a polemical topic. Beginning in 1959, when segments of the middle class began to actively oppose the new revolutionary measures, official rhetoric moved from a position of multiclass inclusion toward asserting that the revolutionary forces were composed predominantly of the peasantry and the working class.[100] Post-1959 official narratives have emphasized the role of the peasantry in the Sierra Maestra in particular, almost to the exclusion of other actors. But scholars have long argued that the anti-Batista forces drew on a multiclass constituency and that the insurrection was best described as "déclassé."[101] As James O'Connor has argued: "There was no single revolutionary class that conducted, or at least gave momentum to, the political rebellion. There were no Cuban counterparts to the peasants in the Mexican and Chinese Revolutions, the urban working class in the Russian Revolution, or for that matter, the urban merchants in the American Revolution." Thus the Cuban Revolution "was neither bourgeois revolution, lower-class rebellion, nor peasant uprising."[102] It was only with the political radicalization after 1959 that the revolution acquired a clear class character.

Within this general scholarly consensus, questions remain about how to define the political role of Cuba's relatively large middle class. Most leaders and many militants of the Sierra and the urban underground were drawn from the educated middle classes, including full-time students, doctors, lawyers, and others from the liberal professions.[103] And in Havana, at least, narrative sources suggest that insurrectionary turbulence often followed the contours of the urban service sectors, drawing on the white-collar employees of Havana's car dealerships and oil company offices, radio stations, and department stores.[104] Yet Cuba's uneven economic development made its large urban middle class precarious, as was the Latin American middle class more broadly.[105] The middle class experienced a kind of collective downward mobility in the 1950s. The historian Jorge Ibarra has argued that the urban middle class's resulting "proletarianization" helps explain its political radicalization and why revolutionary leaders of middle-class extraction such as the Castro brothers could gain such a broad popular following. In other words, Ibarra suggests that revolutionary leaders gained widespread backing in spite of their middle-class background, not because of it.

But the insurrectionary ephemera discussed above suggest that there was also a specifically middle-class appeal in some propaganda, with explicit references to forsaking middle-class comfort—a car, a TV, trips to the beach—and to formal Catholicism, which was predominantly an urban middle-class phenomenon. This raises questions about the class-based appeal of certain constructions of revolutionary masculinity. Elsewhere, the social and economic changes of the 1950s redrew the boundaries of proper manhood. For example, as A. Ricardo A. López has argued for the case of Colombia, the more visible separation of manual and nonmanual labor prompted rethinking about how to define middle-class masculinity.[106] In the case of the United States, Van Gosse has argued that the romantic, rugged appeal the rebel army held for Americans partly derived from the counterpoint the *barbudo* provided to the conformist 1950s company man.[107] Similarly, we might also ask whether the postwar expansion of Cuba's service sector and male office work had a similar effect. A romanticized revolutionary masculinity may have had special resonance, holding out the promise of feeling "a little more manly" to these segments of the urban middle class who were seeking to redefine their status in the face of economic changes.

Agents of Revolution: From General Strike to Military Vanguard

By 1958, we see the rise of the now-familiar iconography of guerrilla struggle embodied in the image of the bearded rebel warrior in the clandestine press. After the 1959 victory, that image and the unlikely story of the small rebel army that overthrew Batista were enshrined in officialist narratives and reiterated in speeches, ceremonies, and various forms of state-sanctioned vernacular visual culture.[108] But in order to understand the rise and consolidation of the heroic guerrilla image, we must first explore the other possibilities that were exhausted along the way.

It was not until mid-1958 that the guerrilla struggle in the Sierra was viewed as strategically more important than the urban struggle by the Twenty-Sixth of July Movement's leadership and in the popular imaginary. Prolonged guerrilla struggle had not been the original intention of the movement. Rather, Fidel Castro and others hoped that the combination of the *Granma* landing and an uprising in the cities led by the Twenty-Sixth of July's urban cadres would spark a mass revolutionary movement to overthrow Batista.[109] But the regular army decimated the *Granma* expedition and the uprising in Santiago de Cuba, forcing Fidel Castro and other surviving expeditionaries to flee to the mountains. From there they began to rebuild their movement as a guerrilla army with peasant support. Yet even then, the Twenty-Sixth of July Movement aimed for a revolutionary general strike supported by the rebel army; they did not plan on a guerrilla overthrow alone. They imagined that mass action culminating in a revolutionary general strike would be supported by armed struggle in the Sierra.[110] As Che's publication *El Cubano Libre* argued, "the revolutionary general strike is the definitive weapon . . . no repressive organization can defeat it."[111]

Beginning in 1955, both the Twenty-Sixth of July Movement and the Revolutionary Directorate sought strategic alliances with organized labor, a crucial participant in any general strike. And in the summer of 1957, a strike nearly spread across the whole island after the killing of the popular urban underground leader Frank País in Santiago sparked a general strike in Oriente Province.[112] But labor leaders and revolutionaries did not always see eye to eye. The predominantly anticommunist insurrectionists feared unions were under the thumb of Communists or corrupt labor leaders. The labor battles of the late 1940s had left the island's once-formidable unions politically polarized and entirely beholden to the state. This was the foundation for the rise of the so-called *mujalista* labor leaders—bureaucratic, self-interested, and corrupt—who controlled the union movement from 1948 to 1958.[113] Then again, the Twenty-Sixth of July Movement made few concessions to labor. By not supporting strikes they viewed as purely economic, the Twenty-Sixth of July Movement effectively asked labor to postpone social demands until after the triumph of the revolution. And in practice, most young insurrectionary leaders, who could be as young as sixteen, lacked the necessary contacts and experience to mobilize organized labor.[114]

Still, reexamining the attempts to organize a revolutionary general strike illuminates the other revolutionary subjects, alliances, and strategies that were envisioned in this period. A handbill printed by the Twenty-Sixth of July Movement, probably from early 1957 during a campaign to sabotage the sugar harvest, reminds us of the other revolutionary imaginaries that preceded the rebel army's victory. It features three men with identical profiles, mouths open as if shouting in unison. Their faces are positioned above a large spinning cog, suggestive of heavy industry. Two of the figures wear hats with different brims, perhaps to suggest employment in different industrial sectors. The middle figure is conspicuously darkened to represent an Afro-Cuban, perhaps influenced by Communist Party depictions of labor, which often explicitly included references to black workers. The Twenty-Sixth of July Movement's bicolored flag hovers above. The handbill envisions an interracial male fraternity of militant labor poised to overthrow the dictator through a general strike in the cities. The plantation zones, meanwhile, would be torched by "peasants [*guajiros*], Cuban workers, [and] militias of the 26 [of July]," the flyer predicted, all following the movement's directive to start "the economic war against the dictator."[115]

Yet as the Twenty-Sixth of July militants geared up for what they hoped would be a final general strike in April 1958, they still had not laid the groundwork for the mass mobilization of labor, and the poorly planned strike took many participants by surprise when it was announced.[116] Some Twenty-Sixth of July Movement militants fiercely opposed an alliance with the PSP; consequently the PSP in Havana did not support the strike (although it did so in much of the interior).[117] The strike also suffered from poor planning, as it was not well announced beforehand. The Twenty-Sixth of July militants simply hoped that last-minute calls to strike and the example of revolutionary violence would prompt mass walkouts. But in the days leading up to the strike, Batista declared a state of emergency, official violence spiked, and the labor federation released an explicit warning that any workers participating in a strike would be summarily fired.[118] And as contemporaries surely observed, working-class militants might be subjected to deadlier police violence than their middle-class counterparts.[119] The strike, when launched, succeeded in other cities across the island, but was quickly put down by security forces in Havana.[120]

The failed 1958 strike left a bitter legacy. The Twenty-Sixth of July's weak relations with organized labor and its conflict with the PSP were painfully obvious in the failed strike. Some revolutionaries forcibly shut down workplaces; others ordered reprisals against workers who did not support the

"Organize the revolutionary general strike that will topple the tyrant!" A Twenty-Sixth of July Movement leaflet circa February 1957 imagines an interracial revolutionary fraternity of striking male workers. (Author's collection)

strike. As one Twenty-Sixth of July leader in Guanabacoa admitted, due to the fact local workers had not been warned about the planned strike ahead of time, "we had to shut down some factories at gunpoint, even though the city was ours."[121] And after the bus drivers' union divided over support of the strike, Twenty-Sixth of July leader Faustino Pérez ordered his action groups to fire on any buses found in operation on the day of the strike.[122] This is why the Communist Party subsequently blamed the Twenty-Sixth of July Movement for "using armed action to intimidate the working class and remove it from the workplace . . . and rejecting the idea of carrying out economic strikes before the general strike."[123]

The PSP later ruefully noted labor's crucial but unacknowledged contribution. As a Communist Party spokesman noted, organized labor may not have played a leading role in the insurrection, but even failed strikes such as that of 1958 had an important impact. "The constant threat of a strike kept a large part of the repressive forces and the military . . . in the cities, impeding their concentration in the zones of armed struggle," the party's national committee wrote in 1959.[124] The attempted general strikes, dismissed as failures, partly ensured the rebel army's freedom of movement and ultimately its victory. But few insurgents saw it that way. Relations between the Communist Party and the Twenty-Sixth of July Movement would take months to recover. For some Twenty-Sixth of July militants, the lesson learned by the failed strike was that Cuban workers were essentially apolitical, dulled by years of "communist sermons" and bureaucratic control. The working class now "measures its triumphs in salary increases," Twenty-Sixth of July member Enrique Oltuski wrote dismissively at the time.[125]

Oltuski, the son of a successful Polish immigrant businessman, later cast organized labor as intransigent in his memoirs. He described a meeting with a leader of the telephone workers to persuade them to join the strike of 1957. He recalled the encounter as taking place in a bar with loud music, shouting children, and men playing dice. During their conversation, Oltuski wrote, the telephone workers' leader was constantly distracted by women walking by in tight pants.[126] In contrast with the worker heroism envisioned in the handbill discussed earlier, Oltuski's description is a caricature of improper working-class masculinity: disorderly, oversexed, too focused on drinking and gambling. Written decades after the events, the anecdote has likely been shaped by postrevolutionary discourse on the problems of republican-era organized labor, yet it gives a suggestive glimpse into the judgment some young middle-class revolutionaries might have shown toward organized labor.

The failure of the April 1958 strike proved a watershed for the revolutionary movement's strategy. As cities were now beset by the furious retaliation of security forces, the Twenty-Sixth of July's leadership largely abandoned the concept of a revolutionary general strike and the struggle in the cities, blaming the urban underground for the strike's failure. It was in the wake of the failure of the revolutionary general strike of 1958 that the Twenty-Sixth of July Movement began to conceptualize a purely military victory based on the rebel army. They thereafter channeled all decision-making power and resources to Fidel and the other Sierra leaders. The urban underground was mostly relegated to provisioning the rebel army. As the historian Julia Sweig notes, "once the vanguard, the urban underground had finally been relegated to the revolution's rearguard."[127] Hopes for a revolutionary general strike had dissolved in state repression, revolutionary inexperience, and the legacy of Cuba's Cold War repression of and polarization of the labor movement. Thus the rebel army did not "bring the Cold War" to Latin America, as is often asserted;[128] the rise of the rebel army was itself shaped by the dynamics produced by the Cold War.

The Triumph of the Heroic Guerrilla

As late as fall 1957, one still finds various revolutionary actors pictured in Twenty-Sixth of July Movement propaganda. For example, one November 1957 flyer advertising the sale of bonds featured drawings of various revolutionary participants: a guerrilla rebel, a saboteur, a propagandist (a man cranking a mimeograph machine), and a well-dressed woman handing something to a man seated at his desk, possibly indicating her role in circulating propaganda or bonds. The figures are of equal sizes, placed at regular intervals across the page, such that no single figure takes visual predominance.[129] Here revolution was imagined as a collective enterprise. But in the wake of the second failed attempt at a revolutionary general strike—that is, in mid-1958—the heroic guerrilla image congealed and spread through the clandestine press and other graphic ephemera, thereafter eclipsing other imagined actors. The rise of the *barbudo* archetype emerged during the shift in power from the cities to the Sierra, and reflected the consequent demotion of the urban underground in relation to the Sierra leadership. The heroic guerrilla was thus not a "natural" expression of the ordeals of the Sierra and the victorious revolutionary movement. Rather, this trope reflected the self-constructed image of a victorious faction, as the Sierra-based portion of the Twenty-Sixth of July Movement sought to establish itself as the center of authority in a large, complicated, island-wide resistance movement.[130]

Judging from the immense impact the image of the *barbudo* made in Cuba and beyond, we know that it was an image with particular power. Still, it remains unclear how exactly Cuban contemporaries understood this image and why it appealed. A close examination of the way the rebel army presented itself through discourse and printed revolutionary ephemera suggests that the image of the *barbudo* resonated with existing masculine ideals such as sexual and military discipline, and righteous violence and deliverance.

The careful crafting of the rebel army's imagery reveals the sensitivity that Fidel Castro and other Twenty-Sixth of July leaders had to the importance of propaganda, perhaps reflecting their upbringing in media-saturated Havana. But given the censorship exercised almost continuously on the mainstream Cuban press in 1957 and 1958, they had to bypass the national press. In December 1956 and the first few months of 1957, as the rebel army was still in the very early stages of consolidation, the movement began a concerted propaganda campaign, inviting several prominent foreign journalists to make a clandestine trip to the mountain-based rebel army. The visits of *New York Times* reporter Herbert Matthews and CBS correspondent Robert Taber in early 1957 were propaganda coups.[131] Thus the first widely seen, sympathetic images of the new mountain rebels were disseminated by the foreign media.

Castro and his cohort took these journalists' visits seriously as an opportunity to craft a certain image, stressing their seriousness of purpose and strong military organization. In particular, they sought to "embellish the 'strength' of the mountain army to make it appear more fearsome than it really was."[132] Establishing their credibility as a military force would help garner popular support and could potentially lead to international recognition as a belligerent force. In one well-known anecdote, Fidel ordered his men to periodically march past Matthews in small bands. Matthews was suitably impressed, never guessing that these various brigades were the same small group of men marching by repeatedly, and that they represented, at the time, virtually the entire membership of the rebel army.[133] In photos, the rebels visually anticipated their triumph, smiling with arms hoisted high above their heads. The imagery from Matthews's visit in February 1957 as well as the news footage taken by Taber and his cameraman Wendell Hoffman in May 1957 provided foundational imagery of the rebel army that would be reproduced and circulated in other media for decades.[134]

Bonds and the clandestine press, which circulated widely in Havana and other urban centers, subsequently became the most important mediums of dissemination of the *barbudo* image. The imagery was meant to transmit a message of strength and courage and to attract greater numbers of Cubans to the anti-Batista struggle.[135] These bonds, in turn, often drew directly on the image that Fidel Castro and others had presented to journalists visiting the Sierra Maestra in 1957. For example, a bond printed in late 1957 by an affiliate group of the Twenty-Sixth of July Movement in New York reproduced a photo of the rebel army taken by Taber and Hoffman.[136]

Many bonds stressed military discipline, which was central to the image of the rebel army as it congealed, featuring similar drawings of the rebel soldier marching in the countryside. One recurring motif was a line of uniformed men marching single file in a mountainous landscape. For example, the one-peso bond marked "Month of the Rebel Soldier," circa 1958, features such a drawing. The men in the drawing look identical, with rifles slung across their backs, wearing matching uniforms, boots, and hats. Their consistent uniforms and tight military formation implied organization, military discipline, and respectability. Such depictions helped cast the rebel army as a "real" army rather than a ragtag bunch of inexperienced youths. Here was a force capable of defeating the regular army. The image is very unlike the "ragged *barbudos* . . . chomping their cigars and darting down green mountain slopes" that international publics later celebrated.[137]

Some ephemera featured imagery of Fidel Castro or real photos of rebel army troops, but bonds and the clandestine press also commonly featured drawings of a generic, unidentifiable *barbudo*. For example, an image used repeatedly on bonds showed a rebel soldier from the back, pointing into the distance, both leading the way for the soldiers behind him and symbolically gesturing toward a brighter national future. One clandestine publication featured a line drawing of a *barbudo* with his face purposefully obscured by a question mark. The caption read, "This rebel soldier could be your son, your brother, or another loved one. Help him by buying bonds."[138] Such depictions posited the *barbudo* as a kind of generic type that any young man might embody. They encouraged identification with the rebel army through familiarity and informality, even implying a literal family connection. The rebels in the Sierra were not foreign agents or rough-and-tumble radicals, the ad implied; they were ordinary men such as one's own son or brother. And in contrast to the explicitly interracial front of striking workers imagined in the 1957 flyer discussed earlier, the men pictured in these images are exclusively light-skinned. These images capture the duality noted by Van Gosse: the *bar-*

A *Twenty-Sixth of July Movement* one-peso bond printed in 1958 features the emerging iconic image of the barbudo. *(Author's collection)*

budos were appealing in that they were rebelling against an established order and yet were "oddly upstanding" and racially coded as white.[139]

Sexuality and Propriety in the Rebel Army

Just as graphic imagery imagined an orderly and disciplined military force, so too did the rebel army depict itself as sexually disciplined. Through the clandestine press and other discursive channels, members of the revolutionary movement fostered an image of their own sexual propriety that reproduced and appealed to cross-class values. As several authors have suggested, prerevolutionary attitudes about gender, family, and sexuality had been changing slowly since the colonial period, and still stressed the importance of female virginity, the patriarchal protection of dependents, and the social centrality of family.[140] While the popular classes exhibited different patterns in practice, particularly with regard to lower rates of formal marriage and larger extended families, they may have largely aspired to similar ideals.[141]

In the Sierra Maestra the rebel army leadership attempted to prohibit sexual behavior it considered improper. In general, leaders disapproved of liaisons with local peasant women and tried to discourage them. The rebels of the Second Front, led by Raúl Castro, received instruction in both politics and "morals," and when entering towns triumphant after battle were instructed not to drink alcohol, engage in "dishonorable acts," or go around in the company of women not affiliated with the rebel army.[142] At other times they tried to encourage formalizing the unions that did exist. For example, in some cases, the rebel army leadership tried to take advantage of the presence of sympathetic priests in the Sierra to legalize unions.[143] Rape of local women, in particular, was severely punished. A few rebel army soldiers in the Sierra reportedly received the death penalty for raping peasant women.[144] To some extent these measures were linked to security, since the rebel army could not afford to alienate the local peasantry through acts of uncontrolled violence. But they also reflected a deeper belief in the need for discipline, both sexual and military.

Claims of sexual propriety were echoed more publicly in the immediate postrevolutionary context. As one former rebel soldier wrote, women among the rebels in the Sierra "were not looked upon as women, but as sisters, as MOTHERS." The author's idyllic portrait of the chaste relations between men and women serves as an important component in reconstructing the sense of brotherhood, family, and solidarity he found within the rebel army. As he recounted: "Despite the long and hard abstention [*ayuno*] from women, the Spartan we all have within us always won out. 'Brother' our sisters would say when speaking to the *compañeros* . . . and that feminine voice . . . was like music from heaven, and one would have to be truly vile to tarnish that music with even the thought of earthly desires. And there [in the Sierra] there was no vileness. Two who were [vile] now rest in tombs. . . . Never did a woman feel more ideally loved, more respected, more protected than the sublime sisters who made that life glorious."[145]

Some young women who had been in the Sierra with the rebels echoed this lofty language. As one woman explained, in the Sierra "what ruled was not just morale. . . . I would call it . . . purity. . . . Respect, decency, order, discipline reigned. . . . We women felt safe, protected, respected. I have never lived in a healthier, purer ambience where sacrifice, abnegation, and even complete immolation were considered natural."[146] Such statements portrayed the Sierra as a domesticated and proper space rather than an uncontrolled space of revolutionary disorder, violence, or radical politics.

The insistence on the young guerrillas' sexual restraint reflects the importance of purity and morality to the rebels' image. A necessarily counterpart to this image was a conceptualization of young women's sexuality that seemed to preclude consensual sex, and centered the mother figure as the

idealized form of women's political contribution. Thus, in contrast to revolutionary movements elsewhere in Latin America during the late 1960s, political mobilization and radicalization were not accompanied by relaxation
or experimentation within sexual relations or by an open questioning of existing sexual proscriptions.[147] The image we now have of the *barbudos* has
been so conditioned by popular memory of the 1960s as a time of sexual liberation in the United States and western Europe that it is difficult to restore
a sense of the sexual discipline and responsibility that characterized their
image in Cuba in the 1950s.

References to religion may also have contributed to the rebel army's broad
public appeal. Oral sources and published memoirs indirectly reveal something of the way the rebel army was perceived by contemporaries. It is commonly asserted by Cubans critical of the revolution that Fidel Castro and
other rebel army members had worn crucifixes while in the mountains in
order to "trick" the public into believing they were Catholics. But once firmly
in power, they cynically ditched their religious medallions.[148] (In the early
1960s, the exile press even juxtaposed photos of Fidel Castro during and after
the insurrection to prove the point.)[149] While this memory may be selective,
it captures at least one aspect of how the rebel army was understood by contemporaries. The image of the guerrilla warrior embodied honor, dignity,
and a quasi-religious redemption. Subsequent generations of Latin Americans saw the radical and bohemian Che Guevara as exemplar of the Cuban
revolutionary movement. But the upstanding company man or former Catholic school student turned rebel was the way many Cubans understood the
barbudo at the time. The rebel army thus grounded and domesticated potentially radical politics in familiar notions of masculine honor and sexual
propriety, making rebellion seem a natural extension of these roles, not the
rejection of them.

By late 1958, the image of the revolutionary as a bearded guerrilla warrior
had been consolidated in clandestine ephemera. The earlier, more varied
depictions of revolutionary agents found in pre-1958 ephemera—such as the
militant striking worker, the urban saboteur, or the female propagandist—
were replaced by a standardized image of the *barbudo*. The appealing image
of the guerrilla warrior helped galvanize and unify a broad revolutionary
coalition. Yet it also implied certain exclusions. The icon of the *barbudo*
tended to venerate rural guerrilla warfare and disdain civic activism, glori-
fying revolutionary violence as a necessary vanguard and implying that civic
activism was merely auxiliary. The logic of guerrilla warfare and revolutionary masculinity was self-perpetuating. It drew new distinctions between

men and women, as well as among men, then fostered explanations of that division that rested on notions of natural difference between women and men, and between men of different "characters." The new emphasis on revolutionary masculinity thereby established hierarchies among men and limited who was defined as a "real" revolutionary. It would cast a long shadow in the decades to come.

3 | MATERNALISM AND THE MORAL AUTHORITY OF REVOLUTION, 1956–1958

In January 1957, nearly a thousand Cuban women gathered before a chapel in the eastern city of Santiago. Most wore black. Some held rosaries. They unfurled banners, raised upended flags, and proceeded to march in silence through the commercial heart of the city. Although this was the largest all-women's demonstration to take place during the insurrectionary period, it was certainly not the only one. Indeed, the period was punctuated by frequent public demonstrations held by women, especially in 1957 and 1958. Events like these were of great importance to contemporaries, seen as forcing concessions from the dictatorship and symbolizing ordinary citizens' anger with increasing government violence. But these protests and other forms of women's activism have not typically been enshrined in the official historical narrative or included in scholarly accounts of the Cuban insurrection. Restoring these forgotten actors helps us reconceptualize women's political agency as well as the dynamics of the anti-Batista insurrection.

This chapter rediscovers the depth and breadth of women's participation in the urban resistance movement after the turn to arms in 1955. Women's participation in the anti-Batista movement is difficult to quantify, first and foremost because of a general lack of reliable statistics about the insurrection. As noted in chapter 2, membership in the urban underground groups, such as the Twenty-Sixth of July Movement or the Revolutionary Directorate (DR), in Havana alone may have reached a peak of 30,000 by late 1958.[1] Anecdotal evidence suggests that women formed between 10 and 20 percent of these urban underground militants.[2] Yet such estimates inevitably leave out the other forms of participation in which women engaged. For example, there were a number of all-women's anti-Batista groups in Havana and Santiago that formed in this period with a combined membership of well over a thousand. These were technically above-ground civic groups that also provided aid and assistance to revolutionary groups and to families of dead or imprisoned insurrectionaries. In addition, probably the largest number of women who collaborated with the anti-Batista resistance did so through the Civic Resistance Movement (MRC), the largely autonomous urban civic wing of the Twenty-Sixth of July Movement, and perhaps with other civic associations. Within this schematic overview there was significant overlap: some women practiced "double militancy," simultaneously belonging to more than one anti-Batista group, as their male counterparts also did, and women involved in underground activity also attended public protests and engaged in civic efforts. Even if we restrict our analysis to formal membership in one or more of the anti-Batista organizations, it is clear that a significant number of women were involved in the broad mass movement to oust Batista. Beyond this we have additional layers of sympathy and participation, including informal support networks, occasional collaborators, and sympathizers, in which women were also involved. We are speaking, at a minimum, of thousands of urban women.

Yet if this is true, why has women's participation not been better remembered? A persistent problem in recovering women in the historical record has to do with existing frameworks for studying the Cuban Revolution. Women's mass participation primarily took place in urban settings, often in public protests, and in roles now understood to be auxiliary or somehow secondary to the military struggle. For example, even women members of the major armed groups such as the Twenty-Sixth of July Movement and DR infrequently bore arms. Instead they concentrated on strategizing, conveying messages, organizing, transporting materiel, providing safe houses, and designing and distributing propaganda, or, in other words, providing "the infrastructure that made combat possible."[3] As a narrow paradigm took shape that equated revolutionary action with guerrilla struggle in the mountains, those actors who did not fit the paradigm were left out of officialist narratives. State-sanctioned histories thus routinely include hagiographic treatment of the so-called heroines of the Sierra, praising the small group of female strategists close to Fidel Castro in the Sierra as important but exceptional actors. Yet they leave out the many more women who participated in or supported the urban anti-Batista resistance.[4]

At the same time, a small but growing body of literature produced by former participants of the urban underground has not treated women's participation as something that requires any particular interrogation or explanation.[5] When women are mentioned at all, it is often implied that they joined the insurrection in ways analogous to those of men—that is, that they joined for the same reasons, motivated by the same fundamental political concerns, although admittedly not in the same numbers, and that their participation was not distinguished by their gender.[6] These various accounts may put a celebratory stress on women's "combativity" and militancy, yet they offer little insight into the way political participation was experienced by women and men.

Beyond Cuba, few feminist historians have taken an interest in excavating women's participation in the anti-Batista movement, as participants were not motivated by feminism per se.[7] The women who copied clandestine flyers by hand, surreptitiously sold bonds, and took risks to hide weapons, visit prisons, and shelter wanted men did so out of a deep concern for their country. They were motivated by outrage over state violence and a principled opposition to dictatorship. They did not include gender equality on their list of demands. As the historian Francesca Miller has written, the generation of Cuban women who joined the struggle "saw themselves as one with the male revolutionaries and did not identify with women as a group."[8]

Nevertheless, this chapter will show that many urban women did mobilize and protest *as women*, especially as "mothers." They used what we might call "maternalist" or "feminine" rhetoric, which appealed to their special moral authority as women. Women across the political spectrum and in various organizations utilized such rhetoric. As other scholars have shown, maternalism can be articulated to either progressive or conservative politics, and to either revolutionary support or critique.[9] (As we shall see, the post-1959 anti-Castro opposition also mobilized maternalist sentiment.) This chapter explores the use of maternalist discourse in a series of all-women's public protests that took place in Santiago, Cuba's second-largest city, in 1957, and in two of the most important all-women's groups that formed to oppose the Batista regime. It shows that some women protesters—particularly women of lengthy political experience—used maternalist politics strategically, consciously manipulating stereotypical images of naivety and innocence to pursue their political work. Maternalism was not the only way in which women engaged politically, but it was a common and effective tactic.

Finally, this chapter examines the experiences of the women who joined the clandestine groups of the urban underground. Maternalist rhetoric was least prevalent among these women, who were predominantly young and unmarried and had little prior political experience. Still, their experience was distinct from that of their male counterparts in important ways, and thus illustrates the utility of employing gender as a category of analysis. Anti-Batista activities became a vehicle for political mobilization and personal empowerment, pushing younger, less politically experienced women to move beyond the prescribed parameters of "decent" women's behavior. That experience proved transformative for them as individuals. It moved them toward a more critical awareness of the limitations of household patriarchy and the private sphere. And it propelled many of them to continue their political activism in different forms after the 1959 victory.

The stories presented here ask us to reconceptualize the anti-Batista insurrection, suggesting that it was more diverse in its actors, locales, and strategies than we have assumed. Women could never embody the hypermasculine image of the guerrilla warrior that came to symbolize the Cuban Revolution, but neither were they marginal to the struggle. As many men took up arms, many women continued in other avenues of organizing and protest. These forms of protest were pivotal in shaping public perception of the dictatorship and the opposition. Women's appeals to their moral authority helped unify the political opposition, drawing together women of different political persuasions and appealing beyond everyday political platforms toward more fundamental images of family. Their public protests and denunciations of state violence were instrumental in establishing a narrative that depicted the insurrection as a moral struggle against a violent dictatorial state, a narrative that helped delegitimize and destabilize Fulgencio Batista's rule.

Protests of Women and "Mothers"

Historians have posited different definitions of maternalism, but a minimal definition "implies a kind of empowered motherhood or public expression of those domestic values associated in some way with motherhood."[10] Maternalism is a variation of what some scholars refer to as "feminine"—as distinct from feminist—consciousness or activism, which embraces and politicizes women's traditional roles and often denounces political or other obstacles to women's ability to fulfill their domestic calling.[11] Maternity in particular has broad cultural appeal, and as the historian Estelle Freedman notes, "motherhood has long endowed women with social power."[12] Beginning in the nineteenth century, women activists staked a claim to political authority based on women's biological difference and the presumed female moral superiority that derived from their nurturing roles as mothers.[13] Maternalist-inflected movements and political discourse persisted from the nineteenth through the twentieth centuries, alongside other rationales for women's mobilization and empowerment, such as feminism. Maternalism has historically had contradictory effects, rationalizing the entry of women into the public sphere while also reinforcing their association with the private and domestic sphere.[14] It tends to present women's activism as something exceptional, necessary only in times of crisis, motivated by disturbances to the sanctity of the home.

Cuban women's use of maternalist rhetoric during the insurrection is particularly visible in a series of public demonstrations that took place in Santiago in 1957. Three major all-women's demonstrations were held in the city in that year. The first and largest protest occurred in the immediate aftermath of a notorious rash of killings carried out by security forces in the cities of Holguín and Santiago (both in Oriente Province) at the end of December 1956. On January 2, 1957, the bodies of several youths arrested during that holiday sweep, including that of fourteen-year-old William Soler, were found in an empty construction lot.[15] In protest, two days later, nearly a thousand women dressed in black, led by the mother of Soler, marched silently from Santiago's central cathedral to the downtown newspaper offices of *Diario de Cuba* to turn over a letter of complaint.[16] There are few detailed firsthand accounts of this early march, subsequently known as the March of the Mothers, but photographs of the protesters carrying a large banner reading "Stop the assassination of our sons—Cuban mothers" were reproduced frequently in subsequent opposition propaganda and in postrevolutionary publications. Thus the event has remained a strong point of reference in memories of the resistance movement in Santiago, despite the limited information about its organization.

A second, very similar protest took place in Santiago some six months later, on June 2, 1957.[17] This time, the protest was sparked by the discovery of four young men, found hanged from trees, whose cadavers showed marks of torture.[18] As the *New York Times* reported: "This caused such a sense of horror and revulsion that a large group of women of the city prepared last Sunday for a demonstration of protest, gathering first for a mass in the cathedral. A number of policemen, armed with submachine guns, were sent into the church to walk around and intimidate the women. The maneuver failed, but when the women tried to form a parade, it was roughly broken up."[19] Some women held placards demanding the removal of newly appointed police chief José María Salas Cañizares.[20] Several dozen women were detained.[21] Police subsequently confiscated newsreel footage of the protest, which may be taken as an indication of the impact that the photos of the first women's march had made.[22]

The third major all-women's demonstration in Santiago was sparked by the police killing of Frank País, the Oriente Province leader of the Twenty-Sixth of July Movement, on July 30, 1957. The protest is well documented

Women protesters walk through a commercial street of Santiago during the famous March of the Mothers, January 2, 1957. (Private collection of Silvia Arrom)

because it coincided with the newly appointed U.S. ambassador Earl T. Smith's scheduled visit to Santiago, which the ambassador decided would be politically unwise to cancel despite the unrest almost certain to be provoked by País's death.[23] About 200 women, most dressed in black, attempted to disrupt his visit to city government officials by gathering in Céspedes Park outside city hall.[24] When Smith appeared they surged toward him, chanting "Freedom." Signs written in English read, "Ambassador, tell your president not to sell any more arms to Batista, since they are used to assassinate the people."[25] Struggling to enter the government building, Smith found himself surrounded by women "shouting and gesticulating." The "general tenor" of their remarks, he later reported, was that Frank País had been "murdered in cold blood" and that Oriente Province was "in open rebellion against [a] bloody dictatorship."[26] As Smith left the government building, a woman thrust a letter into his hands. Signed by "mothers of Santiago," it characterized the struggle as one for human rights and asked the U.S. government to stop selling arms to Batista.[27]

These descriptions provide at least a schematic outline of events. But how should we characterize the politics of these protests? Why did they emerge when and where they did? Why did protesters so frequently define themselves as mothers? And why do we find this public articulation of maternalist discourse emerging particularly in 1957? Although the documentary record on these issues is incomplete, we can piece together the descriptions of the protests with other documents—such as letters, manifestos, oral histories, and published memoirs—to tease out a response to these questions.

First, the timing and location of these protests were related to significant shifts in state violence. The women's protests coincided with the growth and transformation of state violence from occasional killings during rowdy public protests or shoot-outs with armed militants to something resembling more organized mass sweeps and killings of civilians. These extrajudicial killings relied not only on formal security forces but also on growing paramilitary forces, and seemed to indicate the indiscriminate spread of violence to young men, including those not involved in political opposition.[28]

Santiago in particular had felt the brunt of increased police and army violence. The city had been the site of an armed uprising on November 30, 1956, timed to coincide with the landing of the expeditionary forces led by Fidel Castro on the coast of Oriente Province.[29] With this, a new chapter of insurgency and counterinsurgency began, sometimes referred to as the "civil war" of 1956 through 1958. Although Santiago's urban rebellion was quickly put down, and the *Granma* expeditionaries were either killed or scattered to the hills, the events revealed the extent of revolutionary organization that had taken place in the eastern province. Three weeks later government forces undertook a retaliatory sweep of the area, leaving the bodies of some twenty-three men hanging from trees or scattered in outlying areas of the city of Holguín, the second-largest city in Oriente Province.[30] Subsequently known as the Bloody Christmas (Pascuas Sangrientas), the incident marked a particularly important turning point in the form of state counterinsurgent violence, being the first major round of extrajudicial killings in Oriente Province. It was just one week after the Pascuas Sangrientas that William Soler and other youths were found dead in Santiago, sparking the first women's march.

Oriente Province in this period was marked not only by a surge of state violence but also by new forms of violent spectacle. Unlike the Southern Cone counterinsurgent states of the 1970s, which created terror through disappearances, Cuban security forces in the late 1950s intentionally used spectacular displays of violence. For example, the growing use of torture during detentions was publicly demonstrated through the dumping or hanging of torture-marked cadavers along highways or in outlying areas of cities.[31] In a few extreme cases, police undertook hasty executions in public. For example, the July 1957 killing of underground leader Frank País on a residential street of Santiago in broad daylight sparked a general strike in the eastern province that spread across almost the whole island and was the occasion of the third women's protest described earlier. The final culmination of such acts was an October 1958 incident in which the bloodied cadaver of a young rebel was tied to the hood of an army jeep and driven through the streets of Santiago.[32]

These public displays of violence had an enormous impact.[33] As one Santiago resident recalled: "When looking at a cadaver, even though it had gunshot wounds, you could tell [the victim] . . . had been tortured [first]. It was a violent spectacle."[34] Such episodes prompted one journalist to write that Santiago had "one of the most extraordinary atmospheres [he had] ever encountered. . . . Santiago de Cuba is a city living in a state of fear and exaltation."[35] The all-women's protests thus coincided with both a spike in state violence and the rise of dramatic and provocative displays of corpses. The protests and other expressions of outrage testify to the enormous psychological and political impact that increasingly arbitrary and spectacular acts of state violence had on much of the eastern populace.

The timing of these protests may be further explained by organizational developments within the anti-Batista movement. Even though women protesters presented themselves primarily as outraged mothers, the protests described above tended to coincide with the rise of civic anti-Batista organizations in which women participated in great numbers, as well as the expansion of the insurgent opposition groups that drew young men away from public protest into the underground and off to the mountains. The 1957 protests were probably at least loosely organized by the MRC,[36] the civic branch of the Twenty-Sixth of July Movement, established in Santiago in late 1956 to channel the money and political will of the urban middle and upper classes, although in practice its base was broader.[37] But other groups likely collaborated in convening the protests, as happened in Havana and among anti-Batista groups in exile.[38] For example, Santiago had multiple women's civic associations, some of which, in the same period, released demands for the removal of police chief Salas Cañizares, denounced state violence, and called for the cancellation of carnival in protest.[39] These and other civic groups likely mobilized some of their members for participation in the all-women's demonstrations, and surely many other women not affiliated with any particular organization also joined.[40]

The Logic of Maternalism

While these developments explain the timing, location, and trigger of the protests, we must still ask, Why *maternalist* protests per se? Most broadly, women protesters' self-declared status as the mothers and widows of martyrs dovetailed with widely accepted popular ideas about women's political motivations as deriving from a defense of the family. In public, women activists occasionally referenced such ideas directly. For example, shortly after the revolutionary triumph, Dysis Guira explained in an interview that women had joined the insurrectionary struggle "because of the crisis in moral values. The family was disintegrating" as mothers were forced to send their adolescent sons into exile. Women thus joined the struggle from a "desire to save domestic peace and harmony."[41] Statements like these characterized women's mobilization as defensive and largely aimed at restoring the sanctity of the private sphere, a reassuring narrative that reinforced commonplace distinctions between men and women.

⌐Protesting as "mothers" did not contest existing constructions of women as mothers, but ascribed different—that is, collective and public—meanings to motherhood. As Diana Taylor notes in her discussion of the Argentine Mothers of the Plaza de Mayo, "motherhood—as a role—had already been socialized and politicized through patriarchy."[42] These political enactments of "motherhood" always contain a contradiction, for they are the public enactments of a role that is by definition private. For, as Taylor notes, "*good* mothers are invisible." But by appropriating and changing the meanings of motherhood, women protesters "manipulated the images that previously had controlled them."[43] ⌐

Additionally, in this context of rising violence, maternalism likely seemed a relatively safe, nonthreatening platform under which women could insert themselves into an increasingly dangerous political field. In retrospect we know that few Cuban women were tortured or killed by security forces in the 1950s. Yet in the context of rising and seemingly indiscriminate state violence, many women had a different impression.[44] This may help explain why many women protesters preferred to present themselves as moved primarily by sorrow, familial ties, and "universal" human emotions, downplaying their prior and current involvement in organized politics.

Certainly this was a common tactic for individual women activists, who had often been catapulted to action, or at least so they claimed, through the death of a son. In public protests and in letters in Cuba and abroad, these individual women activists pointed to the death of their sons as the source of their moral authority and political agency. For example, in a 1957 letter to First Lady Mamie Eisenhower written "in the name of the mothers of the Island of Cuba," Dora Rosales explained, "This right to represent them [i.e., other mothers] I achieved at high cost: the blood of my son, Joe West-brook Rosales, murdered April 20th last by Captain Esteban Ventura and his henchmen. . . . My voice is not the voice of one woman bereaved, but of many, many."[45]

Yet while Dora Rosales and a few other women protesters were genuinely the mothers of "martyred" activists, most were not. Thus, unlike the better-known Mothers of the Plaza de Mayo in Argentina, for whom motherhood was a literal as well as a symbolic identity, most women protesters in Santiago used references to motherhood metaphorically.[46] Even in petitions and letters signed by women who were clearly *not* the mothers or widows of martyrs, including women who had a clear political affiliation of their own, the justification of women's action through familial ties was also used. For example, one document signed by the women representatives of the various "women's sections" of the insurgent groups began by addressing the U.S. ambassador thus: "As Cuban women and as relatives—mothers, daughters, wives, sisters—of the victims of this tyranny that bleeds our country, we direct ourselves to you."[47] The signatories' claim of familial relations to male victims is almost entirely rhetorical and merely serves to legitimate their political participation. Additionally, we might note that women activists tended to sign various letters and petitions wearing different "hats"—that is, a woman might identify as a grieving mother in one letter, as the female representative of a particular political group in another, and simply as a professional in a third. Women positioned themselves for maximum impact depending on the context of the petition.

Thus we need to understand maternalism as a strategic position, in which women consciously referenced the nonthreatening identity of motherhood. Contemporary and even subsequent accounts might imply that women protesters were naïve, politically inexperienced, and acting spontaneously. For example, the insurgent group Organización Auténtica described the protests thus several months later: "Passersby are beaten for no reason, civic and political demonstrations are dissolved with force, including that of women who had left a mass where they prayed for their dearly departed."[48] Yet it is clear that many of the women protesters had prior political experience.

This much is suggested by the fact that many of the letters signed by various grieving women and "mothers" were laced with sharp references to citizenship, international treaties, and the Cold War, and also utilized the emerging discourse of international human rights, sometimes directly referencing the United Nations' Universal Declaration of Human Rights of 1948. But these references were cast as a "politics of the heart," interwoven with prose that stressed the grief-stricken and to some extent innocent nature of the letters' authors. For example, one letter to the American consul in Santiago read, "This is an appeal to your generous hearts so that you, as citizens of a Democratic Country and always ready to help the oppressed, like you did recently for the Hungarians, help us by all means in your power that these rights be respected."[49] As we saw earlier, some of the women who attended protests in this period would have been affiliated with the MRC. Many others had likely been militants or at least sympathizers of the Ortodoxo or Auténtico parties. Other women protesters had been active in other associations and organizations. For example, Leida Sarabia, a leader of the MRC, had also been a leader of Santiago's Catholic School Teachers (Maestras Católicas) and was involved with the Knights of Columbus.[50] Some young women who eventually joined the Twenty-Sixth of July Movement in Santiago had first been members of Catholic Action.[51] Thus, despite their self-identification as mere mothers, women were pulled into anti-Batista activism by their contacts from various overlapping networks, including political parties; professional associations such as teachers' organizations; cultural or literary groupings; and spiritual or moral organizations, such as lay Catholic groups or the Freemasons.[52]

At least in theory, motherhood as an identity unified women across class lines.[53] Yet there was also a special resonance to violence visited upon middle- and upper-class women and their children. Indeed, some contemporary accounts suggest that the women protesters of Santiago were primarily middle and upper class—members of the *clases económicas*, to use the categories of the time.[54] This was how Ambassador Smith described the women who protested his arrival in Santiago.[55] When Smith later that evening attended a reception that included many representatives of local civic organizations and civil society, he noted that "a sizeable number of wives at [the] party, including those of leading lawyers, doctors, industrialists and merchants told me with great pride that they had participated in [the] demonstration in front of [the] city government building that morning."[56] Surviving photos and film footage of the three public all-women's protests in Santiago show predominantly, but not exclusively, light-skinned, sharply dressed women with high heels, religious medallions, and leather purses.

Oral sources suggest that women of all classes participated in protests in opposition to the Batista government in Santiago, but that middle- and upper-class women took on leadership roles because they had access to resources, such as phones, cars, and leisure time, which could be marshaled toward organizing opposition actions.[57] As one working-class Santiago woman who eventually joined the Twenty-Sixth of July Movement noted, middle- and upper-class *santiagueras* "had access to a telephone, to publicity [channels]. They belonged to the church, [and] had a certain protection from the church. They were also respected by the police, because they were from the city elites. . . . The police didn't mess with them as they did with the students, because they were respected. They were the wife of so-and-so, the wife of such-and-such, the president of [a social] club [or] a big store owner, so they had a social backing that allowed them to undertake good, very strong revolutionary action."[58]

Thus, while protests and revolutionary collaboration drew on a cross-class group of women, elite women were willing to take greater risks because they were better protected and connected; they might be arrested but were unlikely to have real police violence visited upon them, especially middle-aged women. There was even a certain performance aspect among middle-class women protesters who "exaggerated" in their provocation of police, confident they would not be mistreated in return—at least not in their guise of genteel women and mothers.[59] For this reason the police use of fire hoses against the women protesting Ambassador Smith's visit caused a furor and forced Smith to make a statement against police mistreatment of women, giving the incident international repercussions.

We occasionally find expressions of maternalist rhetoric that specifically utilized a class-based discourse of "decency" or "respectability." Protest letters penned by some women activists made veiled reference to violence against the middle class, asserting for example that "the life and security of the best citizens is worth hardly anything," and protesting the killing of two girls "from a nice, decent family."[60] One group of "mothers" drew on discourses of racialized savagery when they complained to the U.S. embassy in Havana that Batista was a "beast" better suited to the "African jungle."[61] And a letter from the middle- and upper-class members of "A Ladies' Institution" to Vice President Richard Nixon expressed disappointment over the U.S. government's inaction toward Batista, noting: "We hoped that the United States would sense some feeling for the lives of the very young people of our unhappy Cuba, Students, Doctors, Lawyers, Engineers, the more cultured class and the idealistics that are being assassinated in hundreds. . . . We hoped [for] . . . an immediate stop to the aid your Government is giving the dictator in our country, who kills, murders, tortures, oppresses and destroys the Cuban home, the Cuban family, the Cuban people."[62] Maternalist expressions of anger over state violence could thus easily echo the relatively elitist strain occasionally articulated within the opposition. And, as other authors have noted, the same broad and unifying appeal of maternalism that gave it its power also made it politically slippery, with conservative as well as progressive implications.[63] Maternalist rhetoric was sometimes limited both by a vision of return to a status quo of peaceful family life and by a tendency to reinforce patriarchal relations in appealing to heads of state as metaphorical father figures and benevolent providers.

Then again, not all "mothers" denounced state violence only. Some groups, such as the women's group Hermandad de Madres Elvira Cape, released statements denouncing both rebel and state violence, and asked all mothers to "practice their parental authority with their children to prevent the repetition of acts that might bring about repression or reprisals, as well as prevent their children from leaving the house at night, under any circumstance."[64] And in one display of maternalist unity, the mothers of martyred revolutionaries publicly met with and embraced the mothers of Batista soldiers killed in the conflict.[65] While maternalist expressions in this period usually contributed to the formation of a broad revolutionary coalition, they were not always contained by prorevolutionary sentiment.

Still, perhaps the most important advantage to mobilizing under the rubric of "motherhood" was its ability to appeal widely to women of different political persuasions, ranging from women on the political left to conservatives, and from active Catholics to members of the Communist Party. Indeed, women of the Marxist Left intentionally appealed to motherhood as a unifying trope as a way to ensure their inclusion in the broader political spectrum of the anti-Batista coalition taking shape. For example, a widely circulated flyer titled "Open Letter to the Cuban People on Mother's Day" was signed by mothers of "martyred" men who had belonged to various and competing political factions, as well as some men with no known political militancy. However, the flyer itself—quite intentionally—makes no overt mention of the men's political affiliation. Their political affiliations can only be deduced from their names, listed next to the names of their mothers.[66] Maternal love is presented here as transcending politics: the signatories self-identify as "women called and united by an immense common tragedy."

Thus maternalist politics posited female grief as a unifying force that transcended immediate political militancy and even politics itself. As Florencia Mallon has observed in a different context, the suffering of wives and mothers could be used "to bond courageous and suffering men."[67]

The original flyer made no mention of the group or author behind the "Open Letter." But it was subsequently revealed that the letter had been printed by the group Opposition Women United (Mujeres Oposicionistas Unidas, MOU), a small, all-women's anti-Batista group that encompassed some members of the Communist Party (about which more subsequently), and that the letter's author was the journalist Mirta Aguirre, a prominent intellectual affiliated with the Communist Party.[68] As discussed in chapter 4, this dovetailed with strategies used by the Cuban Communist Party to appeal to women as aggrieved mothers and homemakers, referencing neighborhood-based issues such as housing and food prices. And although the PSP's leadership did not endorse the armed struggle until the summer of 1958, party members may have seen efforts like these as ways to create a "united" front against Batista.

Maternalism as a political logic could serve as the basis for wide alliances, but it did so partly by effacing women's more formal, ideological political commitments, and instead appealing primarily to sentiment. Opposition groups frequently circulated heart-wrenching, sentimentalized accounts of the impact of state violence written in verse. Ariana Núñez, a member of the Twenty-Sixth of July in Santiago, recalled the use of "poetry that was written for the insurrection, which moved you and made you cry, because they had killed a lot of young people. So that was reproduced, and was sent around by mail."[69] Two such "insurrectionary" poems—one by the Catholic poet and DR affiliate Pura del Prado, the other by Nieves Rodríguez Gómez, who was affiliated with, or at least sympathized with, the Communist Party—utilize similar imagery of suffering mothers while gesturing toward different political solutions.

The 1957 poem by del Prado, written in honor of one of the DR martyrs and circulated in the clandestine press, eschews overt references to political struggle, instead decrying the impact of state violence on the private sphere of familial and romantic ties:

Today I have a sky of melancholy
Above bodies wounded and mournful
Today I have a heart of prison cells
With prisoners bruised with agony.

Today I have long mothers, sobbing,
Girlfriends who never became wives,
Orphans made suddenly and by bullet . . . [70]

This poem can be interestingly compared to a 1958 poem written by Nieves Rodríguez, an Afro-Cuban radio actress and poet who was exiled in Mexico in 1957. Nieves was apparently involved in anti-Batista activity and was likely sympathetic to the Marxist Left. Her husband was a Spanish immigrant who belonged to various cultural organizations related to the Communist Party, and they both published poetry in the Communist Party daily *Noticias de Hoy*.[71] Here Rodríguez uses imagery and even vocabulary remarkably similar to that of del Prado's poem, suggesting that images of female grief and state violence served as lynchpins of revolutionary sentiment. But Rodríguez also sees political repression and economic misery as interwoven, linking images of feminine mourning to the tragedy of structural violence:

At night the prison cells of blue puppets
And stabbing moans assault and exhaust me
And more than that, I'm still hurt by the closed factories
And the legion of aged children that inhabit our Havana
And the men who cease being men
Due to the brutality of a uniformed beast
And the mothers pregnant with sadness
Lit up with hatred, and in mourning . . .
And the prisons that swell day by day
And the poor homes that shrink
And the leaders who go and don't come back
And so many comrades disappeared
And so many comrades extinguished[72]

Thus one of the key attractions of maternalism was that it was politically malleable, compatible with various political positions. The image of women prodded to action through personal loss facilitated wide mobilization and broad alliances by shifting the emphasis of protest from specific political goals to the everyday, unifying experience of sorrow. Women across the political spectrum, from active Catholics to women affiliated with the Communist Party, could and did protest together as grieving "mothers." These appeals to moral authority, righteousness, and shared grief helped transform the anti-Batista insurrection into a moral struggle. Women's interventions were thus centrally important in constructing an oppositional narrative to which various segments of the broad movement against Batista could cohere.

The overall picture that emerges here is not of a mass of "mothers" spontaneously pushed toward protest by egregious examples of state violence, as contemporaries frequently implied. Rather, many of the women protesters had political experience or were at least politically savvy, as we have seen. Women's "maternal" or "feminine" public protest helped consolidate a narrative of revolution and revolutionary agency that reinforced certain traditional gendered tropes, such as the suffering mother pushed toward politics in a last-ditch effort to save her family. Just as the insurrectionary movement's repurposing of traditional masculinity contributed to its widespread appeal, so too did the familiar symbol of motherhood help the opposition gain political legitimacy. Yet there is also significant evidence that women were consciously and strategically referencing the nonthreatening identity of motherhood, using those tropes to further their own political practice.

Maternalism as Strategy in Two All-Women's Anti-Batista Groups

Not all women organized solely under the rubric of motherhood during the insurrection. Among the many groups that formed throughout the course of the insurrection with the expressly stated purpose of opposing Fulgencio Batista's dictatorship, we find a number of all-women's groups.[73] The two most important of these groups were the José Martí Women's Civic Front (Frente Cívico de Mujeres Martianas, FCMM) and the MOU, both based in Havana.[74] Both groups were sympathetic with, but independent of, the Twenty-Sixth of July Movement and the DR, although in some cases members of the all-women's groups simultaneously belonged to those groups. Because we have more information about these formally constituted organizations than about the often amorphous protesters and letter writers discussed above, a close examination of them will give us additional insight into the way women mobilized politically in this period and strategically utilized feminine discourse.

The FCMM was formed in January 1953 by Aida Pelayo, Carmen Castro Porta, and several other experienced women activists, including Pastorita Núñez and Marta Frayde, who eventually split off to form the MOU. Unlike the newly formed male-dominated revolutionary groups of the 1950s, which tended to be led by men in their twenties and early thirties with relatively little previous political experience,[75] the FCMM and the MOU were both multigenerational. They were led by middle-aged women of long political standing, with a rank and file composed predominantly of young women whose activism tended to stem from their participation in high school or university politics. Formed explicitly to oppose Batista, the groups generally followed the antidictatorial, nationalist Left. The women were all, at the time, affiliated with the Ortodoxo Party, which had begun to splinter even before Batista's 1952 coup due to internal rivalry after the suicide of party leader Eduardo Chibás in 1951. The party now suffered more severe strain as members clashed over how to respond to the 1952 coup.

Some of the women founders also had long histories of prior activism. The FCMM's leaders, Aida Pelayo and Carmen Castro Porta, had initially been politicized through the Marxist Left in the turbulent 1930s. Born in 1912 and 1908, respectively, Pelayo and Castro Porta both became interested in politics while students at Havana public high schools during the late 1920s and early 1930s. Both joined various student and international solidarity groups affiliated with the Marxist Left.[76] Pelayo and Castro Porta met and became close friends in the 1930s and worked together for the rest of the decade in solidarity organizations for Spanish Civil War exiles and Cuban political prisoners.[77] Pelayo later worked for the International Red Cross and as a schoolteacher in Havana. Castro Porta had worked for the student magazine *Mella* in the 1930s, where she met many of the luminaries of the Marxist and nationalist Left, and eventually became a journalist for the widely read liberal daily *Prensa Libre*.[78] By the 1950s both women had distanced themselves from the Communist Party and its affiliated groups, and had become members of the women's section of the Ortodoxo Party.[79]

Aida Pelayo had also been attracted to feminism, which was a strong movement in Havana in the 1930s, and which in some currents overlapped with socialism and radical student politics.[80] Feminism in the 1930s had encompassed competing political agendas, including those of elite women who primarily sought the female franchise and those of working-class women who sought the amelioration of labor conditions in predominantly female industries or who linked their criticism of gender inequality to critiques of capitalism and U.S. imperialism. Controversial issues were battled out in congresses held in the 1920s and 1930s. Pelayo was a delegate to the Women's Congress of 1939, which helped secure women the vote.[81] By her own account she became a single mother by choice, marrying the father of her child "for one day" before he returned to Spain to fight in the Civil War, thus technically ensuring the child's legitimacy while also scorning the institution of the bourgeois family.[82]

Pelayo's history with feminism sheds interesting light on the way the FCMM conceptualized women's political participation. The group's discourse could be characterized as "feminine" rather than feminist. In their pamphlets and flyers, the group never referenced gender equity, although they did carefully trace a lineage of women's political action back to the nineteenth century. For example, one FCMM proclamation of 1956, apparently addressed to a broader audience of women (that is, not just its own membership), asks rhetorically, "Wasn't it our apostle [José Martí] who exalted the virtues and sacrifices of Latin American women?" The document then lists female historical figures that joined the continent's wars of independence, often by supporting their men who had joined the war, or by pushing their men to join. It follows that with a list of Cuban women in particular who had fought in the Wars of Independence against Spain. The proclamation ends with a call to action, but in effect asks its women readers to support their revolutionary men—in other words, not to hold back their husbands or sons who might be engaged in the anti-Batista struggle: "Do not censure, Cuban mother, your rebel son in his patriotic passions. Encourage him in his thirst for justice. . . . If your husband . . . fights for the dignity of the Republic, encourage him, uniting his desires with yours. If your brother has embraced the ideal of liberty, follow him [imítalo], dignifying those ties of blood with a more vigorous understanding. Cuban woman, honor your glorious ancestors."[83] Such rhetoric prodded women to enter the political fray, yet also suggested women's political mobilization would follow that of their male relatives, and even that political activity had the potential to unite families. To some extent, the group's public actions also reinforced the idea that women followed their sons and husbands into politics, in that they reached out to other women under the rubric of family-oriented action. For example, the FCMM helped organize mothers of prisoners during a prison hunger strike.[84] They also offered support to families of martyred insurgents by identifying bodies, attending to families during funerals, and bringing food and aid to families. The MOU engaged in similar activities, forming the Asociación de Ayuda a los Presos (Association of Aid to Prisoners) along with the Twenty-Sixth of July Movement, the DR, and progressive lawyers, to organize family members of prisoners.[85] Taken broadly, therefore, the activities of both groups made reference to women's special moral authority rooted in their roles as wives and mothers.[86]

Oral histories also supply evidence that the FCMM leadership consciously manipulated prevailing notions of women's political activism as deriving from protective familial instincts, or of women as generally passive, apolitical creatures. A former MOU member in Havana recalled a revealing incident involving Aida Pelayo. Here the nature of its oral transmission—repeated even among women who were not part of Pelayo's immediate group—gives us a sense of the anecdote's contemporary appeal and subsequent memorability: "Aida Pelayo was protagonist of an incredible anecdote that my sister would tell dying of laughter: [Pelayo] took part in a meeting, and the cops come to dissolve it, and she runs out, but she bumped into a policeman, and she says to him (of course, [Pelayo] was a young woman at that time), she says, 'Oh, sir, protect me! Protect me from all this trouble!' And *she* was the one causing all the scandal and trouble."[87] Pelayo's playacting and the hilarity it provoked among her acquaintances suggest that politically active women were savvy about manipulating such roles and that other women appreciated such shrewdness. Pelayo's early interest in feminism also suggests that, even though the group never directly addressed issues of gender equity, Pelayo and others engaged in a performative, conscious appropriation of maternalist and feminine imagery.

It is also revealing to distinguish between the two groups' public actions and statements and their clandestine activities. Their public activities frequently reinforced women's traditional roles as nurturers, caretakers, and auxiliaries to male revolutionaries. For example, groups like the FCMM and the MOU were best known publicly for conducting charitable visits to political prisoners, helping to organize the mothers of prisoners, helping young widows identify the bodies of husbands, or organizing and attending funerals of "martyrs." But in their cooperation with Havana's underground movement, the groups also organized meetings for leaders of the major rebel groups, procured safe houses for wanted men, relayed messages across the city and throughout the provinces, coordinated between members of action groups in and out of prison, and occasionally transported arms.[88]

Official revolutionary histories now tend to define these types of activities as auxiliary or rearguard, casting "real" revolutionary action as the use of arms. To some extent the women's groups' activities do reflect a reproduction of dominant gender ideology and encouraged a gendered division of labor within the insurrection, as women embraced their role as a support network for the primarily male rebel groups. Nevertheless, such work was also strategically essential. Women often worked behind the scenes as organizers, liaising between opposition groups and laying groundwork for subsequent actions. And often actions that might appear innocent on the surface could have deeper importance. For example, undertaking visits to political prisoners was not merely about raising morale and providing material aid. It also provided crucial information for helping the underground movement verify which men had been detained, and for existing political prisoners to procure confirmation that a new inmate was indeed a member of a revolutionary cell and not a government infiltrator.[89]

Finally, groups such as the FCMM help us understand the widespread acceptance of armed insurrection that we find in Cuba by 1958. The FCMM supported revolutionary violence, imbuing it with the feminine moral authority that they and other women protesters cultivated. As we have seen, throughout the late 1950s, women protesters often spoke in their public statements of "the family" and "the home" in order to denounce the violations of the sanctity of those domestic spaces through state violence. Yet in an insurrectionary context, to uphold family sanctity and to denounce state violence could also implicitly endorse rebel violence. For example, in one manifesto, the FCMM balanced its abhorrence of state violence with its veiled statement of support for armed rebel groups: "Cuban woman! We do not nurse hatred or rancor. We do not call for blood like hyenas, out of barbarity or vengeful rage. But neither can we resign ourselves to the sacrifice of blood from our own veins."[90]

An anecdote concerning FCMM founder Aida Pelayo also clarifies this dynamic. In November 1955, Pelayo was asked to speak at a rally called by members of the "old" political party–based opposition. As the only woman speaker, she found she was expected to speak about "the family and peace." Yet the accomplished orator managed to turn those themes on their head by giving a rousing, tour-de-force speech in which she shouted out the names of young activists killed by security forces, fiercely denounced the regime's violation of the home, and ended with a vow to "revenge the spilled blood of our brothers." The crowd rallied to her speech with shouts of "Revolution!,"[91] which contemporaries would have understood as a call to arms. This incident is particularly revealing: it shows the general societal expectations that women should speak of "the family and peace," the unfixed and potentially disruptive meaning those themes might have in practice, and the use of female moral authority to legitimate revolutionary violence.

Scholars studying "maternal" or "feminine" movements, especially the groups of mothers of the disappeared throughout Latin America, have tended to stress the special affinity maternalist politics has with the politics of "peace." In particular, they note the special potential of women's movements to uphold "life" against dictatorial terror.[92] Yet we must be careful not to read these movements as simple calls for peace or nonviolence. As other scholars have noted, "mothers" have long supported state-directed war efforts, albeit in ways distinct from those used by male leaders and soldiers.[93] As we have seen here, with the FCMM's anguished endorsement of the armed struggle, or in Pelayo's angry public call for vengeance, the acceptance of violent methods of struggle may be an extension of a felt abhorrence for (state) violence; the two are not only not contradictory, they are closely related. The very same logic that endowed women with the special moral authority to denounce state violence as destructive of life and the family could also be mobilized toward supporting political violence.[94] In these cases, maternalist anguish helped present revolutionary violence as a necessary evil to counter the physical annihilation of Cuban youth and the suffering of Cuban mothers and families. Thus the moral authority of women, like the responsible masculine honor of men, helped "domesticate" rebel violence while casting state repression as abhorrent. These women's groups, as well as the collaboratively organized public protests discussed above, collectively stripped Batista of legitimacy and even helped sanction the use of violence against his rule.

The Gendered Experience of the Urban Underground

Although the urban underground has been largely overshadowed by studies of the rebel army, there is recognition, at least in some circles, of the urban underground's importance, and there is a growing body of literature reassessing its role.[95] Still, existing studies focus almost exclusively on well-known male leaders; the relationship of the urban underground with the Sierra leadership; and the action and sabotage brigades, the armed underground cells that coordinated attacks on security forces or sabotage against varying urban targets. Even the most complete studies of the urban underground scarcely mention the presence of women.[96] Such erasure makes it difficult to fully assess women's participation.

Oral sources suggest that many young women were first recruited by men to act as decoys: a man was less likely to be stopped and frisked if accompanied by a young woman pretending to be his girlfriend.[97] But women's involvement often grew steadily from there. Women were less likely to directly take up arms or plant bombs, and more likely to engage in various other roles, sometimes similar to those played by women in the FCMM and the MOU, such as strategizing, printing and distributing propaganda, handling movement finances, relaying messages, arranging safe houses, building bombs, transporting materiel, and other duties.[98] Thus assessing the depth of women's involvement requires looking beyond the action and sabotage brigades.

Although the demographics of the membership of these organizations is still not entirely clear, a rare study conducted by researchers at the University of Havana with some 675 women who had participated in the insurrection in one municipality of Havana helps reconstruct their social profile. Most were in their late teens or early twenties, most were white, and the majority of them—perhaps two-thirds—came from the middle sectors. Primary occupations among those listed in the survey were student, teacher, and women with "no occupation," perhaps housewives or unemployed graduates. Following these categories, the second-largest groups were store employees, industrial workers, and domestic servants. Like their male counterparts in the urban underground, women activists were primarily but not exclusively white and middle class.[99] And, as stated earlier, anecdotal estimates suggest that they formed between 10 and 20 percent of urban underground militants, which would mean as many as several thousand women at the insurrection's peak.[100]

Still, assessments based on formal organizational membership likely underestimate women's real numbers and impact, as women were probably overrepresented in the putative margins of the movement. Oral sources highlight women's roles as occasional collaborators and sympathizers, often not formally affiliated with any group, drawn into sporadic collaboration through personal contacts. As we shall see, these could include middle-aged as well as young women. Two examples will suffice here. In her research, the sociologist Linda Ann Klouzal uncovered the way one informational or "spy" network organized by the Twenty-Sixth of July Movement operated in Havana: it comprised one man, four young women, and three or four older women who lived in different neighborhoods. The operation consisted in advising movement militants when they had been identified by police, based on information the male cell member gleaned through his job at the government Intelligence Office. He passed this information through his mother to one of the cell's young women; she in turn conveyed the information to whichever older woman lived closest to the militant; the older woman then contacted the militant in question.[101]

Another example suggests the prevalence of women as informal and occasional collaborators with the DR. Vicente Robaína, a young law student and member of the DR, helped organize a five-minute work stoppage in 1955 that drew on organized labor and the student sector. In an interview, he described how he relied on a support network of mostly female friends, relatives, and acquaintances, who worked in the small shops clustered in downtown Havana:

> I had friends who were store employees. . . . Some had been students of my mother's. I worked with Casa Cofiño, a hardware store on Neptuno [Street]. There were some women [working] there who I knew didn't support the dictatorship. They weren't communists or with the 26 [of July] or anything like that, but they didn't support [Batista]. We also went to a furniture store, La Moda, on Neptuno and Galiano [streets], where a cousin of my mother's worked as a furniture designer. She and my mother had fought together during the Spanish Civil War, and she fled here when Franco took power. I had a contact in [the shoe store] Flogar, a woman who was also with the DR. And one in [the department store] El Encanto. She wasn't with the DR but she bought bonds from me, hid things in her house. She helped me.[102]

This anecdote is fascinating for the way it turns the everyday image of the "shop girl" on its head, recasting such women as a network of revolutionary collaborators. It also captures the bonds forged across generations, as some women were contacts or longtime collaborators of his mother's, a Spanish Republican exile and schoolteacher. This example suggests that women's participation in anti-Batista activities could be shaped by their overrepresentation in certain sectors, such as retail. Similarly, the Twenty-Sixth of July Movement in Santiago relied on telephone operators—overwhelmingly female—for intelligence gathering. Even some women's lack of formal employment could apparently be turned to the movement's advantage, as in the case of the older women "spies" who used their flexible time at home to relay messages. These examples make clear that women were involved in ways large and small, and performed labor that was essential.

The women members of the male-dominated revolutionary groups did not necessarily see themselves mobilizing as women per se, nor do they now always recognize any gendered particularity to their activism. Yet their participation reveals certain patterns. Women in the urban cells of the Twenty-Sixth of July Movement and the Revolutionary Directorate faced different obstacles, played different roles, and had different experiences than their male counterparts. Sexuality influenced how their participation was viewed and regulated by both their parents and movement leaders. Their socially constructed role as caretakers led them to take on more pronounced public duties in mourning and in support for militants' families, sometimes in collaboration with the all-women's groups discussed earlier. And women's roles within the family—particularly those of young women—required them to negotiate and confront the boundaries of patriarchal authority in order to gain the freedom of movement and association required to undertake political activism. Thus, just as a defense of domestic sanctity might prompt militant public action, as we have seen in the case of maternalist protests, women's public action also first required some negotiation over domestic relations.

For many young women, engaging in any type of political participation required the negotiation of authority within the home. This was especially true for the young, unmarried, middle-class women who comprised the bulk of those who joined revolutionary organizations. Although urban gender relations in the 1950s were not as strict as in earlier decades of the century, adult chaperones still closely regulated contact between young men and women in a courtship context, such as parties and dances held in homes, social clubs, or Spanish immigrant associations. For middle-class families especially, spending time in public ("in the street") had different implications for adolescent men and women. Most young men enjoyed freedom of movement throughout the city, and could spend long hours away from home unaccounted for.[103] But young unmarried women's public movement was still somewhat suspect, and streets and plazas in Havana thus afforded an anonymity and relative privacy that many young women's parents, who hailed from small towns in Spain or elsewhere in Cuba, had not known and felt was threatening.[104] The modern, semipublic spaces of the darkened cinema or the privately owned car posed similar perils. For their part, many high school–aged girls began to chafe at what they felt were antiquated restrictions, influenced by the relative liberty of young women as depicted in Hollywood films and enticed by the ease of traveling from one side of the city to another on public transportation.

Ana Losada Prieto, a young teenager during the insurrection who joined the José Martí Women's Civic Front, recalled an early battle with her father sparked by excessive regulation of her older sister's sexuality. After hours of preparation for an extended-family picnic in the country, her father—who could not go himself because of work—suddenly got cold feet over the presence of his teenage daughter's boyfriend and vetoed the whole outing. Infuriated, Ana "stood up to him," telling him that "everything was ready and that *I was* going. . . . What is all this nonsense, this backwardness, this watching over people? . . . When I have a boyfriend, I won't tolerate having a chaperone."[105]

Conflicts such as these could only be compounded by young women's participation in the insurrection, which involved not only political and physical risk taking, long absences, and unrestricted movement about the city, but also close, unsupervised association with single men. Eneida Hernández, a lower-middle-class Havana teenager who eventually became a cell leader for the Twenty-Sixth of July Movement, recalled conflicts with her mother over visits from a thirty-something political contact of hers, who might stop by the house to ask her for help in hiding a *compañero* wanted by the police or in distributing clandestine publications. In order to avoid provoking her mother, they eventually devised a meeting signal. Her contact would play a particular song on the jukebox in the corner bar across from her house. "You could hear it perfectly . . . so I'd go out yelling, 'Mom, I'm going to the corner for a second!' I'd meet with him, we'd walk around the block, and he would tell me what he needed."[106]

Eneida was increasingly drawn into the struggle and eventually went underground, living in a house rented in a neighborhood far from her parents' home and masquerading as the wife of one of the two *compañeros* she lived there with. Seeking parental approval, she appealed in vain to her mother's own political sympathies: "I told her that [Ortodoxo leader Eduardo] Chibás had died for *something*."[107] Her Twenty-Sixth of July *compañeros* met with her parents to appeal to them in a more traditional language, pledging their paternalistic protection of the young woman. Still, the idea of her daughter living with two unrelated men proved too much for her mother to accept. Eneida finally broke off ties with her family until years after the revolution's triumph.[108]

On the other hand, some women recalled one or both of their parents being supportive of their political endeavors, helping them to hide materials, allowing wanted men to sleep in the family home, or perhaps providing economic support for their political activities.[109] In one revealing story, Marisol Álvarez recalled that her mother was so incensed by her new boyfriend—a student leader at the university—that she took a long trip back to Spain to prepare for the whole family's return to their native country. During her absence, Marisol not only became increasingly involved in the underground herself; she managed to convince her father to support the movement as well.[110] Yet even when they did not face parental disapproval, it was, in general, harder for young women than men activists to hide their political participation from their families.[111] Even older, married women sometimes faced similar disapproval from their husbands.[112] Thus women's activism required some previous battle over the boundaries of patriarchal authority, sparked new conflicts within the family, or perhaps even strengthened familial ties around newfound political solidarities. In other words, their political actions necessarily required them to negotiate and confront the patriarchal relations of the home.

These examples remind us that young women's political activity and sexuality were difficult to disentangle, for the ideological conflation of the public with the political meant that women's freedom of movement always also caused tensions over their sexual freedom. Parents frequently saw their daughters' political activity through the prism of seduction. For example, some women interviewed recalled that their parents blamed their political participation on a "troublemaking" boyfriend who, they believed, had drawn their previously innocent daughter into political—and sexual—trouble. Then again, many young women did experience a simultaneous sexual and political awakening, and in interviews some replicate their parents' belief that it was a particular boyfriend that brought them to political consciousness. This is a connection rarely echoed in interviews with male revolutionaries, whose earliest sexual and political forays also presumably coincided in time. But young men's sexual initiations did not always take place with women they considered their social or political peers.

Interestingly, Twenty-Sixth of July Movement leaders replicated parental concerns over sexual encounters between militants, although not always for the same reasons. Their primary concern was logistical. Urban clandestinity forced young men and women into close quarters, sometimes sharing an apartment for weeks at a time. Movement leaders feared the disruptive impact of romantic rivalries and pregnancies. They correspondingly coached their members to refrain from engaging in sexual relations with others in the movement. According to former militants, when young men and women had to sleep in the same safe house, their more experienced *compañeros* "spoke clearly" to them about the need for restraint.[113] Like leaders of the rebel army, ranking urban underground militants sought to contain their subordinates' sexual exploits, although this was considerably more complicated in the fluid context of the city. Evidently movement leaders also worried that sexual liaisons would threaten the pure, morally correct character of the revolutionaries. The relationship between the young men and women involved in the urban underground was supposed to be "sacred," one former Twenty-Sixth of July member reported; violating that relationship would be considered a "sacrilege."[114]

When movement militants developed committed partnerships with one another, they also struggled with the dilemma of whether or not to engage in premarital sex, often reluctant to violate social conventions, yet unable to marry in such circumstances.[115] The 1988 feature film *Clandestinos*, based on the life of Twenty-Sixth of July member Norma Porras, fictionalizes the choices faced by young women and men in the urban underground.[116] One couple decides not to consummate their relationship until they can get married after the struggle, but the man is killed before the revolution triumphs. Another couple does engage in sexual relations, and the young woman consequently becomes pregnant. As a result, she can no longer be as active in the struggle, and is also estranged from her family, who disapprove of her premarital relations. Thus young women's participation in the urban underground was subject to different forms of sexual policing—from both parents and movement leaders—than that of their male counterparts, and their sexual encounters could have more serious consequences, especially an unplanned pregnancy. Many male insurrectionaries benefitted from a more permissive attitude on the part of their parents, and more often enjoyed sexual relations with women not involved in the movement.

Women militants also faced specific forms of sexual abuse when detained by police, including rape or other sexualized forms of humiliation.[117] Eneida, the teenage cell leader for the Twenty-Sixth of July Movement, recounted that when police captured her and an older woman in an apartment, they gang raped the older woman and stripped Eneida before forcing her into the police car. Once in the police station, they placed Eneida naked in a holding cell with thirty male political prisoners, mostly members of the Twenty-Sixth of July Movement, thus inviting Eneida to imagine being gang raped by her own *compañeros*. She was later raped by police during interrogation.[118] Such tactics show a conscious attempt not only to wound, terrify, and humiliate, but also to pollute ties of political solidarity through sexual innuendo and fear.

Experiences such as these could not be entirely assimilated to those of their male *compañeros*, nor did they fit easily within narratives of male revolutionary heroism and glorious martyrdom. The everyday experiences of young women in the urban underground encouraged a different consciousness. Conflicts with family over political activities illuminated the patriarchal relations of the home; sexual humiliation and rape by police suggested the gendered nature of state terror. These were the insights that eventually led women active in revolutionary movements elsewhere in Latin America to embrace feminism.[119] Yet the Cuban women who joined the revolutionary movement are generally not included in these assessments. As one sociologist has argued, the post-1959 revolutionary state's redistribution of wealth, implementation of relatively egalitarian access to education and employment, and construction of an ideologically antifeminist mass women's organization explain the subsequent "absence of revolutionary feminism in an otherwise ideologically radical society."[120]

This chapter has suggested that, rather than explain the "absence" of feminist consciousness in Cuba or assume that women's political motivations, consciousness, and experiences were somehow analogous to those of their male counterparts, we instead carefully examine the various forms of women's political consciousness that we do find. Few women active in the insurrection articulated a critique of gender inequality. That agenda would come after 1959, from further left. Yet many mobilized as women, particularly as mothers, manipulating and disrupting traditional assumptions of women as apolitical and housebound. And the experiences women underwent as activists sometimes pushed them toward more critical, feminist-inflected understandings of the limitations of household patriarchy. It is not a coincidence that a few of these women, many decades later, formed a short-lived organization that was openly feminist in stance, albeit it rejected the term "feminism" as too confrontational.[121]

The January 1959 triumph of the insurrection prompted an enormous emotional outpouring for those who had been deeply devoted to the cause. In late January 1959, the José Martí Women's Civic Front gathered one last time in Santiago. They marched to a local cemetery bearing a large Cuban flag, flanked by the weeping mothers and widows of the city's young martyrs. Aida Pelayo stood before the crowd and gave a speech with the passion and flair she was known for. Cuba, Pelayo proclaimed, was now truly free. Finally liberated of its yokes and chains, it could embark on its radiant national destiny. And women, she reminded the audience, had participated in every aspect of Cuba's momentous struggle. Yet with a nationalist revolution now in power, Pelayo no longer saw the necessity of an organized women's group; she believed her work was done. With those words, the most important women's group of the anti-Batista insurrection was officially disbanded. But for many other women, January 1959 was just the beginning.[122]

4 | THE NEW WOMAN AND THE OLD LEFT, 1959–1960

In April 1959, a few months after the revolutionary victory, police reports noted that two sixteen-year-old girls from the western province of Pinar del Rio were missing. But they had left behind a letter "in which they explained to their families that they were leaving for an expedition to fight for the freedom of Nicaragua."[1] That two teenage girls thought it appropriate that they should fight for the liberation of a neighboring country gives us a sense of just how much some women were rethinking their own roles in the first months of the revolution. Undoubtedly infused with the passion of the revolutionary moment, they had perhaps been inspired by the tales of women's participation in the Cuban insurrection that flooded the newspapers. Or they may have been enticed by the exiles from other Caribbean nations that now flocked to Havana seeking public support for their home causes. Or they themselves might have participated in Pinar del Rio's anti-Batista movement, and now wished to extend their political engagement to national liberation elsewhere. While we lack further specifics about their case, the two teenagers' horizons and sense of calling had surely been dramatically altered. And in that they were not alone.

The 1959 victory of the revolutionary movement led to a new surge of women's mobilization. Women who had participated in the insurrection now continued their activism in other ways, forming new organizations expressly devoted to furthering the revolution and attempting to spread the revolution's influence as extensively as possible, both socially and geographically. Many women who had not taken part in the insurrectionary conflict were inspired by the new mood of revolutionary rebirth; they too flocked to the new organizations for revolutionary women. This chapter recovers the history of the multitude of new women's groups that formed in the crucial period of revolutionary ferment from the revolutionary triumph of January 1959 to the summer of 1960, when all existing women's groups were collapsed into the new Federation of Cuban Women (FMC). This vast yet forgotten groundswell is key to understanding how and why the revolutionary leadership turned to women's issues in the first place.

These new women's groups mobilized toward a variety of causes, such as defending the revolution, opposing dictators throughout the Americas, advocating solidarity with rural and urban labor movements, or demanding the economic alleviation of working-class women. The groups comprised women of different political persuasions, reflecting the political plurality of 1959 and 1960. Indeed, the very richness of the revolutionary moment lay in the diverse visions and organizations that emerged in parallel—and sometimes in conflict—with one another. Recovering their histories helps us reconceptualize the early revolutionary period: we might see the mid-1960 formation of the FMC and other mass organizations as the closing of a window of politically plural, bottom-up popular mobilization, not the beginning of women's mass mobilization in the revolution.

Within this broad mobilization, two main tendencies were strongest. One comprised the primarily young women affiliated with the insurrectionary movement led by the Twenty-Sixth of July Movement, that is, women of the so-called New Left. The other encompassed the often older women affiliated with the Marxist or "Old" Left, who by and large had not participated in the insurrection. I argue, perhaps counterintuitively, that women affiliated with the Marxist Left generated a more progressive and well-developed platform for women's rights than the women activists of the revolutionary movement. This platform drew on the "party feminism" that had evolved in dialogue with the socialist world during the 1940s and 1950s. Thus we cannot overlook the contribution of the "Old" Left in this early revolutionary period.

Cold War tensions inevitably produced conflict and competition between noncommunist women of the insurrectionary movement and women affiliated with the prerevolutionary Communist Party throughout 1959 and 1960. As the revolution increasingly turned toward the Cuban Communist Party and the Soviet Union for support, women of the Marxist Left rose to leadership positions, eventually sidelining the women who had led the anti-Batista struggle. But the conflict between these two political tendencies was not the whole story. There were also important points of convergence between how women of the Old and New Lefts reimagined women's roles in the revolution. They each raised the issue of what role women should play in the revolution either directly—in rallies, in local meetings, and in national and even international congresses—or indirectly, through their actions, for example by joining a female militia unit. This mobilization occurred during the earliest, most fluid period of the revolution, a time when the new leadership was still seeking to consolidate its rule and was thus necessarily more open and responsive to grassroots demands. Thus the various women's groups that emerged in the earliest period of the revolution—even when in conflict with one another—collectively succeeded in establishing women's rights and gender reform as part of the revolutionary agenda.

Recovering the role of women affiliated with Cuba's prerevolutionary Marxist Left helps us rethink histories of feminism, revolution, and the Old Left in Cuba and beyond. Scholars of women's involvement in Latin American guerrilla movements have argued that their participation led to the rise of "revolutionary feminism," a gradual, organic evolution from "feminine" to "feminist" consciousness.[2] But this chapter shows that we cannot see the trajectory of insurrectionary women in isolation. We need to include the Old Left in our assessments and to see the Old and New Lefts in dialogue and in competition with one another.

Tracing the history of the formation of these women's groups in 1959 and their supersession in 1960 also challenges the dominant narrative of women's liberation from above. That official narrative stresses the role of a visionary leadership in first mobilizing women for the insurrection, and then formalizing that mobilization by founding a mass organization for women in August 1960. The FMC supposedly marked the entry of women into the revolution and, indeed, into national politics for the first time. But this chapter shows that, instead, activist women themselves pushed for inclusion and redress. The impetus for women's liberation thus came from below and from the Left. In response, the revolutionary leadership imposed a top-down, centralized agenda on what had been a far more organic, plural, and at times conflictive grassroots women's movement. In so doing, the leadership promoted a more homogeneous and less radical vision of women's emancipation.

The Marxist Left and the "Woman Question" in the 1950s

To understand the role that women affiliated with Cuba's Communist Party played in developing a vision of women's emancipation in the first months and years of the revolution, we need insight into the way the Marxist Left dealt with these questions prior to 1959. Recent historiography has tended to criticize the conservatism of the Marxist Left in Latin America in the realm of gender relations and especially sexuality.[3] And the history of Cuba's prerevolutionary Communist Party is particularly controversial, for the party engaged in political deals and compromises with Batista that tarnished its reputation. But the prerevolutionary Marxist Left had developed a surprisingly progressive platform for women's rights in the late 1940s and 1950s, and as a result played a crucial role in redefining women's roles after the revolutionary triumph.

Cuba's prerevolutionary Communist Party, then known as the Popular Socialist Party (PSP), was considered one of the strongest Communist parties in Latin America in the 1940s and 1950s, perhaps second in strength only to Chile's. Its strength was partly derived from a political pact with Batista in 1937, as he ascended to power for the first time, which gave the PSP temporary control of the Confederation of Cuban Labor. Although the PSP was not large, and although it lost significant strength during the anticommunist assault of the late 1940s under the Auténtico government, its strength in unions of strategic industries gave it disproportionate power in national politics. It also exercised a strong media presence through its daily paper, *Noticias de Hoy*, and through its highly regarded radio station, Mil Diez. The party's membership in the late 1940s and early 1950s may have fluctuated between 10,000 and 20,000, but electorally Communist candidates could garner upward of 125,000 votes.[4] The majority of its membership was drawn from the urban working class, although some radicalized middle-class intellectuals also belonged and rose to leadership positions.[5]

Women may have comprised nearly half of the PSP's membership in the late 1940s and early 1950s, although some contemporary sources describe women affiliates as the "wives" of PSP members, and it is possible that many of the women counted as PSP members may have been primarily affiliated with the women's organization the Democratic Federation of Cuban Women (discussed later in this chapter).[6] Observers commonly noted that the PSP was "strongest" in women's and youth organizations, as well as in the unions of key industries such as sugar, tobacco, and port workers.[7] A 1951 Communist Party ad gives us some sense of the language and imagery the party used to appeal to potential women members. A man with a hammer and sickle emblazoned on his chest is surrounded by a group of people apparently signing up for party membership. A blonde woman with her back to the viewer features prominently in the center of the ad. The accompanying text assures women readers that the PSP fought for "the full equality of women," including equal pay for equal work and other measures. In addition, the first two slogans featured in the ad note the party's commitment to world peace and to lower prices, issues thought to be of particular interest to women.[8]

Like other Communist parties in Latin America in this period, the PSP had renounced revolutionary violence; it sought to effect gradual reform in the short and medium term through electoral coalitions, union activities, and mass consciousness raising. In foreign policy, the PSP technically sup-

"*Worker, Peasant, People: To Your Party!*" *A 1951 Communist Party electoral ad shows a group of people, including one woman, signing up for party membership. (From Confidential U.S. State Department Central Files, Cuba, 1950–1954 [microform]: Internal Affairs)*

ported the USSR and vocally opposed U.S. imperialism, but in practice the party emphasized national and local issues, which most appealed to its constituency.[9] In addition, despite common allegations that the party was doing Moscow's bidding, it is unclear how much direct communication existed between the PSP and the USSR.[10]

Few historians have studied the way the PSP addressed questions of women and gender, but the party had been active in mobilizing women since the 1920s, perhaps originally in response to the Communist International's 1922 call for Communist parties worldwide to more actively reach out to women and to socialize household tasks.[11] According to Nicola Murray, the Cuban Communist Party led a campaign for equal pay for equal work in the late 1920s, then in 1934 formed the Unión Nacional de Mujeres, which "demanded rights for working and peasant women."[12] Throughout the 1930s, as Cuban first-wave feminism developed and radicalized, other leftist feminist groups emerged, such as the Unión Laborista de Mujeres, led by the socialist Ofelia Domínguez.[13] The feminist movement declined after 1940, but the party continued to advocate for women's legal rights. Indeed, contrary to widespread assumptions about the conservatism of the Marxist Left regarding issues relating to gender, the Democratic Federation of Cuban Women (Federación Democrática de Mujeres Cubanas, FDMC) elaborated a platform of women's rights that was surprisingly progressive for the period.

The FDMC was formed in 1948.[14] The group was active in conferences and campaigns, and had its own publication; it thus gives us further insight into the Marxist Left in this period. The group was technically the Cuban branch of an international Soviet-sponsored group, the Women's International Democratic Federation (WIDF). Although the FDMC had formal organizational autonomy from the PSP, in practice it operated as a women's organization affiliated with the Communist Party.[15] Many of the most prominent women of the PSP also featured in the FDMC, and there was strong overlap between both the membership and the political platforms of the two groups. This relationship has led some commentators to view the FDMC as merely an "appendage" or front organization for the party, with the consequent implication that it could not function as a legitimate forum for women's rights.[16] But in practice the relationship between Communist Party leaderships and party-sponsored women's organizations has varied widely, as scholars such as Francisca de Haan and Elisabeth Freidman have shown. For example, in the case of Venezuela, Friedman shows that the Unión de Muchachas, formed by the Venezuelan Communist Party in the early 1950s, was explicitly designed to foster women's political development as leaders, and the group was given significant autonomy and control over its strategy.[17] In addition, as the pioneering work by the historian Kate Weigand has shown, the Communist Party should not be viewed as a monolith. Indeed, the history of Communist parties elsewhere suggests that issues of women's equality and conceptualizations of women's emancipation could be divisive, and that some women party members faced sanction for their unorthodox interpretations of women's oppression.[18]

Importantly, the Cuban Communist Party in general, and the FDMC in particular, attempted to simultaneously address hierarchies of race, class, and gender. Since at least the late 1930s the party had specifically cast itself as fighting for equal rights for blacks and women.[19] As the historian Alejandro de la Fuente describes, the party pursued these goals in tandem, trying to push for progressive antiracist legislation through affiliated women's and youth groups and through the national Women's Congress held in 1939. The party also provided a platform for the articulation of a critique about the intersection of race, class, and gender. For example, Esperanza Mastrapa, an Afro-Cuban party member and a leader of the FDMC, stated in 1950, "To the inequality that women suffer in all social relations in our country . . . black and mulatto women must add those based on skin color."[20]

The FDMC grew to significant national prominence during a campaign for peace in 1950 and 1951 during the onset of the Korean War, when the Cuban government pledged to send troops to help the U.S. effort.[21] To further the campaign, the FDMC established organizational chapters and "Mothers' Committees" in almost all towns of any size throughout the country and brought hundreds of delegates from all over the island to its March 1951 congress.[22] The group also collected as many signatures as possible for its petitions; the number of signatures garnered suggests that the FDMC was able to reach far beyond the ranks of the PSP, at least for the peace campaign.[23] It is hard to establish how deep or significant the contacts established between urban PSP militants and rural women in such encounters were. Yet it seems significant that, in many rural small towns, the local chapter of the FDMC was the only organization explicitly devoted to issues of relevance to women, and that it appealed to rural women in a specifically political idiom, unlike, say, the faith- and uplift-focused efforts of Catholic Action.[24] As the U.S. embassy noted, "inasmuch as the organization interests itself in topics of general concern to women (children's care, women's rights, cost of living, and education) in many of the localities it probably is considered as *the* women's club of the town."[25] In 1959, in the wake of the revolutionary triumph, women of the Marxist Left would mobilize these island-wide networks.

Guided by its pro-Soviet umbrella group and by images of women's emancipation in the USSR, the FDMC elaborated a local program for women's civil, political, and economic rights. The international WIDF repeatedly asserted that women had rights "as mothers, as workers, and as citizens." The WIDF's 1953 Declaration of the Rights of Women called for the right to work, for equal pay for equal work, for equal rights to social security, and for the rights of women and children to "protection from the State." It also called for equal civil rights regarding marriage, property, and children; the right to vote and hold office; the extension of industrial workers' rights to workers in the countryside; and the right of peasant women to own land.[26] The international Left's systemic perspective led the FDMC to an explicit conceptualization of issues of gender equality or family reform as linked to broader structural problems of Cuba's monoculture, its cyclical employment, and its dependent relation with the United States. For example, the FDMC voiced specific demands to improve the family, including higher salaries, state subsidies for large families and the unemployed, and construction of cheap housing units in both city and country. Yet it also argued that long-term resolution of these problems would require the end of monoculture, agrarian reform, and the protection of national industry.[27]

In applying the WIDF's framework to Cuba's national situation, the FDMC also added some innovative elements, elaborating ideas that were highly progressive in the Cuban context of the 1950s. For example, drawing from ideals circulating among women of the socialist bloc, the group tried to generate a theoretical framework for understanding the position of peasant women, who faced different forms of exploitation from those of their urban counterparts and could be defined simultaneously as housewife, employee, and independent farmer. As one author wrote in the group's publication *Mujeres Cubanas*, peasant women were "a mixture of housewife and estate peon [*peón de la finca*], since to the task of taking care of the children and attending to a thousand obligations in the home, must be added the [task] of caring for animals ... and [harvesting] root vegetables ... and fruits." In addition to being a "loving mother" and "housewife," the *campesina* was also "a kind of worker, without a salary or a boss, without protection or help."[28] Rather than merely assume peasant women would automatically benefit from the material uplift of male *campesinos*, as most leftist parties and regimes throughout Latin America have done, the FDMC tried to recognize the specificity of rural women's exploitation.[29]

The FDMC also found inspiration in news from the Soviet bloc. The group could indulge in romanticized depictions of life in the socialist world. For example, *Mujeres Cubanas* occasionally featured idealized depictions of the conditions of children in the Soviet Union or East Germany, implying that the eradication of capitalism had resulted in a children's utopia.[30] But it could also be more grounded and concrete. For example, the same magazine also penned detailed explanations of the labor and maternity rights women had won in the Soviet Union. It praised the USSR's state-funded childcare services, which relieved women of domestic burdens. And it commended the subsidies granted by the Soviet state to single mothers, who formed a large group in Cuba.[31] Whether or not these provisions were always followed in the USSR, the example of Soviet women's emancipation at least raised the bar on what gains for women seemed possible.

The FDMC also explicitly addressed issues of race and strongly denounced racism in the workplace and beyond. As Mastrapa noted in a 1949 speech, working-class women of color faced a "triple discrimination" based on race, class and gender.[32] The FDMC demanded sanctions against employers who discriminated against dark-skinned women and "measures that will assure the incorporation of black and mixed-race [*mestizo*] women into the workforce, with no other limitations than their own capacity."[33] In contrast to dominant approaches to racial inequality in Cuba, which tended to focus on reform of the public sphere and downplay the need for antiracist consciousness raising, the FDMC also called for a "vast educational campaign" directed toward eradicating backward beliefs and practices that tended to view women as inferior beings and that would erase "absurd differences based on false concepts of racial superiority."[34]

While the FDMC described maternity as a "sacred right" and called for the implementation of various measures to facilitate maternal health and children's welfare, it did not exclusively view women as mothers.[35] The FDMC supported the incorporation of women into paid labor. It demanded the strict enforcement of equal pay for equal work and bemoaned the fact that the immense majority of women workers were concentrated in the most poorly remunerated industries, such as domestic service and food processing. To assist working mothers, it called for the installation of daycare centers and even breastfeeding rooms in factories and, more generally, the state-funded resolution of women's domestic burdens through the construction of daycare centers, cheap cafeterias, and collective laundry facilities in neighborhoods, factories, and rural areas. Yet the FDMC did not exclusively insist on women's incorporation into the paid workforce as a solution to housewives' purported isolation and backwardness.[36] The group seemed to embrace a wide spectrum of women's militancy that included both women workers and mobilized housewives. In fact, it praised militant housewives as crucial and highly effective allies in various labor struggles.[37]

Cuba's Marxist Left in this period may have turned a blind eye to certain controversial issues, particularly sexuality. It never publicly addressed abortion, which was illegal but widely practiced, divorce, which had been legal since the 1930s, or homosexuality, which was practiced relatively openly at least in Havana during the republican period.[38] It did not raise issues pertaining to relations between men and women in the private sphere or scrutinize the behavior of its male members to enforce equality within the home.[39] It never adopted the term "feminism," which it would have denounced as divisive, bourgeois, and imperialist.

But since the decline of Cuba's first-wave feminism in the late 1930s, the PSP and especially the FDMC were some of the only groups in Cuba's political landscape that continued to seriously address issues of women's equality and reach out to working-class women within this rubric.[40] The only other major Cuban organization to do so was the liberal feminist organization the Lyceum, which was predominantly a cultural organization that sponsored talks in Havana and conceptualized its outreach to poor and working-class women through the rubric of professionalized social work.[41] In addition, in its suggestions for eradicating racist *thought*, not merely discrimination in employment and elsewhere, the FDMC at least gestured toward the transformation of the private sphere, not only the public sphere—a radical suggestion in Cuba.[42] Viewed in its historical context, the Marxist Left thus had the most developed and progressive vision regarding women's emancipation in the Cuban political landscape of the 1940s and 1950s. This progressive platform derived from contact with and inspiration from the socialist world.

Through the FDMC, the Marxist Left also facilitated the growth of a cadre of politically experienced radical women who saw issues of gender inequality linked to broader structural problems of capitalism and underdevelopment. After the revolution these women would become key to the broadening of the government's program in 1959 and 1960. Yet, by and large, the Marxist Left did not support the revolutionary insurgency when it erupted in Cuba in the 1950s, and this fact would have strong implications for women's political organizing in the immediate aftermath of the revolution. The PSP's tardy embrace of the revolutionary struggle was bitterly resented by many Twenty-Sixth of July activists, who accused party members of collaborationism and passivity.

When the revolutionary movement abruptly triumphed in January 1959, a window of opportunity opened for the Marxist Left. In the emotional outpouring in the wake of the insurrectionaries' success, veteran Communist leader Elena Gil noted the sudden opportunity for political action, even for those not involved in the insurrection: "It was no longer only the Rebel Army that could undertake the great battles; it was anyone who joined the struggle to fight to defend and consolidate the Revolution. Many of those whom skepticism . . . had distanced from concrete actions during the armed struggle, ashamed of their attitude, [now] proved themselves disposed to undertake any task that the Revolution assigned them."[43] Ostensibly speaking of women, the passage can be interpreted as referring to the PSP's belated support for the revolution. As we shall see, women of the Marxist Left quickly took advantage of the political opening of the revolution to mobilize politically. But the rifts between the PSP and the Twenty-Sixth of July Movement could never be fully reconciled. These relations of mistrust would soon be replicated between women of the Marxist Left and the women who had mobilized to support the revolutionary movement.

"A Very Febrile Year": Women in the Revolutionary Moment

The revolutionary triumph of January 1959 inaugurated a period of breathtaking change, a momentous period of popular euphoria and rapid reforms. As Louis Pérez has written, the first 100 days witnessed a dizzying array of government decrees, leaving the populace alternately stunned and euphoric.[44] Rents were halved. Salaries were raised. Long-resented phone and electric foreign monopolies were intervened. Racially segregated spaces were integrated. Social justice at last seemed tangible. Protected by a brief honeymoon with its more powerful neighbor, the United States, Cuba had not yet witnessed the weighty international repercussions these revolutionary changes would eventually spark.

However, amid this outpouring of reform, the issue of women's rights was notable for its absence. This should perhaps not surprise us: throughout the insurrection, the leadership of the Twenty-Sixth of July Movement, the largest and most prominent revolutionary group, never mentioned women's rights in any of its manifestos or proclamations. As Nicola Murray notes, "the Rebels came to power without any clear policies aimed at changing the position of women."[45] After coming to power in 1959, Fidel Castro made a few brief comments in passing about discrimination against women and Afro-Cubans. But his comments tended to be abstract, and he called for no specific policies of redress.[46] In fact, despite brief comments in January 1959, Castro rarely spoke of women's rights or needs at all during his first two years in power.[47] Furthermore, the revolutionary government had no specific programs of outreach to women *as women* in this period, except for women's sections affiliated with the Twenty-Sixth of July Movement, as discussed subsequently.

It should also be clarified that in this period the leadership never used the term "liberation" or even "equality" when discussing women's issues.[48] These were terms that must have sounded conflictive or extreme to contemporaries. The terms usually used by the leadership were "integration," "incorporation," *superación* (denoting improvement or uplift), or even "redemption."[49] Castro's famous comments that women needed to be "doubly liberated" and that their liberation constituted a "revolution within the revolution" were not made until 1966.[50] Indeed, even in his speech given at the formation of the FMC, the key rationale for the new organization, as Castro expressed it, was that women were "useful" and that the revolution would henceforth "be able to count on one more force, on a new, organized force."[51] While women had been crucial to the revolutionary triumph, especially in the cities, the leadership did not view women as an aggrieved constituency that required specific measures of redress. Given this context, the interventions made by activist women in this period—especially those affiliated with the Communist Party—are all the more notable.

Buoyed by enthusiasm in the revolutionary moment, women affiliated with the Twenty-Sixth of July Movement began to form women's groups in the first weeks and months of 1959. They did so for the first time, since during the insurrection the movement had no specifically all-women's groups, aside from a small platoon in the Sierra Maestra.[52] The written historical record is nearly silent on the composition and activities of these groups, but interviews suggest that they were typically formed by young women who had been involved in the clandestine structure of the Twenty-Sixth of July Movement. Although in many ways they functioned as support groups for the national leadership's initiatives, the groups were also important forums for young women to lead and to mobilize other women. Though sanctioned and encouraged by the national leadership of the Twenty-Sixth of July Movement, the women leaders of these groups seem to have operated with some amount of discretion and autonomy. In sharp contrast to the bureaucratic and centralized structure of the FMC and other mass organizations after 1960, the activities of these groups were improvised, experimental, and inspired.

The two largest Twenty-Sixth of July–affiliated groups that formed were the Women's Revolutionary Brigades (Brigadas Femeninas Revolucionarias) and the Women's Section of the Twenty-Sixth of July Movement (Sección Femenina del 26 de Julio). Interviews give the sense that the impetus to form women's groups emerged simultaneously from women themselves and from the male leadership of the Twenty-Sixth of July Movement. As Martina Granados, a coordinator for the Women's Section of the Twenty-Sixth of July Movement, recounted: "The Provincial Direction of the Twenty-Sixth of July in Havana [Province] . . . had a Labor Section, a Finance Section, a Section of Social Issues, and the Women's Section. That is what they asked me to organize. Because many women [were] saying, we want to continue! . . . And they didn't really know what to do with those women."[53] However, we should balance these assertions by noting the tendency in interviews conducted with prorevolutionary Cubans to exaggerate the presence of the national leadership in nearly every process. For example, there is a tendency to credit the national leadership with all successful initiatives and to downplay or erase grassroots initiatives. (Conversely, it is common to attribute all failed initiatives to Soviet interference.)[54] There is also a strong impulse to stress one's proximity to the national leadership as a way of legitimizing one's participation. Bearing this in mind, it seems plausible that women within the Twenty-Sixth of July Movement were in fact a predominant factor in the formation of the women's groups.

The young women who led these groups were not Marxists, and in many cases considered themselves anticommunists. They identified with the radical nationalism of the insurrection and were motivated by an impassioned sense of duty toward the revolution. The Women's Brigades and the Women's Section were primarily devoted to supporting the new revolutionary decrees and implementing the social justice called for by Fidel Castro in the original Moncada speech. To this end, the organizations supported various mobilizations and attended revolutionary events en masse. In some ways, the groups seemed conceptually modeled on the women's sections of Cuba's prerevolutionary political parties—that is, designed to mobilize women for the party cause without developing a specific program around women and gender. Interviews suggest that they often functioned as a support network, closely following the Twenty-Sixth of July leadership.[55] As Gladys Marel García, a leader of the Women's Brigades, noted, "Che would suggest going to the airport because a member of the government was arriving, so [we would go]." When the agrarian and urban reform laws were announced, she said, they would "rush out" (*se lanzaba*) in support.[56] The Women's Section seemed to operate in a similar way. They would mobilize on behalf of the government "if there was a rally or some demand, whatever there was, [or] a need to support the measures of the revolution, for example the nationalization of properties or when Fidel tried to resign his premiership and we had to rally so he would stay [in power] . . . [1959] was a very, very, very febrile year."[57]

The women who formed these groups had no clearly articulated goals regarding gender equity and did not demand redress for women specifically. Like other women guerrillas in Latin America, the Twenty-Sixth of July–affiliated women's groups' leaders had been motivated to join the insurrection by goals similar to those of their male counterparts, namely, the desire to end dictatorship and exploitation. As Karen Kampwirth argues about women guerrillas in several countries, "gender justice was almost never a factor in their initial decision to join" the insurrection.[58] In interviews with former members of the Twenty-Sixth of July–affiliated women's groups, when asked why they had wanted to form organizations specifically for women in this period, they tend to offer several other overlapping rationales. Some clearly felt a need to digest and share the experience of the insurrection, and in that sense they at least implicitly recognized the particularities of women's experiences, such as their minority status within revolutionary cells, or their imprisonment, during which they underwent different tactics of sexual degradation or rape, including gang rape. Eneida Hernández, a member of a small women's group formed in early 1959 called the Women's Front of the Twenty-Sixth of July (Frente Femenino del 26 de Julio), recounted: "Because I was a member of the leadership [*comandancia*], I knew the women who were more or less [my] close collaborators. . . . I knew there were women in other groups, but I didn't know their names," because of the clandestine structure of the Twenty-Sixth of July Movement. "Many of us women had been imprisoned and for us it was a strong experience."[59]

A second goal was to incorporate more women into the revolution, particularly women of the popular classes.[60] The Women's Brigades were formed by a core of women from the action and sabotage units of the Twenty-Sixth of July Movement, and they were representative of a militantly revolutionary tradition. As the word "brigades" suggests, militancy was key to how the group conceptualized their endeavors. The Women's Brigades commandeered a wing of the Capitolio building in downtown Havana in the earliest weeks of the revolution and proceeded to recruit and aid women, particularly those from the surrounding working-class areas, including the many women employees of the nearby cigar factories and small workshops dedicated to leather and shoe manufacture. They also reached out to the city's army of domestic servants a full two years before the government would establish more institutionalized retraining programs for them. Gladys Marel García described approaching these women with the impassioned prompt: "Which do you prefer: Going to work or going to battle?" (*A trabajar o a la marcha?*) The women who joined forces with the Women's Brigades were outfitted with cots and given access to a cafeteria in the Capitolio building.[61] The Women's Section engaged in similar actions and also worked specifically to incorporate youth. As one woman recalled, "we visited small towns, engaged in [prorevolutionary] proselytism, called on women whenever it was necessary." Many of the young women who joined the Women's Section were students or unemployed, a socially and racially heterogeneous group.[62] If the leaders of the Women's Section lacked long-term experience in civilian organizing, they enjoyed the generalized rush of support for the Twenty-Sixth of July Movement brought on by revolutionary victory.

The mobilization of women-only groups contained an implicit recognition of women's specific roles in the revolution, as well as recognition of specific groups of women within society, especially domestic workers and prostitutes, who required redemption. Yet by and large the groups affiliated with the Twenty-Sixth of July did not embrace a specific, explicit agenda regarding women's rights or needs. As Francesca Miller has argued, it is necessary to distinguish between groups devoted primarily to mobilizing women and groups mobilized to address gender inequality.[63] The orientation of the Twenty-Sixth of July–affiliated women's groups should not surprise us, since there was no explicit or sustained articulation of gender inequality as a problem during the insurrection, from which these women had emerged.[64] That attention to gender inequality would be much more pronounced among organizations led by women who came from the ranks of the Marxist Left.

Women of the Marxist Left and the Revolutionary Moment

By the early months of 1959, women of the Marxist Left were also mobilizing, not only to support the revolution, but also to steer the revolution toward a particular vision of women's inclusion and emancipation. They drew on their old, island-wide networks, adapting their pre-1959 platform to the revolutionary moment. They organized conferences, fund-raisers, and rallies, and occasionally sponsored talks by radical women from other Latin American countries.[65] In so doing, they created forums for thinking through how the revolution could serve women, not simply vice versa. As discussed earlier, women's groups affiliated with the Twenty-Sixth of July Movement clearly raised the issue of women's participation in the revolution. Yet the first explicitly stated demands for gender equity and for alleviating women's traditional burdens came from women of the Old Left.

The actions of women of the Marxist Left can be traced most clearly through the group Revolutionary Women's Unity (Unidad Femenina Revolucionaria, UFR), which formed in 1959. In some ways the UFR was a successor organization to the pro-Soviet FDMC, discussed earlier.[66] Although in practice it tended to serve as a vehicle for women of the Old Left, its propaganda stressed the importance of unifying all prorevolutionary women.[67] Alongside women from the FDMC, it also included some well-known women activists from various insurrectionary groups, such as Opposition Women United (MOU), the Twenty-Sixth of July Movement, and the Revolutionary Directorate.[68] The UFR's very earliest statements reflected these composite origins, drawing on rhetoric from the triumphant revolutionary movement as well as the prerevolutionary Marxist Left. For example, the UFR's announcement for its first national conference, held in the spring of 1959, contained the impassioned denunciation of state violence, glorification of martyrs, and praise of women's sacrifice that had typified the insurrectionary movement. Its initial pronouncements also contained calls for "peace" and "democracy," common watchwords in the global campaigns led by the socialist bloc against nuclear buildup and redbaiting.[69] Their pronouncements soon included a new emphasis on solidarity with antidictatorial national liberation movements elsewhere in the region, in keeping with the ambience of 1959.

Compared to the women's groups affiliated with the Twenty-Sixth of July Movement, the UFR began with a stronger, more explicit vision pertaining to women's rights and needs. Here the influence of the prerevolutionary Marxist Left's program for women is loud and clear. In the announcement of its first national conference, the UFR's organizers were specific about its goals: the conference would lead to the formation of a "powerful, female revolutionary organization," which would work alongside the leadership to consolidate the revolution. At the same time, it would also work "for the specific demands of women,"[70] such as equal protections in the workplace, racial equity, childcare provisions in rural as well as urban settings, lowered costs of necessary goods and of rent, and better schools and parks for children.[71] The initial call for the conference stated: "So that working women have the same rights as men, and may enter all the same sectors of employment without discrimination based on skin color, and so that all the social laws that protect women's work [are honored]; so that there are thousands of daycares [creches] throughout the country where working mothers or campesinas can trust leaving their children; for [these reasons] we must support the revolution." The UFR thus positioned itself as something of a pressure group rather than simply a support group, stating that "women need to unite in order to consolidate [and] defend [the revolution], and hold the revolution to its promises [hacer que la revolución cumpla sus postulados]."[72] That is, women needed to support the revolution, but also to help shape it and hold it accountable. By extension, the group implied, women's support for the revolution was conditional.

Like the women's groups affiliated with the Twenty-Sixth of July Movement, the UFR focused on mobilizing women of the popular classes in particular. In the spring of 1959, the UFR called a series of conferences at which women from across the island could converge to debate their needs and demands in the context of the new revolution. In March 1959, the UFR held its first provincial-level conferences in Las Villas and Havana provinces. In April it held a national conference, attended by more than 500 delegates sent from all over the island by local chapters of the UFR and by other women's organizations, especially those on the Left. The attendees included women famed as *combatientes* in the Sierra Maestra, various peasant associations and representatives from labor unions, and delegates who hailed from factories and sugar mills. More than a year before the formation of the FMC, the UFR conferences provided a rare public platform for the open debate of working-class women's specific demands.

At the national conference held in April 1959, leaders and delegates coincided in their broad demands for economic justice, education, urban development, services for working women, and a manageable cost of living. Within that broad consensus, however, there were nuances. The Havana-based leadership proposed initiatives that would mobilize urban women to support agrarian reform and help "needy" peasant families, as well as training programs that would teach dressmaking or home economics, all suggestions that revealed a paternalistic strain.[73] In contrast, delegates tended to raise concrete measures that would alleviate their daily challenges as working-class wives and mothers, provide education for children, and extend urban infrastructure to underserved rural areas and impoverished urban *repartos*.[74] Delegates demanded daycare centers and cafeterias (*comedores populares*) with discounts (*bonificación*) for poor families.[75] And in both Havana's provincial conference and the national conference, delegates from the working-class Havana neighborhood Regla pointed out the urgent necessity of *bodegas* that stayed open past 7 P.M. in poor neighborhoods.[76] In the latter conference they also proposed a creative solution: staffing night *bodegas* with unemployed workers affiliated with the Retail Employees' Union.[77] In contrast to the tone and substance of the FMC's congresses after 1960, which often focused on foreign policy and other priorities of the national leadership, here delegates debated and suggested solutions for the everyday problems of working-class women.

The proposals advanced by delegates also transcended women's practical gender interests—or rather, they defined those interests very broadly.[78]

They demanded economic redistribution, not simply retraining for poor women. Delegates from Las Tunas Province supported the initiative of two local peasant associations to request that state inspectors visit "idle lands" belonging to Central Manatí, obviously with the hope that such lands would be redistributed among local residents as a result. This focus on the implementation of agrarian reform was echoed in other regional UFR activities. For example, in Camagüey, women affiliated with the UFR marched alongside residents of *reparto* Guernica who demanded that lands held by local Batista-era politicians be expropriated "and that the property titles be given to them," that is, to the local residents.[79] Other delegates to the national conference discussed the idea of forming a pineapple-canning factory as a cooperative.[80]

The Marxist Left in this period may even have explored the notion of the redistribution of domestic labor between women and men, a topic not publicly discussed in Cuba again until the mid-1970s. While covering a visit of peasant women to Havana for a week of Latin American solidarity initiatives, a journalist for the Communist Party's daily noted that it was "interesting" that these same *campesinas* had performed all necessary labor for both farmland and home when their husbands had traveled to Havana last year. "Now their husbands, as the women made their journey, took care of their houses and children in turn."[81] While the article did not directly call for women and men to share domestic burdens, it implied that such an arrangement was not unrealistic, and subtly linked male participation in childcare and housework to the revolution. The implication was that domestic labor might be shared prior to, or in lieu of, the collectivization of housework.

Finally, it was the Marxist Left that pioneered the idea of women as a coherent sector with shared problems and demands. In June 1960, a long, unsigned editorial in *Noticias de Hoy* enumerated women's specific needs and proposed that "we women, who have a series of demands as such," meet with Fidel to negotiate solutions, just as other sectors had.[82] The payoff, the author suggested, would be well worth it. "Imagine when there are popular laundries, when there are popular cafeterias, when there are kindergartens and children's rooms in the great factories where women will work in growing numbers. What wouldn't we be able to do with the free time we would have?"[83]

Thus in the earliest months of the revolution, women affiliated with the Marxist Left had articulated a program for women's rights that anticipated and in many ways surpassed programs launched by the revolutionary government in subsequent years. The UFR articulated a multifaceted social and economic platform that was partly dedicated to supporting or "defending" the revolution, but also went beyond it. It provided a space for the articulation of working-class women's demands, and for interaction among women from various social classes and regions. Their collective demands included access to public education in poor and rural areas; state-funded release from domestic burdens via daycare centers and popular cafeterias; lower prices for necessary goods; and *bodegas* with more flexible hours to ease the burden on working families. They had raised the prospect of women workers forming cooperatives for both production and consumption, and they demanded the redistribution of farmland even before the passage of the first Agrarian Reform Law. And they had done so in a context in which the revolutionary leadership had scarcely addressed the issue of women's needs.

Divergences

There is a tendency among some former members of the Twenty-Sixth of July Movement to view the UFR as a "Trojan horse" for the PSP, a vehicle through which women of the prerevolutionary Communist Party manipulated their way to power. Indeed, they have good reasons to, for eventually women affiliated with the prerevolutionary Marxist Left were awarded prominent positions in the women's mass organization and elsewhere in government, while many women leaders of the Twenty-Sixth of July Movement were passed over.[84] Oral histories with former members of the Twenty-Sixth of July convey a frustrated sense of displacement as the Communist Party became increasingly influential between 1959 and 1960 and depict the PSP as a usurper, thus intentionally disrupting an official history that suggests that the PSP smoothly and harmoniously took its rightful place in leadership after 1959.[85] These are powerful counterhistories, rich with implications. They harbor the idea that PSP members "Sovietized" the nationalist Cuban Revolution—that is, subordinated it to the USSR, introduced intolerant views, and sanctioned political repression. Publicly submerged for decades, that narrative reemerged in the 1990s after the demise of the USSR. Since then, a slow consensus seems to have been building within Cuba that blames the USSR's influence for derailing the development of what might have been a more tolerant and authentically Cuban form of socialism.

In order to understand these competing narratives, it is important to note that they reflect a period of broader competition between the Twenty-Sixth of July Movement and members of the PSP, as both jockeyed for position and influence within the new revolutionary government.[86] The broad nature of the antidictatorial struggle had subsumed different political positions oughout late 1958, but it was nearly inevitable that those differences would urface after the revolutionary triumph. Thus, throughout 1959 and 1960, ompeting factions of the broad anti-Batista revolutionary alliance struggled to define the direction of the revolution. As international pressure mounted and the U.S. government moved toward an openly interventionist stance, a schism emerged in 1960 between a "radical" faction of the Twenty-Sixth of July Movement, willing to ally with the PSP, and a "nationalist" faction of the movement that refused to. Eventually, that nationalist wing of the Twenty-Sixth of July Movement either warily accepted this growing alliance or broke ranks with the revolutionary government entirely and left for exile or joined the anticommunist armed opposition. It was within this broader political context that friction between the different women's groups arose, since women from the Twenty-Sixth of July Movement and the Marxist Left tended to belong to different revolutionary organizations: the Women's Brigades and the Women's Section of the Twenty-Sixth of July Movement, and the UFR, respectively.

Given what is at stake in this debate, it is important to treat these historical issues carefully. What exactly were the political divergences between women of the Marxist Left and women of the Twenty-Sixth of July? The most important political division concerned relations with the Soviet Union. This issue encapsulated two related problems: international alliances in the Cold War and the internal political structure of the new revolutionary polity. Gladys Marel García, a founder of the Women's Brigades, described their own politics as *martiana*—that is, nationalist and anti-imperialist, but not pro-Soviet. In this view, Cuba should be "neither a colony of Russia nor a colony of the United States."[87] While the UFR does not seem to have addressed the USSR directly in its pronouncements in this period, we know that the prerevolutionary FDMC shared a celebratory vision common in left-leaning women's groups in the 1950s, which praised the Soviet family and the lesser burdens on Soviet women.[88] And Cuba's Communist Party served as an important interlocutor between the new revolutionary leadership and the Soviets in this period.

Regarding the internal structure of their respective organizations, it is possible that there were also some differences in terms of how leaders from each group conceptualized relationships with their bases. For example, some of the young Twenty-Sixth of July women attempted to pioneer more egalitarian relations between leaders and participants. As García recalled, she sought to forge a relationship "de tú a tú"—that is, a relationship of equals—

with the poor women she and the other Twenty-Sixth of July female leaders were trying to mobilize.[89] These efforts may have had their limits. Anecdotes suggest that youth and relative inexperience hampered these young women, who tended to be educated and at least lower-middle class if not more affluent. In their most nostalgic, confident recollections of their interactions with women and men of the popular classes in the euphoric days of 1959 and 1960, they perhaps conflate easy rapport with shared democratic decision making. Other women have less triumphalist memories, recalling moments of skepticism, rejection, or conflict as they visited poor neighborhoods.[90] Furthermore, it is unclear how women of the popular classes might remember those interactions.[91] Yet the young women leaders of the Twenty-Sixth of July Movement affiliates at least evinced a desire to pioneer more egalitarian horizontal relations. They expressed a more spontaneous style of leadership and more openness toward experimentation, perhaps a legacy of the exceptional experience of having participated in a successful insurrection. Furthermore, they were imbued with a deep sense of passion and an acute awareness of the historical grandeur of the revolutionary moment.

Women politically formed by the prerevolutionary Communist Party likely had a more hierarchical notion of organization. Generation may also have been a factor in this respect. Women of the PSP tended to be much older than women of the Twenty-Sixth of July, who were in their early twenties or even late teens and, as García conceded, simply "did not have an international-political vision."[92] They had earned their stripes in the exceptional environment of the urban underground or the rural guerrilla struggle, and often had difficulty translating their clandestine organizing skills into the quite different political environment of 1959 and 1960. Carlos Franqui noted that this was a general trend among the young insurrectionaries: "As fighters they were terrific—they had resisted torture, prison, any number of fights—but they had no idea what power was, what politics was."[93]

Conversely, the older women of the PSP often brought decades of organizing experience to the table, including deeper working-class contacts. Those decades spent in labor organizing and subject to party discipline were visible in their leadership skills, organization, and strategy.[94] They insisted on the procedural aspects of constructing an organization, such as calling congresses, electing delegates and leaders, publishing a magazine, collecting dues, and renting offices.[95] Thus differences between women of the PSP and those of the Twenty-Sixth of July had strong overtones of a generational conflict: the discipline and structure of the Old Left against the innovation of the New Left.[96] The youth critique of PSP conformity and passivity is reflected in interviews in references to PSP members as "sheep," moving blindly in a flock, following their leader.[97]

Still, the sharpest point of contention between women of the Marxist Left and women of the insurrectionary movement seems to have been in the struggle over who would take leadership positions of the new revolutionary organizations. Specifically, many members of the Twenty-Sixth of July Movement vehemently opposed Communist Party members taking on leadership positions within the new revolutionary institutions that were then in formation. There was a perception among the Twenty-Sixth of July *combatientes* that the PSP had not actively attempted to dislodge Batista and, worse, may have actually been complicit with him, as it had in the late 1930s. The anti-Batista narrative generated during the insurrection, which stressed the bravery, sacrifice, and violent martyrdom of the revolutionaries, disdained the long, gradual struggle for social justice through institution building, political compromises, and strategic alliances that the Communist Party leaders embraced. Many Twenty-Sixth of July members viewed such strategic alliances as *politiquería*, shrewd politicking. And they could not forgive the Communist Party's transgressions in initially dismissing the visionary military action led by Fidel Castro as "putschism." For their part, many PSP members must have disdained the youth and inexperience of the Twenty-Sixth of July members, and perhaps felt suspicious of the personalistic charisma, spontaneity, and improvisation shown by the Twenty-Sixth of July's leadership.

In effect, women of the PSP and the Twenty-Sixth of July Movement employed competing narratives of "revolution" or "struggle" (*lucha*). Many PSP militants saw themselves as veterans of a long march toward socialism that included global struggles against fascism, imperialism, and the anticommunist witch hunts of the Cold War. Most Twenty-Sixth of July members, in contrast, were youths in their early twenties or late teens, many of whom barely perceived a political horizon beyond the toppling of Batista until January 1959. To the extent that they traced their political lineage back historically, they saw their precursors in the nationalist Wars of Independence. Reflecting these different vantage points, women of the Marxist Left and the insurrectionary Left attempted to discredit each other using different languages. The PSP used the language of class, accusing the young women of the Twenty-Sixth of July of being "bourgeois," a potential danger to the revolution.[98] Their critique was less about literal social origin than about political identity. That is, the Twenty-Sixth of July had not, by and large, embraced a "worker's" identity.

For their part, the women of the Twenty-Sixth of July Movement accused the PSP of carpetbagging, trying to appropriate leadership of a revolution they had not made. The Twenty-Sixth of July militants' focus on the anti-Batista insurrection as the only claim to political legitimacy made the PSP's claim to political centrality simply unintelligible. For example, García recalled a confrontation with an older man of the PSP who tried to rationalize Communist leadership of a new revolutionary organization by referencing the party's important global role in the fight against the Nazis during World War II. García responded with incredulity, unable to see the relevance of these past international histories and replying angrily that the real revolutionaries were those who had joined the struggle against Batista. Similar miscommunication was evident when a journalist interviewed María Núñez—a member of the prerevolutionary PSP in Santiago, a leader of the FDMC and subsequently of the UFR—after she had been named head of a women's militia training school in late 1960.[99] When the journalist asked Núñez about her "previous activities," Núñez replied simply, "I did everything, wherever I was needed. I've been working for the Revolution for 30 years."[100] Thus the conflict represented the clash of two different narratives about revolutionary action, leadership, and legitimacy.

Convergences

The tensions of the Cold War almost inevitably resulted in conflict between women of the UFR, many of whom were affiliated with the Marxist Left, and women who had been politicized through their participation in the insurrection, many of whom viewed communism—at least in its contemporary Soviet iteration—as a threat. Yet there is a problematic tendency among historians to reproduce the binary schema of the Cold War in their scholarship. This, in turn, has often blinded historians to instances of convergences and cooperation between, say, Catholic and Communist women in western Europe in the postwar period.[101] Similarly, despite tensions between the women affiliated with the Twenty-Sixth of July Movement and those affiliated with the PSP, it must also be recognized that women activists shared many goals in this period. This is visible in parallels between the programs embraced by the Women's Brigades and the UFR, such as the mobilization of poor women, the "rehabilitation" of prostitutes, or support for agrarian reform. Although interviews with former participants may focus on the competition for control of the women's movement, we might ask instead how women's mobilization affected the broader political panorama in which it took place. If we bring the various women's organizations of 1959 and 1960 into the same analytical frame, we can argue unequivocally that organized women of different political stripes together defined an agenda of women's rights at a time when the revolutionary leadership had relatively little to say about the matter. Women activists—collectively—articulated a program that included broad political demands in keeping with the revolutionary moment as well as specific demands relevant to women, especially working-class women.

One principal demand that was shared by the UFR, the Women's Brigades, and the Women's Section of the Twenty-Sixth of July was the formation of a female militia. There was apparently strong backing for the idea at the UFR's national conference. Conference delegates passed a resolution "demanding the creation of popular militias made up of women to undertake military training and to defend the revolution with arms, if necessary."[102] The delegates enthusiastically signed a petition for a women's militia and turned it over to Che Guevara, who attended the conference.[103] Additional demands and motions were sent to respective ministries and departments by commissions of UFR women.

Again, understanding the broader context will help us appreciate the importance of this demand. It is true that Fidel Castro had consented to the formation of an all-women's battalion in the Sierra, the Mariana Grajales Brigade. While Fidel recognized the ability of women to continue bearing arms, at least in the abstract, he also explicitly conceptualized women as a reserve force of militia. As he stated in a 1960 speech, women "should be those that substitute [for] the combatants, when they fall, if we have to fight," and that they would allow the revolution to double the number of combatants if necessary.[104] In this view, women combatants were, by default, a temporary or emergency force.

Furthermore, Castro's repeated anecdotes about the difficulty of convincing his male comrades in the Sierra to accept the Mariana Grajales Brigade reveal the general atmosphere of derision toward women combatants that prevailed within the ranks of the Twenty-Sixth of July Movement.[105] While it is true that in the early days of the revolutionary triumph there was a certain celebratory tone regarding female *combatientes*, for example in the mass media, such celebration was also partly based on the assumption that women's military participation had been temporary, and reveals a view of women *combatientes* as something of an endearing curiosity. At other times they were ridiculed and even sexually fetishized, as a comic strip printed in *Revolución*—the daily newspaper of the Twenty-Sixth of July—clearly demonstrates. The comic shows a male military instructor recoiling in surprise as a sexy, buxom woman shoulders a gun in a trench, while two women clad in tight military garb, brandishing guns, look on in the background.[106] The comic is striking for its categorical denial of women's political engagement, suggesting that women joined the revolutionary movement for male sexual attention. Later, when the popular militias formed, other comic strips and jokes similarly revealed a sense of societal unease with the new figure of the female militia and anxiety over the sexual transgressions that militia service was imagined to precipitate.[107]

The proposal for the formation of a women's militia was more than simply a demand for military training. It was also an indirect assertion about women's rights. While it was couched in deferential language that recognized the tenuous position of the Cuban Revolution and women's desire to defend their country, and occasionally referenced "mothers'" desire to protect their children, it also had deep implications. It was a striking demand in the sense that it had no corollary in prerevolutionary traditions of charity and social work designed to uplift subaltern women; nor did it conform to the traditional roles of women as revolutionary auxiliaries who either provided first aid or offered symbolic support as the mothers of martyred patriots. The establishment of a women's militia provided, instead, a very public and visible statement about women's militant defense of the revolution. In the mood of Cuba in 1959, when one's revolutionary credentials were virtually predicated on the willingness to take up arms, this was nothing less than an argument for women's citizenship in the new revolutionary polity.

The demand for a female militia was not merely rhetorical. By January 1960, the new women's militias of the UFR and the Women's Section of the Twenty-Sixth of July Movement marched publicly during an enormous parade held in Santa Clara, presided over by two commanders and attended by Che, on the anniversary of the revolution's triumph.[108] The UFR's special publication for International Women's Day in March 1960 featured three young women proudly marching in military formation on its cover, two porting rifles, and the third carrying a flag.[109] Clearly the formation of a women's militia was, by that time, a central part of the UFR's identity and perhaps part of its appeal in recruiting new members. Although by early 1960 women's

Unidad Femenina, *March 1960, cover. The UFR's publication features young women marching with rifles and flags. (Movimiento Femenino Collection, Instituto de Historia de Cuba)*

militias apparently existed only in Havana and Las Villas, the UFR vowed to organize them across the whole island.[110]

The spectacle of uniformed women marching to support the revolution apparently prompted some disapproval or even verbal attacks. As one former UFR member recalled, when the group marched in the street some people would yell, "There go the prostitutes."[111] And as women joined the new militias, revolutionary detractors apparently also linked participation in the militia with improper sexual mores. One woman recalled, "We had to show [in response] that all that was a lie, that the most moral women, the most virtuous, were those that were [fighting] for the ideals [of the revolution]."[112] This backlash may have reflected escalating political tensions as the revolutionary program radicalized, here expressed as a critique of sexual deviance. Yet even among revolutionary supporters, women militia members were sometimes described as either antifeminine or, at the other extreme, as the comic strip mentioned earlier suggests, sexually fetishized.[113] Thus both political friends and foes might caricature women's military mobilization as inappropriate sexual adventurism.

As Mary Nash has shown in her research on the Spanish Civil War, public opinion of women militia members may change sharply over time. The Spanish *miliciana* was briefly celebrated as an optimistic figure exemplifying Spanish resistance to fascism. But as the war continued, *milicianas* were increasingly discredited and accused of prostitution, suggesting that they were motivated by material rather than political concerns and that their presence corrupted and debilitated male soldiers.[114] Similarly, the Cuban press briefly hailed the novelty of the women *guerrilleras* who had fought in the Sierra, but as the reality of long-term popular mobilization for national defense set in, women *milicianas* could also become objects of derision. Given this context of disdain, women's participation in defense represented a double challenge, in the sense that it both subverted traditional gender roles and implied a strong political commitment to the revolution in a polarizing period.

Mobilization from Below, "Unity" from Above

By early 1960, both the Women's Brigades and the UFR proved themselves able to mobilize thousands of women, including many poor urban and rural women. Undoubtedly the majority of those women had not participated in the insurrection and were thus being drawn into the revolution for the first time. The picture emerging here questions standard histories of women's mobilization in the revolution, which assume a top-down institutional mobilization through the formation of the FMC. It has long been assumed that the idea of forming a women's mass organization came from Fidel Castro, who created the FMC by decree in August 1960 and drafted his presumably somewhat reluctant sister-in-law Vilma Espín as its head. In fact, she has often been quoted as expressing surprise when Fidel approached her about a women's organization in mid-1960. As Lois Smith and Alfred Padula wrote in their classic account of women in revolutionary Cuba, "when Castro created the FMC, Espín remembered thinking, 'Why do we have to have a women's organization? I had never been discriminated against.' "[115] But in fact, Espín must have first come across the idea of a women's organization in the summer of 1959, while being courted by women of the UFR, who invited Espín to their events and even named her honorary vice president.[116] This generative role of women of the Marxist Left goes against the grain of a less dominant narrative, also articulated by Espín in the 1980s, that posits the FMC as the organic and inevitable outgrowth of women's mobilization in the Twenty-Sixth of July Movement during the insurrection.[117] While recognizing the important impetus of women themselves, the latter account nevertheless overlooks the crucial role of the Marxist Left in this period in advancing an agenda "for the specific demands of women."[118]

In fact, the story of women's mobilization in the revolutionary moment raises new questions about why the FMC was formed. Clearly it was not merely intended to mobilize women, who had mobilized themselves in significant numbers already. Instead, the revolutionary leadership presumably intended to harness and channel the growing constituencies that groups such as the UFR and Women's Brigades were developing. The leadership also likely hoped to unify the diverse women's movement that had emerged, and to thereby prevent conflict and rivalry.[119] In fact, the explicit government statements about the FMC *unifying* women's groups in 1960 remind us that the FMC was, at least initially, truly conceived of as a federation. However, the FMC would not only bring together women of different organizations. It would also dissolve all prior organizations and subsume their various visions to a single, government-mandated platform— perhaps a more limited platform than some women had imagined. Thus we should not view the creation of the FMC as the culmination of the widespread women's mobilization of 1959 and 1960. In some ways, it was the taming of that mobilization.

In addition, by forming the FMC the government implicitly formalized— we might even say co-opted—the organic network that was then emerging among different women's groups, who began reaching out to one another horizontally during the first year of the revolution in power. In fact, the substance of the women's early demands explored here throws into relief the timidity and paternalism evident in the FMC's subsequent programs. Some of the most ambitious programs for women's organization and mobilization were first articulated by women themselves in 1959. And the important vision—however inconsistently expressed—of a working-class woman's simultaneous right to motherhood, to childcare, to work, and to political engagement first emerged from the grassroots initiatives of women themselves, not from the leadership. But, as in other social revolutions, the more far-reaching and radical visions of the revolutionary moment were constrained as the revolution consolidated.[120]

Ultimately, most of the women who took up prominent positions in the FMC were longtime activists of the Marxist Left who had risen to leadership positions first in the FDMC, in the 1950s, then in the UFR in 1959 and 1960. Indeed, it is worth highlighting the fact that, with the exception of Vilma Espín and a few others famous for their involvement with the rebel army, the most important women leaders of the insurrection against Batista did not feature prominently in the FMC.[121] The process by which female leaders of the insurrection were sidelined in favor of women of the Marxist Left has always been opaque, but the history of the UFR helps fill in the gaps in this transitional period: the group provided an important institutional platform for women of the PSP who had not participated in the insurrection.

The rather timid policies of female uplift that the FMC ultimately embraced likely reflect the limits of those men at the nation's helm who determined the FMC's agenda. Yet, in their midlevel positions, women activists of the prerevolutionary Marxist Left directed and must have helped conceptualize the vast programs that trained, oriented, and served hundreds of thousands of Cuban women in subsequent years.[122] And while women of the Marxist Left certainly jockeyed for power in the first months of the revolution, they were not simple usurpers who profited from Cuba's new friendship with the USSR. This chapter has argued that women of the Marxist Left actually had something to offer, namely, a more coherent and radical demand for women's rights that they had developed in dialogue with the socialist world throughout the 1950s.

While the activist women discussed in this chapter all eventually joined the FMC, it is clear that not all women initially welcomed the formation of a single, unitary women's organization. Nor did they likely applaud the dissolution of their prior organizations. When Marina Azcuy, head of the FMC in Pinar del Rio, arrived for a constitutive meeting of a local chapter, she was angered to find women seated separately in groups that corresponded to their prior affiliations: the Women's Section of the Twenty-Sixth of July Movement, the José Martí Women's Civic Front, the Revolutionary Directorate, and the PSP. "No, here we're [all] *Cuban* women," she scolded them.[123] "I'm here to constitute the organization created by Fidel; think about it and when you reach an agreement we'll come form the Federation of Cuban Women, the revolutionary [women]." Azcuy did not live to see it happen.[124] "Unity" could be decreed, but harmony would be a process.

5 | FROM THE CONSUMER'S REVOLUTION
TO THE ECONOMIC WAR, 1959–1962

On April 13, 1961, flames engulfed the Havana department store El Encanto. The fire quickly burned the structure to the ground, killing the store's manager, Fe del Valle, a woman subsequently enshrined in the revolution's growing pantheon of martyrs.[1] The fire was the result of arson, one of a growing number of sabotage attacks carried out in the period. While at first glance the department store might seem an odd target, its destruction in fact resonated deeply with *habaneros*. Five stories tall, covering a whole city block, and with nearly a thousand employees, the store was Havana's largest and finest, a monument to midcentury visions of modernity and cosmopolitanism.[2] During their first two years in power, the Cuban revolutionary leaders embraced a more democratic version of those visions, promising widespread prosperity and abundance. But El Encanto's incineration coincided with and symbolized the decline of the revolution's early promises, and marked the rise of a new revolutionary creed of austerity and sacrifice.

This chapter explains how and why those early visions of the revolution's promise changed. It does so by focusing on the issue of consumption, including luxury items as well as basic necessities such as food. I argue that an early, consensus vision of modernity, progress, and a higher standard of living characterized the years 1959 and 1960. But as the revolution radicalized, pushed forward by growing shortages, it moved from its early promise of generalized prosperity toward one of equality in prolonged material hardship. By 1961 the leadership proffered a new vision of social justice, economic sovereignty, and national liberation combined with internal political discipline. Such visions deeply appealed to some Cubans yet profoundly dismayed others. As shortages mounted, the emerging anti-Castro opposition upheld different ideals of modernity, which to some extent overlapped with Cold War definitions of market-based freedom and procedural democracy emanating from the United States. In other words, the meaning of the revolution and the social model it promised was partly debated and contested through the country's relation to consumption.

The early revolutionary vision of prosperity and modernization implied a special role for consumers, especially urban consumers, who were seen as engines of economic growth and industrialization. In particular, the leadership viewed women as the city's paradigmatic consumers. Focusing on consumption thus illuminates the complex ways in which the revolutionary leadership appealed to women as revolutionary participants in this period. Unlike most scholarship on women and the revolution, which focuses on the revolutionary leadership's drive to incorporate women as laborers throughout the 1960s and 1970s, this chapter argues that in the early period of 1959 to 1962, Cuban leaders more often appealed to urban women as consumers.

But as shortages of food and other necessary goods spread, and the leadership began to praise shared and equal austerity, women's roles as consumers correspondingly became more conflictive. By 1961 revolutionary leaders enjoined women to consume less rather than more. Women themselves frequently pressed the leadership with consumer-oriented requests, but they positioned themselves as demanding and boisterous consumers who demanded redress. As a result, in this period the figure of the urban female consumer became more threatening, a counterpoint to the "new" revolutionary woman who embodied self-sacrifice and revolutionary loyalty.

A focus on consumption also helps illuminate the way changes introduced by the revolution differentially affected women and men, as well as country and city, since the issue of consumption had particularly powerful ramifications for urban women's daily lives. When some necessary goods sporadically became scarce in the urban centers in mid-1959, it was women who altered their recipes and spent more of their time going from store to store. When more serious shortages began in 1961, especially in Havana, it was primarily women who were forced to spend ever-larger portions of their day standing in long food lines.[3] And when shortages reached their apex in 1961 and 1962, fanning anger among urban consumers, it was often women who led organized demonstrations and spontaneous scuffles in food lines. As has historically been the case in other situations of conflict or war where consumption patterns were disrupted, urban women became increasingly important actors in this context, and their demands and protests commanded attention from the revolutionary authorities.[4] Examining struggles over consumption and employing gender as an analytical frame thus shed new light on the actions of the revolutionary leadership and the everyday experiences of women and men.

Modernity, Revolution, and Development

The revolution came to power amid a euphoric sense of expectation and the optimistic hope that Cuba's long night of underdevelopment and misrule was finally over. In January 1959, there was near-total consensus among Cubans about the warped development path the country had taken and about the need for agrarian reform, economic diversification, and industrialization.[5] If there were powerful pockets of opposition to the idea of agrarian reform among large plantation and ranch owners, especially in the easternmost provinces, there was also an aspiring urban bourgeoisie based in Havana, with interests in commerce and urban real estate. The urban bourgeoisie to some extent viewed the large agrarian export interests as a backward and irrational form of economic development. For some urban sectors there was also a certain nationalist attraction to the idea of Cuba as a rising industrial powerhouse, the "Japan of the Caribbean," so to speak.[6] There was, therefore, a multiclass urban constituency that backed the early revolution's goal of agrarian reform. This constituency encompassed a political spectrum that ranged from a Catholic-infused vision of social justice to a desire for personal enrichment and even regional domination.

Ideas about modernity, progress, and democracy in prerevolutionary Cuba were bound up in complex ways with ideas about mass consumption and "Americanization." Louis Pérez has documented the overwhelming influence of American consumer culture in twentieth-century Cuba, arguing that imported goods and forms of entertainment dominated the urban centers and even reached far into rural areas. The American neocolonial domination of the island nation was, as Pérez points out, truly hegemonic, establishing the terms within which Cubans viewed their country's development and their national identity. These patterns were facilitated by Cuba's unusual historical development, which had created a population that was predominantly urban despite the country's economic dependence on export agriculture; a relatively large urban middle class; and a service sector that was growing at a much faster rate than manufacture. The island's physical proximity to the United States, its unequal absorption within American trade relations, and its saturation with American commercial culture all generated a sense of entitlement and expectation—especially among the urban middle sectors—that was perhaps unequaled in the region.[7]

In 1959 many Cubans believed the revolution would now mean the culmination of "Americanized" consumption, not its rejection. They imagined a comfortable and dignified standard of living made more widespread and equitable by the elimination of backward economic structures and the nationalization of foreign monopolies. For this reason the political scientist Sam Farber has dubbed the first two years "the consumers' revolution."[8] This vision did not imply obsequiousness to U.S. markets; many Cubans hoped national industry would surge and that the island would enjoy more equitable trade relations with its northern neighbor. As one 1960 advertisement put it succinctly, "a nation with its own industries is a free nation."[9] In that spirit the earliest months of the revolution witnessed jubilant Buy National campaigns. Appeals to the public to purchase nationally made goods were made through government ads and even through musicals with names like *Consuming Cuban Products* and *Operation Cuban Industry*.[10] Perusing used-book stalls in Havana some fifty years later, one could still find paperbacks from 1959 with the phrase "Made in Cuba, by Cuban Workers" imprinted on the back flap.

The first few months of the revolution were thus characterized by a generalized euphoria as the rebels took power and promised to restructure Cuba's stagnant economy in order to encourage industrialization and end cyclical unemployment and poverty. While these intentions harbored radical potential, the depth and detail of the planned measures were not yet clear. The revolutionary leadership's modernizing, developmentalist intent was sometimes expressed in contemporary Cold War discourse that stressed the need to raise the standard of living of the poor in order to prevent the rise of communism. For example, this was how Fidel Castro presented the revolution's goals when visiting the United States in April 1959. He proclaimed: "There is only one way to make wealth and that is to establish industry. And there is only one way to establish industry; that is by obtaining factories and machinery; and the only way to buy them is by having dollars. We must have a market for our goods."[11] Real democracy, Castro asserted, was "not possible for hungry people." Both bread and liberty were necessary.[12]

Government plans for transforming the economy included an idealized vision of harmonious new relations among producers, consumers, and the state. It was a win-win situation: the agrarian reform would not only result in more equitable land tenure, Cuban leaders assumed; it would also produce higher yields. The elimination of structural inefficiencies and "parasitical" middlemen would mean higher prices for agricultural producers and lower prices for urban consumers. The island's resultant ability to produce rather than import its foodstuffs, the thinking went, would thus allow it to put its foreign reserves toward investment in industry.

Two newspaper illustrations from 1959 capture these ideas, as well as the different political tones they could encapsulate. In the first, printed in the Communist Party daily *Noticias de Hoy*, a peasant is shown brandishing a knife and fork, about to dig into a roast pig labeled "latifundios" (large agricultural estates). The caption reads, "The roast pig of the Year of Liberty," as 1959 had been officially dubbed. The implication is that *campesinos* would benefit handsomely from the agrarian reform. They would now consume more; in fact, they would figuratively eat the vast plantations that had previously squeezed them off lands, in a vision that implied significant class conflict in the countryside. Another illustration, also printed in *Hoy*, is an ad for popular festivities to be held in one of Havana's covered food markets. A drawing shows a folkloric musician figure playing a guitar next to fruits and vegetables. The ad captures the imagined combination of revelry, prosperity, increased food consumption, and urban-rural harmony that animated the first two years of the revolution.[13] It reflected the idea that multiple groups would benefit from the agrarian reform: the rural peasantry through redistribution of lands and direct access to urban markets; the urban consumer through cheaper prices for agricultural goods. It was an idyllic vision of a national market, free of foreign imports, in which producers and consumers would become partners in national development.

The "New Woman" as Revolutionary Consumer

Women figured powerfully in this schema. Higher consumption among the urban populace hinged on the urban woman as consumer. Simply by purchasing, she would fuel the country's industrialization and prosperity. As Fidel Castro said in a speech to tobacco industry representatives in 1959, "Cuban women are helping us extraordinarily in the decision to consume Cuban products."[14] And a lighthearted poem entitled "Nation and Production," printed in the newspaper *El Mundo*, trumpeted:

Peasants, workers, and students
along with housewives have sworn
. . . to acquire Cuban goods.[15]

In the first two years of the revolution, promotional ads appealed to women to help the nation industrialize by consuming. For example, a 1960 ad placed by the nationalized Cuban electric company features a serious-looking young white woman with her arms full of packages.[16] The text explains the roles of the agriculturalist, the worker, and the consumer, extolling the importance of the last figure, who was obviously imagined as female. The agriculturalist "makes the earth produce," the text enthused; technicians and workers helped industrialize the country. "But the most essential thing to complete the economic cycle and the progress of the country is you, the consumer! . . . If you consume the products of our soil, you are helping, as much as anyone, the development of our agriculture. If you buy articles made in Cuba, you are helping, as much as anyone, in the industrialization of the country. The more national products you consume, the more work and wealth there will be in our countryside, the more industry will give jobs to more Cubans."[17]

Another ad from the following year encouraged women to shop in the newly nationalized department store Fin de Siglo. In one corner of the ad we see a cartoonish drawing of a slim, stylish white woman presiding over a tower of packages decked out in wrapping paper and ribbons, carried by a man presumably meant to be her husband. The opposite corner of the ad features a drawing of two men in overalls tending to an enormous machine. The two images are connected by a circle of flying banknotes and coins. The caption reads: "The people's money returns to the people [when] purchasing in nationalized stores."[18] The ad promised that by shopping in discriminating but enjoyable ways—indeed, by buying more than before—women would contribute to the country's industrialization. Ads like these reflected the widespread early optimism that the transition from monoculture to diversified industrialization might be attained simply by consuming, and that women's roles were central in this process.

The emphasis here on leisurely shopping and discretionary spending seems aimed at middle-class women in particular. The Fin de Siglo shopper's short blond hair, hourglass figure, and heels mark her as an idealized 1950s housewife: white, middle-class, stylish. Yet other Buy National campaigns stressed the importance of consuming Cuban-made staples that working-class women also purchased, such as rice. Campaigns thus appealed to women of diverse class and race backgrounds as consumers, although middle-class women, white women, and housewives—overlapping but not synonymous categories—best fit an idealized conception of the urban shopper.

Much scholarship on women and the Cuban Revolution has taken it for granted that the leadership primarily wanted to incorporate women into the revolution as workers, urging women into so-called productive labor, both waged and volunteer.[19] Leaders believed their incorporation into the workforce would simultaneously liberate women from the depoliticized

USTED TAMBIEN

puede ayudar

A DAR EMPLEO A MAS CUBANOS

El agricultor, con su denodado esfuerzo, hace producir nuestra tierra... el industrial, el técnico y los obreros industrializan el país... el comercio pone al disfrute del pueblo toda esa producción... Pero, lo más esencial para completar el ciclo económico y el progreso de la nación, es usted: **El Consumidor!**

Si usted consume productos de nuestra tierra, está contribuyendo, como el que más, al desarrollo de nuestra agricultura. Si usted compra preferentemente artículos fabricados en Cuba, está ayudando, como el que más, a la industrialización de nuestro país. Mientras más productos nacionales se consuman, más trabajo y más riqueza habrá en nuestros campos, más industrias darán empleo a más cubanos, y más movimiento tendrá nuestro comercio.

EN SUS MANOS ESTA AYUDAR A DAR EMPLEO
A MAYOR NUMERO DE CUBANOS:

¡CONSUMA
PRODUCTOS
CUBANOS!

ESTE ES UN MENSAJE DE *Cía. Cubana de Electricidad*

"You too can help give work to more Cubans." An ad placed by the nationalized electric company shows a young woman shopping for the good of the nation. (Printed in Bohemia, *January 1960; courtesy of Instituto de Historia de Cuba)*

domestic sphere and help the country achieve economic sovereignty. Women's liberation, in this view, would thus be an automatic side effect of the country's economic productivity. Leaders were likewise dismissive of housework, which they viewed mainly as a drain on women's labor time, and which they assumed would somehow eventually be collectivized.[20]

But a closer look at the first two years of the revolution shows that some of the leadership's earliest appeals to women were made in the language of consumption. Specifically, in this early period, revolutionary consciousness for women was linked with correct consumption practices rather than being strictly or even primarily related to their incorporation into waged labor. A focus on consumption shows the changing ways the leadership viewed women's potential contributions to the revolution over time: as we shall see, once serious shortages began, and as women made increasingly aggressive demands over provisions, the figure of the female consumer could become more threatening. While the leadership tended to imagine the "new woman" in this early period as a conscientious consumer more than as a dedicated laborer, at least in the cities, the emphasis on men's incorporation in the revolution stressed full employment and increased rates of production. The revolutionary leaders thus reproduced the gendered division of male production and female consumption. That is, they appealed to women and men to help Cuba attain true sovereignty, by struggling— respectively—in the battles of consumption and production.

It is true that the leadership occasionally emphasized wanting to incorporate women into "productive" labor in order to simultaneously liberate women from the depoliticized domestic sphere and help the country achieve economic sovereignty, even in this early period. Yet in practice such rhetorical appeals seem to have been made primarily during formal speeches and not in the form of mobilizational propaganda addressed directly to women, at least in the early 1960s. In reality, few channels for creating work opportunities were established in urban settings in this period and, at any rate, there was no "overwhelming demand" among women for work.[21] And while there were several major job training programs for women of the popular class in this early period, these exceptions in themselves are highly revealing of the revolutionary leaders' limited vision. For example, the government sponsored massive programs to train women to work in the new daycare centers and to retrain domestic servants for jobs in the service sector. The government also established schools for young rural women, who were brought to Havana with much fanfare to be trained as seamstresses. Yet sewing was, in any case, a traditional recourse for popular-class women unable to find formal employment. Sewing was often done as piecework within the home, and was a form of employment both unprotected and poorly remunerated.

These government training initiatives thus tended to shift women from informal, precarious segments of the service sector to more formal, better-protected segments of the same sector. This was of course clearly preferable, although it did not undermine the identification of these fields as "women's work."[22] Furthermore, there was a tendency in these programs to concentrate on the most exploited and least protected women, who had engaged in forms of labor the leadership considered denigrating, namely, prostitutes and domestic servants.[23] Thus the retraining initiatives carried overtones of moral redemption, and were, in some cases, more about political formation and the raising of working-class women's consciousness than about effective job training.[24] It is important to look beyond these specific initiatives, which targeted a relatively small portion of the working-age female population, in order to understand the other ways the leadership appealed to women in this period, including urban middle- and working-class women. As we have seen, the earliest revolutionary policies presumed women's roles as consumers. The issue of consumption would quickly become more conflictive.

The Problems of Urban Provisioning

The early, optimistic visions of the harmonious rise in employment, production, and consumption soon proved hard to implement in practice. As early as the summer of 1959, shortages of some staple food items began in urban centers. There were several factors behind this development. The progressive social legislation of the first few months quickly contributed to climbing consumption in both urban and rural areas. With government-decreed salary raises and rent reductions, the country's popular classes had money to spend as never before. Rural markets in particular were expanding in response to rising local wages, cheap government-supplied credit, stable prices for produce, and the early redistribution of lands to tenant farmers that took place through the Agrarian Reform Law of 1959.[25] Produce that had once reached the city was now being consumed locally, inverting the traditional consumption hierarchies of country and city. Yet overall production did not rise correspondingly, partly due to the reticence of plantation and factory owners. With an eye on the political forecast, some plantation owners preferred to wait rather than replant, while some ranch owners began to slaughter cattle, fearing the imminent loss of their lands. And some urban vendors—for example, clothing vendors—took advantage of the seller's market, preferring to liquidate their back stock rather than reorder or produce, waiting to see how the political situation would stabilize.[26]

In addition, existing agricultural production and distribution chains were disrupted by the new revolutionary measures. The Agrarian Reform Law of May 1959 was a watershed in this regard: it definitively altered Cuba's political landscape. Although an agrarian reform program had long been expected, and had in fact been one of the principal promises of the revolutionary movement, the proposals put forth by the Twenty-Sixth of July Movement had often lacked specifics. The new law was more radical than expected and introduced a surprisingly predominant role for the state. It limited land holdings to 1,000 acres, except for sugar or rice plantations, which could extend to three times that amount. Expropriations would be indemnified, but through twenty-year bonds with property values calculated based on declarations in prior tax returns. Furthermore, expropriated properties might not simply be subdivided and redistributed; instead, some large estates would now be administered by the state.[27] It now became clear that the largest plantations would inevitably be affected and that the countryside might be dominated by the state, not a class of new small farmers. In response, the first organized political opposition formed, beginning with cattle ranchers in the eastern province of Camagüey.[28] The agrarian reform also had unexpected results among smaller and medium-sized producers, as some lost their existing outlets to urban vendors, began to fear instability and possibly further nationalizations, or simply chose to sell their produce closer to home, where rural markets were expanding.

In addition to these internal problems, conflict with the U.S. government was on the rise. The agrarian reform inevitably began to affect plantations owned by U.S. corporations, and as such it pushed the U.S. government's policy from tense coexistence toward covertly planning the revolutionary government's overthrow.[29] Cuba depended entirely on the United States as a market for its sugar. In turn, the island imported products ranging from cars, refrigerators, and tractors to staple foods such as rice and lard.[30] Any reduction of the American importation of sugar would be potentially catastrophic. In the wake of the agrarian reform, confrontations with the U.S. government became increasingly severe. President Eisenhower eventually refused to purchase some 700,000 tons of sugar that had formed part of previous annual agreements with Cuba, and then unilaterally terminated diplomatic relations. Without markets for its sugar and with foreign reserves dwindling, the island was left unable to import the primary food products it relied on, most urgently lard. Throughout the tumultuous year of 1960, all these problems combined, and the pinch was soon felt in Cuban kitchens, stores, factories, and fields.

Shortages Begin

By the spring of 1959, tension was already growing between urban shop owners and consumers as prices began to rise. By the summer of 1959, Havana was experiencing sporadic shortages of some staple items, such as potatoes. And over the course of the next year—from the summer of 1959 through the summer of 1960—the first serious and sustained problems in urban provisioning began. As tensions over food prices and availability escalated, women began to present consumer-oriented demands to the revolutionary leadership.[31]

For urban women of the popular classes, the price of staple foods had long been a fixture of their everyday demands. Many hoped that the revolution would rein in prices, and in the early months of 1959 they began to draw the country's new leadership's attention to the issue. At the Revolutionary Women's Unity (Unidad Femenina Revolucionaria) conferences held at the provincial and national level, as discussed in chapter 4, women delegates denounced high food prices and the inconvenient hours of neighborhood shops.[32] Many smaller, local organizations also appeared to voice similar demands. For example, newspaper photos from 1959 capture the dozens of small neighborhood-based committees, mostly comprising women, which sprang up in peripheral neighborhoods to demand better access to services and goods. Some of these committees demanded investigations into the price of necessary food items at their nearby markets.[33]

But the rising food prices that began in the spring and summer of 1959 seemed to threaten the revolution's promise. Women writing in the Communist Party daily *Hoy* called on other women—"housewives" and "feminine organizations"—to be vigilant in their dealings with food vendors.[34] As one self-proclaimed housewife asked in a 1959 editorial, "Why are the scales of the butchers hung so high that we can't see if the weight is exact or not?" She proposed that the scales be hung "at the height of a short person," and that each neighborhood should designate one person to serve as a "secret inspector" to keep an eye on vendors tempted to cheat their customers. She also appealed to the country's new leaders for redress. "Meat is a principal food item and since it's so expensive, the poor can only buy [the worst cuts], and only a little and not every day," she wrote. "They should at least weigh it correctly, right Fidel?"[35] Her gentle prodding hinted that the revolution needed to work more firmly in the defense of women and the poor. Furthermore, her stance suggested qualified, not unconditional, support for the leadership's policies, a position at odds with the near–hero worship cultivated by the revolution's self-declared vanguard.[36] Thus in conferences, letters to newspapers, and small neighborhood rallies, women called on the revolutionary leadership to act.

The leadership did act, but gradually. Throughout 1960 and 1961, as food lines lengthened and tensions rose, the revolutionary government responded to the mounting challenges in provisioning the urban population with two approaches: first, a series of legislative attempts to stop price hikes and shortages by targeting shop owners, and second, public exhortations to restraint made through various media outlets to the Cuban populace. It is possible that these two approaches were primarily addressed to different sectors—that is, that the new legislation was aimed at placating urban women of the popular classes, while public exhortations to consumers mostly targeted middle-class women with discretionary budgets. Yet there was also significant overlap between the two.

As food prices rose, the government first placed price ceilings on certain food items—such as rice, milk, bread, and beef—and then introduced a limit on the profit margins permitted to wholesale and retail outlets.[37] In late January 1960 the government introduced the first sanctions to punish so-called crimes against the popular economy, such as hoarding or price gouging.[38] These measures were mostly targeted toward penalizing shop owners for not adhering to proper weight and price scales and busting "speculators" for hoarding scarce items.

These new government directives gave ammunition to conflicts unfolding in workshops, on plantations, and in factories. The new measures designated certain practices as "crimes," such as withholding necessary products from the market, and reified the actors engaged in such practices as "speculators" detrimental to the revolution. Workers swiftly appropriated this newly sanctioned language and sought to bring the force of the law to bear on their employers, presumably with an eye toward government intervention. For example, rice workers in Manzanillo denounced plantation owners for using poor sales as an excuse to paralyze production, and the workers of a Havana *almacén* denounced the shop's owners for "speculating" with potatoes and then decamping to Miami.[39]

In particular, the new measures seem to have unleashed a veritable war between women shoppers and urban vendors, to judge from the flurry of sanctions against shop owners for overpricing, underweighing, hoarding, and other infractions that took place over the next months. The prosecution of food vendors reached its zenith in the fall of 1960, when Havana inspectors made thousands of inquiries, issued hundreds of fines, and in some cases detained shop owners.[40] It is possible that some of these infractions were uncovered by state inspectors making their regular rounds. But the spike in sanctions must also reflect the use that Havana residents, most likely working-class women, made of state inspectors in this period.

Throughout 1960, the leadership also simultaneously exhorted the populace to exercise self-restraint, asking consumers not to overpurchase and warning vendors not to overcharge. Through op-eds, printed propaganda, popular songs, radio spots, and posters, the government appealed to shoppers to consume only what they needed.[41] Exercising self-restraint implied raising *conciencia*—revolutionary consciousness—about these issues, that is, calling for consumer self-restraint for the greater good of the collective. Women were viewed as crucial agents of *conciencia*, and government cajoling particularly targeted the urban women or "housewives" who did most of the shopping.

By the spring of 1961, new problems emerged as U.S.-Cuban relations reached a historic low. The defeat of the April 1961 U.S.-engineered Bay of Pigs invasion gave the Cuban Revolution a certain political stability. The reorganized army and new militias had successfully flexed their muscle, and the island could rest assured that it would not suffer another invasion in the near future. Moreover, the declaration of the revolution as "socialist" implied an alliance with the Soviet Union and the island's eventual incorporation into the planned economy of the socialist bloc. Yet it would be years before the Soviet Union could adequately provision the island, and in the process, it introduced a far more complicated system of trade and distribution, already emerging by 1961. As one journalist described it in 1964: "Orders previously made by U.S. brand name and catalogue number, and fulfilled in a matter of days by the Miami ferry, now had to be made months ahead, with unfamiliar specifications, and dispatched across the world. Long accustomed to the ferry service, Havana lacked warehouse space to store goods from thousands of miles away, and while United-States-made plants began to fall to bits through lack of equipment, the docks became jammed with undistributed cargo."[42]

In addition, after the failure of the Bay of Pigs, the U.S. government focused on forcing the Cuban Revolution toward implosion through an economic embargo. The policy took advantage of Cuba's historic dependence on U.S. markets to cripple the Cuban economy. It was hoped that creating widespread conditions of economic misery would create an uprising from within, prompting the populace to turn against the revolutionary leadership.[43] Military action had given way to economic warfare.

As shortages spiraled throughout 1961, many women were forced to spend ever-larger portions of their day standing in line for foodstuffs. Despite government attempts to stem the tide, shortage seemed to have a momentum all its own. The shortage of one product (say, potatoes) quickly led to the shortage of another (say, yucca), as people were forced to find substitutes. And as more businesses were accused of hoarding and speculating, the government was forced to resort to intervention more frequently, setting up government-run "people's stores" (*tiendas del pueblo*) in their places.[44]

Meanwhile, urban residents sought ways to make do. In the process, they often anticipated subsequent government policies. For example, long before the government announced generalized rationing in March 1962, various grassroots initiatives, almost surely spearheaded by local women, sprang up to ensure the fair and equal distribution of foods in stores. Some neighbors fashioned their own makeshift ration cards and compiled rotating lists of who had permission to buy on a particular day.[45] In the summer of 1961, following the formation of mass organizations such as the neighborhood-based Committees for the Defense of the Revolution (CDRs) and the Federation of Cuban Women (FMC), the leadership called on these newly formed groups to keep organized watch over bodegas to make sure people were purchasing in "normal" rather than "excessive" amounts.[46] But it is likely that government enlisting of the mass organizations merely gave official blessing to activities already in practice. And the utilization of the mass organizations as local vigilantes implied primarily mobilizing women, for CDR membership in this period was predominantly female.[47]

Scholars sometimes depict the dynamic of the early revolutionary period as one in which the populace was always running "behind" the leadership.[48] As Sam Farber has argued, "the radicalism of the leadership . . . filtered down to the masses of Cubans, who always remained 'behind' the various measures Castro periodically and unexpectedly produced after long night sessions of the revolutionary leadership."[49] The leaders, in this view, announced more and more radical measures, which the general public struggled to digest. But when it came to the question of provisions, grassroots actors—especially urban women—often outpaced leaders' directives. They confronted vendors, called on state inspectors, weathered interminable lines, improvised distribution schemes, and demanded increased state intervention.[50] The government slowly acceded to their demands.

Visions of Revolution: From Prosperity to Austerity

As shortages deepened, they challenged the leadership's early, optimistic visions of the prosperity the revolution would usher in. In late 1960 and early 1961, as shortages of staple items in Havana became severe and long lines snaked outside food stores, the issue of consumption was increasingly politicized. By early 1961, the first suggestions were made—at least behind closed doors—that a system of rationing might be necessary.[51] Pressed forward by events, the revolutionary leadership's ideal of widespread improved consumption and prosperity began to shift to one of shared austerity, sacrifice, and hardship, at least in the short term. The leadership's ideas about women's roles as consumers also correspondingly changed. At the same time, as the early revolutionary consensus began to fray, critics of the revolution began to articulate divergent views of urban modernity, particularly the relationship the country should have with consumer goods. These debates about consumption had profound implications for broader issues of social equality, political economy, and even national identity.

Until mid- or late 1960, the revolutionary government had clung to a vision of prosperity despite mounting problems of provision. For example, an August 1960 ad placed by the newly nationalized Cuban Petrol Institute, when the Cuban government was embroiled in a heated conflict with the U.S.-owned refineries on the island, unrealistically promised readers that, despite the conflict, "industry, transport, public services, comfort in domestic life . . . all the machinery of a modern country" would keep functioning. The ad showed a miniature city, complete with skyscrapers, docking ships, container-laden trucks, and airplanes prominently circling overhead, the very epitome of urban modernity. The image of Havana as a bustling modern city proffered in the advertisement was a vision widely shared by *habaneros* of nearly all political persuasions in 1960.

But by March 1961, faced with mounting food shortages, the leadership began to address the problem of provision more systematically, and tempered promises of future prosperity by promising that shortages would be borne equally. Speaking virtually on the same day, Fidel Castro and Che Guevara addressed the problems directly. At a youth congress, in response to a spontaneous shout from the audience about the long food lines, Fidel called on youth to be the "most ardent defenders of the revolution" in the lines as well as in their schools and neighborhoods, a comment that seemed to equate revolutionary support with endurance in food lines.[52] Che Guevara, speaking at the national sugar workers' meeting in Santa Clara, promised that, even if there was scarcity, the prices of necessary goods would be fixed, and the government would punish lawbreakers, speculators, and "all those who try to profit from the sacrifice of the people."[53] Roughly a week later Fidel again warned that there might be shortages, but promised that the government would "try to avoid speculation and disorder, and before those disorders occur, in which some people buy [supplies] for six months and others are left with nothing, we are disposed to ration those articles."[54] It was the first public mention of the possibility of rationing. Yet it was not until March 1962, a full year later, that generalized rationing was implemented.[55]

An inchoate critique of U.S. consumption patterns, mass culture, and political power had been slowly evolving in Cuba since the mid-1950s, as we saw in chapter 1. Since coming to power in January 1959, Fidel Castro had occasionally raised these ideas. He made several references in his speeches to the country's warped economic development, occasionally blaming the excessive consumption of U.S.-made luxury products for the inability of the country to import or produce many necessary goods. For example, he asked in a speech in July 1959, "Why were we [importing] Cadillacs when what we needed were tractors?"[56] His comments implied Cuban shortcomings, such as poor policy choices, as well as unchecked market forces. He described it as a kind of national moral failing, and did not consistently blame the United States for the vast political and economic power it wielded over the island.

But by 1961 we see a clearer linking of U.S. imperialism to certain local patterns of consumption. Leaders of the Communist Party, which was then in political ascendency, offered a sharper critique of mass consumption. They believed that Cubans' reliance on American-made consumer goods had corrupted them, identifying them with U.S. consumer capitalism and corroding their nationalist identity. Consumption of U.S.-made goods was thus the most devious form of imperialism, for it produced a colonized mind. As Communist Party leader Carlos Rafael Rodríguez complained, "one of the most ominous forms of imperialist penetration in Cuba has consisted in the submission of the Cuban to the patterns of Yankee consumption . . . that blind acceptance of all things American [lo norteño], planted in our subconscious by the press, radio, TV and film." Rather than a source of modernization and an improved standard of living, Rodríguez viewed the penetration of U.S. goods as an insidious form of social control and even a problem of national security. "There are men who are disposed to shoulder a rifle, but they find it impossible to shave without Gillette," he said, adding that these two things were part and parcel of the "same battle," that is, the battle against imperialism.[57] Thus the new, gritty reality of shortage and austerity revealed the gravity of Cuban consumption patterns. A weakness for imported consumer goods could subvert even the bravest man's performance in battle.

The consuming habits of women, in particular, received increased scrutiny. Left unchecked, women shoppers' actions could have devastating consequences. As Interior Minister Máximo Berman said in a televised appearance, "the housewife [has] contributed to shortages without realizing it." Most housewives typically used one box of detergent per week, he explained. But as the detergent shortage began, some housewives went to another bodega each day to purchase an additional box. They did so out of a natural desire to protect themselves from shortage, but in the process they collectively aggravated the country's crisis. Thus he requested that people "purchase only what they really need." But mere exhortations to morality in purchasing were not sufficient. Berman also called on the public to monitor the consuming practices of others: "[We ask] that they . . . denounce hoarders and speculators, who are a product of the counter-revolution."[58]

The interior minister's comments revealed an important shift. The leadership no longer conceptualized actions such as hoarding and speculating as mere "crimes against the popular economy." Rather, by the spring of 1961 they were seen as generalized efforts to subvert the entire revolution; in other words, they formed part of a counterrevolutionary movement. Berman made his comments on the eve of the U.S.-sponsored Bay of Pigs invasion, when the nation was on war footing. By this time, having "excess" food in one's house was virtually considered evidence of counterrevolutionary activity.[59] And as Fidel Castro proclaimed several months later, speculators were "the number one enemy of the revolution."[60] Furthermore, Berman hinted ominously that even well-intentioned individual women shoppers could collectively aggravate shortages during this time of crisis. It was the first public suggestion that "housewives" might unintentionally—or perhaps even deliberately—threaten the revolution.

The leadership's new, more austere vision of consumption had particular ramifications for women's behavior. Unlike earlier euphoric ideas that women might contribute to the revolution by shopping, leaders now stressed restraint. Women were still envisioned as consumers, but—as Vilma Espín pronounced in late 1961—the true revolutionary woman consumed only what was necessary.[61] The leadership hoped women would voluntarily embrace austerity and reject the seductions of American consumer culture and its associations with modernity. And while men were routinely featured in posters or ads holding tools and rifles to indicate their role in the "battles" of production and defense, women were now enjoined to find creative solutions to cooking dilemmas as a way of contesting imperialism.

This idealized vision of revolutionary womanhood was dramatized by the personal conversion experiences of young *habaneras* in the literacy campaign that took place during 1961, as food shortages reached their apex. As one young girl from a middle-class neighborhood in Havana wrote from her rural posting in the literacy campaign in the summer of 1961, she had at first been frightened to leave Havana, but now realized that things like new dresses and shoes were unimportant, and that her true calling was to help the peasants, herself, and her nation. "Now I can say that I truly feel the Revolution. . . . I can say with my head held high that I am a revolutionary and no one will ever be able to confuse me."[62] Another newspaper article described how teenage girls, "previously fans of rock, chewing gum, and American music," now returned from the literacy campaign transformed by a redemptive experience in the countryside. One of the girls pledged, "We won't go back to being princesses [*pepillas*], now we'll be soldiers for the nation and the revolution."[63] The young woman had experienced a revolutionary transformation from consumer-oriented urbanite to self-sacrificing "soldier."

These narratives obviously reflect emerging official discourse and may even have been scripted.[64] Nevertheless, they suggest that, by 1961, a clear understanding had evolved of frivolous consumption and "revolution" as mutually exclusive concepts. Yet, at the same time, the quotes capture the widespread suspicion that women, particularly young women of the urban middle sectors, were those most easily seduced by imported American products and frivolous consumption in general.[65] Thus these secular conversion narratives provided important public templates. They showed that even teenage girls could voluntarily move from the realm of frivolous leisure to militant dedication and self-abnegation by participating in revolutionary campaigns.

Yet these very same narratives raised the possibility that not all women would evolve into such devoted revolutionary beings. A poem written in the mid-1960s by the prorevolutionary Luis Suardíaz captures this concern. The poem describes a young secretary that the narrator remembers seeing

ASI TAMBIEN SE DERROTA AL IMPERIALISMO   *Por Adigio*

"You defeat imperialism like this too." A woman is *"armed" with a frying pan and sports a round of cutlery as ammunition. The book under her arm is titled* How to Cook without Oil. *(Illustration by Adigio Benítez, printed in* Noticias de Hoy, *July 12, 1961; courtesy of Instituto de Historia de Cuba)*

around town before the revolution, eating ice cream at the cafeteria counter in Woolworth's, riding in a convertible, or dancing in nightclubs. He wonders if she has left the country:

> Would she be likely to put up
> With voluntary work, queues, ration books
> A possible shortage of chocolate cake?
> It may simply be a prejudice of mine . . .
> But people like her
> Are incapable of the slightest sacrifice.[66]

The poem was consistent with a certain disdainful tone toward women's efforts that we find elsewhere in this period, indicative of the more aggressive language toward women that emerged with the turn toward austerity. A 1961 graphic printed in the newspaper *Hoy*, for example, showed a line of people in the foreground (composed of both men and women, although most of the city's shoppers were women) with an image of a falling guerrilla in the background. The caption read, "The sacrifice of those that fell was greater!"[67] The image was intended to shame complaining consumers into stoicism by contrasting the trivial frustration of standing in long lines with the heroism of giving one's life in battle. The graphic also bore a subtext about the different sacrifices required of men and women, suggesting to women that their sacrifices were less meaningful than the military sacrifices made by men. In a more lighthearted tone, a stanza printed in the newspaper compared a middle-aged shopper to her militia son, making this point even more clearly:

> If her son offers his life
> standing, with Czech weapon in hand
> how can his lovely mother
> let herself be defeated
> by the shortage of butter?[68]

One unnamed CIA source also reported that cars with loudspeakers circulated past long lines outside markets, warning shoppers not to "complain" about food lines because "it would be worse if you had to form . . . lines . . . to identify the corpses of your children."[69] Whether comparing urban women shoppers to the mothers of martyrs or to the martyrs themselves, the government often belittled the daily struggle of procuring food and other necessary items as trifling.

These examples suggest an abiding concern about whether women were capable of "sacrifice"—and, by extension, whether they could be true revolutionaries. While publicly exhorting women to embody the new revolution- ary codes of self-sacrifice and modest consumption, leaders also seemed to harbor a nagging doubt that perhaps women were not prepared to make the sacrifices necessary for the revolution.

Austerity and Its Discontents: Contested Visions of Modernity and Consumption

Official slogans trumpeted that Cubans might lack soap, but they were full of courage.[70] Yet not everyone saw virtue in austerity. As the revolutionary leadership's vision praising revolutionary sacrifice congealed, it confronted a spectrum of countervisions expressed either in private, in sporadic public outbursts, or in increasingly organized oppositional activity. The focus and catalyst of these critiques were often the shortages of foods and other nec- essary items, yet they were not primarily about the literal insufficiency of sus- tenance.[71] Various observers noted that the amount of available foodstuffs was usually sufficient, but that variety was greatly limited and that urban Cubans could not procure the foods they were used to. As one letter for- warded to the CIA noted, "large quantities of Soviet canned goods stay right there on the shelves because people do not want to buy them. I cannot say that we are hungry, but . . . a great need is arising."[72] Rather, the critique ex- pressed by some urban, especially middle-class, *habaneros* wove several strands together, including changes to daily life and the visible transforma- tion of the city, and they linked these changes to a broader critique about the revolution's perceived reversal of urban modernity.

It is from this perspective that we can understand the frustration ex- pressed by some *habaneros* as the everyday comforts and privileges of urban middle-class life were undermined. In letters written in 1961 and 1962, writers mentioned over and over again how much their daily lives had changed. For example, one man wrote a parody of an average day in revolutionary Cuba, contrasting the victorious slogans with the arduous reality. "You wake up early . . . and opening a stream of cold water in the shower, shout at the top of your lungs: *Patria o muerte!* Then you carefully [lather with] one thirti- eth of a bar of soap."[73] Sitting down to a "vigorous breakfast that will help production in your workplace," the narrator described carefully counting drops of milk for his coffee. His satiric chronicle suggested that the daily comforts of prerevolutionary life—such as a hot shower or coffee with milk—were on the wane, while demands placed on citizens—including political participation and workplace productivity—were rising.

Shortages also meant the absence of familiar imported goods that had been a staple of urban middle-class diets and, to some extent, identity. Cuba's particular historical development as a sugar-monoculture producer dominated by large modern plantations, without a significant peasant population engaged in subsistence agriculture or production for local markets, meant that it had never been food-sufficient. Even *campesinos* depended on imported foodstuffs, such as dried cod.[74] The geographic proximity and political dominance of the United States made it the source of much of the island's imported foodstuffs. Many middle-class *habaneros* had grown up eating the canned fruits and vegetables produced by American corporations like Del Monte, and letters from the period reveal that many Cubans considered canned condensed milk a dietary staple.[75] Thus food shortages challenged established class-based modes of consumption. The middle class could not obtain foods in the same quantities, even with recourse to the black market, and could not procure foods of familiar brands.

Critics of the revolution also mourned the fact that Havana's city center, long a site for experiencing and imagining modernity as well as procuring goods, was being physically transformed by the revolution. The transformations engendered by the revolution had changed the city in more ways than one. Long a site of leisure and consumption, and the location of sporadic political protests under Batista, Havana's famous downtown shopping thoroughfare now also became the site of sustained political mobilization and conflict. The nationalization of the major department stores in the fall of 1960 left them physically altered, draped both inside and out with Cuban flags, banners announcing their nationalization, and signs bearing revolutionary slogans.[76] The thousands of employees, mostly women, who staffed the counters and sewing workshops of the department stores were themselves divided. Most supported the revolution, but others, who strongly identified with the former owners and managers, felt increasingly isolated from their coworkers.[77] The demographic composition of consumers shifted, one magazine reported, as what were once the most exclusive stores now found themselves "taken over" by a "jumbled public" of all ages, phrases that may have been euphemisms for the rural popular sectors brought to Havana for various programs early in the revolution, or for darker-skinned, working-class *habaneros*.[78] Such coded language also referenced the racial imaginary attached to certain visions of modernity and consumption, where the shoppers of the most "modern" department stores and supermarkets were imagined as white women. As the revolution's early tremors began to shift the race and class character of the city's commercial districts, some *haba-*

neros found the changes exciting and welcome. Others found them disquieting, and claimed that their city's main drags and its shoppers had changed beyond recognition.

As the structural transformations introduced by the revolution affected distribution and consumption, Havana's downtown stores were faced with depleted stock and were no longer able to showcase the latest fashions and products. Some Cubans lamented these changes. "The . . . lovely shop-window displays that we loved to watch at night, newspaper, radio and TV advertising, all that has disappeared!" wrote one man to a friend abroad. "You go into any kind of store and you find the shelves 75% empty and the sales people idle, short-tempered and rude."[79] By 1961 the once-vibrant department store windows had been superseded by other commercial activity, such as the bustling street stalls that now sold printed copies of revolutionary laws, books about the Soviet Union, and revolutionary insignia "so that our Havana sidewalks really have a quite different aspect than they used to," as one letter noted.[80] Other Cubans reiterated how shocked and discomfited they felt as they witnessed transformations to the city. In early 1962, one exile publication ran a photo series of the city center, prompting its readers: "*Habanero*, you've passed by this corner a thousand times. It was the commercial center of your capital. You and your whole family would go there. Bet you don't even recognize it today, right?"[81]

These different visions of consumption and urban modernity were not simply battles of ideas. They were literally explosive issues, fought out on Cuba's urban landscape through a series of sabotage attacks that shook Havana's downtown department stores. The attacks began around Christmas 1960, two months after many of the stores had been nationalized. The bombings escalated in the first months of 1961, leading up to the Bay of Pigs invasion of mid-April 1961. The firebombing of the department store El Encanto that April was the most devastating of these attacks. But many other stores were also attacked in this period, beginning with a bomb or flammable substance set off in the Flogar department store on Christmas Eve 1960, resulting in several injuries; arson at the department store La Época just one week later; and an attempt to place a bomb in the downtown Sears in September of 1961.[82] In March 1961, a coordinated sabotage attack was launched simultaneously against both downtown branches of Woolworth's.[83]

Why department stores? They had no strategic importance, unlike the myriad sabotage attacks on crucial industries, such as sugar, and important infrastructure and transportation services, such as trains, bridges, and electric generators, that took place in this period. In addition, Havana had no lack of politically symbolic structures, such as the Capitolio building, the National Palace, or the municipal buildings along the Plaza de Armas, all of which were just blocks away from the main department stores. Yet there were very few sabotage attacks on those traditional buildings of government. In some ways, Havana's commercial drags had a more visceral and contemporary importance.

Department stores and supermarkets embodied a particular vision of urban modernity and cosmopolitanism. El Encanto, Silvia Pedraza argues, was "more than a store, it was a symbol of the hopes and aspirations middle-class Cubans had, wanting to be part of the world that they saw as modern and civilized."[84] The American chain stores also carried great symbolism. Sears, for example, was seen as the pinnacle of modern consuming practices in the 1950s.[85] The large, multistory department store featured modern American appliances and was one of the first stores to feature electric escalators and air conditioning, the latter a major attraction in a tropical country.[86] Such innovations converted shopping from a simple exercise in consumption into a form of diversion. Likewise, Havana's commercial districts, including the older commercial strips of La Habana Vieja and the newer development emerging along the main drag known as La Rampa in Vedado, were a source of pride for many Cubans.[87] Browsing the shop windows that lined the commercial drags of the center was a pleasant pastime, as was sitting at the modern, U.S.-style lunch counters of diners and cafeterias. The destruction of these temples of modernity conveyed a sense that Cuba's progress and development had been derailed by the revolution.

Charges of the country's increasing "backwardness" in consumer goods had profound political implications, representing for some Cubans a temporal slide back to the premodern. As one exile periodical lamented in 1962, "Cuba has returned to the colonial period: from the rapid automobile to the slow animal-drawn carriage; from the supermarkets with varied foods to the ration card; from fine dresses and shoes to primitive attire; from air conditioning to the hand-held fan; from civilization to the cave; from liberty to slavery."[88] Such criticisms viewed progress and modernity as bound up with increased consumption, and judged Cuba's declining material standards—at least for the urban middle class—as both evidence of and metaphor for the disappearance of political freedom. These visions clashed sharply with the emerging revolutionary ideals of freedom as liberation from imperialist domination and capitalism, and shared austerity as evidence of revolutionary commitment.

This vision of urban modernity and cosmopolitanism had particular resonance with Havana's middle class. Indeed, middle-class denunciations of shortages and urban destruction reveal how frequently criticism of the revolution was expressed as resentment over the experience of a kind of downward mobility. There were also certain racial connotations to "modern" versus "backward" forms of consumption. A 1957 cover illustration of the popular magazine *Carteles* clearly captures the racialized imaginary of "modern" shopping in the 1950s.[89] It features a plump Afro-Cuban woman decked out in bright folkloric attire, standing near the checkout counter of an American-style grocery store, the kind then spreading to affluent areas of Havana. She has inappropriately piled her groceries into a basket balanced on her head, the kind traditionally used by street vendors. In the background, white women with shopping carts gape at her in surprise. The contrast between the white and black women shoppers reminds us of the extent to which images of progress and modernization during the Republican period relied on racialized others.[90] The implied absurdity of the scenario in the illustration helps us understand the shock and disorientation with which some middle- or upper-class *habaneros* responded to the new "jumbled publics" now invading their familiar commercial spaces, and their sense of being forced "backward" toward premodern and racially coded consumption practices.[91]

Although support for the revolution was generally high among the urban and rural working class in this period, popular critiques of the new consumption regime emerged as well. There is some evidence that the leadership expected the urban popular classes to be less impatient with shortages and to accept or even embrace rationing. In fact, rationing may have been presented with different rationales to different publics. In Fidel Castro's televised speeches it was presented as a necessary evil that would at least alleviate housewives. As Castro explained, women "won't have to spend long hours in the markets and other establishments waiting for their turn. . . . Now they will know that the bodega-owner and butcher and vegetable-vendor have their share reserved."[92]

But in assemblies held in the poorest Havana neighborhoods, low-level functionaries also described rationing as a positive measure, embodying social justice and equality. One CDR leader recalled announcing that "the Revolution wouldn't permit [some people to have] more and others less or nothing, like before; everything was going to be distributed in equal shares, equitably."[93] They then asked all those in favor of rationing to raise their hands. Leaders also assumed that, despite shortages, the poorest sectors were still eating better than before. As Fidel Castro called out confidently to an assembly of peasants, "Did you eat meat [and] drink milk daily [before the revolution]? Did you have eggs every week?"[94] In a reversal of the middle-class critique of downward mobility, the leadership frequently implied that popular support was at least partly premised on a rising standard of living, whether in the present or the near future. In fact, it is likely that for the poorest Cubans, consumption did rise, even in this period of turmoil and shortage.

Yet the picture was complicated. For one thing, rationing did not ensure equal consumption, not even in its design. Some groups enjoyed higher rations, such as the leadership and youths who joined certain prestigious political campaigns.[95] City dwellers were allotted higher rations than rural residents.[96] Certain items were rationed only in major cities, and others only in Havana.[97] And the food equality theoretically imposed by rationing was circumvented by various problems in practice. The government's first attempts to implement rationing were chaotic, as distribution chains broke down or were mired in inefficiency, sometimes inadvertently favoring those who had certain resources—such as a refrigerator—over those who did not.[98] There was apparently widespread popular disgruntlement with the fact that goods promised on the ration book were not always available in practice. Thus even revolutionary supporters referred to the ration book as "the deceiver," because it "promised but didn't deliver."[99]

Thus disgruntlement and critique related to consumption had multiple axes. If a deep attachment to U.S.-made consumer goods may have characterized the middle and upper class somewhat more than the popular classes, one might argue that the question of equality in consumption was a more vexing issue that stirred deeper popular discontent. Members of the popular classes, as well as the more affluent Cubans who identified with the revolution's promises of social equality, may have chafed at the actual inequality in consumption that they witnessed in everyday practice. Indeed, both Cuban exiles and the U.S. government saw the opportunity to create propaganda that publicized not simply shortage, but inequality in consumption. In proposals to destabilize Cuba in the aftermath of the failure of the Bay of Pigs invasion, Brigadier General William Craig recommended interjecting small, one-line radio broadcasts into official station breaks, including sentences such as "Castro and his henchmen feed off the land while we are rationed."[100] Exile publications also played on this theme. For example, a 1965 pamphlet entitled *There Is None (No Hay)* juxtaposed photos of empty stores with Fidel Castro relishing a heaping plate of food.[101]

Black Markets in Country and City

Differential access to goods extended beyond the realms of official distribution. In particular, middle- and upper-class *habaneros* enjoyed more resources with which to procure scarce items through the black market, such as cash and cars for trips to the nearby countryside. The ability of those with more resources to procure more and better foods may have angered poorer Havana residents, for these unregulated practices made a mockery of the new social equality presumably ushered in by the revolution. As one man noted in a letter, "the word *compañero* abounds, but everyone scoffs at it [*se burlan de ella*]. You can only get [goods] with money and connections."[102] In letters to friends and relatives abroad, Havana residents of means noted their own recourse to the black market, while recognizing the social inequalities these actions inevitably reproduced. As one woman reported, lines to purchase just two eggs per person stretched for hours, while her friend's husband managed to purchase one hundred eggs on the black market "at a premium price, of course."[103]

The government tried to stamp out the black market, but this in turn raised other problems.[104] In particular, by trying to repress speculation, new laws unintentionally alienated small farmers who sought to sell meat and produce in private transactions. Officials occasionally imposed draconian punishments for unauthorized slaughter and sale of livestock, although it is difficult to determine whether these were systematic or isolated incidents.[105] In addition, laws were often unclear or unevenly enforced. For example, a government pronouncement of late 1961 suggests that the leadership felt it was necessary to clarify things. The statement reassured peasants that they had the right to kill pigs over 150 pounds to eat them themselves, or sell pork to the proper government office for "fair prices" and immediate payment. "But we are asking the *campesinos* not to sell piglets [or fattened pigs] to intermediaries who will use them to speculate."[106]

By the summer of 1962, new legislation stipulated that buying more than twenty-five pounds of food directly from private farmers was punishable with up to six months of jail time.[107] Rumors of even more severe penalties flew rapidly. Stories circulated that black marketers, including those peasants who slaughtered their own livestock without permission, would be shot.[108] In May 1962, the National Institute for Agrarian Reform issued a ruling emphasizing "respect" for the small private farmer, and "making it clear that he must be allowed, within limits, to slaughter his own livestock and dispose of it locally," in an apparent attempt to reassure small farmers and rein in those local officials who had imposed detention for unauthorized slaughter and sale.[109] While food shortages were the source of discontent in urban areas, rural areas in this period were more often affected by the disorder that resulted from disruptions to prerevolutionary forms of production and distribution, and by overzealous official attempts to stamp out the black market.

The black market was not only shaped by supply and demand. Politics also entered the picture, as individuals and groups tried to channel goods toward those who shared their political sympathies. With the introduction of lard rationing in mid-1961, and generalized food rationing by March 1962, the leadership implemented a Census of Consumers, carried out by neighborhood CDRs, to determine each neighborhood's needs. As a result, those suspicious of the revolutionary government viewed the imposition of rationing as a method of social control. "Lard will only be distributed among the sympathizers of the regime," one predicted. "Anyone feared as a counterrevolutionary or hostile toward the regime will never get a ration-card."[110] Some thus feared that the government would utilize food shortages to enhance its power and punish its enemies.

At the same time, organized opponents of the regime also dealt in the black market. They hoped shortages would work to their advantage both by creating widespread discontent and by channeling consumers toward their own networks of goods and thus funding their political activities.[111] As one man noted in a letter, "in the country and in the shops, the only ones who get anything . . . are those who are known as 'worms' "—the revolutionary leadership's epithet for its opponents—"otherwise you starve."[112] Another "worm" concurred, noting, "Those of us who are well accredited as 'worms' and who can pay for it, still get good meat."[113] Black marketers sometimes preferred dealing with those who were disgruntled with the revolution, either due to shared political sympathies or, more pragmatically, because it was unlikely such people would report them to authorities.

Food shortages and the leadership's attempt to control those shortages through rationing thus met with discontent and opposition among different sectors for different reasons. For some, particularly some sectors of the urban middle class, shortages and rationing were the antithesis of a view of modernity as prosperity and urban development. For others, perhaps particularly the urban popular classes, shortages and the inequities that could result circumvented the revolution's promises of social equality. And although much of the rural popular class likely benefitted from early redistributive measures, and did not face the same food shortages as their urban counterparts, at least some small farmers viewed the increasing official scrutiny over slaughter and sale as an unwanted intrusion of the state. The problems of provision were thus influenced by multiple factors, such as class, region, and political alliances.

Women and the Conflicted Politics of Provision

Still, women—that is, urban women of all classes—were affected in particular ways by transformations to consumption, though not because they were more easily swayed by the seductions of consumer culture, as caricature might have it. Entrusted by tradition with the reproductive labor of the home, women were designated as being responsible for a household's daily domestic labors, either by cooking, cleaning, washing, and caring for children themselves, or by supervising the servants who undertook such tasks. They were thus directly and immediately affected by price hikes, food shortages, and the immense time and effort required to procure necessary goods. As shortages spiraled in 1961 and 1962, urban women were thrust to the forefront of the crisis. They voiced critiques, demanded solutions, led disturbances in lines, and organized large-scale protests. In the process, they pushed the leadership to respond.

Some women criticized changes to provisions in ways that engaged broader Cold War debates. As familiar staples either disappeared or were replaced by Soviet or Chinese versions, women had to adapt in the kitchen. Prorevolutionary publications published new recipes and encouraged women to find creative substitutes.[114] Yet some consumers ridiculed the new imported products with critiques that had clear political overtones. As one woman complained, "the miracles of socialism are apparently restricted to rocketry, but when it comes to making flour and packing meat they are a flop." She found the cooking oil, chickpeas, and dishcloths imported from Russia and China to be worthless.[115] Such dismissals may have reflected real differences in production quality, but they also referenced Cold War propaganda that praised the wonders of American durables and perishables against those of the Soviet Union.[116] These debates often focused on whether socialism or capitalism more effectively alleviated women's household labor. Women were not only the subjects of these debates, but also their presumed audience, as international exhibits were often particularly tailored to appeal to women, showcasing time-saving domestic appliances.[117] As the historian Victoria de Grazia argues, in the 1950s and 1960s, the well-stocked kitchen, packed with modern appliances, was "mobilized as an icon of the

Western way of life."[118] The kitchen stood for America's relatively high standard of living and its rational, managerial housewives. The Cold War raised questions everywhere about how best to define modernity and progress in relation to consumption practices, and how women would be implicated in these issues.[119] In Cuba, these questions took on particular urgency as the island moved toward an alliance with the Soviets.[120] As Cuban women critiqued the changes around them, they joined a global conversation in which such issues were already intensely politicized.

Women of all class and racial backgrounds were affected by the increasing time required to procure provisions. During the earliest shortages, women of means may still have been able to send their servants to stand in line on their behalf.[121] But throughout 1961 the wealthiest Cubans emigrated, and domestic servants were recruited into government retraining programs.[122] Thus the more affluent women who remained on the island could no longer outsource domestic labor to servants. As Muriel Nazarri has argued, the loss of a servant class meant that middle- and upper-class women were more affected by the revolution than their male counterparts, as women's status in particular was defined by access to servants.[123] Domestic labors formerly outsourced along class, and often racial, lines were now broken down along gender lines. Yet, at the same time, political events were rapidly compressing the material distinctions among classes. And although poor and working-class women benefitted in general from the revolution's early redistributive measures, the amount of time required to procure food also rose. Thus by 1961 and 1962, women of all classes struggled in long food lines, as contemporary letters attest.[124]

Women noted that their daily lives were radically altered, as they were forced to spend ever-larger portions of their day standing in line for foodstuffs or spending long hours going from store to store to hunt for necessary goods. For middle-class women in particular, the time spent traversing the city—"in the street," as it was popularly and somewhat derisively described—could be a shocking disruption to their former lives.[125] It also provided a new kind of collective experience, though not the kind endorsed by the leadership. "You can't imagine how many of us women were in the street yesterday," one woman marveled.[126] Another woman similarly noted that "to eat you have to spend [all] your time in the street," because some items were sold in the morning and others in the afternoon, and nothing could be procured without a lengthy stint in line.[127]

The atmosphere in the food lines became increasingly tense. Letters described the mood of the crowds standing in line as "worse every day."[128]

Tensions flared and spilled over into popular disturbances. In letters, Havana residents reported various incidents of violence, including "daily fist fights" in bakeries and women who "fought, squabbled, [and] pulled each other's hair" during scuffles in stores.[129] Security forces occasionally had to intervene to restore order in situations bordering on riots, with particularly grave incidents in centrally located neighborhoods of Havana in which security forces fired shots into the air.[130]

Some of these scuffles took on a decidedly political cast, as women of different political persuasions confronted one another, or women in lines physically attacked policemen, militia members, or CDR leaders.[131] Both revolutionary leaders and emerging opposition leaders viewed the lines as an opportunity to proselytize. One FMC official optimistically described the food lines as potential sites of female solidarity and consciousness raising, "true assemblies" in which FMC members would teach "housewives" the reasons behind the shortages.[132] Some anti-Castro groups also imagined organizing demonstrations in food lines, where disturbances often happened spontaneously.[133] In at least some cases, clashes were sparked by discrepancies over what had caused the shortages. For example, in the summer of 1961, crowds in lines attacked a government car with a loudspeaker that was blaming food shortages on "imperialist action."[134] In an era in which political rallies were increasingly choreographed, Havana's tumultuous food lines became mass public gatherings for unscripted political conversation and conflict.[135]

There were also organized protests. In the summer of 1961, protesters in Manzanillo and Santiago demonstrated with pots and pans, and a large crowd gathered outside the Presidential Palace in Havana to protest food shortages.[136] These food-related protests seem to have been predominantly led by women. Certainly some opposition sympathizers were convinced that women, who bore the heaviest burden of daily scarcity, were correspondingly more critical of the revolutionary government than men on the whole. According to one CIA source, the long lines in Havana had pushed many women toward the opposition. "Cuban women have become the leaders of opposition activity and urge their husbands to undertake action to alleviate the present situation," the source noted. Lines at stores stretched four to five blocks, he said, and church attendance, which was predominantly female in Cuba, was "at an all-time high as a demonstration of opposition to the government."[137]

The revolutionary leadership must have felt threatened by these food protests. We can surmise as much from the heavy-handed government reaction to the largest food protest of the period, which took place in Cárdenas, a port city on the northern rim of Matanzas Province, about a hundred miles east of Havana, in June 1962. The protest took place several months after the introduction of ration cards and after growing tension in food lines, but was apparently sparked by the opening of a well-stocked grocery store for foreign technicians only.[138] What began as a peaceful procession of women protesters apparently turned more volatile, and prompted the government to send in army troops and tanks as a show of force.[139] Estimates about the number of women protesters subsequently varied from 200 to 1,000.[140] Women protesters were either predominantly of the popular classes or a mixture of working- and middle-class women. For this reason President Osvaldo Dorticós warned that the revolution would not countenance "street provocations" undertaken by "crooks" (*maleantes*) or "lumpens," without mentioning the participation of the bourgeoisie.[141]

The ensuing government reaction seemed patently out of proportion for what was, by all accounts, a public protest of civilian women. In an overwhelming military display, government troops drove tanks throughout the streets of Cárdenas and staged flyovers with MiG jets. President Osvaldo Dorticós and rebel army commander Jorge Serguera were dispatched to the town to publicly warn against any further "provocations."

There may be several reasons for this surprising reaction. First and foremost, Matanzas was one of the provinces where peasants were taking up arms against the revolutionary government. Matanzas farmers had been relatively prosperous before the revolution, and the province, like other western provinces, was marked primarily by small and medium-sized farms rather than large estates (*latifundia*). Thus, when the leaders of agrarian reform in the province moved to back agricultural workers who demanded the socialization of the small farms where they had been employed, many private farmers felt that the revolution was not in their interests.[142] As the political scientist Jorge Domínguez has shown, cooperative farms, welcomed in some places, were elsewhere imposed on local farmers against their will; this, it seems, had been the situation in Matanzas.[143] In addition, local officials who feared the consequences of food shortages in urban centers cracked down on peasants by arbitrarily confiscating peasant produce, and at times by forcing peasants to harvest crops prematurely.[144] All these pressures—as government officials subsequently admitted—pushed some small private farmers in Matanzas to take up arms against the revolution.[145]

While this peasant insurrection was theoretically confined to rural areas in the southern part of the province, not in the countryside immediately surrounding Cárdenas, the national leadership may have feared that the province's rural conflicts might articulate with urban discontent. Ominously, there had apparently been food protests in other cities throughout the province in recent weeks; the Cárdenas protest was simply the largest of several. In the city of Matanzas, about twenty miles west of Cárdenas, reportedly "crowds composed mainly of women had gathered to yell 'We're hungry' while beating on pots and pans."[146] The large protest in Cárdenas was also apparently the culmination of several days of protest in the city, which provincial authorities had been unwilling or unable to stop.[147] In addition, the province's capital city, Matanzas, had seen a series of disturbances in the spring of 1962, including several sabotage attempts and a rash of arrests.[148] National authorities may thus have feared that expressions of urban opposition, including food protests, might combine with rural grievances and snowball into a multiclass, province-wide opposition movement and perhaps even spread to the neighboring province of Havana.

The spectacular show of force certainly sent a clear message that the government would not tolerate further large food protests, and perhaps implied that rural disturbances risked provoking the national leadership's wrath as well. The stamping out of the Cárdenas demonstration put an end to the era of turbulent reactions to food shortages. In ensuing months and years, food provision for the most part stabilized, as the island formalized trade relations with the Soviet bloc. Yet some chronic distribution problems remained, and would become a permanent feature of Cuban daily life.[149]

The Trouble with Housewives

The Cárdenas incident and other food-related protests capture the centrality of urban women actors in this crucial period and the way they responded to the crisis in provisions. When their interests were threatened, women pushed the state for redress. They demanded lowered prices for necessary goods and state regulation of interactions between vendors and consumers. Women used the channels established by the state when they could; but when these were no longer sufficient, they also went beyond them. When the revolutionary authorities passed new legislation against hoarding and price gouging in early 1960, infractions against store owners soared. With the formation of the mass organizations later that year, women used these organizations, as the state authorities in fact requested they do, to monitor transactions in local stores. When shortages and long lines became intolerable, women engaged in street protests and caused disturbances in lines that helped move the revolutionary government toward a program of widespread rationing. In other words, women pushed the revolutionary leaders to take action on these issues, and they thereby shaped the development of the revolution in a crucial period of definition and consolidation.

Yet in this same period we also see the emergence of a new government concern over women or "housewives" who were not sufficiently incorporated into the revolution. This represented a shift away from an earlier, more optimistic approach to women as consumers. As shortages began to deepen by 1961, they raised the possibility that women might be unfavorably disposed to endure scarcity. The leadership now correspondingly eyed women consumers more warily, concerned with how problems with provisioning might compound with women's purported social isolation. This anxiety was one of the factors reflected in how the "new woman" was imagined in this period. If the new woman was a young, politically engaged, self-sacrificing "soldier" for the revolution, her antithesis was the older housewife, the woman who neither studied nor worked, who defended her own family's interests against those of the collective. Women like these were now viewed as "unincorporated" and therefore potentially dangerous. As visions of the revolution's goals began to diverge, and as a militant opposition began to take shape, women's political loyalties became a key question.

FMC leaders expressed concern about housewives' potential misunderstandings, particularly housewives of the popular classes. One FMC official warned that their "lack of a habit of reading" could be detrimental to their political education.[150] The Communist Party's newspaper similarly entertained the idea that "isolated" working-class housewives might be angered by food shortages and vulnerable to rumors. Housewives were too busy with domestic labor to participate in other activities, the newspaper warned. They spent their days in the home or in tasks related to housework, and were thereby susceptible to claims made by oppositionists, shop owners, and priests. "They . . . do their shopping in food stores, fruit stands, the market, in clothing stores, etc.," all places where they might hear, "and occasionally echo, the rumors that [our] hidden enemies are spreading."[151] Housewives would have to learn to deflect (rather than echo) rumors of permanent scarcity spread by the friends or acquaintances that they might come across while doing their daily shopping. There was thus a certain anxiety over the fact that rumors and counterrevolutionary sentiments might be easily reproduced within social spaces not linked to the state, such as the private home, the neighborhood streets, the food market, the corner store, and the church—all spaces the revolution had not yet conquered, and where old loyalties prevailed.

Housewives were becoming a problem. Here we see the seeds of an idea that reached its apex after the failure of the major 1970 sugar harvest, when officials publicly denounced housewives as idle, blaming their alleged refusal to labor for the harvest's failure to reach its target.[152] But if we scrutinize the period 1960 to 1962, when concern over housewives was first voiced, we might hypothesize that those criticisms may have represented a backlash against the obvious political agency exercised by those very same women, rather than reflect their purported apathy and disengagement. Government portrayals of women as isolated, confused, disengaged, or unable to sacrifice may have explained away the uncomfortable fact that some women voiced criticisms, protested, and sympathized with the political opposition.

6 | THE DESTRUCTION AND SALVATION OF THE CUBAN FAMILY, 1959–1962

Shortly after coming to power, the new revolutionary authorities embarked on a series of measures to fortify the family. Mass weddings legalized informal unions. New legislation enforced protection for children born out of wedlock. Newly subsidized leisure activities and urban housing were designed to encourage a healthy and dignified family. Yet by 1960 the growing ranks of the disaffected and the increasingly organized political opposition charged that the revolution was destroying the family. How can these two seemingly divergent claims be reconciled?

This chapter examines transformations to the Cuban family, both real and imagined, intentional and unintentional. Following Anita Casavantes Bradford's pioneering study of children in the early revolution, published in 2014, this chapter argues that struggles over idealized visions of marriage, children, and the family were key to competing notions of the nation's future in this period.[1] Although the revolutionary leadership and the growing ranks of the disaffected initially shared liberal ideals of family fortification, those ideals were soon strained by the rapid changes of the period. Throughout 1960, the new mass organizations and revolutionary campaigns increasingly mobilized women, adolescents, and children, inadvertently challenging traditional family structures in the process.[2] In this context of rapid transformation, both revolutionary leaders and those who began mobilizing against the revolution increasingly appealed to "the family" as a way to justify their positions. In so doing, they sharpened their visions of how the state might remold the family. By 1961 the revolutionary leadership had moved from reformist notions of family uplift toward a more strident and interventionist vision of popular motherhood, strong working-class families, and patriotic childhood. At the same time, Cubans suspicious of the revolutionary leadership increasingly feared that the new government would displace the rights and duties of parenthood and the patriarchal family onto an authoritarian state.

This fear reached its culmination in a campaign of rumors about the abolition of Patria Potestad. Patria Potestad was a legal term encompassing various parental rights over one's children, including custody. From mid-1960 through 1961, organized opponents of the revolution with the CIA's backing intentionally spread rumors that the revolutionary government would soon end parents' legal custodial rights to their own children. It was said that all children over the age of five would be forcibly removed from the family home, sent to schools in the countryside for indoctrination, inducted into the militias for military training, and, finally, sent to the Soviet Union for further exposure to Marxism. These rumors, while apparently unfounded, had serious practical consequences. They helped convince many parents that their children would be safer abroad, and thus contributed to Operation Peter Pan, a secret program operated by the U.S. State Department in conjunction with U.S.-based Catholic relief agencies and the underground anti-Castro movement in Havana.[3] This program consisted of the clandestine evacuation of 14,000 unaccompanied, mostly urban, middle-class Cuban children to the United States. Parents believed these relocations would be temporary. They hoped to either bring their children back to Cuba after the revolution's swift overthrow or join their children in exile. Instead, Operation Peter Pan resulted in permanent emigrations and often in painful, years-long separations between children and their parents.

Gender and sexuality determined the pattern of these fears over familial destruction. The plights that might befall prepubescent children, adolescent boys and girls, and adult women were viewed as distinct. Parents focused on the political indoctrination of young children, especially as private education was abolished. When it came to teenage boys, they worried that they would be trained to fight in foreign wars. But fears over the removal of teenage girls from the home focused more on potential sexual transgressions: parents feared that adolescent girls' mobilization through government campaigns would result in either sexual promiscuity and pregnancy or militarization and hence masculinization.

Similarly, the heightened focus on children inevitably meant that changes to adult women's roles were given special scrutiny. Women in their current or future role as mothers were seen as the lynchpins of the family, and deviation from their traditional roles was imagined to facilitate the disintegration of the family unit. For this reason, changes that in retrospect seem relatively innocuous—such as women performing voluntary manual labor, joining a mass organization, engaging in paid labor for the first time, or simply being encouraged to more frequently leave the house for "the street"—could be read as symptomatic of deeper and more threatening changes. For if women could be subverted from their traditional calling as mothers and home-makers, families might then be abandoned to the whims of the state. The specter of state intrusion into the domestic sphere thus seemed to position mothers as the state's natural antagonists, and the emerging anti-Castro op-position accordingly imagined women at the vanguard of anticommunist resistance.

The conflict over the roles of women, children, and the family also influ-enced the racial imaginary of the period. Anti-Castro propaganda tended to depict the family under siege as white, middle-class, and nuclear.[4] In many ways, ironically, this bolstered the revolutionary leadership's increasing por-trayal of exiles and oppositionists as economic elites incapable of accepting the racially inclusive project of the revolution. And while state-sanctioned propaganda still often depicted imagined revolutionary subjects as white, this was beginning to change, as new actors—such as the Afro-Cuban liter-acy brigade volunteer Conrado Benítez—were publicly celebrated as the embodiment of revolutionary abnegation.[5]

Rumors over the state's appropriation of children should not surprise us. As the historian Karen Dubinsky notes, social and political upheavals often generate anxieties that are expressed in apocalyptic stories about missing children. From rumors of children stolen by the monarchy during the French Revolution, to fears of Communist "baby snatchers" during the Cold War, the plight of children has historically carried an enormous symbolic impact.[6] The particular dynamics of the Cold War, with its simultaneous emphasis on the need for domestic security and the pervasive threat of global annihi-lation, generated an even more intense focus on children's protection in the capitalist West.[7] For different reasons, children in the socialist world and in the revolutionary upheavals of the decolonizing world were also endowed with special importance. Children were the future citizens, the "new men" and "new women" who would construct a more just future society. They had to be educated in new revolutionary values in order to transcend the tradi-tion that weighed down older generations.[8] In 1959 Cuba found itself at the crossroads of these different currents. As a result, children—and by exten-sion the family—were invested with enormous symbolic significance.

This chapter suggests that perceived threats to children, the family, and conventional forms of marriage and sexuality were an important motor of disaffection and exodus in the crucial period of the revolution's definition and consolidation. These perceived threats also helped the growing organized opposition congeal. Just as the politically plural anti-Batista movement had papered over differences with a discursive focus on manly martyrdom, grieving motherhood, and distraught families, so too did allegations about the destruction of the family lend coherence to the poorly unified and politically diverse anti-Castro movement. And they fueled the articulation of a more conservative, Catholic-inspired vision of womanhood and family within the anti-Castro movement. Taking allegations of family destruction seriously thus helps us recapture the moral anticommunism that was especially characteristic of the middle sectors, who feared intimate transformations to the family and the self as well as broad economic and political changes. Studies of the anti-Castro movement have been so dominated by the polarized "official" accounts of the island and exile leaderships that they have hardly moved beyond caricatured explanations of opposition motivation.[9] But as this chapter suggests, the lasting identification of anti-Castroism with the defense of the family, traditional gender roles, and Catholicism, and the lasting allegations of exiles that socialism has been accompanied by sexual promiscuity and weakened family structures, must be seen as the products, not the causes, of the period's political conflict.[10]

Operation Matrimony: Moderate Family Reform, 1959–1960

There is a sizable sociological literature on the Cuban family after the revolution, especially concerning state policies toward the family.[11] Most of this literature takes a long view, charting a shift from leaders' more "radical" approach toward the family in the 1960s, when the state was thought to take precedence, to a renewed emphasis on the individual family unit in the 1970s. Yet a close look at the earliest family-related initiatives of the revolution restores the complexity and political plurality of the revolution's first two years. It recovers the persistence of liberal notions of family reform and demonstrates the revolutionary leadership's transition from those early reformist positions to a more interventionist, forceful, and politicized position that championed the working-class family and the "right" to motherhood.

In fact, a close examination of the events of the first two years of the revolution suggests that the measures undertaken by the government in this period seem, if anything, remarkably moderate. The programs instigated in 1959 and 1960 suggest that the revolutionary government envisioned building a new society partly by modernizing and improving the working-class family. Early government initiatives attempted to create stable working families through programs to end free unions among the popular classes and to provide wholesome family entertainment, thus drawing working-class men away from the libertine environment of neighborhood bars. These moralizing uplift projects suggest that revolutionary leaders initially embraced liberal notions of family reform and working-class improvement, for these initiatives were not geared toward radical transformation of family structures or gender relations. Yet these initiatives also had radical potential. They gave women leverage within patriarchal relations by providing new state allies. They sidestepped the Catholic Church and implied that the state might take a greater role in rationalizing and modernizing the domestic sphere.[12]

Explicit government concern over the family surfaced in the summer of 1959, when the Ministry of Justice initiated a plan to formalize free unions and encourage the registration of children with local civil authorities. These measures were at least partly spearheaded by Alfredo Yabur Maluf, a forty-year-old middle-class lawyer of Lebanese descent.[13] Yabur was one of a handful of moderate ministers appointed in 1959. Although he had been loosely affiliated with both the Revolutionary Directorate and the Twenty-Sixth of July Movement, he was, as the historian Hugh Thomas notes, "no revolutionary."[14] The measure was greeted with encouragement from the liberal press, which praised the revolutionary government's concern with stabilizing the Cuban family, especially the rural family. As one columnist in the daily newspaper *El Mundo* noted, "in the foothills of the Sierra Maestra, men and women do not contract matrimony to establish a home and create a family. They simply 'get together' [*se arriman*], the popular term which in the countryside is used for concubinage." Such couples rarely inscribed their children into the civil registry, he explained. More seriously, the facility of such cohabitation often led to one man having children with various women. Although the Catholic Church had long sought to change the situation, "now it falls to the State, armed with the resources and means that come with power, to put an end to this as far as humanly possible."[15]

Eventually known as Operation Matrimony, the initiative prompted mass weddings involving hundreds of couples, many of them long-term partners with multiple children. Some mass weddings legalized hundreds of unions at a time: a September 1960 newspaper article claimed that more than 500 couples had recently been married in an act held at the Cuban Workers' Confederation and that more than 4,000 couples had been married in the rest of the island.[16] Collective weddings were held in Havana as well as in the countryside among workers at sugar mills and peasants who worked in other forms of agriculture. Often Justice Minister Yabur himself traveled across the provinces, officiating in local town halls. Prior to his arrival, local officials spread word of the impending collective wedding among inhabitants of their region, so that on the appointed day couples arrived from isolated rural areas. Following the secularized rituals—which often included singing the anthem of the Twenty-Sixth of July Movement as well as the national anthem—authorities held brief public festivities before guiding the newlyweds to the proper office to inscribe their children in the civil registry.[17] The number of unions ultimately legalized through Operation Matrimony may have reached 400,000.[18] As the historian Carrie Hamilton notes, early revolutionary support for marriage contributed to Cuba's formal marriage rates rising to one of the highest in the world during the 1960s.[19]

Operation Matrimony had several aims. From the perspective of the revolutionary leadership, it would help document and regulate existing unions, bringing them under the purview of the future state bureaucracy. As such it would facilitate the distribution of land titles and urban housing under the new revolutionary laws, which were explicitly designed to benefit families and households rather than individuals. The program also had protective and moralistic dimensions, often stressed in the liberal press. Increasing rates of legal marriage was seen as a way to protect women and children from abandonment or from severe poverty in the event of widowhood and to ensure inheritance.[20] It was also seen as a way of instilling proper moral conduct into the more relaxed social mores of the countryside. As one article explained, "when a man and woman feel united with all the legal requisites, they feel fortunate, complying with all the demands of citizenly morality and at the margin of social sanction, in a favorable mood that consolidates the family."[21] Thus Operation Matrimony partly conformed to liberal notions of social welfare and class uplift, notions shared by some of the revolutionary leadership and its liberal supporters.

The mass weddings could also carry an overt political tone. In these collective events in which up to hundreds of popular-class couples sang the Twenty-Sixth of July anthem and pledged their marital values before officials of the revolutionary state, the protagonists seemed to be embracing the revolution as well as marriage. Indeed, photographs of marriage ceremonies from 1959 and 1960 suggest that weddings of young couples in this period could be tinged with celebratory references to the revolution. Photos in the press captured young male members of the rebel army getting married in rebel uniform, or even marriages in which both bride and groom were in uniform.[22] While mass marriage initiatives stemmed from an existing liberal preoccupation with legality, images and perhaps the meanings of marriage ceremonies were also changing as they incorporated new symbols of political mobilization.

Why did couples join these collective weddings? Some scholars have suggested that many Cuban women were anxious to have formal papers.[23] Oral sources suggest a combination of reasons, including political inspiration and the logistical and financial ease of the new ceremonies. For example, Norberta Rivas, a working-class Afro-Cuban woman from Havana interviewed in 1979, never formalized her first partnership. "We didn't get married . . . because we couldn't. With what money? That was costly, because you had to pay the judge, you had to prepare all the paperwork, you had to get birth certificates of both parties, all of that was costly."[24] Rivas's parents accepted her cohabitation as long as it was "with the idea to [eventually] get married."[25] Years later, after the revolution, her second longtime partner suggested they get married in one of the new collective weddings. By that time they had been living together for some thirty-five years; she was about sixty, and he was roughly seventy-five. They had no biological children but had raised an informally adopted daughter (*hija de crianza*). They only married after the revolution, Rivas explained, "because we had never thought of doing it [before]. We lived well like that, we went everywhere [together] like a married couple."[26] Her partner was a Spanish immigrant who worked for the municipality; his friends, mostly black Cubans employed by the city government, never inquired about the couple's legal status. "He introduced me as his wife, there was no discrimination in that sense."[27]

Rivas's story suggests that while working- and lower-middle-class *habaneros* preferred legal marriage, especially for a young woman, they accepted cohabitation in practice, and unwed couples faced minimal social stigma from their peers.[28] Rivas and her partner may have been primarily motivated to join a collective wedding by political considerations, since both were dedicated revolutionary supporters, as well as the fact that it was free and convenient. State officials helped the couple prepare the necessary paperwork and summoned them by telegram to a collective wedding on a particular date.[29] Rivas enjoyed the collective marriage ceremony, which was held at Havana's Workers' Palace in the presence of Minister Yabur himself. But she did not tell any of her friends. "I did it hush-hush, because [people] would have made fun of me," she confessed, more sheepish than proud to finally tie the knot. "Two old folks!"[30]

Housing, Leisure, and the Revolutionary Family

In retrospect, we can see Operation Matrimony as part of a series of early reforms intended to bolster and improve the popular-class family. The years 1959 and 1960 also witnessed initiatives to introduce healthy popular pastimes and more modern family housing. The vision of moderate family reform embodied in these initiatives partly reflected the strength of liberals in the new administration in this early period. As Louis Pérez has written, many of the reforms of 1959 were "devised and implemented not by radicals, but by liberals, Protestants, and graduates of U.S. schools, who, in fact, carried the moral of North American value systems to their logical conclusions."[31] The ministries that led these reforms were all headed by figures affiliated with the prerevolutionary Ortodoxo Party or with the Twenty-Sixth of July Movement, including Justice Minister Yabur, Housing Institute director Pastorita Núñez, and Minister of Public Works Manuel Ray—that is, figures of the Center-Left, not the most radical flank of the revolutionary coalition.

The revolutionary provision of housing was imbued with several layers of meaning. On the one hand, the urban reform of 1959 reflected the long-standing concern among Cuban social reformers that housing scarcity and speculation in Havana had led to overcrowding, inflated rents, and unsanitary and "promiscuous" conditions among the urban working class.[32] The Twenty-Sixth of July Movement's earliest political program, as pronounced by Fidel Castro in a 1953 speech, revealed an acute awareness of the urban housing problem in particular, while also acknowledging the inferior and unstable housing in the countryside.[33] Urban slum dwellers and to some extent rural squatters (*precaristas*) had, in this view, long been victims of unrestrained market abuses, and the forced lowering of rents and government construction of affordable housing were the natural first steps toward implementing social justice.

On the other hand, a more paternalistic political logic persisted alongside what one could call the more rational economic discourse toward housing outlined above. This other logic implied that the popular classes received housing in exchange for service to the revolution, either as a reward for their participation in the insurrection against Batista (this was the subtext of many of the early development initiatives in the Sierra Maestra) or to ensure their subsequent defense of the revolution if and when the U.S. government invaded the island. The idea was visualized in an advertisement placed by a nationalized paint company in late 1960, by which time rumors of an imminent military invasion were widespread. A drawing shows a man in militia uniform with a rifle standing guard in the foreground. In the background another man paints a tract house, characteristic of the low-cost housing then being constructed by the new housing institute, Instituto Nacional de Ahorro y Vivienda (INAV). The ad's text reads, "One with the rifle . . . the other with the paintbrush, both help protect the house the Revolution gave you."[34] Thus male heads of households simultaneously became property owners and citizen-soldiers by receiving a home from the government in exchange for armed defense of the revolution.

The notion that the provision of housing gave ordinary Cubans a spiritual as well as material stake in the revolution was discursively linked to notions of family. Indeed, government discourse was quite specific about *families* as the recipients of housing. (In fact, single individuals were last in line to receive housing through the urban reform.)[35] For example, in a November 1960 speech to Cuban workers employed at the U.S. naval base at Guantánamo, Castro asked them to make certain sacrifices in order to avoid exacerbating tensions with the U.S. government.[36] In exchange, he promised the construction of new housing units in a speech that loosely yet unequivocally associated the ideas of family, patriotism, and honor with the revolutionary state's provision of housing. As Castro explained, the beneficiaries of the housing reform would receive more than simply a physical dwelling, more than "a material piece of property." The families that lived in these houses, whom he described as the children and wife of "a worker," would be given more than the opportunity to live in a pleasant home. "We also want to let you have the honor of what this means to you and to the family of each one of you. . . . These are not just houses . . . they are more like medals which the revolution has pinned on the chests of the true revolutionaries, the true patriots, the true Cubans."[37] Castro's speech reinforced the notion of a male "worker" or head of household whose family the revolution recognized and honored with housing.

One finds a related reference to new homes as providing Cuban families with a stake in the revolution, and therefore something to fight for, as well as becoming the metaphorical site of struggle against the foreign invader, in a series of ads placed in newspapers by the INAV, directed by Pastorita Núñez, one of the few women leaders of the insurrectionary period to be rewarded with a prominent government position in 1959. The ads refer to a house of one's own as a "trench" from which to defend the revolution. In response to "foreign aggressions," one ad explained that the INAV had constructed and distributed 124 housing units: "124 more families that now have their trench. 124 families that now have a house of their own. Let them come! So they can see a united people gaining their liberty and a revolutionary government working tirelessly!"[38] The distribution of housing presumably ensured the loyalty of Cuban families who would now struggle to defend their new social rights. Thus the revolutionary leadership viewed the provision of housing not simply from the pragmatic perspective of necessary shelter, or only as a fundamental human right and a necessary component of social justice, but also as reflecting and even constructing the new revolutionary subjects and the revolutionary family.

The government announced ambitious projects for building several planned communities in its first years in power. Although these were not always carried out, the plans for these new "cities" in 1959 and 1960 reveal the leadership's vision of the rationally ordered community, family, and citizen that would characterize the new Cuba.[39] For example, plans for the so-called City of Construction, a planned development of roughly ten large housing units to be built from scratch in an undeveloped area of Havana to house construction workers, reveal the influence in Cuba of the various projects of utopian social engineering that were then widespread in Latin America.[40] The proposed community—marked by clean lines, integration of buildings and gardens, planned traffic flows, and so on—reflects the modernist influence that underlay other projects for ideal cities, such as Brasília, the most obvious contemporary model.[41] One contemporary economist criticized the seemingly bourgeois mentality behind such plans, noting that housing units were "designed with an abundance of fixtures and gadgets, almost all of them of U.S. manufacture," and that these early projects "reflected American middle-class standards rather than an attempt to meet the needs of a country as poor and short of housing as Cuba."[42]

Even more revealing is the plan for the apartment interiors: a tasteful modern single-family apartment, with three bedrooms, spare contemporary styling, and a rationally ordered spatial layout. The plans also included the creation of a recreation area with a theater, a pool and other sports facilities, and "popular laundries" that would help liberate women from their domestic burdens.[43] Plans for new housing thus also implied the remolding of working-class families, who would enjoy the efficient, labor-saving services that liberated women and the healthy pastimes that strengthened rather than debilitated working men.

Similarly, by constructing Workers' Social Circles (Círculos Sociales Obreros), desegregating beaches, and encouraging "popular tourism," the government attempted to provide family-oriented, healthy leisure activities for the popular classes, while it simultaneously limited sites of "vice" such as pool halls and—with far less publicity—circumscribed prostitution.[44] The Workers' Social Circles converted former sites of elite associations into workers' clubs. Before their formation, according to Fidel Castro, the working class (that is, working-class men) had no place to socialize: "They had to go to the *bodega* on the corner to drink a beer."[45] For a modest membership fee, the new social circles would provide a wide array of sports facilities and training, offering workingmen and their families the chance to learn previously elite sports such as fencing, swimming, gymnastics, and judo.[46] The Workers' Social Circles were intended to provide a site for festivities, including limited alcohol consumption (permitted on weekend afternoons only), and also to encourage more intellectual pursuits by providing libraries, reading rooms, and lectures on theater and other fine arts. Their construction paralleled the closing of racially segregated private social clubs, including, eventually, Afro-Cuban associations.[47]

To some extent such initiatives suggest that the government in its early days conceived of working-class uplift partly as remaking popular-class families in a middle-class image. Appeals to new forms of leisure were often specifically family-oriented and emphasized the new accessibility of pursuits formerly restricted to the middle classes and elites. For example, advertisements for "popular tourism" featured a white nuclear family with suitcases and a beach ball about to board a bus rather than a private car. "Now everyone can travel [even] without having money," the ad explained. Another ad featured photos of racially integrated groups of Cubans at the beach, hotels, restaurants, and other recreational areas. The Institute of Tourism promised to "keep constructing new places of recreation, rest, and distraction so that you, Cuban, can enjoy them with your family."[48]

The family uplift projects initiated by the revolutionary government in its earliest months were not aimed at radical transformation. Rather, they sought to bolster a heterosexual, nuclear family, with legally married partners and a male worker at the helm. Yet the early government initiatives also had more transcendent potential. They reclaimed, at least symbolically, sites of elite leisure and identity formation for the working class. They encouraged racial integration in spaces of public socialization rather than simply at sites of employment or in political associations—a practice that was evidently a novelty for some Cubans, who referred to the new social clubs as *congrí* (rice and beans)—that is, a mixture of black and white.[49] And the reforms at least opened the possibility that women could be liberated from domestic labor through collectivized state services. As political conflict mounted after 1959, such programs took on ominous tones, and interactions between the state and the family soon became a flash point for conflict.

The Revolutionary Roles of Children and Youth

By 1960 some sectors began to perceive the new revolutionary government as a threat to the family, a charge soon exploited by a major rumor campaign about the abolition of Patria Potestad. This fear was found especially, but not exclusively, in Havana's middle class. Yet fear over state control of the family was not, in general, precipitated by the moderate programs for family reform outlined earlier. Instead, other campaigns that targeted or otherwise involved children or adolescents set off alarms. Major sources of friction in the period included the establishment of public daycare centers, the conflict between revolutionary authorities and Catholic schools, and the mass literacy campaign of 1961. It is unclear whether the leadership anticipated that these initiatives might affect the family in unwelcome ways; the measures were primarily intended to facilitate women's employment, expand education, or politically orient youths. Yet these programs indirectly affected families by mobilizing adolescents and threatening to bring young children into greater contact with the state. Cumulatively, and experienced in the context of transnational anticommunist narratives, these programs led some Cubans to view the state as attacking the family—or at least encroaching on the domestic and private sphere.

One major factor in producing anxiety over the state's influence over children and youths was the growing conflict between the revolutionary leadership and the Catholic hierarchy. The clash between church and state was not unleashed immediately. Indeed, the revolutionary goals of constructing "new men" and "a new Cuba" initially resonated with many Catholics, although they interpreted these phrases differently. Throughout 1959 and 1960, those Catholics with a social calling heartily supported the revolution's goals of ending poverty and extreme inequality, combating racism, and devoting oneself to the greater good of the collectivity.[50]

But political transformations in this period soon touched off a confrontation between revolutionary authorities and the institutional church, heightened when the Catholic Church held a large conference in Havana in November 1959 that demonstrated its strength.[51] Tension increased over the next six months, as Catholic clergy made increasingly strident declarations against communism and the revolutionary leadership and the Communist Party responded in kind.[52] By the summer of 1960, fervent revolutionaries and anticommunist Catholics were coming to blows outside churches during mass.[53]

Denunciations by the hierarchy and by lay Catholics in the growing political opposition frequently focused on the new revolutionary government's destructive impact on children and the family. The pastoral letter "Por Dios y por Cuba," released by Santiago archbishop Enrique Pérez Serantes, argued that communism "denie[d] the existence of the matrimonial link, and its indissoluble nature." Another collective letter issued by the church hierarchy stated that communism "[drove] women to leave their home in order to undertake, away from their house, the harshest tasks," and ignored families' wishes for their children's education.[54] And the Catholic intellectual Andrés Valdespino wrote in an editorial that the "ten commandments" of atheistic communism included "spy on one's parents" and "practice free love and scorn 'conjugal fidelity' as an obsolete bourgeois [practice]."[55]

As political opposition increased, some of the most militant anticommunist activists emerged from Catholic high schools, which the revolutionary leadership now denounced as hotbeds of conspiracy and misguidance.[56] In November 1960 a student strike led by Catholic school students touched off a series of revolutionary reprisals against Catholics militants, especially in the provinces.[57] The Catholic Church, now on the defensive, reasserted its power to shape children and youths.[58] In one revealing incident, Catholic activists hung leaflets around Havana the day before catechism classes were held that showed a child's face with the caption "Will this child be a believer or an atheist? It depends on you." The leaflets had been printed by the Junta Catequista Diocesana, an underground Catholic anti-Castro organization.[59] Revolutionary militias tore them down and replaced them with similar posters reading "Will this child be a patriot or a traitor? It depends on you." Catholics and revolutionaries—categories that were increasingly mutually exclusive—found themselves locked in a struggle over the nation's future, its children.

In addition to the growing conflict between church and state, the announced formation of state-run daycare centers also raised a red flag among some Cubans. As discussed in chapter 4, the most strident public calls for state-funded daycare centers first came from below beginning in 1959, when women of the Marxist Left in particular took advantage of the revolutionary opening to press for government attention to women's domestic burdens. They raised the importance of laundries, popular cafeterias, and daycare centers.[60] Prior to 1959, Cuba had only a few dozen public crèches, "charity orphanages" for the children of the poorest. There were no other public school programs for children before kindergarten, and there were no kindergartens outside the urban centers.[61] After the formation of the Federation of Cuban Women (FMC) in mid-1960, Clementina Serra was tasked with developing the new daycare centers, to be called Children's Circles (Círculos Infantiles). Serra had no experience in childcare per se, but as a member of the prerevolutionary Communist Party she had long worked on women's issues and had been provincial coordinator for the party in Camagüey Province.[62] The first Children's Circles formally opened in April 1961.[63]

No matter how nonthreatening the rationale used to publicly justify daycare centers—such as their "protection" of children or support for widows, for example—the Children's Circles touched a nerve.[64] Suspicions over the reasons for establishing a state-run daycare program must have been widespread, at least to judge by the numerous explanations of the purpose of the new daycare centers provided by the revolutionary government in print, in public speeches, and on television in the fall of 1960. In December 1960, several female panelists addressed public anxieties over daycare on a popular television show. Serra, director of the Children's Circles, explained that they would primarily help working mothers "without diminishing at all the natural love between parents and children, while also creating a more advanced youth, which the liberated country needs."[65] The speakers stressed the good formation children would receive in daycare centers, guided by professionally trained staff.

Interestingly, public government justifications of the Children's Circles did not use language about women's liberation. As noted in chapter 4, the revolutionary leadership rarely if ever used such language in this period. When government pronouncements on daycare did mention the need to unburden women, they tended to stress either the dire economic strains on working mothers or the attractions of "rational" home management.[66] But more frequently they described initiatives such as the construction of childcare centers as the cheapest and most effective way to facilitate women's integration into the labor force as the economy industrialized. As both Fidel Castro and Che Guevara argued, it made no economic sense for one woman to work while paying another woman to care for her child, for the net "loss" of women workers to the "productive" economy was the same. Collective childcare provided by the state, on the other hand, could achieve economies of scale.[67]

Yet some Cubans nevertheless viewed the new daycare centers with suspicion, interpreting the government's provision of childcare as merely disguised efforts to gain control of children. By 1961 some critics charged that the new daycare centers were simply a pretext to remove children from the family home in order to "poison their infantile souls with lies about communism." The exile publication *Bohemia Libre* warned, "Every Cuban child who enters a [state-run daycare center] will return converted into a spy against his own family."[68] In this view, daycare centers were not only a way of reducing the family's influence on a child; they were also a way for the state to infiltrate and perhaps ultimately destroy the family. As organized anti-Castro groups began to emerge, some took advantage of and bolstered those fears. As the anti-Castro group Rescate warned in its bulletin, "they are preparing a campaign called 'For the Emancipation of Women,' to oblige all children to be inscribed in a kind of census, with the intention of classifying them to intern them in state institutions, separated from their parents."[69] Such calls ironically conceded a radical feminist intent to government initiatives, linking them to intentional efforts to disrupt families. Some clandestine anti-Castro pamphlets likewise interpreted calls for gender equity within the household as "exhortations to married women to not respect their husbands" and as evidence that "Communism uses the weaker sex to develop the theory of Marx and Engels against family unity."[70] In this view, any perceived alteration of established family patterns was evidence of deeper machinations to produce family conflict and increase social control.

The 1961 Literacy Campaign

The construction of public daycare centers and the gradual curbing of the Catholic Church's public power raised suspicion among some Cubans. But the revolution's new educational initiatives proved a watershed in creating anxiety over state intrusion into the family. The first efforts to reform and expand education began in 1959 and 1960. As the revolutionary leadership sought to transform education to make it available to the poor, especially in underserved areas, it first established enormous "school-cities" (*ciudades escolares*), large residential educational camps, often in the countryside, where children from the surrounding rural areas would temporarily reside for schooling. The measure raised the specter of the militarization of young boys and their "brainwashing" in Marxist ideology far from their families, despite the government's description of the school-cities as predominantly intended to provide education for children in rural regions that had little or no educational infrastructure.[71] In fact, the government itself often described these initiatives in martial language. It likened the experience of rural children in the new schools and that of young people in the various new associations such as youth brigades for voluntary labor, the Association of Rebel Youth, and the youth sections of the popular militia, to the experience of rebirth that members of the rebel army had undergone through the physical rigors and comradeship they had found in the Sierra Maestra. The school-cities were also one of the new initiatives that began to mobilize urban middle-class teens and young adults, such as college students, some of whom volunteered to travel to rural zones such as the Sierra Maestra in 1960 for initial teacher training courses that included quasi-military endurance hikes. Many of them subsequently asked to work as volunteer teachers in the region.[72]

The first efforts at extending rural education were staffed primarily by volunteers, including Twenty-Sixth of July Movement militants. But the massive, island-wide literacy campaign of 1961 introduced a new paradigm that proved a turning point in mobilizing youth for the revolution. The plan, as announced by Fidel Castro in the fall of 1960, was highly ambitious and also highly disruptive. The school year would end early, and all schools would remain closed for the following eight months, during which time students from sixth grade and up could be mobilized for the campaign. Thus urban children as young as thirteen departed for the countryside to live and work with peasant families for months while they taught their hosts to read.[73] The scale of the mobilization was enormous. The campaign successfully utilized the newly formed mass organizations and the emerging government publicity machine. Eventually more than a million Cubans took part, either as students or *brigadistas*, as the young literacy teachers were dubbed. The literacy campaign mobilized more Cubans than any other single revolutionary program and had an enormous social impact.[74]

Beyond its sheer scale, the project of bringing knowledge to the countryside was deeply political. The revolutionary leadership viewed the campaign as an extension of the fabled encounter of rural and urban combatants in the Sierra. Young civilians could now replicate the purifying and politicizing experience of the rebel army members by joining the "army" of educators. The redemption and recognition of the peasantry, whom the leadership credited with having sacrificed greatly for the insurrection, were also a powerful motive. More broadly, the campaign placed rural illiteracy within a larger narrative of capitalist exploitation and underdevelopment. In many ways, the campaign was the culmination of the revolutionary transformation of education, which the leadership now definitively associated with national liberation, the end of capitalist exploitation, and subaltern empowerment.[75] The campaign was more than simply an educational initiative; it was a kind of political crusade.[76] This was reinforced by the fact that the literacy campaign kicked off just as the Bay of Pigs invasion began.

Despite the near-universal agreement on the need to improve rural education, the way the literacy campaign was conducted sparked distrust among some urban parents. It prompted a spectrum of reaction, ranging from mild disapproval to zealous opposition. Some parents opposed the literacy campaign because they objected to the removal of young teenagers from the protection of the family home, not because they necessarily opposed improving rural education. They disapproved of their children living with strangers and doing manual labor such as cane cutting, especially in rural regions, which some viewed as "unsanitary" and "primitive."[77] Some parents also criticized the fact that the leadership insisted on continuing with the literacy campaign during the Bay of Pigs invasion. For more conservative critics of the revolution, the whole initiative smacked of a world upside down, in which middle-class urban children were sent to the countryside for indoctrination and rustic labor, while peasant girls were being put up in the most luxurious hotels in Havana to receive classes in literacy and dressmaking.[78] Thus for some Cubans, these educational initiatives upended country and city, banishing urban children to a countryside that was imagined as a disordered, primitive, or dangerous space.

For others, the mobilizing of young students and their long stint away from home in some quasi-military "camp" raised the possibility of indoctrination.[79] As one woman in Camagüey wrote in a letter, the literacy campaign had at first seemed "admirable" to her. "But now when I see groups of children marching down the street, shouting 'To the Wall!' ['*Paredón! Paredón!*'] or 'Viva Nikita!,' then all the beauty disappears."[80] She rued the specter of children marching in military formation, calling for violent retribution or praising Soviet leaders. In a similar vein, a Havana man wrote, "The worst thing of all is the damage being done to the minds of Cuban children and youths. They are the section of the population most heavily indoctrinated, and as their minds are weak and easy to convince it's only logical to think that the seed will bear fruit more rapidly [among them]." He interpreted their jubilant street celebrations upon their return to Havana as evidence of the fact that they had been "thoroughly indoctrinated."[81] While official propaganda focused on the magical encounter of enthusiastic urban youths and grateful peasants, counternarratives of the literacy campaign stressed state control and brainwashing of youths.

The literacy campaign also dovetailed with the state's increasing tendency to appeal to youths as political agents in their own right. Photos of the literacy *brigadistas* show how young they were: mostly teenagers, with some perhaps as young as twelve. As Anita Casavantes Bradford argues, the revolution refashioned children's lives in ways that "challenged middle-class understandings of childhood as a time of dependence, innocence, and play."[82] The youth of many new teachers, as well as new coming of age rites associated with political performance, made "the rite of passage to adulthood as much about the child's relationship to the state—and the authority conferred by his or her assumption of duties to the revolution—as it was about any developmental milestone."[83]

The participation of teenage girls in the literacy campaign caused particular consternation among urban parents, even among some who otherwise supported the initiative.[84] The idea of teenage girls living in the countryside, unaccompanied by older relatives and in the presence of unknown peasant men, suggested that the literacy campaign might threaten traditional practices of chaperoning and shielding young women. Even for the revolution's staunch supporters, this could be hard to swallow.[85] For example, one former *brigadista* recounted that her own mother, the head of a major public high school in Havana at the time, held a special assembly for parents to assuage their fears and persuade them to give their children permission to participate. And yet she herself had not yet signed the release forms for her own two daughters, ages thirteen and fourteen, to go.[86]

Sexuality was the sticking point. Rumors abounded of girls coming back from the literacy campaign pregnant, as did accusations of promiscuity among the young *brigadistas*.[87] It was jokingly said that if 1961 was the "Year of Education," 1962 would be the "Year of Maternity."[88] (Indeed, the first few years of the revolution did witness a baby boom, although for other reasons, such as the more rigorous enforcement of the ban on abortion, the disruption of sales of birth control, and a general excitement about the future among revolutionary supporters.)[89] Less humorously, it was alleged that the government was establishing residential centers—perhaps even abortion clinics—for the teenage girls who came back pregnant after sexual encounters with locals, with their fellow *brigadistas*, or with the older foreign technicians who were said to have accompanied them.[90] These negative fantasies were haunted by racial specters, as white middle-class parents particularly feared interracial unions.[91]

If some parents merely feared their daughters' vulnerability due to the lack of family supervision, a more extreme view held that young girls were *actively* being taught to engage in premarital sex. According to James Baker, director of an American school in Havana and eventually an instrumental figure in Operation Peter Pan, during the literacy campaign "girls who had been carefully chaperoned all their lives were taught that sex was a natural need, which should be satisfied, as was hunger for food." As a result of this "campaign to break down . . . family values," he alleged, so many teenage girls returned to Havana pregnant that a special abortion clinic was established.[92]

Revolutionary authorities tried to deflect some parents' criticisms by announcing various concessions: girls would be housed with peasant families in small villages in safe areas. Boys, on the other hand, might be sent to more remote areas, where they slept in rural schools or other community buildings.[93] Special offices were set up to keep family members informed about the young *brigadistas*' whereabouts and activities.[94] With great fanfare, Fidel Castro invited a group of mothers of *brigadistas* on a surprise visit to the training camp in Varadero, all expenses paid, on Mother's Day 1961.[95] Parents were even allowed to accompany their children as long as they signed up to be literacy workers too.[96] As the Cuban literary critic Luisa Campuzano has argued, the state thus offered a patriarchal "revolutionary pact," in which it promised to uphold and respect existing gender roles and reproduce the paternal authority of the home by explicitly promising to protect the *brigadistas*.[97] Some parents were mollified by these concessions. Others sought informal ways to strategically place their children near relatives in rural areas.

The most anxious parents undertook protests. Groups of women traveled to the *brigadista* training camp in Varadero beach in order to reclaim their children or denounce their daughters' "seduction" by fellow *brigadistas*.[98] And some angered parents found common ground with the organized anti-Castro opposition. Opposition propaganda fanned parents' fears by indulging in speculation about the worst repercussions of the literacy campaign. Stories of the lost innocence and destroyed families that lay in the wake of the literacy campaign continued to circulate into the mid-1960s, suggesting that these dramatic stories formed something of a parable about the revolution's destruction of the family. For example, the pamphlet *Cuba: Anécdotas de la enseñanza comunista*, published by a group of anti-Castro educators, tells the dramatic story of one idealistic fifteen-year-old girl who wanted to "contribute to the construction of a new Cuba" and volunteered for the literacy campaign in the Sierra. She returned home months later, pregnant after being raped by a militia member. Her father, a doctor in Las Tunas, was so distraught that he committed suicide with a shot to the head. The young girl followed suit by dousing herself in alcohol and lighting herself on fire. "The literacy campaign, a pretext for immorality and the uprooting of youths from the family's protection [*potestad hogareña*] bore its impressive fruits," the pamphlet concluded.[99]

The Gender Chaos of Revolution

Like a kaleidoscope, opposition allegations embellished and distorted, but they also reflected genuine changes. While the leadership did not preach free love in the literacy campaign training camps, it is true that many young women and girls who participated in rural educational initiatives defied traditional gender roles and expectations.[100] By leaving home unattended, asserting their desires to participate even when their parents disapproved, and adopting quasi-military uniforms and gear, young women *brigadistas* transgressed contemporary middle-class gender norms.[101] Ironically, their cosmopolitan, middle-class bearing and habits—such as smoking and wearing slacks—also caused consternation among the more traditional peasants, who "saw in the [female] literacy teacher the liberal, libertine woman from Havana."[102] Caught between disapproval on two fronts, young women literacy workers must have felt they were striking out into uncharted cultural territory and must have experienced a particularly heightened kind of self-awareness as a result. And for some youths, those exhilarating forays into new locales and new personal roles, unaccompanied by family, must have provided opportunities for sexual experimentation.[103]

As the revolution became increasingly anticapitalist and anti-imperialist, with the leadership publicly embracing socialism by May 1961, some young people questioned the future of sexuality and marriage. The Association of Rebel Youth—soon to be rechristened the Union of Communist Youth—addressed these questions directly in a 1961 Valentine's Day edition of their publication *Mella*. The cover featured an idealized image of the new partnership. Two young, white *milicianos* in gender-specific uniforms hold hands and gaze at each other longingly. A sketchy background scene suggests a future of industrialization and dignified workers' housing. The magazine's editorial explained that its cover image represented "love between revolutionaries," which should be based on common political ideals, not materialistic expectations.[104] A long article walked readers through a classic Marxist explanation of how the family and the bourgeois institution of marriage emerged historically as a vehicle for passing on private property.[105] But this prompted the question: If two young revolutionaries loved each other, yet scorned bourgeois marriage, what then? The article argued that a true revolutionary should seek love and commitment with a partner who held similar political ideals. They should emulate "proletarian marriage with love." "And free love? Well, free love has never been revolutionary, it's the decayed fruit of petty bourgeois ideology, unstable, vacillating, ambiguous. It's the idea of the 'rebels without a cause,' who don't aspire to change society, only to justify their sexual libertinage. . . . This has nothing to do with the revolutionary ideology of the working class, which has never proposed free love."[106]

In retrospect, this vision of disciplined, monogamous, intraracial, heterosexual love hardly seems threatening. Yet the passage indeed questions traditional or "bourgeois" marriage. For example, the emphasis on political compatibility above other criteria implied that youths might seek partners of different social backgrounds whom they met in the new mass organizations, beyond the bounds of traditional familial networks and without parental approval.[107]

Similarly, while opposition claims of political "indoctrination" were exaggerated, it is clear that the revolution's educational initiatives and especially its new mass organizations were intended to serve as platforms for the rudimentary political orientation of youth. The literacy campaign of 1961 was decidedly political in its intent to uplift rural areas, empower with knowledge, and form future revolutionary subjects. The campaign was explicitly viewed by the leadership as helping to construct future revolutionary subjects both in the countryside and among the young urban cadres who were the campaign's foot soldiers.[108] And it did indeed prove a life-changing experience for many *brigadistas*, although this was due less to the political content of the teaching materials they were given and more to a combined sense of coming of age, bearing witness to rural poverty, and participating in a vast political movement.[109]

By mobilizing and politicizing the younger generation in particular, the revolution's initiatives could also have the effect of introducing generational rifts. For example, one woman recalled the ramifications of her decision to join the literacy campaign. An orphaned fifteen-year-old being raised in Havana by her grandmother, she was inspired by the fact that all her classmates had signed up to join the literacy campaign. She was determined to go as well, despite her grandmother's opposition, even at the risk of forfeiting family unity. "[My grandmother] said, 'If you leave this house you won't come back to it, and you won't be part of the family anymore.' So I said, 'OK, I may not be part of the family anymore, but I'm going.' "[110] The anecdote

The 1961 Valentine's Day edition of Revista Mella *offers an image of courtship in the new Cuba: two militia members holding hands. (Private collection of Anna Veltfort)*

gives us a sense of the high stakes and sense of passion of the period, as family members, often of different generations, took competing positions.

Indeed, interviews and contemporary letters suggest that clashes between children and parents were frequent in this period, since younger people tended to be more supportive of the revolution than their elders. Alfonso Jiménez, a Santiago youth who initially supported the revolution, recalled that he and his mother "had fights all the time," as his mother denounced the government for having nationalized some of the family's property. "And I would say, 'Look mom, it's our turn! [nos tocó!] It's for the good of the country!' "[111] By mobilizing and politicizing the younger generation in particular, the revolutionary changes often strained relations between parents and their adolescent children.

Perhaps inevitably, the state began to encroach upon the private sphere as the revolution centralized and consolidated. As Smith and Padula note, "Through a range of economic and social policies, the Cuban government literally and figuratively entered the home and became, for good or ill, part of the family."[112] Public daycare centers, new rural schools, and other initiatives that mobilized children and youths were new channels through which the revolutionary leadership could take a far more active role in the formation of future citizens. And by nationalizing private social clubs and private schools, the leadership simultaneously shut down the most important socializing agents of the urban middle and upper class. For some Cubans, these transformations were experienced as an assault on their existing social networks, the disintegration of the prerevolutionary social worlds from which they had drawn their identities. This sensation helps explain the common allegations among exiles that the revolution had "destroyed the family" and introduced divisions or "hatred." As one Cuban exile explained in the 1960s, "suddenly a brutal change came into our lives. Our democratic, religious, and cultural institutions were crushed overnight. There was complete disunity in the Cuban family—fathers against sons, brothers against brothers, childhood friends converted into enemies."[113] Even initiatives that may not have been intended to affect the family—such as the literacy campaign or other volunteer efforts—inevitably drew women and children from the family home. Thus the previously "private" worlds of the home, church, or neighborhood might now be experienced as a terrain of social conflict and state intrusion.

Anxiety over these changes was compounded by the fact that these social transformations coincided with political polarization, a growing conflict with the U.S. government, the nationalization of large properties, and changes in access to information that may have encouraged the proliferation of rumors. Indeed, the leadership's general lack of transparency regarding its decision making occasionally resulted in awkward coincidences between rumors and reality. For example, as Fidel Castro admitted, "rumors" that the government was conducting a census of children were in fact true, but he blamed a midlevel official within the administration of the Children's Circles for undertaking said census without permission from above. Such bureaucratic errors, Castro admonished, "fit the counter-revolution like a glove" in its quest to "confuse the masses."[114] At the same time, throughout 1960, many Cuban newspapers and magazines entered into direct conflict with the government. As these conflicts escalated, they culminated in government intervention. Once nationalized, a newspaper's overall tone and appearance, not to mention its editorial positions, changed drastically.[115] In the same year, the CIA established a radio signal on Swan Island from which it broadcast anti-Castro programs, often given to hyperbole. Thus, by mid-1960 many Cubans had access to competing sources of information, perhaps none of which seemed entirely credible. The resulting accumulation of suspicion and hearsay contributed to the spread and reception of rumors about Patria Potestad, which seemed emblematic of a broader onslaught on an entire way of life.

Such concerns may have had special resonance for the urban middle class, but they were not limited to it. In 1969 the sociologist Geoffrey Fox conducted a series of interviews with recently arrived working-class Cuban men in Chicago and found that many expressed intense anxiety over their loss of control over women's lives. Although they did not necessarily view this as part of an international "Communist" plot, they resented what they experienced as a changing balance of power within previously patriarchal family relations. These days, as one interviewee said, "neither the father, nor the mother nor the husband rules [a woman]." They repeatedly expressed opposition to the idea of women performing "rough" work, such as agricultural labor, which they viewed as defeminizing and therefore threatening to existing gender roles. And their fundamental belief that women would naturally fall prey to the sexual advances of men in public settings without the protection of their male relatives left them overwhelmed by women's autonomous participation in the bevy of new revolutionary activities such as the militia, the mass organizations, and voluntary labor.[116] While these same émigrés critiqued other issues, such as the state control of unions, food rationing, and in some cases racial desegregation, changes to gender roles seemed to strike a special chord, inciting nearly universal condemnation.

As Fox concluded, "'Women's liberation,' to the extent it had occurred in Cuba, created extreme discomfort among these working class men and may even have been the main source of their rage and a contributing factor to their total rejection of the revolution."[117]

Gender transgressions are seemingly central to how revolutions are experienced by their detractors. Thus critics of the Cuban Revolution caricatured the leadership as somehow inappropriately gendered, such as in comic drawings of a slender and effeminate Raúl or an overbearing and emasculate Vilma. They alleged that revolutionary initiatives were provoking inappropriate forms of sexuality, such as promiscuity among teenage girls on the literacy campaign. Or they claimed that the revolution would separate parents and children in the Patria Potestad rumor campaign. These associations were not limited to Cuba. As Greg Grandin has noted in the case of Guatemala's 1954 revolution, coffee planters claimed that if the Guatemalan reformer Jacobo Arbenz won the presidency, "women would be raised up to the same height as men and children would be taken away."[118] So, too, did an imagined connection between rural revolutionary campaigns and women's compromised chastity find expression elsewhere. In Karen Kampwirth's study of the Nicaraguan revolution, one of her interviewees argued that the Sandinistas "prostituted young girls by sending them off to harvest coffee, where they had to practice free love. That was what made [the Sandinistas] fall."[119] The focus on the reversal of gender roles or upheaval in the family draws its power from the implication that revolution is unnatural, for it upends God-given, time-honored sexual differences and destroys that most intimate and meaningful of units, the family.

The Patria Potestad Rumor Campaign of 1960–1961

As we have seen, the vast societal changes of the first few years of the revolution laid the groundwork for anxiety over changes to parental authority, children's education, and youth sexuality. These burgeoning anxieties were sharpened into fear and even hysteria over state destruction of the family by the Patria Potestad rumor campaign, a program of intentional misinformation carried out by the burgeoning anti-Castro movement. The rumors alleged that the leadership had drafted but not yet made public a new law to remove all children over the age of five from their families. The state would then indoctrinate them in some state-run facility and eventually transport them to the Soviet Union for further training.[120] In effect, the rumors claimed that responsibility for and authority over children—encapsulated in the legal concept Patria Potestad—would pass from individual parents to the state.

The rumors began circulating in exile publications in the summer of 1960,[121] then were broadcast that fall on Radio Swan, the exile-run station based on an island off the coast of Honduras with support from the CIA.[122] Word of the impending abrogation of Patria Potestad then spread further by word of mouth, by phone, and by flyers and handouts distributed throughout the country in churches and other locales. Some flyers reproduced a document that appeared to be an actual draft of a law signed by Fidel Castro and other leaders. The rumors waxed and waned throughout 1960, reemerging in the summer of 1961.[123]

Initially, organized anti-Castro groups spread the rumors intentionally. The rumors then gained a life of their own, snowballing into widespread belief as individuals persuaded by the rumors repeated them to friends and family. But the campaign may have been originally conceived of by the CIA, which drew on its recent experience of the destabilization and overthrow of the Guatemalan government in 1954. Themes involving women, children, the elderly, and religion were thought to be particularly effective, and the CIA hoped to mobilize women and the church hierarchy in the anticommunist struggle.[124]

Still, we should not conceptualize the campaign as something imported by the CIA wholesale into a new context, nor did the CIA simply create these fears out of thin air. The CIA drew on and exploited local concerns.[125] Nevertheless, the CIA's involvement lent ammunition to those existing anxieties. The CIA offered funding, infrastructure, political support, and protection to the small anti-Castro organizations that disseminated the rumor throughout the island. More importantly, the CIA helped map local concerns over the family onto the broader East-West ideological conflict, connecting events in Cuba to a well-established anticommunist narrative that the U.S. government had helped disseminate globally.

As historians such as Mary Brennan and Laura Belmonte have shown, in the 1950s, U.S. government agencies depicted the family as a crucial locus of struggle between communism and democracy. They portrayed the United States as a haven for the middle-class nuclear family, while alleging that Communist governments "divided families in order to fill distant factories, collective farms, and the military."[126] CIA director J. Edgar Hoover was particularly instrumental in articulating communism as a godless threat to the family. Under communism, Hoover explained in 1956, children " 'would be placed in nurseries and special indoctrination schools.' Women, relieved of child-care responsibilities, would go to work in factories and mines with the men."[127] The emphasis on women being forced to perform hard labor under communism revealed the class and racialized fears inherent in American anticommunism. As Brennan notes, such manual labor was often performed by immigrants or nonwhites. The notion that "middle-class white women might be thrust into the gutters to pick up trash or driven onto the assembly line" was nightmarish.[128] The focus on morality and the family meant that, within militant anticommunist circles, mothers were seen as lynchpins of anticommunist resistance, the very foundations of a strong America. Conversely, women who failed to raise their children correctly might leave them open to Communist indoctrination.[129]

Agencies such as the United States Information Agency (USIA) made a concerted effort to circulate these ideas globally through films, comic books, and posters which claimed that Communist regimes turned children against their parents, made young women "slave laborers," and destroyed families. For example, posters distributed in Asia showed Communist soldiers forcibly separating a woman from her children, a nightmarish image that would now reappear in Cuba and throughout Latin America.[130] Although scholarship on anticommunism in Cuba in the late the 1940s and early 1950s focuses almost exclusively on battles for control of organized labor, we might assume that Cuba's close historical ties with the United States and the USIA's work with Cuban media outlets facilitated the local reproduction of these images.[131]

In Havana, especially within Catholic middle-class circles, the Patria Potestad rumor campaign produced fear bordering on frenzy. Interviews refer to the "collective hysteria" that marked many middle-class households at the time.[132] Rumors claimed that children left unattended on the streets could be picked up by government trucks and disappeared, eventually resurfacing in socialist countries. As one Havana man wrote in a letter to a friend: "The nephew of the guy who cleaned for you was taken, because he went to the *bodega* to get change and was found alone. They're picking up kids as if they were dogs, and disappearing them. There's panic over it."[133]

Even more revealing is the number of young children—over 14,000, mostly from middle-class Havana families—sent unaccompanied to the United States through Operation Peter Pan, a joint initiative involving an underground network within Cuba, the Catholic Church in Miami, and the U.S. government.[134] While specific rumors over Patria Potestad were not the only factor in parents' decision to send their children, they are frequently mentioned in interviews along with a series of other concerns regarding danger to women, youth, and the family. For example, when asked in an interview why his parents had decided to send his younger siblings abroad, Alfonso Jiménez recalled their fear caused by constant rumors of children being forcibly taken from their homes and sent to Russia, as well as an anti-Castro flyer that featured an image of a woman being forced to perform hard labor—evidence of dangerous and unnatural defeminization, and perhaps symbolic of racial darkening, as discussed above.[135]

Mothers in the Front Line of Defense

The Patria Potestad rumor campaign had particular implications for women. Apocalyptic claims about the destruction of the family pivoted around changes to gender and sexuality, particularly the fear that women's revolutionary transformation would render them unable to protect the family from the state. The pamphlet *El comunismo destruye la familia en Cuba*, published by an anti-Castro group in exile, demonstrates how these charges all came together. The forced defeminization of a woman through militarization, heavy labor, and removal from the home changed her physical appearance and her sense of self. "With her femininity destroyed, she transforms from a being endowed with the ability to give life into an abject animal, instrument of death." She now only vaguely remembered the former attractions of family life, "because for a Communist, there is nothing other than the Party."[136] Another exiled anti-Castro group referred simultaneously to defeminization and sexual violation, arguing that "under the terrible communist Cuban regime, women are submitted to a military system, are obligated to wear rough uniforms, use rifles and machine guns, and to satisfy the perversions [*aberraciones*] of the vile red leaders."[137] Since women anchored the family, their forced transformation and abandonment of the home led to the family's implosion.

This chain of logic ensured that the opposition press frequently focused on women's military training and the purported gender-bending it caused. For example, the bulletin *Acción Cubana* captured one man's impression of a "chaotic and repugnant" Cuba as he watched militia members aggressively search people at the airport: "Pants on the legs of women and long manes on the heads of men are seen everywhere," he recounted.[138] Similarly, a brief editorial entitled "Little lady [*cubanita*], why have you fallen into this?" in the exile magazine *Bohemia Libre* was illustrated with an image of two women with long rifles. The editorial urged women not to collaborate with the revolutionary regime, citing proper gender roles: "Don't abandon your place, little lady. Your place is in your home, or your school, or in your work place. Not in the street, giving or taking orders. Not spying on anyone. Not turning anyone in. Haven't you been told that that was never a dignified activity for women [*oficio para las cubanas*], little lady?"[139] The conversion of innocent young girls into violent revolutionaries or counterrevolutionaries, the disdain for the gender-bending appearance of the new female militias, fears over the disintegration of marriage and the family, and women's physical transcendence of their traditional spaces all combined into a narrative about the sexual disorder unleashed by the revolution.

The burden of sustaining the family against these destructive forces seemed to fall disproportionately on women. Both the growing anti-Castro movement and the CIA may have seen women as natural antagonists. According to one CIA source, "Cuban women have become the leaders of opposition activity and urge their husbands to undertake action to alleviate the present situation."[140] The radio broadcasts and printed materials disseminating the Patria Potestad rumors often prodded mothers into the symbolic front line of defense, referencing women's allegedly natural instinct to protect their children and the family home. Radio broadcasts included shrill exhortations directly addressed to mothers. "Cuban mothers," one broadcast exclaimed, "don't let them take your children away! The new law of the Revolutionary Government will be to take them away from you when they turn five and return them at age eighteen, by that time converted into materialist [i.e., Marxist] monsters. Fidel will turn into the supreme mother of Cuba."[141] The image of Fidel as "supreme mother" raised the frightening prospect of the state, embodied in the revolution's highest leader, replacing the nurturing role of a mother and family. Alongside frequent references to Raúl Castro's purported effeminacy or homosexuality in the exile press, such charges sought to discredit the revolutionary leadership by alleging gender inversion and sexual transgression.[142]

The rumor campaign appealed to women with apocalyptic imagery, describing the anti-Castro struggle as one of life or death. It suggested that a mother should be prepared to sacrifice her own life for her family and for the anti-Castro cause. As one broadcast said, "Cuban mother, the government can take away your clothes, your food, and even kill you, but the right to raise your child can't be taken away by anyone. . . . Offer your life to a just cause like ours, before turning your child over to the beast."[143] The broadcasts and printed materials appealed to women, sometimes in oblique terms, to support one of the opposition groups then growing in strength. At the same time, the pronouncements characterized the anti-Castro struggle as something otherworldly, beyond everyday politics: a struggle for the soul. As one full-page ad in the magazine *Bohemia Libre* read: "Cuban mother . . . the classic dictatorships of Cuba . . . could only take away your child's life. The Castro dictatorship aspires to more: it aspires to take away his soul—that is, his religion, his sense of nationality, his dignity as a free person."[144] Women themselves sometimes reproduced the extremity of such claims. In one widely repeated story, fifty women in the town of Bayamo made a pact to kill their own children "rather than hand them over to Castro."[145] Opposition propaganda that exhorted women to undertake passionate and even violent displays of protective motherhood thereby reified the notion of women as self-sacrificing defenders of family.

Anti-Castro groups' more specific demands could also have serious consequences for women. For example, Cuban mothers were exhorted not to send their children to the "cemetery of souls" (public schools). As one editorial in *Bohemia Libre* proclaimed: "Cuban mother, the police state won't be able to do anything if you comply with your Cuban and Christian duty: refuse to let them take children from your tutelage. . . . Don't be afraid, against the general resistance of Cuban mothers, the police system can't do anything."[146] Removing a child from a public school or from a private school that had been nationalized was a situation not long tenable; it seemed to be premised on an expectation of either imminent exile or governmental overthrow. Furthermore, as the revolutionary leadership increasingly called on children to demonstrate patriotism and even "heroism," removing a child from school might generate unwanted attention from the authorities. As one Ministry of Education ad warned, citing Fidel Castro, "a child who doesn't study isn't a good revolutionary."[147]

Removing young children from school also sometimes forced a mother to leave her workplace. For example, one Havana woman worked as a nurse until the nationalization of schools, after which she stayed home with her five- and six-year-old children until she finally sent them alone to the United States as part of the Peter Pan exodus.[148] Her experience suggests that, at least in some cases, the fear sparked by rumors over government brainwashing of children and family destruction actually created the very insular domestic sphere they claimed to protect. Thus could claims of the destruction of the family help conjure an idealized family into being.

In fact, the revolutionary government and the burgeoning opposition mutually reinforced one another in their depiction of the opposition as predominantly white, Catholic, middle-class, or elite, and even, to some extent, dominated by women or mothers. For its part, the revolutionary

Y ADEMAS, SACRILEGO!...

"And what's more, sacrilegious!" A Cuban woman fends off Fidel Castro with a cross as he destroys a church. (Cover of Bohemia Libre, *January 22, 1961; courtesy of the Cuban Heritage Collection, University of Miami Libraries, Coral Gables, Florida)*

DEFIENDE A TU HIJO

MADRE CUBANA,
te corresponde una heroicidad más
en la hora tétrica de la Patria. Las
dictaduras clásicas de Cuba, al recu-
rrir al terror, sólo podían arrancar la
vida de tu hijo. La dictadura castrista aspira a más: aspira a arrancarle
el alma — es decir, su religión, su
sentimiento de nacionalidad, su dig-
nidad de persona libre. Mediante
un diabólico proceso de adoctrina-
miento, la tiranía castrista pretende
inculcar en el alma de tu hijo el más
grosero ateísmo, un sentimiento de
internacionalismo al exclusivo ser-
vicio de Rusia y la última partícula
de conciencia individual. ¡DEFIEN-
DE A TU HIJO, madre cubana! Si
el estado totalitario hace de tu hijo
un ser totalitario, ¡TU HIJO SERA
UN MONSTRUO!

"Defend your child." An editorial calls on mothers to undertake "one more heroic act" in the country's time of need. Like other opposition imagery, the drawing features a woman who appears to be white and Catholic. (From Bohemia Libre, *October 23, 1960; courtesy of the Cuban Heritage Collection, University of Miami Libraries, Coral Gables, Florida)*

leadership endeavored to portray the opposition as restricted to economic elites at a time when the revolutionary government was in fact also faced with growing opposition from organized labor.[149] For example, Fidel Castro's characterization of those skeptics and naysayers who spread rumors against the revolution by telephone is revealing. He denounced the medium as well as the message when he imputed a class and gendered character to the spread of rumors. Who was behind such rumors? he asked rhetorically. "The women who have three telephones in their house. . . . The men who don't have to work . . . who drink high balls in the aristocratic clubs. . . . The women who have three or four maids."[150] Ironically, Castro was lambasting one of the very methods through which his own revolutionary movement—especially its women members—had countered the claims of the *batistato*. His description of malicious rumors also strove to contain them within the paradigm of an organized campaign, when clearly rumors are powerful precisely because they can enter the everyday circuits of oral culture and generate spontaneous reiterations, even if, as in the case of the Patria Potestad campaign, they originated in radio broadcasts and printed flyers.

However, despite Castro's allusions, the rumors about the abrogation of Patria Potestad apparently appealed to women beyond the elite. The Communist Party newspaper warned of the need to reach out to isolated working-class housewives, who were too burdened by domestic labors to participate in the revolutionary process or even read the newspaper, and thus found themselves at the mercy of the gossips they ran across in the bodega.[151] Those local gossips tried to "touch the most sensitive point for a mother: the loss of her child." Thus it was necessary for revolutionary women to divulge and explain the revolution's good works, because "although we [i.e., revolutionary women] are clear about what's happening, a great number of women are not. . . . The gratitude of Cuban mothers toward the revolution and Fidel should have no limits."[152] The fact that Fidel Castro and other officials denounced the Patria Potestad rumors in numerous public speeches and other media suggests the rumor campaign's wide reach and staying power.

In addition to references to class, opposition propaganda in this period always featured white Cubans in drawings and photos. The pamphlet *Communism Destroys the Family in Cuba* featured a photo of a blond girl cradling a doll, juxtaposed with a quote attributed to Lenin that reads "Give me the children for four years and the seeds I plant will never be uprooted."[153] In another image, a *Bohemia Libre* cover depicted a white boy in the countryside behind barbed wire with armed guards visible in the distance. The

"He must be saved!" A young white boy is trapped behind barbed wire in the countryside, with an armed guard in the distance. (Cover of Bohemia Libre, *January 15, 1961; author's collection)*

superimposed text reads, "He must be saved!"[154] The opposition propaganda's discursive emphasis on the nuclear family, formal marriage, and Catholicism, characteristics that described Cuba's middle and upper classes especially, also served to delineate the class and racial character of the family under threat. As the campaign of rumors unfolded, it constructed an image of the family as white, middle-class, Catholic, and nurtured by a mother who was predominantly confined to the home, where she tended her spiritual duty of raising children. In Cuba, as elsewhere, the notion of the idealized family as a bulwark against communism was forged in the struggles of the Cold War.[155]

Democracy, Freedom, and the Family

As the revolution radicalized and polarized throughout 1960 and 1961, questions swirled over what kind of political and economic system might best "defend" the family. Was the family best protected by a free market, private property, and low-cost consumer goods, or by a protectionist, redistributive state? For some Cubans critical of the direction the revolution was taking, the state's increasing role in both education and the distribution of goods signaled a violation of their definition of freedom. As a Havana woman who described herself as "one hundred percent anti-communist" denounced in an interview: "They indoctrinated the children. They incorporated them into indoctrination groups. . . . There was no milk for children over six years of age. It was whatever they wanted to give. . . . In Cuba before the revolution there was a lot of freedom. You could buy whatever you wanted, eat what you wanted, raise your children your own way."[156] For this young mother, material shortages, political proselytization, and youth mobilization all blurred together into an assault on personal freedom and family autonomy.[157] Her experience reflected the interrelated ideas of freedom and consumption that were prevalent in prerevolutionary Cuba.

As Louis Pérez has argued, "'democracy' and 'freedom' meant different things to different people; the terms had long been associated with a material condition, implying convenience, comfort, and contentment."[158] Some anti-Castro organizations reflected these intertwined concepts of consumption, childrearing, and political freedom. As a group called the Cuban Freedom Committee alleged in a pamphlet, families were being pulled apart by political pressures as well as by "assaults on the family's property and the scarcity of consumer goods."[159] These views dovetailed with American early

Cold War notions of consumer freedom and "people's" capitalism, which viewed families as strengthened by access to cheap consumer goods.[160]

As organized political opposition to the revolution gained momentum, the defense of the family from a predatory state became something of a mantra for opposition leaders. The concepts of youth indoctrination or state control of children were so ingrained in opposition thought by early 1961 that they featured prominently in the political manifestos of many anti-Castro groups.[161] In fact, the focus on state control over the family proved to be generative. Allegations of familial destruction provided a shared theme and sensibility among politically diverse opposition groups. Although militant opponents of the revolution could be found at various points along the political spectrum, from right to left, the emphasis on protecting the family resonated with most tendencies.

For liberal anticommunists, state encroachment on the family was seen as part of the foundation of an authoritarian regime. For example, the Revolutionary Democratic Front, the broad anti-Castro umbrella group mentored by the CIA, announced in the crucial weeks leading up to the Bay of Pigs invasion that its postrevolutionary government would end political tyranny, guarantee free enterprise, restore legitimate property rights, and end the militarization and indoctrination of children and youth, instead "encouraging [their] moral formation."[162] Such statements reveal the intense concern that existed within the anti-Castro movement over the social and political influence over youth in this period, which would continue among political exile groups long after the anti-Castro movement declined in the early 1960s. For Catholic anticommunists, on the other hand, the "atheistic" state formation of children was seen as a threat to the human soul. As the prominent Catholic intellectual Andrés Valdespino argued, the most serious crime of the Castro regime was the attack "on the very soul of the people . . . the character of its children. . . . It's not a crime against material goods or tangible things. It's a crime against the values of the spirit."[163] And Catholic lay organizations in exile posited a "Christian vision" of womanhood that stressed the importance of virginity, humility, self-abnegation, and sacrifice for the family.[164] In contrast to the liberal opponents of the revolution, who tended to stress the neutralization of republican institutions and legal frameworks, Catholic anticommunists offered a more metaphysical, transcendent critique.

As allegations about the revolutionary destruction of the Cuban family became staples of the emerging opposition movement, the revolutionary leadership was pushed to more clearly delineate its own defense of the working-class, "socialist" family. For example, in a November 1960 speech, Castro ridiculed rumors that the revolution would abolish Patria Potestad, stating that instead the revolution was saving, educating, and empowering children. He noted that orphaned or abandoned children had been housed in state-run shelters and that children of the impoverished countryside now had access to much-needed "school-cities." Beyond education and shelter, Castro pledged that the revolution would guarantee all children "human warmth," so that they would "feel important, start to feel like someone beginning in childhood [*sentirse algo desde niño*]."[165] His defense revealed the different way he and his critics conceptualized the protection of children and family rights. While opposition leaders demanded family autonomy and self-determination, Castro viewed the "real" protection of children as the guarantee of their physical and emotional well-being, whether that was provided by the individual family or by the state.

A month later, again dismissing rumors over the abolition of Patria Potestad, Castro expounded on the defense of working-class motherhood, describing women's universal and sacred right to be mothers, which was violated in a class society. His speech is worth citing at length for its clear delineation of the revolutionary defense of motherhood and family:

> The revolution wants not just to protect children, but to protect *the rights of human beings to have children, to be parents*. The selfish society in which we lived [prior to the revolution] took away more than *patria potestad*; it deprived millions of humble people of the right . . . to have children. The cruel society in which we lived prohibited a domestic servant from having children . . . prohibited a female worker with poor earnings from having children . . . it deprived a widow of the right to work, because . . . she had no one to leave her children with to go to work, and . . . this put that woman in the worst dilemmas. . . . That was the cruel society in which we lived, which obliged many women to [abandon] their children in [public orphanages], because they had nowhere else to take them. In the cruel and inhuman society in which we lived, only the rich had the right to have children, *comfortably*; the poor who had children paid for it in misery . . . [it] *deprived millions of women of the sacred and natural right to have children and be mothers.*[166]

The Cuban leadership's discursive defense of working and poor mothers reinscribed the sanctity of motherhood. Yet it provided a class-based defense of the family, emphasized women's participation in labor markets and their right to work, and raised at least the promise—if never the full realization—of collectivized solutions to domestic labor, including childcare. For, as Castro suggested, working-class women might have children, but they could only *be mothers*—"comfortably"—by shifting some portion of their domestic burdens to the state.

Castro also depicted the working class and the Marxist Left as those most ardently devoted to the family with assertions about the working-class propensity to have large families, Cuban socialists' devotion to their children, and the strength and unity of the Soviet family. In a long September 1961 speech denouncing the Patria Potestad rumor campaign, he alleged that the Cuban "aristocracy" had only one or two children at most, and were therefore presumably not very family-oriented. "Those who really have children are the revolutionary classes . . . the workers and peasants." The revolution was being waged "precisely so that they can bring bread to their children . . . house their children in a dignified home . . . [give their children] food, a school, and a future."[167] In the same speech, Castro refuted enduring assumptions about communism being against the family.[168] For example, he noted that the veteran Communist Party labor leader Lázaro Peña and his wife Zoila were inseparable from their eight-year-old son. Despite Peña's hefty responsibilities, Castro explained, he "takes their son around with him all day, with the deepest affection that a father can feel for a son."[169] And he scorned U.S. Cold War propaganda that portrayed the Soviet Union as having destroyed the institution of marriage: "The historical truth is actually this: that the most solid matrimony in the world is Soviet matrimony, and the country that has the lowest percentages of divorces [and] separations in the world is . . . the Soviet Union."[170] Borrowing talking points from Cuba's Marxist Left, which argued that socialism encouraged the strongest families and the most egalitarian marriages, Castro's comments indicated that henceforth the revolution would invoke the socialist world as its familial model.[171]

The intensifying conflict of the first years of the revolution pushed both revolutionary supporters and detractors toward more developed stances on the role of children and the family vis-à-vis the state. Questions over the family were connected to broader questions about politics and economics, and by extension to competing notions of freedom, democracy, and justice. In this battle of ideas, revolutionary opponents—including both those affiliated with the liberal, secular opposition and those that had emerged from Catholic student activism—found common ground. A resurgent Catholicism stressed family and faith as bulwarks against communism, and liberals saw the family as a building block of civil society. Thus anticommunist Cubans of different political leanings embraced the family as a refuge from and locus of resistance to the state, and elevated "defense of the family" to a primary goal. Partly in response to this more conservative vision of the family embraced by its opponents, and partly in response to prodding from women activists as described in chapter 4, the revolutionary leadership now moved toward sharper definitions of working women's rights and increasingly positioned itself as a champion of the working-class or "socialist" family. Thus the conflict sparked by the revolutionary victory of 1959 was not only a struggle over property rights, national politics, or international relations. It also unleashed a struggle over constructions of femininity and masculinity, of marriage and the family.

CONCLUSION

On December 17, 2014, President Barack Obama announced that the United States would resume diplomatic relations with Cuba after more than 50 years. The U.S. government thereby sought to "begin a new chapter among the nations of the Americas," as he put it. Although the exact details of this re-engagement and how it will impact Cuba remain to be seen, it felt like the end of an era. The subsequent months witnessed a vast stream of international media commentary, an explosion of foreign visitors to the island, and much speculation about Cuba's future. As the island stands on the threshold of a new epoch—if that is indeed what we are witnessing—it will be important to more fully assess the historical legacy of the revolution.

Like most revolutions, the Cuban Revolution ultimately restricted power to a small cohort. The massive social transformations it engendered generally subsided after the first decade, when the revolution became more institutionalized and bureaucratic and repressive tendencies proliferated. The most radical expectations raised by the revolution were not ultimately met, due to limitations imposed by both external aggression and the internal process of state formation that followed the revolutionary vacuum of power. The economic decline of the 1990s compromised and to some extent even dismantled many of the revolution's most fundamental and respected accomplishments. It is now patently obvious that the revolution was never able to produce a perfectly egalitarian society.

But the Cuban Revolution also, like most revolutions, threw open the political horizons of the nation. In the sudden illumination of the revolutionary moment, Cubans envisioned a new polity that was much more inclusive, egalitarian, and democratic. While the revolution never fully erased old hierarchies, it nevertheless encouraged Cubans to question and challenge them in a way that very few other political movements in history have managed to do. The revolutionary government largely abolished private property and the profit motive, and it confronted powerful transnational corporations in Cuba and entrenched interests abroad. It gave opportunities to new actors, both individuals and entire social groups, who rose to new national prominence. Perhaps most fundamentally, the revolutionary opening prompted the articulation of new ideas about rights and needs. The demand for those rights quickly radiated outward, raising the political stakes throughout the region by suddenly widening the scope of the possible. The Cuban Revolution thus permanently transformed the consciousness of an entire generation in Latin America.

Women were in the front lines of shaping this truly revolutionary process. While never numerous in the iconic battles of the Sierra Maestra, at least not as combatants, women were ubiquitous in the revolutionary struggle of the urban centers. They played strategic roles as liaisons and as strategists, staffed safe houses and distributed propaganda, raised funds and smuggled the most precious of resources, information. They formed all-women's anti-Batista groups such as the José Martí Women's Civic Front and Opposition Women United. They also took part in broader revolutionary groups such as the Twenty-Sixth of July Movement or the Revolutionary Directorate. They often conceptualized their own participation as maternal figures who wielded special moral authority, which they mobilized to demand an end to state violence, respect for human rights, and the implementation of democracy.

After the revolution's triumph, many women continued organizing apace, now turning toward a more consciously gender-specific agenda or mobilizing around issues pertinent to women as culturally ordained heads of household reproduction, especially food provisioning and neighborhood vigilance. Women of the old, Marxist Left were often central in this process. While the Communist Party was wary of armed revolution and did not support the Twenty-Sixth of July Movement until mid-1958, the party played an important role in helping to publicly articulate the need for equality between men and women in 1959. Still, not all women's participation was "radical" or prorevolutionary. Many women also organized against the revolution or in positions not always easy to characterize as being on the Left or the Right, for example, by protesting against food shortages. But one thing is clear: women often took the initiative, and in doing so they pushed the new revolutionary government to appeal to them as revolutionary actors. They did so directly, by organizing and petitioning the government, or by pressing certain issues forward through their actions. They also did so indirectly, by proving themselves fierce critics—opponents who needed to be co-opted and who therefore forced the state to organize prorevolutionary women in response. Taken together, their actions broadened the scope of the revolutionary platform, especially regarding problems within the private sphere, such as food provisioning, domestic labor, and childrearing, and they proved that women would be strategically important actors as the revolution evolved. This book thus challenges persistent myths of the revolution's "liberation" of women from above, showing that women were far more proactive in contributing to the revolution and demanding their own rights than has been acknowledged.

Rethinking the role of women actors also leads us to unravel the central role played by gendered imagery and discourse in the revolutionary process. During the insurrection to oust Fulgencio Batista, rhetorical appeals to Batista's destruction of masculine honor and the Cuban family helped forge a hegemonic discourse of rebellion that stressed the moral grandeur of the struggle. In a historical context in which violence had been discredited in Cuban politics, the emergence of a hypermasculine guerrilla warrior figure, self-disciplined and sexually restrained, lent credibility and wide appeal to the insurgent Twenty-Sixth of July Movement. Despite what we may now think of as the transgressive or radical appeal of the *barbudos*, in retrospect it is surprising how much the revolutionary movement relied on familiar imagery and discourse regarding masculine honor, sexual discipline, and even Catholicism and paternal duty.

Similarly, after the revolution, the leadership and its critics both struggled to raise the banner of morality and family defense. Fears over the destruction of the family and the corruption or brainwashing of children spread widely, especially within the urban middle class, and helped forge a moral anticommunism with broad appeal. By the same token, the revolutionary leadership also struggled toward a stronger definition of women's rights, children's duties, and the revolution's reformation of the family. The mobilization, radicalization, and polarization of the period are often told as a simple story about class interests coming into inevitable conflict. But this book suggests that deep fault lines also appeared around the issues of gender, the family, and daily life. These conflicts over idealized constructions of femininity, masculinity, marriage, family, and children strongly influenced the way political developments took place and left long legacies. The hypermasculinity of the guerrilla and the "new man," fears over revolutionary sexual promiscuity and the crumbling of the family—all these images continue to haunt contemporary discourse within and beyond Cuban shores.

The official, state-sanctioned narrative about these processes has too often eclipsed the actors and stories included in this book. The focus on the *barbudo* has erased those who did not fit the model of the rural guerrilla, such as middle-class Catholics, the civic resistance, the urban underground, or those who opposed the use of force. The new *oficialista* narrative that emerged thus effectively replaced a messy story of wide and varied popular participation with the neat, teleological notion of a revolutionary vanguard, that is, the cohort of political leaders or intellectuals blessed with superior knowledge of the political conjuncture that is destined to lead the masses. Among these many other forgotten actors, women's activism in particular was easily dismissed in the heady first years of the revolution's victory, as heroic armed struggle and volatile public protest increasingly came to define the essence of rebellion. Cuba's post-1959 glorification of armed struggle thus effectively wrote many women out of the official historical narrative and cast women's "liberation" under socialism as the result of the postrevolutionary state's enlightened paternalism, not women's own activism. By extension, a paternalistic political discourse emerged that viewed women as the mainly passive recipients of revolutionary generosity and cast them as those who had ostensibly "benefitted the most" from the revolution.[1] Restoring a sense of complexity to the story of the revolution is thus more than an empirical corrective; it also has political implications. For as Carlos Monsiváis has noted, "patriarchy is nothing if not an endless strategy of concealment."[2]

By centering women and gender, this book heeds the admonition of the Cold War historian Odd Arne Westad, who has suggested that "gender relations were closer to the core of the conflict both in terms of representation and in language than we have previously thought."[3] Indeed, I have argued here that close attention to gendered imagery and language is crucial to an analysis of the Cuban insurrection and revolution, since it provides keys to understanding political mobilization and political identity. Using gender as an analytical lens gives us a fresh perspective on the Cuban Revolution by raising questions about changing strategies of insurrection, class and class identity, ideas and practices of consumption, revolutionary support and opposition. The recovery of these complex stories is necessary to fully understand the epic changes that buffeted this small island nation throughout the second half of the twentieth century. As Cuba faces the future, it will be crucial to reflect honestly and critically on this revolutionary past.

NOTES

Abbreviations Used

CUSSDCF	*Confidential U.S. State Department Central Files*
CHC	Cuban Heritage Collection, University of Miami Libraries
HMP	Herbert L. Matthews Papers, Rare Book and Manuscript Library, Columbia University Library
IHC	Instituto de Historia de Cuba
NARA	National Archives and Records Administration
NLCLC	*New Leader* Collection of Letters from Cuba, Tamiment Library/Robert F. Wagner Labor Archives, New York University

Introduction

1. Fidel Castro, speech, December 9, 1966, in *V Plenaria Nacional de la FMC* (pamphlet) (Havana: Minind. Ecag. Taller, n.d. circa January 1967). I have appropriated this phrase for the title of the book because it captures well the complex layers and competing agendas within the revolutionary process. But I hope to provide a more critical inflection to the phrase's implication regarding the top-down liberation of women.

2. For an excellent deconstruction of the revolution's official story or "grand narrative," see Guerra, *Visions of Power*. Guerra interrogates not only state discourse and media representations, but also rallies and other choreographed political acts of the early 1960s to show how the leadership constructed an official narrative that posited the unquestionable leadership of Fidel Castro and unanimous popular support for his leadership.

3. Important exceptions include the small group of women who collaborated closely with the rebel army in the Sierra, some of whom went on to preside over cultural and mass organizations. And although critical counternarratives of the revolution have always existed, they tend to replicate the focus on Fidel Castro and the other revolutionary leaders, and not to challenge the official discourse on women's emancipation.

4. *My Dear Uncle Sam* . . . (flyer) (Nicaro area, Oriente Province: n.p., n.d., circa 1959), attached to Department of State memo dated November 16, 1959. English in original. Consulted on microfilm in the collection *Confidential U.S. State Department Central Files, Cuba, 1955–1959: Internal Affairs* (hereafter CUSSDCF, *Cuba, 1955–1959*).

5. Early scholarly publications on the Cuban Revolution included Draper, *Castroism*; Thomas, *Cuba*; and Zeitlin, *Revolutionary Politics*. Classic monographs on the region inspired by the revolution include Wolf, *Peasant Wars*, and Womack, *Zapata and the*

Mexican Revolution. For an overview of historiography on Cuban history, see Louis Pérez, *Essays on Cuban History*.

6. Domínguez, *Cuba*; Fagen, *Transformation of Political Culture*; Farber, *Revolution and Reaction*; Lewis, *Four Men*; and Lewis, *Four Women*.

7. Molyneux, "State, Gender, and Institutional Change."

8. Randall, *Cuban Women Now*; Bengelsdorf, "On the Problem of Studying Women in Cuba"; and Murray, "Socialism and Feminism." See also Smith and Padula, *Sex and Revolution*.

9. Coco Fusco's 1998 article was the first to note the resurgence of prostitution. Fusco, "Hustling for Dollars." See also Bengelsdorf, "[Re]Considering Cuban Women," and Maxine Molyneux, "State, Gender, and Institutional Change."

10. See, for example, Díaz Castañón, *Ideología y revolución*.

11. The transition from women's history to gender history was most notably sparked by the pathbreaking work of Joan Scott. See her collection of essays, *Gender and the Politics of History*.

12. The most important scholarship of recent years in this vein includes Guerra, "Gender Policing"; Molyneux, "State, Gender, and Institutional Change"; and Serra, *New Man*. See also Bunck, *Fidel Castro and the Quest for a Revolutionary Culture in Cuba*; Young, *Gays under the Cuban Revolution*; and Lumsden, *Machos, Maricones, and Gays*.

13. Serra, *New Man*; Bengelsdorf, "On the Problem of Studying Women in Cuba"; Molyneux, "State, Gender, and Institutional Change." Subsequent scholarly studies have adopted similarly complex approaches. See, especially, Andaya, *Conceiving Cuba*; Fernandez, *Revolutionizing Romance*; and Hamilton, *Sexual Revolutions*.

14. Kampwirth, *Feminism*; Shayne, *Revolution Question*.

15. Kampwirth deemed Cuba's top-down approach to women's uplift a form of "patriarchal feminism"; Kampwirth, *Feminism*, 191. See also Shayne, *Revolution Question*; Molyneux, "State, Gender, and Institutional Change"; and Randall, *Gathering Rage*.

16. For a critique of the Cuban electoral system and women's disproportionately low representation in positions of authority, see Luciak, *Gender and Democracy*. New work on the revolution that offers more sophisticated insight into women's agency includes Guerra, *Visions of Power*, and Herman, "Army of Educators."

17. Joan Scott famously admonished historians not to simply "add women and stir." See also Tinsman, "A Paradigm of Our Own."

18. The quote is from the pioneering study by Brown, *Good Wives*.

19. Ibid., 4.

20. Early studies that transcended this approach include Nelson, *Cuba*; Karol, *Guerrillas in Power*; Fagen, *Transformation of Political Culture*; Wright, *Latin America in the Era of the Cuban Revolution*; Carlos Franqui, *Diary*; Domínguez, *Cuba*; Paterson, *Contesting Castro*; and Farber, *Revolution and Reaction*. For a recent new wave of social histories on the Cuban Revolution, see De la Fuente, *A Nation for All*; Guerra, *Visions of Power*; Casavantes Bradford, *Revolution*; Herman, "An Army of Educators"; and Benson, *Antiracism in Cuba*.

21. Rafael Rojas has described this interpretation of history as *caudillista*, drawing on the Spanish word *caudillo* or strongman. See his *La máquina del olvido*.

22. Guerra, *Visions of Power*, 8.

23. See, for example, the accounts offered in Randall, *Cuban Women Now*, 3–32; and Mary-Alice Waters's introduction to Espín, de los Santos, and Ferrer, *Women in Cuba*, especially 34–35. These accounts closely follow the way women's liberation is narrated in the speeches of Cuban officials. While each author stresses the immense participation of women in the evolution of the FMC and other initiatives, they also fall back on reflexive praise of the leadership, particularly Fidel Castro, and locate the seeds of the revolution's ultimate liberation of women in his visionary decision to incorporate women into their own guerrilla army unit. A typical official declaration of women's top-down liberation and resulting gratitude can be found in the final statement of the Fifth Plenary Session of the Federation of Cuban Women's National Committee in 1998: "After 1959, Fidel gave us women the privilege of being the first to advance. . . . We are now worthy, complete, educated, and free: that is the greatest victory that we have attained through the revolution. . . . In the past we were excluded, subordinated and oppressed, and our work always went unnoticed, but now we are the visible protagonists of a heroic exploit" (cited in Kampwirth, *Feminism*, 188).

24. The belief that women were more susceptible to counterrevolutionary mobilization has been prominent among (male) leftists and revolutionaries in Latin America throughout the twentieth century. This stems from the ideas that women are more isolated in the home and thus less politically conscious and that they are more influenced by the clergy. While these claims are largely spurious, it is true that women are often incorporated into revolutionary projects in ways different from that of their male counterparts due to both the gender conceptualizations of revolutionary leaders and to women's traditional role in shouldering the domestic labors of the home. The polemic role of women in revolution has been debated particularly in studies of the Mexican and Chilean revolutions. See Becker, *Setting the Virgin on Fire*; Boylan, "Gendering the Faith"; Olcott, *Revolutionary Women*; and Tinsman, *Partners in Conflict*. For the case of Nicaragua, see Lancaster, *Life Is Hard*.

25. See especially Gosse, *Rethinking the New Left*; Katsiaficas, *The Imagination of the New Left*; and Isserman, *If I Had a Hammer*. On the Latin American New Left, see Grandin, *Last Colonial Massacre*; Gould, "Solidarity under Siege"; Zolov, "Expanding Our Conceptual Horizons"; Markarian, "Sobre viejas y nuevas izquierdas"; and Marchesi, "Geographies of Armed Protest."

26. The phrase is from Gosse, "A Movement of Movements."

27. Evans, *Personal Politics*.

28. See Molyneux, "State Socialism and Women's Emancipation," and Randall, *Gathering Rage*. As the anthropologist Jafari Allen writes, the measures to ameliorate the problems faced by women introduced by the FMC "have not gone far enough, precisely because of the enduring analytic frame that finds gender ideology a mere superstructural reflection rather than a productive relation." Allen, *Venceremos?*, 115.

29. See, for example, Gotkowitz and Turits, "Socialist Morality"; Guerra, "Gender Policing."

30. For recent scholarly approaches to urban revolutionary movements, see Marchesi, "Geographies of Armed Protest" and "Revolution beyond the Sierra Maestra"; and Weld, *Paper Cadavers*.

31. Franqui, *Diary*; Morán Arce, *La Revolución cubana*; Sweig, *Inside the Cuban Revolution*. See also Cuesta Braniella, *La resistencia cívica*; and Nieves and Feijóo, *Semillas de fuego*.

32. See Hamilton, *Sexual Revolutions in Cuba*, which notes the slow transformation of ideas about sexuality. The anthropologist Nadine Fernandez, looking at the intersection of race, gender, and sexuality (particularly the still charged notion of black men with white women), uncovered the persistence or reproduction of reactionary and even violent behavior in this realm, including among the most stalwart revolutionaries. See Fernandez, *Revolutionizing Romance*.

33. See Green, "Who Is the Macho Who Wants to Kill Me?"; Cowan, "Why Hasn't This Teacher Been Shot?"; and Guerra, "Gender Policing."

34. Guerra reports that Che distributed the contents of the Bureau for the Repression of Communist Activities in Havana archive to Communist Party militants; *Visions of Power*, 78.

35. For the best collections of the clandestine press of 1952–59, see the Prensa Clandestina collection at the Instituto de Historia de Cuba (hereafter IHC), the Herbert Matthews Papers at Columbia University (hereafter HMP), and the Carlos Franqui Papers at Princeton University. Additionally, many clandestine periodicals and flyers are appended to contemporary Department of State dispatches.

36. Casavantes Bradford, *Revolution*, 128.

37. For exile periodicals, I have relied heavily on the excellent collection held by the Cuban Heritage Collection at the University of Miami Libraries (hereafter CHC).

38. For example, Elizabeth Sutherland Martínez, *Youngest Revolution*, and Ernesto Cardenal, *En Cuba*.

39. Important academic studies conducted in this period with impressive access include those of Verena Martínez-Alier, Richard Fagen, Oscar Lewis, Douglas Butterworth, and Maurice Zeitlin. During the Gray Period, some sympathetic scholars based in Latin America continued to undertake oral history work, including Margaret Randall, Laurette Séjourné, and Eugenia Meyer.

40. I have utilized the Instituto de Historia's excellent periodical collection, including their collection of clandestine periodicals, as well as the Fondo del Movimiento Femenino.

41. This may have been related to the process of identifying and awarding veteran status to former participants of the insurgent groups, which involved soliciting autobiographical statements about each person's participation, corroborated by a designated committee. The papers (fondos) of insurgent groups and individual leaders are held in the high-security archive of the Consejo del Estado. It is not open to the public, but several scholars have published accounts based on their access. The

collection was created in 1964 by Celia Sánchez, although it was not properly organized as an archive until 1993. On the Office of Historical Affairs of the Consejo del Estado, see "Un tesoro para todos los tiempos," *Trabajadores*, January 5, 2014, accessed at http://www.trabajadores.cu/temas/oficina-de-asuntos-historicos-del-consejo-de-estado-oahce/. For a work that draws heavily on the Consejo del Estado archives, although with no footnotes, see the biography of Celia Sánchez by Álvarez Tabío, *Celia*. See also Sweig, *Inside the Cuban Revolution*.

42. See especially García Oliveras, *José Antonio Echeverría*; Nieves and Feijóo, *Semillas de fuego*; Cuesta Braniella, *La resistencia cívica*; Nieves Rivera, *Rogito*; and Castro Porta, *La lección*.

43. Cuban research institutes may not encourage oral history interviews, but they are nevertheless conducted by many Cuban researchers and some foreign researchers. Although all those interviewed here participated willingly, I have used pseudonyms unless otherwise noted to protect the interviewees' privacy. Interviews were almost always conducted in the person's home, and lasted between one and three hours.

Chapter 1

1. For example, Hugh Thomas describes the early opposition group Movimiento Nacional Revolucionario as "one of the many tributary movements of what ultimately became Castroism" (Thomas, *Cuba*, 797). Many accounts of the anti-Batista resistance gloss over this period quickly, providing detailed information only about the 1953 Moncada attack. For a recent example, see Gott, *Cuba*. The most detailed accounts of the 1950s, which explore civic activism as well as the formation of the insurrectionary groups, are found in Thomas, *Cuba*; Domínguez, *Cuba*; and Ibarra Guitart, *El fracaso de los moderados*.

2. See Guerra, *Visions of Power*, 37–74.

3. There is an unfortunate paucity of scholarship on the 1940s and early 1950s. Studies that do exist tend to focus on the high politics of the period's parties rather than on mass *chibasismo*. See Ameringer, *Cuban Democratic Experience*, and Grau Alsina, *Mongo Grau*.

4. Ehrlich, *Eduardo Chibás*, 92. Ehrlich also cites another survey showing that women exceeded men in their support of Chibás after his 1949 acquittal. See ibid., 292n11. One factor in reaching female publics may have been Chibás's concerted use of the radio, a medium that may have reached women more effectively than print; he was one of Cuba's first politicians to do so (Thomas, *Cuba*, 751).

5. For example, the newsweekly *Bohemia* reported that in a march organized by the party in Santiago in late 1955, "predominaban la mujer y los jóvenes" ("En Cuba," *Bohemia*, November 13, 1955). See also Ehrlich, *Eduardo Chibás*, 139.

6. Álvarez Tabío, *Celia*, 124–30.

7. Cuadras also formed a small, all-women's anti-Batista group called Mujeres Humanistas. See the memoirs of Cuadras compiled by Cabrales (Cuadras de la Cruz and Cabrales, *El rostro descubierto*).

8. Castro Porta, *La lección.*

9. For a list of later MRC activities that correspond closely to earlier actions described here, see interviewee cited in Serra, "El Movimiento de Resistencia Cívica en la Habana," in Oltuski, Rodríguez Llompart, and Torres-Cuevas, *Memorias de la Revolución,* 238.

10. Pérez-Stable, *Cuban Revolution,* 52.

11. Two surveys conducted in 1949 and 1951 by the island's most important magazine, *Bohemia,* found that Batista was second in popularity only to the strident populist leader Eduardo Chibás. On the February 1949 survey, see Ehrlich, *Eduardo Chibás,* 209. A 1951 survey showed in addition that Batista's base of support extended throughout the whole island, as opposed to the regional support held by other political figures. On the 1951 survey, see Álavez Martín, *Eduardo Chibás,* 146.

12. For these revisionist approaches to leaders often being misunderstood as merely repressive or manipulative, see Gould, *To Lead as Equals*; Turits, *Foundations of Despotism*; and Derby, *Dictator's Seduction.* For a related analysis of the power of Peronism, see James, *Resistance and Integration.*

13. See Whitney, *State and Revolution*; and Argote-Freyre, *Fulgencio Batista.* Quote from Arboleya, *La contrarrevolución,* 27.

14. See Whitney, *State and Revolution,* chap. 7.

15. Interview with Marta Sánchez, Union City, N.J., March 2008.

16. The Cuban constitution did not permit reelection.

17. See Department of State, memo, "Political Situation in Cuba: Meeting at Montreal of Opposition Groups," June 8, 1953, in *Confidential U.S. State Department Central Files, Cuba, 1950–1954: Internal Affairs* (hereafter CUSSDCF, *Cuba, 1950–1954*).

18. *Chibasismo* is still awaiting a scholarly reappraisal. Interviews and memoirs make it clear that Chibás inspired a passion that cannot be explained by his formal policy-related platform, which is difficult to differentiate from that of the Auténtico Party. See Ehrlich's *Eduardo Chibás* for a step in this direction.

19. The State Department saw anti-Batista activity during the first few years after 1952 as primarily coming from the Ortodoxo Party, with some movement also from university students, the Auténtico Party, and to a lesser extent labor unions and the PSP. See memo from Office of Middle American Affairs (MID) to Bureau of Inter-American Affairs (ARA), subject: "Opposition to Batista Administration in Cuba," May 15, 1952, unsigned. Memo from MID to ARA, subject: "Opposition to the Batista Administration in Cuba," April 7, 1952. Dispatch from Havana Embassy (unsigned) to Department of State, CUSSDCF, *Cuba, 1950–1954.*

20. Bethell and Roxborough, *Latin America*; Grandin, *Last Colonial Massacre.*

21. It was in this period that we find the first bursts of regional, armed, antidictatorial expeditions, such as the Caribbean Legion—a group of young pan-Caribbean activists, including Fidel Castro, who launched an unsuccessful attempt to overthrow Trujillo. See the essays in Sosa, *Insurrección y democracia.*

22. Domínguez notes, "Batista had greater political support among the poor than among the rich" (*Cuba,* 122). Boris Goldenburg writes that Batista in 1952 "still [enjoyed] considerable popularity among the Cuban lower classes" ("Rise and Fall of a Party," 77).

23. Bonachea and Valdés, introduction to *Revolutionary Struggle*.

24. For overviews of this period, see Thomas, *Cuba*; Pérez-Stable, *Cuban Revolution*; and Pérez, *Cuba: Between Reform and Revolution*. See also Ibarra Guitart, *El fracaso de los moderados*.

25. See, for example, Thomas, *Cuba*, 793–95.

26. Weeka (weekly interagency summary analysis) Report no. 22, Havana Embassy to Department of State, dispatch no. 2,036, May 29, 1952, 2.

27. Havana Embassy (signed Earl T. Crain) to Department of State, "Observance of Cuban Labor Day on May 1," dispatch no. 1,707, May 4, 1953, CUSSDCF, *Cuba, 1950–1954*.

28. Interview with Marisol Álvarez, Havana, January 2006. State Department officials also reported student disturbances, including women passing out "bits of crepe" (i.e., black ribbon to symbolize mourning) and playing "funereal music" on loudspeakers to mark the first anniversary of the coup. See memo from Havana Embassy (signed Earl T. Crain) to Department of State, subject: "First Anniversary of March 10 Coup: Presidential Speech and Student Disorders," dispatch no. 1,405, March 11, 1953, CUSSDCF, *Cuba, 1950–1954*.

29. Interview with Pilar López, Miami, February 2008; Weeka Report no. 22, Havana Embassy to Department of State, dispatch no. 2,036, May 29, 1952, 2.

30. Weeka Report no. 22, Havana Embassy to Department of State, dispatch no. 2,036, May 29, 1952, 2.

31. On an anti-Batista student march held on the anniversary of Tony Guiteras's death, see telegram no. 743 from Havana Embassy (signed Beaulac) to Secretary of State, no subject, May 8, 1952, CUSSDCF, *Cuba, 1950–1954*. On the procession of several hundred students on the anniversary of the 1871 execution of protesting medical students, which ended in gunfire between students and police, see telegram no. 233 from Havana Embassy (signed Gardener) to Secretary of State, no subject, November 27, 1956, CUSSDCF, *Cuba, 1955–1959*. In Santiago, students held a ceremony to swear to uphold the ideals of José Martí on the hundredth anniversary of his birth in January 1953, an act that was understood as a denunciation of Batista's coup. See Álvarez and López Fonseca, "La recepción martiana en la Universidad de Oriente," 110.

32. Michelle Chase, "Women's Organizations," 440–58.

33. Eliseo Riera-Gómez, "Rivers of Blood," article appended to letter from Riera-Gómez to Representative William Lantaff, May 8, 1953, CUSSDCF, *Cuba, 1950–1954*.

34. Havana Embassy to Department of State, subject: "First Anniversary of March 10 Coup: Presidential Speech and Student Disorders," dispatch no. 1,405, March 11, 1953, CUSSDCF, *Cuba, 1950–1954*.

35. Stoner, *From the House to the Streets*.

36. Printed in *Batalla*, January–February 1953, cited in Cuesta Braniella, *La resistencia cívica*, 15.

37. English translation included in dispatch no. 2185 from Havana Embassy (signed Walter P. Houk) to Department of State, subject: "Opposition Chain Letter," June 25, 1952, CUSSDCF, *Cuba, 1950–1954*. My italics.

38. In 1951, for example, the entire city of Pinar del Rio attempted to declare itself *ciudad muerta* in support of demands of tobacco growers. See *Noticias de Hoy* (hereafter *Hoy*), December 13, 1951. See also Winocur, *Las clases olvidadas*.

39. Cuesta Braniella, *La resistencia cívica*, 63.

40. MRC handbill, circa March 1957, cited in ibid., 96.

41. Interview with Rosario Navarrete, Havana, July 2007; Díaz Vallina, Dotre Romay, and Dacosta Pérez, "La mujer revolucionaria."

42. MRC handbill "Dia del Decoro," circa May 10, 1957, cited in Cuesta Braniella, *La resistencia cívica*, 114.

43. Transcript of Tad Szulc interview with Vilma Espín, 91; Tad Szulc Collection of Interview Transcripts, CHC.

44. On the strength of rumors, see "En Cuba," *Bohemia*, August 4, 1957, 88, cited in Cuesta Braniella, *La resistencia cívica*, 154–55; and Morán Arce, *La Revolución cubana*, 100–101. On the package of emergency decrees, including one against spreading rumors, see memo from Havana Embassy (signed Daniel Braddock) to Department of State, "Decree-Law Issued Pursuant to Law of National Emergency," dispatch no. 831, April 17, 1958, CUSSDCF, *Cuba, 1955–1959*.

45. Interview with Ramona Betancourt, Havana, September 2005.

46. Cited in Cuesta Braniella, *La resistencia cívica*, 197.

47. Radio Rebelde broadcast transcript, April 10, 1958, Carlos Franqui Collection, 1952–81, Manuscripts Division, Department of Rare Books and Special Collections, Princeton University Library. See also the interview with Haydée Santamaría in *Revista Santiago*, no. 18–19 (June–September 1975): 33.

48. This reference is made frequently in oral histories and *testimonios* by former militants, and is occasionally referenced in official speeches. See, for example, testimonies gathered in Nieves and Feijóo, *Semillas de fuego*. The memoirs of Twenty-Sixth of July leader Enrique Oltuski contain this typically brief aside: "Someday I would like to write an entire book about Cuban women, because they have played such an important role [in the urban underground]. . . . Until that book is written, however, let me say that these young women were students, housewives, and workers, and at this time their primary role was to accompany the men on trips and actions and to transport secret documents, money, and arms. . . . These women were very important in collecting money, transporting bullets, delivering secret messages—all sorts of things. Some of them participated in sabotage as well." Oltuski, *Vida Clandestina*, 126.

49. Klouzal, "Rebellious Affinities," 139–40; Lewis, *Four Women*, 372–73; Cruz Díaz, *Chicharrones*.

50. For comparisons, see the descriptions of women's activities in Friedman, *Unfinished Transitions*, 109, and in Shayne, *Revolution Question*, especially 5 and 37–38. Shayne argues that women in revolutionary struggles often manipulate their assigned gender roles in order to carry out strategically important tasks.

51. See Miller, *Latin American Women*. For studies of the Catholic Church as a conduit for women's politicization and entry into guerrilla and other revolutionary movements in the second half of the twentieth century, see Kampwirth, *Feminism*;

Shayne, *Revolution Question*; and Bayard de Volo, *Mothers of Heroes and Martyrs*. The Cuban case is slightly different, due to the fact that the revolution occurred prior to the rise of liberation theology.

52. Cuadras de la Cruz and Cabrales, *El rostro descubierto*, 95. See also 57–58 for a description of such practices before the insurrectionary period.

53. Castro Porta, *La lección*, 222.

54. The Juventud Obrera Católica later became an important source of militants during the formation of the Twenty-Sixth of July Movement.

55. Interview with Carmelo Jiménez, Miami, November 2005.

56. Mary Kay Vaughan argues that the new urban spaces of consumer culture were "not so much a [strictly] feminine phenomenon . . . as . . . an arena through which women moved noticeably into public spaces." See Vaughan, introduction to Olcott, Vaughan, and Cano, *Sex in Revolution*, 23.

57. See Rosenthal, "Spectacle, Fear, and Protest," 41–46.

58. On the rise of the concept of an armed vanguard and the attendant demotion of the urban struggle to support functions only, see Franqui, *Diary*; Sweig, *Inside the Cuban Revolution*; and Morán Arce, *La Revolución cubana*.

59. Cuesta Braniella, *La resistencia cívica*, 74.

60. *Resistencia*, July 15, 1958, cited in Cuesta Braniella, *La resistencia cívica*, 288.

61. Pérez, *Cuba under the Platt Amendment*.

62. Pérez, *On Becoming Cuban*, 281. See also Derby, *Dictator's Seduction*, for the way this process unfolded in the Dominican Republic.

63. Pérez, *On Becoming Cuban*, 10.

64. See Derby, *Dictator's Seduction*, 66, on the relationship between consumption and urban space.

65. Pérez, *On Becoming Cuban*, 320.

66. Derby, *Dictator's Seduction*, 61. Derby suggests that the penetration of the marketplace into society was also seen as sapping the physical strength of men, feminizing the nation. Ibid., 48.

67. Pérez, *On Becoming Cuban*, 461–62.

68. Ibid., 471–73.

69. Ibid., 14.

70. They may have also contained an implicit racial critique, as many of the musicians and performers of popular music in the period were black. On the postrevolutionary tendency to view *música bailable* as superficial and apolitical, and the racial implications of that disdain, see Perna, *Timba*.

71. *Batalla*, January/February 1953; cited in Cuesta Braniella, *La resistencia cívica*, 15.

72. Movimiento de Resistencia Popular, "Chibás ordena: Cubano, cumple con tu deber!" (handbill), attachment to memo from Havana Embassy (signed Earl T. Crain) to Department of State, "Expressions of Discontent under the Batista Regime," dispatch no. 1,532, March 20, 1952, CUSSDCF, *Cuba, 1950–1954*.

73. But for the use of the Capitolio as the site of early protests, see interview with Miguel Guillén, Havana, January 2006. On actions against hotels, see Schwartz,

Pleasure Island, 174. It was not until the late 1950s—with the rise of tentative alliances between insurgent groups and organized labor—that the conflict would eventually spread to the more industrial, farther-flung, poor and working-class areas of the city.

74. The consumption patterns the flyers describe, including access to disposable income and luxury purchases, are also implicitly middle class in their associations. The influence of the Ortodoxo Party in early protest activity may also give some indication of the social background of early protesters. As Jorge Domínguez has noted, the concentration of Ortodoxo votes in Havana and Oriente Province, where most of the country's middle class resided, "suggests that . . . the appeal of reformist moralizing was a peculiarly middle-class concern." Domínguez, *Cuba*, 113.

75. On distributing flyers and other opposition ephemera in central streets of Havana and Santiago, I have relied on a joint interview with Dolores Domínguez and Caridad Arango, Havana, July 2007, and an interview with Ariana Núñez, Havana, July 2007.

76. Interviews with Rogelio Gil, Miami, November 2005, and Miguel Guillén, Havana, January 2006.

77. Weeka Report no. 14, Havana Embassy to Department of State (signed Earl T. Crain), dispatch no. 1,645, April 4, 1952, 2, CUSSDCF, *Cuba, 1950–1954*.

78. Memo from Havana Embassy (signed Earl T. Crain) to Department of State, "Anti-Batista Leaflets Circulated," dispatch no. 1,571, March 25, 1952, CUSSDCF, *Cuba, 1950–1954*.

79. See Rosenthal, "Spectacle, Fear, and Protest." Although Batista did not begin consistently imposing press censorship until 1956, the construction of a visible community of protesters was nonetheless important in this early period.

80. See Pérez, *On Becoming Cuban*, for a discussion of urban modernity in early twentieth-century Cuba. In the case of Mexico in the 1930s, the historian Anne Rubenstein notes that the use of movie theaters as the site of protest "was to make a statement in itself, an implied connection between a local political issue . . . and broader social concerns over cultural modernity and sexual morality." Rubenstein, "Raised Voices in the Montecarlo," 316.

81. Oltuski et al., *Memorias de la Revolución*, ix, 254–55.

82. "0-3-C Flyer," Ernesto Chávez Collection, folder 3, George A. Smathers Libraries, University of Florida, Gainesville. Also reproduced in Cuesta Braniella, *La resistencia cívica*, appendix (unpaginated).

83. Lina Patriz (pseudonym for Selina Bernal), Secretaría General de Propaganda del Directorio Revolucionario, "Go Home, Mr. Nixon" (leaflet), June 1, 1958. From the private collection of Federico Larrazabal.

84. For an influential account of republican-era corruption, see Roig de Leuchsenring, *Males y vicios de Cuba republicana*, 249–54. Norberto Fuentes penned a similar critique of the corruptive influence of mob-owned casinos in "Vida libre al sindicato del juego," *Revista CUBA*, March 1968, cited in Séjourné, *La mujer cubana*. The U.S. press in the same period published exposes of mob influence in Havana. See for example Ernest Havemann, "Mobsters Move in on Troubled Havana," *Life*, March 10, 1958, 32.

85. Interview with Miguel Guillén, Havana, January 2006.

86. This was distinct from the concept of action used by other constituencies, such as Catholic Action. According to Julio Moreno, in Mexico, Catholic Action "defined 'action' not as violent confrontation but as careful planning and networking and coercing people, institutions, and organizations into supporting its cause." Moreno, *Yankee Don't Go Home!*, 224.

87. Interview with Valeria Espinoza, Havana, July 2007.

88. Interview with Eneida Hernández, Havana, July 2007. As Sam Farber notes, the tendency to glorify action and denigrate theory had a long history in populist political culture in Cuba. Farber, *Origins of the Cuban Revolution*, 41.

89. Interview with Valeria Espinoza, Havana, July 2007.

90. Moro, *Nostalgias*, 201.

91. *Sierra Maestra* (Florida), July 1958.

92. Cited in Pedraza, *Political Disaffection*, 50.

93. Eneida Hernández, personal communication.

94. Anonymous personal communication, August 2011.

95. Interview with Valeria Espinoza, Havana, July 2007.

96. Interview with Valeria Espinoza, Havana, July 2007.

97. Interview by Tuka de Alvarado, circa 1959, Dysis Guira Collection, CHC.

98. Moro, *Nostalgias*, 205.

99. An English version of the speech is available at http://lanic.utexas.edu/project /castro/db/1973/19730727.html (accessed May 22, 2014). A copy of the poster is available in the Commonwealth and Latin American Archives Project; see http://polarch.sas.ac .uk/pages/oclae_poster_coll.htm.

Chapter 2

1. "Carta a un cubano," (flyer) (n.p.: n.p., n.d., circa August 1958), reprinted in Cuesta Braniella, *La resistencia cívica*, 353–54.

2. See Zolov, "Expanding Our Conceptual Horizons." The so-called *foco* theory spread through the publications of Che Guevara and Régis Debray but was often reinterpreted by local actors. See Marchesi, "Revolution beyond the Sierra Maestra," and Marchesi, "Geographies of Armed Protest." On the impact in the United States, see Gosse, *Where the Boys Are*.

3. Mallon, "*Barbudos*, Warriors and *Rotos*"; Sorensen, *A Turbulent Decade Remembered*; Saldaña-Portillo, *The Revolutionary Imagination*; Gosse, *Where the Boys Are*; Green, "Who Is the Macho Who Wants to Kill Me?" For studies on Cuba, see Guerra, "Gender Policing"; Serra, *New Man*; and Lumsden, *Machos, Maricones, and Gays*.

4. Mallon, "*Barbudos*, Warriors and *Rotos*," 180–81, 183.

5. Gosse, *Where the Boys Are*, 2–3.

6. Evans, "Sons, Daughters, and Patriarchy," 337.

7. Zolov, "Expanding Our Conceptual Horizons," 69.

8. On the escalation of violence, see Thomas, *Cuba*, 875; Chase, "The Trials," 166–70.

9. Domínguez, *Cuba*, 126.

10. Bonachea and San Martín, *Cuban Insurrection*, 264.

11. Guerra, *Visions of Power*, 16. See also Thomas, *Cuba*, 984.

12. LaCharité, *Case Studies in Insurgency and Revolutionary Warfare*, 94.

13. Farber, *Revolution and Reaction*, 9.

14. Pérez-Stable notes that "liberals, radicals, and communists coexisted loosely within the opposition movement"; *Cuban Revolution*, 58.

15. For example, Fidel Castro made inconsistent statements about the nationalization of industry, a divisive issue. See Thomas, *Cuba*, 992.

16. Pérez-Stable, *Cuban Revolution*, 59.

17. "Patria nueva," in García Oliveras, *José Antonio Echeverría*, 96.

18. Oltuski, *Vida Clandestina*, 96–97.

19. Interview with Miguel Guillén, Havana, January 2006.

20. Tosh, *Manliness and Masculinities*, 5.

21. Letter printed in Castro Porta, *La lección*, 92.

22. Bonachea and Valdés, *Revolutionary Struggle*, 107.

23. Organización Auténtica, *Manifiesto* (pamphlet) ([Havana?]: n.p., May 1957), HMP, box 8.

24. Oltuski, *Vida Clandestina*, 61.

25. Marquitos eventually became a highly controversial figure: he was executed in 1964 after a lengthy public trial, convicted of having infiltrated the DR on behalf of the PSP and presumably having supplied police with the locale of a safe house the group operated, resulting in multiple deaths. His case is usually seen as revealing the conflicts among the PSP, the Twenty-Sixth of July Movement, and the DR that persisted after 1959.

26. Sandals—as well as long hair—were denounced as "decadent" male attire in the early 1960s by the revolutionary leadership. See Franco, *Decline and Fall*, 94. See also Guerra, *Visions of Power*, 248–49.

27. Guerra has shown that homosexuality was understood by the revolutionary leadership to be related to "intellectualism." See her "Gender Policing," 271, 283.

28. "Segunda vista del quasi-religious contra el delator Marcos Rodriguez," *Bohemia*, April 3, 1964, 41–42.

29. Ibid.

30. Ibid. This view was echoed in somewhat different terms by Che Guevara, who famously remarked to a PSP leader, "You are capable of creating cadres who can endure the most terrible tortures in jail, without uttering a word, but you can't create cadres who can take out a machine gun nest" (*Reminiscences*, 201). He viewed it as the strategic misconception of the Communist Party: they wanted to struggle against imperialism but suffered from "an inability to envisage the possibility of taking power" (ibid., 201–2).

31. Letter from Pura del Prado to Dysis Guira, March 26, 1964, Dysis Guira Papers, CHC.

32. De la Torre, *La lucha*, 87–88.

33. Cited in ibid., 92.

34. This tension harkened back to older leftist ideas about self-control and self-discipline, and was reflected in the New Left as tension between bohemianism and individual self-liberation. See Zolov, "Expanding Our Conceptual Horizons."

35. As one friend in the movement recalled, Fontán appreciated "universal" poetry, "but always insisted that his [real] poems were . . . those he could perform in the language of his black world, tinged with the embers of the *solar* and the *rumba*. . . . 'That's my world,' he would say." Cited in Niurka López, "Hortensia: La mamá de Fontán," in Nieves and Feijóo, *Semillas de fuego*, 1:143.

36. On the organization of the urban Twenty-Sixth of July Movement, see Morán Arce, *La Revolución cubana*, 220; and Sweig, *Inside the Cuban Revolution*.

37. "Fontán en el recuerdo," in Nieves and Feijóo, *Semillas de fuego*, 1:136.

38. Ibid., 1:135.

39. Ibid., 1:136.

40. Ibid., 1:137.

41. Interview with Miguel Guillén, Havana, June 2007.

42. For other stories of social and political "passing," see chapter 3, where a revolutionary activist passes as an "innocent" woman, and memories of "Noel" recounted in Nieves and Feijóo, *Semillas de fuego*, 2:97.

43. On the construction of revolutionaries as white and of Afro-Cubans as correspondingly pro-Batista, see de la Fuente, *A Nation for All*, 250–52; and Benson, *Antiracism in Cuba*.

44. Lumsden argues that for Fidel Castro and other Cuban machos who shared his worldview, "there was no place within a revolution for males who don't reflect the values of an 'ultra-virile country, with its army of men'" (Lumsden, *Machos, Maricones, and Gays*, 53). Gotkowitz and Turits also noted the belief—articulated by Fidel Castro some years later—that gay men were somehow constitutively incapable of discipline. Discipline, as discussed later in this chapter, was viewed as a crucial revolutionary characteristic. See their "Socialist Morality," 11–12.

45. As Gail Bederman argued in her classic work, "Manhood—or 'masculinity,' as it is commonly termed today—is a continual dynamic process. Through that process, men claim certain kinds of authority, based upon their particular type of bodies. At any time in history, many contradictory ideas about manhood are available to explain what men are, how they ought to behave, and what sorts of powers and authorities they may claim, as men." Bederman, *Manliness and Civilization*, 7.

46. On the efficiency of the Havana police force, see Suárez Suárez and Puig Corral, *La complejidad de la rebelión*, 105–6.

47. Carmen Castro, "Relatos de la lucha revolucionaria," *Prensa Libre*, February 27, 1959, 18.

48. Nieves and Feijóo, *Semillas de fuego*, 1:130–31.

49. "Nuestros combatientes: Mario Hidalgo," *Resistencia*, August 5, 1958.

50. Bonachea and San Martín, *Cuban Insurrection*, 102.

51. Office memo from DRA (Robert A. Stevenson) to INR (Ambassador Hugh S. Cumming), subject: "Dr. Ernesto Guevara, Second in Command of Rebel Troops," April 7, 1958, 2, CUSSDCF, *Cuba, 1955–1959*.

52. See, for example, letter from René Ramous Latour to Che Guevara, December 19, 1957, in Franqui, *Diary*, 273.

53. "A la ciudadanía," *Resistencia*, February 1958, reprinted in Cuesta Braniella, *La resistencia cívica*, 351–52.

54. See accounts in Nieves and Feijóo, *Semillas de fuego*, 1:164 and 2:70, 78. Also recounted in interview with Samuel Rodríguez, Miami, March 2006.

55. On use of death anniversaries and death imagery, such as symbolic coffins containing the 1940 constitution, in student and other protests, see Suchlicki, *University Students and Revolution*; Bonachea and San Martín, *Cuban Insurrection*; Gladys Marel García, *Insurrection and Revolution*; and Castro Porta, *La lección*. See also Julio García Oliveras, *José Antonio Echeverría*.

56. The funeral of Frank País was said to have 60,000 attendees. Sweig, *Inside the Cuban Revolution*, 48.

57. See testimonies compiled in Cruz Díaz, *Chicharrones*.

58. As reported in *Resistencia*, November 1, 1957, and in Department of State, memorandum of conversation with John L. Topping and Terrence G. Leonhardy, "Cuban Revolutionary Activities," October 1, 1957, CUSSDCF, *Cuba, 1955–1959*. See also Carmen Castro, "Relatos de la lucha revolucionaria," *Prensa Libre*, February 27, 1959, 18.

59. Memo from American consulate, Santiago (signed Oscar Guerra), to Department of State, "Political and Other Events in the Southern Part of Oriente Province," dispatch no. 15, October 22, 1957, CUSSDCF, *Cuba, 1955–1959*.

60. Cardenal, "Epitaph for the Tomb of Adolfo Baez Bone," from his *Epigramas* (1961), consulted at http://www.poesi.as/ec610029.htm (accessed May 7, 2015).

61. See Bayard de Volo, *Mothers of Heroes and Martyrs*, especially 44.

62. Verdery, *Political Lives of Dead Bodies*, 32–33.

63. On imagery of male heroism in the Wars of Independence, see Ferrer, *Insurgent Cuba*.

64. Pérez, *To Die in Cuba*, 331, 333.

65. Nieves Rivera, *Rogito*, 49.

66. Ibid., 43.

67. Ibid., 44.

68. Ibid., 60.

69. See, for example, the extensive coverage of the funeral of Frank País in *Revolución*'s special supplement and the description of the death of Twenty-Sixth of July leader Tony Alomá in *Sierra Maestra* (Matanzas), October 5, 1958.

70. On the use of funerary wreaths, see Cruz Díaz, *Chicharrones*, 44–46.

71. Memo from American consulate, Santiago (signed Bernard Ferminella) to Department of State, no subject, dispatch no. 2, July 18, 1958, CUSSDCF, *Cuba, 1955–1959*.

72. The handful of women killed in the urban anti-Batista struggle fit uncomfortably with the notion of "revolutionary martyrs." In general, their "martyrdom" makes sense

only when framed in terms of sexual exploitation. For example, official narratives now routinely celebrate the Giral sisters, who were raped and killed by security forces, but in tones of pathos and sexual victimization rather than bravery or military glory. See, for example, Nieves and Feijóo, *Semillas de fuego*, 2:161–65.

73. Aretxaga, *Shattering Silence*, 49.

74. Ibid., 50. See also Aretxaga's study of the important role of women during funerals of the Basque separatist movement, *Los funerales*.

75. See Nieves and Feijóo, *Semillas de fuego*, 1:164 and 2:78. Wanted men occasionally undertook significant risks to attend. See, for example, ibid., 2:144.

76. See Natalia Bolívar's description of an altercation between police and women activists of various groups during the tumultuous burial of Directorio Revolucionario leader Mario Reguera, which she describes as "a march of women." Hilario Rosete, "Con Natalia Bolívar," *Alma Mater* (Havana: University of Havana, 2002), http://www.afrocubaweb.com/bolivar.htm. See also the detailed description of interactions between women activists and police in Josefina Rodríguez Olmo, "A los heroes les enterró el pueblo," *Tribuna de la Habana*, April 14, 2007.

77. See testimonies compiled in Franqui, *Diary*; Nieves Rivera, *Rogito*; and Nieves and Feijóo, *Semillas de fuego*. It is worth noting that political masses and funerals had provided women with "appropriate" platforms for public intervention during the anti-Machado struggle of the 1930s, and likely earlier. On the participation of women as speakers at political funerals in the 1930s, see Stoner, *From the House to the Streets*, 117.

78. On police attempts to carry out quick burials and militants' attempts to stop them, see Mirtha Rodríguez Calderón, "El hombre que salvó a los muertos," in Nieves and Feijóo, *Semillas de fuego*, 2:71–80. See also Nieves Rivera, *Rogito*, 46; Bolívar interview in *Alma Mater*; and "Caida de un valiente," *Sierra Maestra* (Camagüey), November 10, 1958.

79. The phrase comes from Luzzatto, *The Body of Il Duce*, which explores the struggle between Fascists and anti-Fascists in occupied Italy to either denigrate or honor the bodies of militants.

80. Nieves and Feijóo, *Semillas de fuego*, 1:198.

81. Interview with Pilar López, Miami, February 2008.

82. For example, Vilma Espín purposefully intervened in the funeral of Frank País to have him dressed in a rebel army uniform rather than a suit. Cited in Hart, *Aldabonazo*, 115–16. See also Bonachea and Valdés, *Revolutionary Struggle*, 101.

83. Letter from Dora Rosales to editor of the *New York Times*, April 27, 1957, HMP, box 1, folder "Correspondence 1957 Jan.–April."

84. Interviews and memoirs make clear that death rituals were quite consciously about the restoration of masculine honor after police emasculation, even when these rituals were conducted in private. See, for example, Castro Porta, *La lección*, 123.

85. See de la Torre, *La lucha*, 84–86.

86. Cited in Nieves and Feijóo, *Semillas de fuego*, 2:70.

87. Letter cited in ibid., 2:167.

88. The phrase comes from a banner held by a group of women in an undated photo, circa early January 1959, published in *Rebelde 6*, 1959. Barbara Weinstein notes similarly, in her discussion of the 1932 regionalist rebellion in São Paolo, a general sentiment that it was "preferable to lose a son in battle than to have a family dishonored by cowardice." Weinstein, "Inventing the 'Mulher Paulista,'" 36.

89. "Carta a un cubano," printed by MRC circa August 1958, reprinted in Cuesta Braniella, *La resistencia cívica*, 353–54.

90. Farewell letter from Che Guevara to Fidel Castro, April 1, 1965, available at https://www.marxists.org/archive/guevara/1965/04/01.htm.

91. Joining the insurrection could imply separation, death, or in some cases something like abandonment. A Bienestar Social agent traveling through Oriente Province in early 1959 noted the presence of some children of rebel soldiers left in orphanages after, for example, their father joined the rebel army and their mother was subsequently killed, or occasionally a father who had joined the rebels and then had gone to Havana upon victory without taking or advising his family. Elena Moure, "Confidencial informe, castigo físico de niños en alberge," February 20, 1961, Orden 244, Legajo 14, Ministerio de Bienestar Social Papers (Fondo), Archivo Nacional de Cuba.

92. This confluence is also notable given that some men later felt that Che's example of masculinity was restrictive, in the sense that it could provide models for a revolutionary warrior or worker but not for a male caregiver. According to Monseñor Carlos Manuel de Céspedes, interviewed by Abel Sierra Madero, "For Che the new man . . . was [he who was] capable of giving his life in guerrilla [warfare], [or] of working in the fields, not the man who had to take care of someone elderly . . . or selflessly help a neighbor, nothing like that." Sierra Madero, "La política, la religión y el hombre nuevo," *Diario de Cuba*, January 5, 2014, http://www.diariodecuba.com/cuba/1388872692_6561 .html (accessed January 21, 2014).

93. For example see Oltuski, *Vida Clandestina*, 74. Several priests became intimately involved in the movement, hiding or even recruiting revolutionaries. See Kirk, *Between God and the Party*, 49.

94. See American consulate (Santiago) dispatch, August 22, 1958, which describes how a Baptist minister and a bank worker, neither involved in politics, were forced underground after being arrested and beaten (CUSSDCF, *Cuba, 1955–1959*).

95. See *Aldabonazo*, August 25, 1956, and *Acción*, June 9, 1958.

96. "Entrevista con las hermanas de Castro," *Patria* (New York), April 1, 1957, in HMP, box 8.

97. "Ciudadano . . . ," flyer, circa 1957, printed by Movimiento de Resistencia Cívica, in series U.S. Embassy, Havana, Cuba: Classified General Records, 1940–61, box 5, file 350: "Cuba Opposition," RG 84, National Archives and Records Administration (hereafter NARA).

98. Friedman, *Unfinished Transitions*; see also Manley, "Intimate Violations."

99. Friedman, *Unfinished Transitions*, 111.

100. See Draper, *Castroism*, 23.

101. See ibid., 57–134.

102. O'Connor, *Origins of Socialism*, 42.

103. Ibid., 43; Morán Arce, *Revolución cubana*, 47.

104. See, for example, both volumes of Nieves and Feijóo, *Semillas de fuego*. As Jorge Ibarra notes, these sectors were among the most vulnerable of Cuba's working population, with fixed salaries and without union representation. Ibarra, *Prologue to Revolution*, 86.

105. Gould, "Solidarity under Siege," especially 349–50.

106. Ricardo A. López, "It Is Not Something You Can Be or Come to Be Overnight."

107. Gosse, *Where the Boys Are*.

108. Guerra, *Visions of Power*.

109. Bonachea and Valdés, *Cuban Insurrection*; Sweig, *Inside the Cuban Revolution*.

110. On strategy, see Bonachea and San Martín, *Cuban Insurrection*, 208–9; and Nieves and Feijóo, *Semillas de fuego*, 1:110–12.

111. Cited in Bonachea and San Martín, *Cuban Insurrection*, 202.

112. On the attempted general strike of August 5, 1957, see letter from Havana embassy (signed Allan Stuart) to William Wieland, Department of State, August 5, 1957; and telegram from Havana embassy (signed Smith) to Department of State, no subject, no. 93, August 6, 1957, CUSSDCF, *Cuba, 1955–1959*.

113. Sims, "Cuba."

114. Interviews with Rogelio Gil, Miami, November 2005, and with Alfonso Jiménez, West Palm Beach, February 2008. See also Sims, "Cuban Labor and the Communist Party," 53–54.

115. Twenty-Sixth of July Movement, "A organizar la huelga general revolucionaria que derrocara la tirania!" (handbill, circa 1957), author's collection.

116. See Sweig, *Inside the Cuban Revolution*, 157–58.

117. García Montes and Alonso Ávila, *Historia del partido Comunista de Cuba*, 525.

118. Bonachea and San Martín, *Cuban Insurrection*, 206. These were not empty threats. The flood of demands for reinstatement by laid-off workers that followed the 1959 triumph suggests that employers used political involvement as a pretense for layoffs.

119. Oltuski, *Vida Clandestina*, 134; interview with Ariana Nuñez, Havana, July 2007.

120. Sectors that struck included bank workers, electric workers, some bus drivers, some shop owners, restaurant workers, telephone workers, textile workers, and cigarette workers. Nieves and Feijóo, *Semillas de fuego*, 2:105.

121. Ibid.

122. Oltuski, *Vida Clandestina*, 119.

123. Sweig, *Inside the Cuban Revolution*, 155.

124. Conclusions of Pleno del Comité Nacional del Partido Socialista Popular, May 25–28, 1959, *Hoy*, June 7, 1959, 7.

125. Quoted in ibid., 146–47.

126. Oltuski, *Vida Clandestina*, 118.

127. Sweig, *Inside the Cuban Revolution*, 153. On this transition, see also Bonachea and San Martín, *Cuban Insurrection*; and Nieves and Feijóo, *Semillas de fuego*, 1:110–13.

128. For a recent reiteration, see Brands, *Latin America's Cold War*.

129. "Pueblo, esta es tu revolucion. Ayudala!," flyer, circa November 1957, Twenty-Sixth of July Movement, in series U.S. Embassy, Havana, Cuba: Classified General Records, 1940–61, box 5, file 350, "Island Reports, 1956–8," RG 84, NARA.

130. As Mike Gonzalez has argued, Cuba's new revolutionaries importantly broke away from the inaction and bureaucracy of the Old Left, but in the process they also abandoned Marxist assumptions about the necessary centrality of the working class to a revolutionary process. "It was in this sense that the message from Cuba, enshrined in the image of the heroic guerrilla, could acquire such importance as the living embodiment of an alternative [to Stalinism], whereby the emphasis on consciousness and will could avoid the problems and contradictions arising from the distance between the revolutionaries and the class which they claimed to represent." Gonzalez, "Culture of the Heroic Guerrilla," 68.

131. Paterson, *Contesting Castro*, 75–79.

132. Ibid., 85.

133. Thomas, *Cuba*, 919–20.

134. Paterson, *Contesting Castro*, 85. See, for example, the famous January 1959 poster designed by Eladio Rivadulla, which uses an image taken from the film footage of the Taber interview. Poster reproduced in Cairo, *Viaje a los frutos*, appendix (unpaginated).

135. López Rivero, Marqués Dolz, and Purón Riaño, *Emigración y clandestinidad*, 104. In May 1957, the Twenty-Sixth of July Movement ordered the first runoff of bonds, then ran off several more in 1958. See ibid., 93–94.

136. Ibid., 31, 44n16.

137. Gosse, *Where the Boys Are*, 2.

138. *Resistencia*, October 15, 1958, 20.

139. Gosse, " 'We Are Highly Adventurous,' " 251. Gosse argues that the revolutionaries were viewed by Americans as almost white, or "Latin."

140. Hamilton, *Sexual Revolutions in Cuba*; Safa, "Hierarchies and Household Change"; de la Torre Mulhare, "Sexual Ideology in Pre-Castro Cuba"; Fox, *Working-Class Émigrés*.

141. Fox, *Working-Class Émigrés*; Butterworth, *People of Buena Ventura*; Hamilton, *Sexual Revolutions in Cuba*.

142. *El Mundo Ilustrado* (supplement to *El Mundo*), January 18, 1959, 12–13.

143. Thomas, *Cuba*, 1011.

144. On the death penalty for rape, see Código Penal de la Sierra, reprinted in *Prensa Libre*, January 20, 1959, 2; Judson, *Cuba and the Revolutionary Myth*, 131; and Franqui, *Diary*, 182. Interview with Carmelo Jiménez, Miami, November 2005.

145. Arnaldo Rivero, "La disciplina revolucionaria en la Sierra Maestra," *Humanismo* (Mexico City), nos. 53–54 (January–April 1959): 372–73.

146. *El Mundo Ilustrado*, January 18, 1959, 12–13.

147. On sexuality and the revolutionary Left in Brazil in the late 1960s, see Langland, "Birth Control Pills and Molotov Cocktails." On Chile, see Mallon, "*Barbudos*, Warriors and *Rotos*."

148. Among many possible examples, see John Jeremiah Sullivan, "Where Is Cuba Going?," *New York Times Magazine*, September 23, 2002, 35; and Belli, *The Country under My Skin*, 5.

149. "La farsa de las medallitas al cuello," *Bohemia Libre*, February 12, 1961, 3.

Chapter 3

1. Bonachea and Valdés, *Revolutionary Struggle*, 264.

2. My interviewees suggested that perhaps 10 to 20 percent of the underground "action groups" were composed of women. Joint interview with Eneida Hernández and Federico Larrazaba, Havana, September 2005; interview with Eneida Hernández, Havana, July 2007; interview with Miguel Guillén, Havana, June 2007.

3. The quote comes from Paula Schwartz's study of women in the French resistance during World War II in her "Redefining Resistance," 142.

4. Stoner, "Militant Heroines and the Consecration of the Patriarchal State"; Thomas-Woodard, " 'Toward the Gates of Eternity.' "

5. Notable publications on the urban underground include Oltuski, *Vida Clandestina*; Sweig, *Inside the Cuban Revolution*; and Nieves and Feijóo, *Semillas de fuego*.

6. For example, Vilma Espín noted famously that during the insurrection, "nobody ever considered being a woman a problem. And I don't mean just in terms of organizing, because there were women who were heads of action, too. . . . Women had a very important place and were very active during [the final phase] of the struggle." Espín, de los Santos, and Ferrer, *Women in Cuba*, 188.

7. An exception is by the sociologist Klouzal, "Rebellious Affinities."

8. Miller, *Latin American Women*, 142. See also González Pagés, *En busca de un espacio*, 113.

9. Boylan, "Gendering the Faith"; Power, *Right-Wing Women in Chile*; Gonzalez-Rivera and Kampwirth, *Radical Women in Latin America*.

10. Weiner, "Maternalism as Paradigm," 96.

11. Kaplan, "Female Consciousness and Collective Action." See also Maxine Molyneux's distinction between "practical" and "strategic" gender interests. Molyneux, "Mobilization without Emancipation?"

12. Freedman, *No Turning Back*, 65.

13. Ibid., 64–68.

14. Ann Allen, "Maternalism in German Feminist Movements."

15. Thomas, *Cuba*, 912.

16. I have not been able to locate the letter, and apparently it was not printed in its entirety in *Diario de Cuba*.

17. This protest has not been enshrined in either popular memory or subsequent scholarly accounts, perhaps because police so quickly broke it up, or because no media images of the protest circulated, or because its similarity to the first protest has merely caused memory of the two incidents to combine. I have found mention of it only in contemporary reports from the *New York Times*. Norman LaCharité's detailed early

study notes that "several protest marches staged in Santiago de Cuba in 1957 began when groups of women dressed in mourning marched in the streets," yet does not specify the dates or number of such protests. LaCharité, *Case Studies in Insurgency and Revolutionary Warfare*, 108.

18. State Department officials reported "further evidence of terrorism on the part of law enforcement officials," including four young men found dead in Santiago and possibly two found hanged near Guanabacoa (a town near Havana), May 29, 1957 (CUSSDCF, *Cuba, 1955-1959*).

19. Herb Matthews, "Populace in Revolt in Santiago de Cuba," *New York Times*, June 10, 1957, 1, 10. See also "Batista Police Aid Protested in Cuba," *New York Times*, June 3, 1957, 4.

20. "Batista Police Aid Protested in Cuba," 4.

21. Joint Weeka Report no. 23, dispatch no. 830 from Havana embassy to Department of State, June 5, 1957, 2, CUSSDCF, *Cuba, 1955-1959*.

22. "Police Seize Newsreels," *New York Times*, June 9, 1957, 13. The documentary *Doctrinas del Corazon* (2012) includes brief footage of this protest.

23. On these events, see Department of State, memorandum of conversation, "Political Situation in Oriente; Ambassador's Visit to Santiago," August 1, 1957; telegram from Havana embassy (signed Smith) to Department of State, no subject, no. 79, August 3, 1957 (hereafter cited as Telegram no. 79 from Havana embassy, August 3, 1957); and memo from ARA (signed Mr. Snow) to Secretary of State, "Ambassador Smith's Remarks at Santiago de Cuba," August 5, 1957; both in CUSSDCF, *Cuba, 1955-1959*.

24. "Cuban Women Defy Jets of Fire Hoses to Attack Regime," *New York Times*, August 1, 1957, 8.

25. Cruz Díaz, *Chicharrones*, 50.

26. Telegram no. 79 from Havana embassy, August 3, 1957.

27. Ibid.; United Press, "Declaraciones del Embajador," *El Crisol*, August 2, 1957. See also Francis McCarthy, "Cuba Chief Suspends Constitutional Rights," *Washington Post and Times Herald*, August 2, 1957, A13.

28. On the rise of paramilitary groups in Oriente Province, see multiple Department of State accounts, including letter from Santiago consul Oscar Guerra to consul general of Havana embassy James Brown, July 2, 1957, in series General Records of the Department of State, Subject Files Relating to Cuba 1951-57, box 1, file "Consulate Santiago Reports 1957," RG 59, Lot 59 D 2, NARA; letter from Park Wollam to Terrence Leonhardy, June 4, 1958, reprinted in Department of State, *Foreign Relations of the United States*, 103-5; and letter from Camagüey consul Paul Tate to consul general of Havana embassy James Brown, October 31, 1958, in series U.S. Embassy, Havana, Cuba: Classified General Records, 1940-61, box 5, file 350, "Island Reports, 1956-8," RG 84, NARA.

29. Due to miscommunication, the *Granma* landed a few days later instead.

30. The incident took place on December 24, 1956. Accounts regarding the numbers of men and their alleged political involvement vary, but the men killed were apparently of different political persuasions, from moderate to radical, including Twenty-Sixth of July militants, Communist labor leaders, Ortodoxos, and men apparently

unaffiliated with any political group. See William Gálvez, "Pascuas Sangrientas," *La Jiribilla*, 2007, http://www.lajiribilla.co.cu/2007/n304_03/historia.html (accessed January 25, 2012).

31. Cruz Díaz, *Chicharrones*, 117; Nieves and Feijóo, *Semillas de fuego*, 2:75-76.

32. Memo from American consul, Santiago, to Department of State, "Revolutionary Actions—Oct. 2-6, 1958," dispatch no. 93, October 6, 1958, CUSSDCF, *Cuba, 1955-1959*.

33. One young member of Catholic Action recalled, "We had to pray very hard in order to not be won over by violence when we saw the soldiers driving around with the cadaver of a young man whom they had let bleed to death tied to the front of their truck." As cited in Fernández Soneira, *Con la estrella*, 418.

34. Cruz Díaz, *Chicharrones*, 117.

35. Herb Matthews, "Populace in Revolt in Santiago de Cuba," *New York Times*, June 10, 1957, 1, 10.

36. Some authors credit the MRC with organizing the March of the Mothers. See Morán Arce, *La Revolución cubana*, 82; and Cuesta Braniella, *La resistencia cívica*, 64. Other sources credit the Twenty-Sixth of July Movement. See Klouzal, "Rebellious Affinities," 104-5. The José Martí Civic Front for Women also claimed to have helped organize the March of the Mothers. See Castro Porta, *La lección*, 147. As noted earlier, the protest of early June 1957 has not entered official histories, and its organization is less clear.

37. Cuesta Braniella, *La resistencia cívica*, 173.

38. As suggested, for example, in Cuadras de la Cruz and Cabrales, *El rostro descubierto*, 132. There is evidence that women's organizations in Havana worked together to organize protests. For example, on the protests held in Havana on July 26, 1957, women from the Twenty-Sixth of July Movement and MOU participated. See "Entrevista: Elvira Díaz," *Unidad Femenina*, circa March 1959, 14. Women's sections of the movement in exile were also expected to work with the women's sections of other opposition groups. See "Mujeres cubanas en acción contra la dictadura," *Batalla* (New York), July 7, 1957, HMP, box 8. See Friedman, *Unfinished Transitions*, 117-18, for very similar processes in the anti-Pérez Jiménez struggle in Venezuela.

39. R. Hart Phillips, "Cuban Civic Units Oppose Carnival," *New York Times*, June 22, 1957, 6; Phillips, "Cuban City Tense on Eve of Rally," *New York Times*, June 30, 1957, 4; "Una protesta de las madres," *Diario de Cuba* (Santiago), January 3, 1957, 1-2.

40. See, for example, testimonies in Cruz Díaz, *Chicharrones*, 49-50.

41. "Por qué luchó la mujer cubana?," *La Mujer* (Buenos Aires), January 20, 1959. Guira was an organizer for the DR and the girlfriend of DR leader Joe Westbrook, whose killing by Havana police became a cause célèbre.

42. Taylor, *Disappearing Acts*, 193-94.

43. Ibid., 195.

44. Joint interview with Dolores Domínguez and Caridad Arango, Havana, July 2007; see also Franqui, *Diary*, 443-44.

45. Letter from Dora Rosales de Westbrook to Mamie Eisenhower, June 3, 1957, CUSSDCF, *Cuba, 1955-1959*. English in original.

46. There is extensive scholarship on the Madres de la Plaza de Mayo, including Taylor, *Disappearing Acts*; Guzman Bouvard, *Revolutionizing Motherhood*; and Navarro, "The Personal Is Political."

47. Letter to U.S. ambassador from various women representatives of rebel groups, August 5, 1957, from series U.S. Embassy, Havana, Cuba: Classified General Records, 1940–61, box 5, file 350: "Cuba Opposition, 1957," RG 84, NARA.

48. Organización Auténtica, *Manifiesto* (pamphlet) ([Havana?]: n.p., May 1957), HMP, box 8.

49. Letter from Rosario García viuda de Pais to wife of Consul Oscar Guerra, March 12, 1957, General Records of Department of State, Subject Files Relating to Cuba, box 1, RG 59, lot file no. 59 D 2, NARA.

50. Identified as such in memorandum of conversation with José Ruiz Velasco (Santiago physician), September 27, 1957, RG 84, Embassy correspondence, file 350, Cuba Opposition, 1957, NARA. On Sarabia's role in the MRC, see interview with Ariana Núñez, Havana, July 2007.

51. Interview with Ariana Núñez, Havana, July 2007.

52. In this they were similar to their male counterparts. See, for example, one man's description of his social world and the various threads by which he was pulled into revolutionary activity in Suárez Suárez and Puig Corral, *La complejidad de la rebelión*.

53. Mary Kay Vaughan argues in her discussion of postrevolutionary Mexican state formation that a series of new laws aimed at rationalizing family life "created new status and entitlement for women as mothers, a democratizing category that cut across class lines." Vaughan, introduction to Olcott, Vaughan, and Cano, *Sex in Revolution*, 28.

54. In reference to the March of the Mothers, an exile paper stated, "The protest in Santiago included the best of society, even the women of the Bacardí family and others were there, asking for the end of the horrifying assassinations of youths and children." *Patria* (New York), April 1, 1957, HMP, box 8.

55. "Found square in front municipal building occupied by large group middle and upper class women, many dressed in black." Telegram no. 79 from Havana embassy, August 3, 1957.

56. Ibid. Herb Matthews, who was well connected in Santiago, commented regarding a protest letter penned by a group of women that they were "Cuban women of society and wealth, including a number in the teaching profession." Letter to Vice President Richard Nixon from "A Ladies' Institution," June 16, 1958, included as attachment to letter from Herb Matthews to Vice President Nixon, June 30, 1958, CUSSDCF, *Cuba, 1955–1959*.

57. It is clear that at least some women of the popular classes also joined these protests. For example, women residents of the poor Santiago neighborhood Chicharrones described joining the marches of mothers. See Cruz Díaz, *Chicharrones*, 48–49.

58. Interview with Ariana Núñez, Havana, July 2007.

59. Ibid. See also descriptions of protests by Vilma Espín in the interview printed in *Revista Santiago*, June–September 1975.

60. Letter to Vice President Richard Nixon from "A Ladies' Institution."

61. Cited in de la Fuente, *A Nation for All*, 253.

62. Letter to Vice President Richard Nixon from "A Ladies' Institution."

63. See authors cited in note 9 of this chapter.

64. "Una protesta de las madres," *Diario de Cuba* (Santiago), January 3, 1957, 1–2.

65. Ibid.

66. The letter bears thirty-seven signatures and is illustrated with a photo of the March of the Mothers of January 1957. Men killed belonged to organizations including the Twenty-Sixth of July Movement, DR, and Organización Auténtica, as well as the "old" parties like the Ortodoxos and Auténticos.

67. Mallon, "*Barbudos*, Warriors and *Rotos*," 214.

68. See *Las mujeres en la revolución cubana* (pamphlet) (Havana: n.p., n.d., circa early 1960s), which reprints the letter with the attributions mentioned earlier. A copy of the original flyer, with no authors attributed, can be found in HMP.

69. Interview with Ariana Núñez, Havana, July 2007.

70. Printed in *Batalla* (New York), July 7, 1957, HMP, box 8.

71. Biographical information found in "Poetisa cubana visitará Manabí," *El Mercurio* (Cuenca, Ecuador), January 12, 2014, 11A; "Nieves Rodríguez Gómez," Wikipedia entry consulted June 5, 2014. On Adolfo Martí Fuentes, see biographical entry in EcuRed, www.ecured.cu/index.php/Adolfo_Martí_Fuentes (accessed June 5, 2014).

72. Nieves Rodríguez, "Carta desde Mexico" (1958), reprinted in *Hoy*, January 14, 1959.

73. There were many all-women's opposition groups during the insurrectionary period, but it is unclear from existing documents how consolidated, how large, or how lasting they were. For a list of women's groups who mobilized against Batista, see *Las mujeres en la revolución cubana*. Additionally, some of the armed rebel groups formed women's sections, which undertook tasks similar to those described in this chapter. On the women's section of the DR, see "Quedó constituido el comité femenino del Directorio Revolucionario," *13 de Marzo*, March 1958. The Twenty-Sixth of July in Havana also formed a temporary "comando femenino" in the days leading up to the failed general strike of April 1958, to assist in making Molotov cocktails, seeking safe houses, and providing aid for the wounded. It was led by one of the older women also affiliated with the FCMM, Pastorita Núñez, later named minister of public housing. See Nieves and Feijóo, *Semillas de fuego*, 1:78–79.

74. I have discussed these groups with more detail in Chase, "Women's Organizations."

75. The Organización Auténtica and Triple A may be partial exceptions, but these were groups largely funded by older members of the Auténtico Party, while the active militant base was mostly made up of young men.

76. Pelayo joined the Communist Youth League in 1928 (Maloof, *Voices of Resistance*, 55). Castro Porta became involved in the student group of the University of Havana, the Directorio Estudiantil Universitario (Matilde Salas Servando, "Una historia sin vacilaciones, ni descanso," *Alma Mater*, July 24, 2008). By the early 1930s, Aida Pelayo belonged to the Marxist student group Ala Izquierda Estudiantil, and Castro Porta worked with Defensa Obrera Internacional (DOI), an internationalist aid group

affiliated with the PSP (Maloof, *Voices of Resistance*, 55). Robert Alexander describes the DOI as one of the Communists' principal front groups. See his *Communism in Latin America*, 276. See also Yolanda Ricardo, "Carmen Castro Porta (Neneína, 1908–1985)," in her *La resistencia en las Antillas*, 210–12.

77. Castro Porta, *La lección*, 27–28, fn1; Maloof, *Voices of Resistance*, 55; Salas Servando, "Una historia"; Marlene Irene Portuondo Pajon, "La mujer cubana y la defensa de la República española," *Tiempo en Cuba* (2002).

78. Castro Carmen, "Como fue ajusticiado el coronel Cowley," *Prensa Libre*, February 18, 1959, 19.

79. Gladys Marel García, "Género, historia y sociologia."

80. Stoner, *From the House to the Streets* and "Ofelia Dominguez Navarro."

81. On the congress, see Stoner, *From the House to the Streets*, 189–90. In a 1992 interview she referred to herself as "still" a feminist—an extremely rare comment in the Cuban context. Maloof, *Voices of Resistance*, 56.

82. Maloof, *Voices of Resistance*, 56.

83. "Mensaje a las mujeres cubanas," circa 1955 or 1956, reprinted in Castro Porta, *La lección*, 287–91.

84. Interview with Miguel Guillén, Havana, June 2007.

85. On MOU activities, see *Las mujeres en la revolución cubana* and interview with Natalia Bolívar published in *Alma Mater* (University of Havana), 2002, http://www .afrocubaweb.com/bolivar.htm (accessed May 7, 2015).

86. Indeed, in one interview I conducted in Havana in 2005, an elderly man recalled the group's name as the "Madres Martianas," a revealing slip.

87. Interview with Lola Zanetti, Havana, July 2007.

88. Castro Porta, *La lección*; various interviews.

89. The cell structure of the insurrectionary groups prevented men from knowing more than ten or twelve of their comrades. Thus, when a new detainee arrived, the existing prisoners—who were internally organized into their respective revolutionary groupings—needed confirmation of his identity and militancy before including him in their group strategizing sessions. Interview with Miguel Guillén, Havana, June 2007.

90. "Mensaje a las Mujeres Cubanas," reprinted in Castro Porta, *La lección*, 287–91.

91. Castro Porta, *La lección*, 97–99.

92. As Jean Franco has argued about the Madres de la Plaza de Mayo, for example, they pioneered a political practice "in which the rights (and rites) of kinship were given precedence over the discourse of the state." "Going Public, Reinhabiting the Private," in Franco, *Critical Passions*.

93. Ruddick, *Maternal Thinking*, chap. 6.

94. Bayard de Volo, *Mothers of Heroes and Martyrs*, 41–43.

95. See Sweig, *Inside the Cuban Revolution*; Nieves and Feijóo, *Semillas de fuego*; Rodríguez Astiazaraín, *Episodios*.

96. Bonachea and San Martín, *Cuban Insurrection*; Sweig, *Inside the Cuban Revolution*.

97. Interview with Eneida Hernández, Havana, July 2007.

98. Germán Arcienagas, "Las heroinas," *Prensa Libre*, January 21, 1959, 2.

99. Díaz Vallina, Dotre Romay, and Dacosta Pérez, "La mujer revolucionaria." The study was based on interviews with former women combatants residing in one municipality in Havana (Plaza). It revealed that the vast majority of the women— 82 percent—were white, that 70 percent were either middle class or working class (without further breakdown), and that 49 percent had completed either high school or college. The study is difficult to contextualize, however, because it does not indicate how veteran status was established, how representative Plaza might have been relative to other municipalities of Havana, or how the various municipalities compiled their statistics. Studies of insurrectionary participation in other Latin American countries suggest that women of the middle sectors were more common than working-class women. See Jacquette, "Women in Revolutionary Movements in Latin America," and Lobao, "Women in Revolutionary Movements."

100. Based on the estimate provided by Bonachea and San Martín that total underground membership reached 30,000 by late 1958. (See chapter 2.)

101. Klouzal, "Rebellious Affinities," 139–40. See a similar account in Lewis, *Four Women*, 372–73. Oral histories collected by Cruz Díaz suggest that the informally and semi-employed urban poor of Santiago collaborated with the movement in similar fashion. Cruz Díaz, *Chicharrones*.

102. Interview with Vicente Robaína, Havana, January 2006.

103. Interview with Rogelio Bárcena, Washington, D.C., September 2011.

104. The children of Spaniards were overrepresented in the urban opposition. For a list of revolutionary leaders who were first-generation Spanish Cubans, see Bonachea and Valdés, *Revolutionary Struggle*, 4.

105. Interview with Ana Losada Prieto, Havana, September 2005.

106. Interview with Eneida Hernández, Havana, September 2005. Other women interviewed similarly mentioned the stress of constantly deceiving suspicious parents, e.g., interview with Rosario Navarrete, Havana, July 2007.

107. A reference to Eduardo Chibás, figurehead of the Ortodoxo Party, whom her mother followed so devotedly that she withdrew from all political activity after his death. Chibás had committed suicide in 1951, but his death was assimilated by his followers to the concept of martyrdom in political struggle.

108. Interview with Eneida Hernández, Havana, September 2005.

109. Interviews with Rosario Marín, Havana, August 2005; Ana Losada Prieto, Havana, September 2005; Marisol Álvarez, Havana, January 2006; and Lola Zanetti, Havana, July 2007.

110. Interview with Marisol Álvarez, Havana, January 2006.

111. Some male revolutionaries I interviewed said their parents did not know of their involvement in rebel activity until they were arrested. Others reported that their parents were against their activity because they feared for their physical safety.

112. For example, in at least one case, a married woman's husband forced her to abandon the FCMM after a protest with the group landed her in jail. Other women activists, whose husbands were less interested in politics or were hostile to their wives'

involvement, later divorced. (Interviews with Rosario Marín, Havana, August 2005; Rosario Navarrete, Havana, July 2007; and Ana Losada Prieto, Havana, September 2005.)

113. Joint interview with Eneida Hernández and Federico Larrazaba, Havana, September 2005.

114. Interview with Carmelo Jiménez, Miami, November 2005. It is unclear to what extent the movement also frowned upon male romantic relations with women not involved in the movement.

115. See, for example, the chaste description of courtships within the urban Twenty-Sixth of July Movement included in the *testimonio* published by Nieves Rivera, *Rogito*, 66, 81.

116. In multiple interviews, former women movement members praised this film as highly realistic. Memoirs capture similar scenarios. See ibid., for example.

117. The topic has remained taboo on the island. It is also clear that some imprisoned men were raped, but this not been publicly spoken of, nor did I broach the subject in my interviews.

118. Interview with Eneida Hernández, Havana, September 2005. For mention of gang rape conducted by army soldiers in Santiago, see "Notes on Visit from Evaristo Vicente," September 27, 1958, box 1, folder "Notes," HMP.

119. As Francesa Miller and others have argued, "in Latin America it was this generation of women who became the fiery feminists of the 1970s." (Miller, *Latin American Women*, 147.) Karen Kampwirth's seminal study documents the transition many women guerrillas made from "feminine" to feminist organizing. "In other words, they made a transition from one kind of women's organizing to another" (Kampwirth, *Feminism*, 8). For scholarly works that trace many women's journey from national liberation to feminism, see ibid. and Shayne, *Revolution Question*.

120. Shayne, *Revolution Question*, 136.

121. The organization was known as Magín. See Fernandes, "Transnationalism and Feminist Activism."

122. Castro Porta, *La lección*, 243.

Chapter 4

1. Manuel Cruz Merlo, "Síntesis de policía," *Prensa Libre*, April 5, 1959, 10.

2. See especially Kampwirth, *Feminism*; Shayne, *Revolution Question*; and Friedman, *Unfinished Transitions*.

3. See, for example, Rosemblatt, *Gendered Compromises*; Tinsman, *Partners in Conflict*; see also Green, "Who Is the Macho Who Wants to Kill Me?"

4. These figures are from Goldenburg, "Rise and Fall of a Party." See higher figures in Sims, "Cuba." Contemporary American observers put the number of members much higher, near 150,000. See Havana embassy (signed Earl T. Crain) to Department of State, "*Carteles* Interviews United Press Correspondent McCarthy on Communist Menace in Cuba," airgram no. 416, August 22, 1950, CUSSDCF, *Cuba, 1950-1954*.

5. For example, prominent middle-class members included Juan Marinello, Carlos Rafael Rodríguez, and Elena Gil. A rare surviving list of presumed Communist Party members who were arrested during an event in Havana to celebrate the World Partisans for Peace Congress on November 7, 1950, notes the detainees' names, occupations, ages, and places of residence. All were male; most were between their mid-twenties and mid-forties; most occupations included trades such as construction workers and other day laborers, cobblers, painters, cooks, and mechanics. Nearly all lived in the working-class neighborhoods of Luyanó, Sitios, or El Cerro. Enclosure to airgram from Havana embassy to Department of State (signed Henry Hoyt), November 30, 1950, subject: "Arrest of Cuban Communists and Mexican, Brazilian and Costa Rican Delegates to Second World Partisans of Peace Congress," CUSSDCF, *Cuba, 1950–1954*.

6. Robert Blake, "The Communist Party in Cuba," typed report, March 1947. In series Office of Middle American Affairs, Cuba 1955, box 1, file "Communism," RG 59, NARA. Blake notes, "Party Workers . . . told this writer that about three-quarters of the members were urban workers and their wives." On membership numbers, see also Havana embassy to Department of State, "*Carteles* Interviews United Press Correspondent McCarthy."

7. Memo from ARA—Mr. Sayre—to MID—Mr. [Bill] Connett, "Statement on Communism—Your Memo of Feb[.] 9," February 10, 1955, RG 59, Office of Middle American Affairs, Cuba 1955, box 1, file "Communism," NARA. See also U.S. embassy to Department of State, "*Carteles* Interviews United Press Correspondent McCarthy."

8. Attachment/enclosure to memo from Havana embassy (signed Henry Hoyt) to Department of State, "Transmitting Copies of Communist Propaganda Which Has Been Circulated in Cuba," dispatch no. 333, August 27, 1951, CUSSDCF, *Cuba, 1950–1954*.

9. Blake, "The Communist Party in Cuba."

10. Thomas, *Cuba*, 697.

11. Weigand, *Red Feminism*, 20. Most scholarly work on the prerevolutionary PSP focuses on its role in the 1933 revolution, its strength in labor unions, and its slow conversion to the revolutionary cause. Goldenburg, "Rise and Fall of a Party"; Sims, "Cuba"; Rojas Blaquier, *El primer partido comunista de Cuba*.

12. Murray, "Socialism and Feminism," 62.

13. Stoner, *From the House to the Streets*, 172–80.

14. Havana embassy (signed Henry Hoyt) to Department of State, "Federación Democrática de Mujeres Cubanas," airgram no. 56, September 1, 1950, CUSSDCF, *Cuba, 1950–1954*. According to Nicola Murray, the existing Unión de Mujeres Nacionales was rechristened the FDMC in 1948. Murray, "Socialism and Feminism." See also González Pagés, *En busca de un espacio*.

15. Havana embassy to Department of State, "Federación Democrática de Mujeres Cubanas."

16. Quote from Thomas, *Cuba*, 846. See also García Montes and Alonso Avila, *Historia del partido Comunista de Cuba*, 442–43.

17. Francisca de Haan has cautioned that scholars should not assume that local affiliates of the WIDF were "controlled" by their respective national Communist

parties. Rather, she has documented that there was great variation in the relationship local affiliates of the WIDF had with the local Communist parties, ranging from autonomy to tight supervision. De Haan, "Communist Feminists?"; Friedman, *Unfinished Transitions*, 114–16.

18. On the Communist Party in the United States (CPUSA), see Weigand, *Red Feminism*; on the Brazilian Communist Party, see Miller, *Latin American Women*, 104.

19. Thomas, *Cuba*, 713.

20. De la Fuente, *A Nation for All*, 231. See also Benson, *Antiracism in Cuba*; Brunson, "Constructing Afro-Cuban Womanhood." Sánchez Mastrapa was expelled from both the Communist Party and the FDMC in 1950 for reasons that remain unclear. See memo dated September 20, 1950, CUSSDCF, *Cuba, 1950–1954*. See also "Expulsada de la FDMC por sus actuaciones Esperanza Sánchez," in *Mujeres Cubanas*, November 1950, 11. All copies of *Mujeres Cubanas* were consulted on Stoner, *The Women's Movement in Cuba: The Stoner Collection on Cuban Feminism* (hereafter *The Stoner Collection*).

21. Havana embassy to Department of State, "Federación Democrática de Mujeres Cubanas."

22. Ibid.

23. In 1952 the magazine was stated to have a circulation of 12,000, but the editors noted that not all members of the FDMC were receiving the magazine, and, conversely, not all those reading the magazine were members. "*Mujeres Cubanas* cumple dos años," *Mujeres Cubanas*, August 1952, 13.

24. Havana embassy to Department of State, "Federación Democrática de Mujeres Cubanas." On Catholic Action's efforts in the countryside in this period, see Fernández Soneira, *Con la estrella*.

25. Havana embassy to Department of State, "Federación Democrática de Mujeres Cubanas."

26. "Resoluciones del Congreso Mundial de Mujeres, 5 de Junio 1953, Copenhague," printed in *Mujeres Cubanas*, August 1953, 27.

27. "Acuerdos del Consejo," *Mujeres Cubanas*, January 1951, 5; "Convención Nacional en Defensa del Hogar," *Mujeres Cubanas*, August 1953, 5; "Programa de la FDMC," *Mujeres Cubanas*, February 1953, 14–15.

28. Nelita Martín, "La mujer campesina," *Mujeres Cubanas*, September 1950, 10.

29. On the Chilean agrarian reform, see Tinsman, *Partners in Conflict*.

30. In the fall of 1950, the FDMC sponsored an exhibit titled "How Children Live in the Soviet Union," shown in Havana and Matanzas. See "Actividades de la Federación Democrática de Mujeres Cubanas" (no author), *Mujeres Cubanas*, November 1950, 6–7; and "La FDMC a traves del pais" (no author), *Mujeres Cubanas*, December 1950, 6–7.

31. See, for example, Salud Rodríguez, "El cuidado de los niños en la Unión Soviética," *Mujeres Cubanas*, November 1950, 5; and "La constitución soviética y los derechos de la mujer" (no author), *Mujeres Cubanas*, December 1950, 5. On the prevalence of single mothers in prerevolutionary Cuba, see Smith and Padula, *Sex and Revolution*, 21.

32. See Brunson, "Constructing Afro-Cuban Womanhood," 282–87, quote from 286.

33. "Programa de la FDMC."

34. See de la Fuente, *A Nation for All*; Benson, *Antiracism in Cuba*. Quote from "Programa de la FDMC."

35. Specifically, the FDMC called for widening the Workers' Maternity Law, establishing maternity rooms in rural areas, distributing free milk to poor women who were breastfeeding, and home care services paid for by the state. For children, it demanded the construction of daycare centers, parks, and swimming pools, provision of free breakfast and lunch programs in public schools, and increased rural schooling. See ibid.

36. For the different perspective of the Chilean Communist Party, see the excellent study by Rosemblatt, *Gendered Compromises,* especially pp. 108–9. She shows that the Chilean Communist Party sought to derail feminist projects by emphasizing the importance of women's solidarity efforts for their male *compañeros* on strike and rejecting feminist calls for equal pay, nurseries, and improved infrastructure in poor neighborhoods. In contrast, the FDMC seemed to embrace various struggles for women's empowerment.

37. One might also contrast this to the highly negative depiction of housewives as lazy and bourgeois that characterized the post-1959 revolutionary government, especially in the late 1960s and early 1970s, and its attendant view of "housewives" and "revolutionaries" as nearly mutually exclusive categories. See Padula and Smith, *Sex and Revolution,* 100. See also Serra, *New Man,* 117–18.

38. On the relative openness of gay culture in nightlife and intellectual circles, see Lumsden, *Machos, Maricones, and Gays,* 33–36.

39. See Weigand, *Red Feminism,* for a discussion of how CPUSA members in the same period raised these issues in party publications and elsewhere.

40. I have here drawn on the pioneering interpretations of Kate Weigand, who argued that the CPUSA was important in sustaining a radical critique of gender relations throughout the inhospitable 1950s and thus laid the groundwork for the emergence of second-wave feminism. Weigand, *Red Feminism.*

41. On the activities of the Lyceum, see Guerrero, *Elena Mederos.*

42. De la Fuente, *A Nation for All.*

43. Gil, "Apuntes para mi hijo," 97.

44. Pérez, *Cuba: Between Reform and Revolution.*

45. Murray, "Socialism and Feminism," 63.

46. On the women's platoon known as the Mariana Grajales Brigade created within the rebel army, see Puebla and Waters, *Marianas en combate.* Leyva Pagán argues that at the formation of the Mariana Grajales Brigade, Fidel Castro gave a stirring, impassioned speech denouncing women's historic exploitation and inequality, and pledging the "revindication" of women upon the revolution's triumph. Leyva Pagán, *Historia,* 234.

47. It was more common for the new revolutionary government to address family reform programs, as I discuss in chapter 5.

48. While these terms were in fact rarely used anywhere in the 1950s, it is important to note that Cuba's Marxist Left did use the slogan "Equality in practice, not merely in

law," and according to Jorge García Montes and Antonio Alonso Ávila, the FDMC pontificated about "the 'liberation' movement of women in the Communist world." *Historia del partido Comunista de Cuba*, 402–43.

49. See the Castro speech reprinted in Guerra López, González Plasencia, and Hernándes Denis, *Fidel*, 1:15–16.

50. See *V Plenaria Nacional de la FMC* (pamphlet) (Havana: Minind. Ecag. Taller, n.d. circa January 1967).

51. See Castro speech in Guerra López, González Plasencia, and Hernándes Denis, *Fidel*, 1:71.

52. During the insurrection, women militants of the Twenty-Sixth of July Movement had not been organized separately, although there was occasionally considerable overlap between some revolutionary cells and occupational sectors—such as telephone workers or education students—that thereby ensured that some underground groups were almost entirely female. Fidel Castro entertained the idea of incorporating the José Martí Women's Civic Front as the Women's Section of the Twenty-Sixth of July, but the proposal never came to fruition. See his letter in Castro Porta, *La lección*, 91–96.

53. Interview with Martina Granados, Santo Domingo (conducted by telephone), February 2012.

54. For a typical example, see Blanco and Benjamin, *Cuba*, 62–63.

55. According to the historian and participant Marel García: "The main activities of the Brigada Femenina Revolucionaria involved supporting the laws set forth in the Moncada Program, . . . supporting the revolutionary government and the Ministry of Social Welfare through all kinds of mass activity and mobilization, and, in particular, supporting agrarian reform through mobilizations in the agricultural cooperatives and people's farms. The Brigada Femenina Revolucionaria also engaged in housing campaigns, civilian and military training of women, the redevelopment of the poor and insalubrious neighborhood of Las Yaguas, the rehabilitation of prostitutes and thieves, and the . . . literacy campaign." García, "Gender," 384–87. The activities listed ran parallel to those spearheaded by the revolutionary government in this period.

56. Interview with Gladys Marel García, Miami, December 2011. See also García, "Gender," 384–87.

57. Interview with Martina Granados, February 2012. She is referring to Fidel Castro's brief resignation in 1959, in protest over actions of the figurehead president Manuel Urrutia, who was thereafter pushed out of government.

58. Kampwirth, *Feminism*, 8. Yet importantly Kampwirth argues that even when women's liberation was not stated as an explicit goal, revolutionary demands for equity "contained the seeds of feminist consciousness and organizing, seeds that often germinated after the military stage of the guerrilla movements had ended or subsided" (ibid., 3).

59. Interview with Eneida Hernández, Havana, July 2007.

60. García, "Gender" 384–87.

61. Ibid.; interview with Gladys Marel García, Miami, December 2011.

62. Interview with Martina Granados, February 2012.

63. Miller, *Latin American Women*, 138.

64. This explains participants' subsequent vehement rejection in interviews of any attempt to characterize their work as feminist-inspired.

65. Prominent leftist women visitors included Argelia Laya of Venezuela and Marta Borges of Mexico.

66. In keeping with the generalized euphoria over the rebel triumph, and perhaps to tone down its connections with the PSP, the UFR downplayed its roots in the prerevolutionary organized Left, preferring to stress its weaker connections with insurrectionary groups. The UFR claimed to be a successor to an anti-Batista group formed during the insurrection, the MOU. The MOU had been founded during the insurrection by Marta Frayde, a gynecologist, but Frayde had been given a prominent position as director of a hospital in Havana in January. The name of the group was changed to reflect the fact that it was no longer in opposition to the government and was now a legal, aboveground organization. But in reality it was a new organization that brought together women from various insurrectionary groups as well as women of the prerevolutionary PSP who had not participated in the insurrection. Perhaps the attraction for the UFR's organizing committee of claiming the MOU was that the MOU had been the women's anti-Batista group farthest to the left, and included women loosely affiliated with the PSP or considered fellow travelers. For more information on the MOU, see Chase, "Women's Organizations."

67. The exact relationship between the UFR and the Communist Party remains controversial. Some sources flatly assert that the UFR either was secretly controlled by the Communist Party or was an open subsidiary of the party. A memo from the Havana committee of the PSP mentions the UFR prominently in its description of outreach to women, suggesting very close organizational links. See "Comité Provincial de la Habana (I) del Partido Socialista Popular: Informes de los trabajos realizados durante la semana comprendida entre los dias 4 al 10 de Octubre de 1959," IHC, Fondo Movimiento Femenino, RG 104.2/82. But the UFR also drew women of the revolutionary Left who were not PSP members, much as the MOU had. (See note 70 of this chapter for names of UFR founders.) Asela de los Santos asserts that the UFR "was an organization of left-wing women—not necessarily Communist but women with progressive ideas." Quoted in "It Gave Us a Sense of Worth," in Espín, de los Santos, and Ferrer, *Women in Cuba*, 108.

68. The original organizing committee included Carlota Miró, Alicia Agramonte, Alicia Hernández Jiménez, Candelaria Rodríguez, María Núñez, Elvira Díaz, Marina Azcuy, Esther Noriega, Gloria Cuadras, Dalia Villaverde, Olga Luisa Borrero, Graciella Hereaux, Zoila Pérez, Natalia Bolívar, Angelina Luna, and Onelia Aguilar. See *Unidad Femenina Revolucionaria, Primera conferencia nacional por la paz y la libertad. Convocatoria* (pamphlet) (n.p.: n.p., March 1959), IHC, Fondo Movimiento Femenino, 1/10:16/1.1/1-2.

69. The announcement for a provincial conference to be held in March 1959 noted, in addition to specific material demands, "We women also want Democracy to reign in our country, [we want] liberty, progress, independence, and that Peace be the light that

shines today and always in our homes, in our homeland." *Primera Conferencia Provincial de las Villas de Unidad Femenina Revolucionaria* (pamphlet) (n.p.: n.p., n.d., circa March 1, 1959), IHC, Fondo Movimiento Femenino, 1/10:15/4.1/1-2.

70. "Unidad Femenina Revolucionaria: Primera Conferencia Nacional, 11 y 12 abril, 1959," *Unidad Femenina* (circa March 1959), 8.

71. Unidad Femenina Revolucionaria, *Primera Conferencia Nacional: Porque la Revolución cumpla sus postulados* (pamphlet) (n.p.: n.p., n.d., circa March 1, 1959), IHC, Fondo Movimiento Femenino, 1/10:16/1.1/1-2.

72. "Unidad Femenina Revolucionaria, Primera Conferencia Nacional por la paz y la libertad. Convocatoria. 38 & 29 Marzo," typed manuscript, undated, IHC, Fondo Movimiento Femenino, 1/10:15/1.1/1-3. Subsequently printed as Unidad Femenina Revolucionaria, *Primera Conferencia Nacional*.

73. "Discurso de María Núñez en la conferencia," *Unidad Femenina*, circa August 1, 1959 (date illegible), 9, 36, 37, *The Stoner Collection*.

74. "Unidad Femeninia Revolucionaria: Sus avances en la provincia de la Habana," *Unidad Femenina* (circa March 1959), 8, 12–13.

75. María Núñez, "Las experiencias de la conferencia de la UFR," *Hoy*, May 24, 1959, 8.

76. Ibid. The term *bodega* referred to small neighborhood shops that primarily sold dried staples such as beans and rice.

77. Women's continued demands for *bodegas* with nighttime hours remained unsatisfied for the next several decades. Smith and Padula, *Sex and Revolution*, 142.

78. On "practical" versus "strategic" gender interests, see Molyneux, "Mobilization without Emancipation?" Molyneux defines practical interests as those oriented to relieving women's traditional burdens, and strategic interests as those that challenge the gendered division of labor and women's subordinated position in society.

79. "Unidad Femenina Revolucionaria en Provincias," *Unidad Femenina*, circa March 1959, 22.

80. Núñez, "Las experiencias de la conferencia."

81. Enrique Mesa, "Mujeres campesinas visitan la Habana," *Hoy*, March 31, 1960, 8.

82. "Las mujeres debemos hablar con Fidel" (unsigned editorial), *Hoy*, June 5, 1960, 6.

83. Ibid.

84. Smith and Padula note: "Most of the women who participated in the guerrilla struggle disappeared from public view after 1959. A few went on to hold modest positions" relative to their male counterparts. *Sex and Revolution*, 32.

85. It must be noted here that these issues are complicated by limited written documentary evidence and the presence of conflictive narratives. In addition, because the women affiliated with the Communist Party tended to be older than the women of the Twenty-Sixth of July, I have not been able to document their stories through interviews. The analyses proffered here are necessarily constrained by these limitations.

86. On this process, see especially Farber, "Cuban Communists in the Early Stage of the Revolution."

87. Interview with Gladys Marel García, Miami, December 2011. The reference is to the teachings of the nineteenth-century nationalist leader and poet José Martí.

88. See Pojmann, "For Mothers, Peace and Family."

89. Interview with Gladys Marel García, Miami, December 2011.

90. Interview with Eneida Hernández, Havana, June 2007.

91. In an anthropological study of former slum dwellers relocated after the revolution, Douglas Butterworth documented significant frustration in the superiority and discrimination displayed toward them by middle-class officials of organizations such as the FMC. Butterworth, *People of Buena Ventura*.

92. Interview with Gladys Marel García, Miami, December 2011.

93. Franqui, *Family Portrait*, 51.

94. For example, Clementina Serra made various suggestions for mundane organization building at the UFR conference, including things like establishing an office, disseminating a publication, charging membership dues, and the like.

95. This organizational diligence has left the activities of the UFR far better documented than the activities of the women's groups affiliated with the Twenty-Sixth of July movement.

96. On the cultural shift between the Old and New Left, see Zolov, "Expanding Our Conceptual Horizons." For a cautionary critique of overly rigid analytical separations of the Old and New Left, see Markarrian, "Sobre viejas y nuevas izquierdas."

97. Interview with Gladys Marel García, Miami, December 2011.

98. Interview with Gladys Marel García, Brooklyn, June 2012. See also the comments made by Asela de los Santos on the prehistory of the FMC: "A unification process began [among women's groups]. But it wasn't a rose-strewn path. . . . It's not surprising there would be initial misunderstandings and divisions, snubs: this one's labeled communist, that one's bourgeois, whatever." (Espín, de los Santos, and Ferrer, *Women in Cuba*, 110.)

99. Núñez is mentioned extensively in FDMC and UFR materials and in *Hoy*. See, for example, "Grandes avances de Unidad Femenina en Pinar del Rio," *Unidad Femenina*, April 1, 1959, 16–17. She is identified as a national organizer of the UFR in *Hoy*, March 1, 1960. See also "Entrevista con Maria Núñez," *Hoy*, August 30, 1959, 6. She is identified as part of the national council of the FDMC in "Acuerdos del Consejo," 5. She is identified as a Santiago PSP member in Suárez Suárez and Puig Corral, *La complejidad de la rebelión*, 161.

100. In original Spanish: "Hice de todo, dondequiera que me necesitaban. Hace treinta anos que trabajo en la Revolucion." Quoted in María Luisa Domínguez Roldán, "La mujer cubana responde 'Presente,'" *Bohemia*, December 11, 1960, 34.

101. Tambor, "Red Saints," 431.

102. Núñez, "Las experiencias de la conferencia."

103. "La idea de crear las milicias populares femeninas surgió de la conferencia de UFR," *Hoy*, May 8, 1959, 4.

104. See Castro speech in Guerra López, González Plasencia, and Hernández Denis, *Fidel*, 71. See also the January 1, 1959, speech where he announced, "We will

have, organized and ready, reserve forces [*reservas*] of female combatants." Reprinted in ibid., 15. Interestingly, although in speeches made after 1959, Castro indirectly took credit for the formation of the Mariana Grajales Brigade, he was in fact petitioned by women members of the movement in the Sierra to form the unit. See Puebla and Waters, *Marianas en combate*, 46. Finally, it is worth noting that in 1959, women who had fought in the Mariana Grajales Brigade were put to more traditionally feminine tasks, such as locating children in remote locales for the new revolutionary schools.

105. Isabel Moya, "Alas desatadas," *La Jiribilla*, January 3, 2009, http://www.lajiribilla.cu/2009/n400_01/400_05.html#_ftnref16.

106. Printed in *Revolución*, January 12, 1959, 12.

107. For example, in another cartoon that made light of these fears, one man exclaims to his friend: "Man, did I play my cards wrong! I convinced my wife that I had joined the militias and had to train at night" (i.e., as cover for his sexual dallying). "So what happened?" "She signed up too!" (i.e., implying that his machinations might now result in he himself being cuckolded). *Bohemia*, April 10, 1960, 126.

108. See photo on page 7 of *Hoy*, January 5, 1960.

109. *Unidad Femenina Suplemento Gráfico*, circa March 1960, IHC, Fondo Movimiento Femenino.

110. *Hoy*, February 9, 1960.

111. Cristina América García Anaya, testimony compiled in Séjourné, *La mujer cubana*, 188.

112. Cited in ibid., 182.

113. Ana Gus, "Como visten hoy las cubanas," *Bohemia Libre*, September 24, 1961.

114. Mary Nash, "Milicianas and Homefront Heroines" and "Women in War."

115. Smith and Padula also noted: "The FMC was reportedly Fidel Castro's idea. FMC chief Vilma Espín once observed that during the . . . insurrection women didn't talk about 'inequality or discrimination' or about 'feminine emancipation.'" *Sex and Revolution*, 36. See also the longer quote from Espín where she states that "it hadn't even remotely occurred to me that a women's organization should exist." Espín, de los Santos, and Ferrer, *Women in Cuba*, 28.

116. "Actividades de UFR en Yaguajay," *Hoy*, August 8, 1959, 8; and "La visita de la compañera Vilma Espín," *Unidad Femenina*, circa August 1959, 6, 34.

117. See "With No Preconceived Structure or Agenda: Interview with Vilma Espín," in Espín, de los Santos, and Ferrer, *Women in Cuba*, and the introduction by Waters in the same volume.

118. The phrase is from "Unidad Femenina Revolucionaria: Primera Conferencia Nacional."

119. The formation of the FMC paralleled formation of other so-called mass organizations in the period, such as the militia and the CDRs. On this process, see Fagen, *Transformation of Political Culture*, especially chap. 4.

120. For other studies that show initially radical visions of women's emancipation— often proposed by women leaders or grassroots activists—that were tamed or left

unrealized during the subsequent process of state formation, see Wood, *The Baba and the Comrade*; Olcott, *Revolutionary Women*; Harsch, *Revenge of the Domestic*.

121. The best-known figures of the urban insurrection included Gloria Cuadras, María Antonieta Figueroa, Aida Pelayo, Carmen Castro Porta, Marta Frayde, Elvira Díaz, Natalia Bolívar, Mirta Rodríguez Calderón, Norma Porras, and Asela de los Santos. Only the "heroines of the Sierra" (Celia Sánchez, Haydée Santamaría, and Vilma Espín) were given prominent positions. For a list of FMC officials named during the organization's formation, see "Unificado el movimiento de las mujeres revoluciona-rias cubanas," *Hoy*, August 24, 1960, 1, 15. For a list of FMC functionaries in Oriente Province, see the "Para la mujer" section in *Hoy*, August 30, 1960, 8.

122. The vast retraining program for domestic workers was headed by PSP veteran Elena Gil. The formation of daycare centers was led by PSP veteran Clementina Serra. The training of women militias was at least partly led by María Núñez, a member of the PSP, the FDMC and leader of the UFR. Dressmaking classes for peasant women were headed by Alicia Imperatori of the Twenty-Sixth of July Movement and Esther Noriega of the PSP. The women's magazine *Mujeres* was edited by Mirta Aguirre and Elsa Gutiérrez, both of the PSP.

123. In original: "No, aquí estamos las cubanas." Blanchie Sartorio, "De juguete hermoso a compañera," *guerrillero.cu* (Pinar del Rio), August 23, 2010 (accessed September 2010). Azcuy was also one of the original signatories of the UFR's organizing committee.

124. Ibid. Azcuy was killed in an August 1960 car crash.

Chapter 5

1. See the biography of Fe del Valle at http://www.ecured.cu/index.php/Fe_del_Valle _Ramos (accessed June 18, 2013).

2. Alfonso Chardy, " 'Cuba of Yesteryear Died' with Destruction of El Encanto Store," *Miami Herald*, December 24, 2008, www.miamiherald.com (accessed June 18, 2013).

3. Smith and Padula note, "Shopping meant standing in line, and it was usually women who waited." *Sex and Revolution*, 151.

4. See Bentley, *Eating for Victory*; Davis, *Home Fires Burning*.

5. Unlike some Latin American countries, the Caribbean islands did not experiment with Import Substitution Industrialization in the 1940s. Puerto Rico's industrializa-tion through Operation Bootstrap in the same period employed a different model, essentially treating Puerto Rico as an offshore special economic zone for U.S. manufacture. On the various sectors that supported industrialization, see Herminio Portell Vila, "Industrializacion," *Bohemia*, December 6, 1959, 30, 135, 146. As he notes, the National Association of Industrialists of Cuba, the Cuban Workers' Confederation, and the revolutionary government all agreed on the urgency of industrializing the country.

6. Personal communication, Teófilo Ruiz, January 2008.

7. On the postwar growth of the urban middle sectors throughout Latin America and their expectations of political democracy and higher living standards, see Bethell and

Roxborough, introduction to *Latin America*. On Cuban particularities within this general panorama, see Pérez, *On Becoming Cuban*, and Ibarra, *Prologue to Revolution*.

8. Farber, *Revolution and Reaction*, 221.

9. "Una nación con industrias propias es un pueblo libre," advertisement for the nationalized gas and alcohol company José Arrechabala, *Bohemia*, April 3, 1960, 47.

10. The Casino Capri hosted a musical titled *Consumiendo productos cubanos*. See advertisement in *Prensa Libre*, April 24, 1959, 3.

11. E. W. Kenworthy, "Castro Declares Regime Is Free of Red Influence," *New York Times*, April 18, 1959, 1, 10.

12. Dana Adams Schmidt, "Castro Rules Out Role as Neutral; Opposes the Reds," *New York Times*, April 20, 1959, 1, 5.

13. See *Hoy*, December 24, 1959, and June 26, 1959.

14. "Address Delivered by Dr. Fidel Castro to the Representatives of the Tobacco Industry," April 8, 1959, http://lanic.utexas.edu/project/castro/db/1959/19590410.html (accessed May 7, 2013).

15. "Patria y producción," *El Mundo*, May 10, 1959, A10.

16. "Usted también puede ayudar a dar empleo a más cubanos," Cía Cubana de Electricidad advertisement, *Bohemia*, March 20, 1960.

17. Ibid.

18. "El dinero del pueblo al pueblo vuelve," department store Fin de Siglo (Nacionalizado) advertisement, *Bohemia*, July 2, 1961, 119.

19. Important early studies include Bengelsdorf, "On the Problem of Studying Women in Cuba," and Smith and Padula, *Sex and Revolution*.

20. For example, Vilma Espín blamed scarcity as one factor in perpetuating the role of women as "a slave to the house" (*esclava del hogar*), tied to the kitchen and the children. Vilma Espín, "La mujer en la revolucion cubana," *Cuba Socialista*, December 1961, 59–67, quote 66.

21. Lewis, *Four Women*, xviii. There were a few small-scale pilot programs to incorporate rural women into agricultural work through cooperatives. A 1961 pilot program in Caney, Oriente, trained seventy women in aviculture, wine production, and other small-scale, home-based forms of agricultural production. The Plan Banao program in Sancti Spiritus trained women who had previously been housewives to plant specialty produce such as strawberries and asparagus. See *V Plenaria Nacional de la FMC* (pamphlet) (Havana: Minind. Ecag. Taller, n.d. circa January 1967); see also Sutherland Martínez, *Youngest Revolution*, 59. As Nazarri and others have noted, many working-class women withdrew from the labor force in this period. Nazarri, "The 'Woman Question' in Cuba."

22. As Carollee Bengelsdorf argued, the fact that "traditionally private women's work" was now collectivized and carried out by women in public only "serve[d] to reinforce the sexual division of labor." Bengelsdorf, "On the Problem of Studying Women," 126.

23. For use of the term *denigrante*, see Elena Gil's comments quoted in Séjourné, *La mujer cubana*, 144.

24. See speech by FMC head Vilma Espín in *V Plenaria Nacional de la FMC*. See also Elena Gil's remarks in Séjourné, *La mujer cubana*, 144, on domestic workers.

25. On these early measures, see Benjamin, *No Free Lunch*, 18.

26. Personal communication, Sam Farber, April 2006.

27. On the agrarian reform, see especially O'Connor, *Origins of Socialism*; Domínguez, *Cuba*, 423–63; and Padula, "Fall of the Bourgeoisie."

28. Thomas, *Cuba*, 1215–18; Padula, "Fall of the Bourgeoisie."

29. Farber, *Origins of the Cuban Revolution*, 80–84.

30. About 30 percent of the food consumed in Cuba was imported, including many staples that could have been produced on the island, such as rice, lard, dairy products, eggs, and vegetables. See Benjamin, *No Free Lunch*, 9. Of those imported food products, some 70 percent came from the United States (ibid., 20). About 80 percent of Cuban imports overall came from the United States. In addition, Cuba exported many raw products to the United States, then imported the processed final product. For example, Cuba exported tomatoes, then imported tomato paste. For an overview, see ibid., 8–14; see also Boorstein, *Economic Transformation*, 70, 94–97, 114.

31. For an early report on the rising prices of staples foods produced in Cuba such as beans, potatoes, and rice, see Gervasio Ruiz, "No se puede pedir que suban los sueldos y bajen los precios," *Carteles*, May 31, 1959, 30–31.

32. The various establishments where Cubans purchased food in this period included *bodegas* (local stores for canned or dried foods and sweets, including imported goods), *almacenes* (local stores for grains, such as beans and rice), *mercados* (large covered markets selling fresh meat and produce), and various other local vendors such as butchers, bakers, and vegetable stalls (*puestos*).

33. For example, the Marianao Comité Cívico Revolucionario de Barrios de Ceiba y Colombia expressed various demands for "improvements," including investigating the Mercado de Buenaventura, "with the aim of lowering the prices of articles of basic necessity," improving the state of schools, and repairing certain local streets. *Hoy*, April 15, 1959, 2.

34. Celia Yaniz, "Entre nosotras," *Hoy*, March 6, 1959; Justina Álvarez, "Contra el alza de los precios: Las amas de casa deben estar vigilantes, las organizaciones femeninas en la defensa de las amas de casa," *Hoy*, May 28, 1959.

35. Yaniz, "Entre nosotras," *Hoy*, March 6, 1959.

36. Guerra, *Visions of Power*.

37. The government set official prices for rice, milk, bread, and beef products in March 1959, then extended those official prices to butter, pork, cheese, potatoes, and other necessary goods such as soap in May 1959. For an overview, see Benjamin, *No Free Lunch*, 22. For specific price caps, see "Economia," *Hoy*, August 15, 1959, 4; "Rebajado el precio de la papa," *El Mundo*, January 12, 1960, A1. See list of price ceilings on seafood printed in *El Mundo*, January 8, 1960, B6; "Afectado el abasto de café," *El Mundo*, October 30, 1959, A1. See also Yaniz, "Entre nosotras," *Hoy*, March 6, 1959.

38. "Sancionarán a los que atenten contra la economía popular," *Hoy*, January 30, 1960, 1, 5.

39. "Maniobra contra la economía popular patronos arroceros de Manzanillo," *Hoy*, February 28, 1960, 10; and "Huyen hacia Miami los patronos del almacén de viveres 'el Tigre,'" *Hoy*, June 21, 1960.

40. "Sancionarán a los que atenten contra la economia popular," *Hoy*, January 30, 1960, 1, 5; "Sanciones a detallistas por violar disposiciones oficiales," *Hoy*, June 24, 1961, 5; "La lucha contra la especulación," *Hoy*, September 8, 1961, 5.

41. See, among many possible examples, the editorial "El ahorro, obligación nacional," *Hoy*, August 1, 1961, 1.

42. James Cameron, "Cuba's Fumbling Marxism: An Eyewitness Account," *Atlantic*, September 1964.

43. Welch, *Response to Revolution*, 98.

44. Benjamin, *No Free Lunch*.

45. Comités de Defensa de la Revolución, *Memorias 1962* (Havana: Ediciones Con la Guardia en Alto, 1963), 62.

46. See "Vigilarán los CDR ventas que efectuen las bodegas," *Hoy*, August 6, 1961, 3; "La revolución en el Mercado Único," *Hoy*, June 3, 1961, and August 6, 1961; "Acabarán los CDR con la especulación," *Hoy*, December 10, 1961. The FMC also announced that it was watching merchants to ensure they were respecting government-set prices. See American embassy, Havana (in Miami, ARA: Miami) to Department of State, dispatch no. 124 (Cuban Series), subject: "USIA-Miami Monitoring Report on Cuban Government Microwave Broadcasts, May 12, 1961," May 24, 1961, *Confidential U.S. State Department Central Files. Cuba, 1960–January 1963, Foreign Affairs* (hereafter CUSSDCF, *Cuba, 1960–January 1963*).

47. See "Presencia de la mujer en los Comités de Defensa," *Bohemia*, September 28, 1962, 72–73, which notes that by the CDRs' second anniversary, nearly 1.5 million Cubans in total had participated, including a million women. At the first FMC Congress of 1962, the organization stated a need to more clearly distinguish its own tasks from those of the CDRs. See "Autocriticó la FMC su trabajo de organización," *Hoy*, September 30, 1962.

48. That is, in contrast to other revolutions, such as the Chilean Revolution, where the popular base pushed the leadership toward more radical positions. See, for example, Winn, *Weavers of Revolution*.

49. Farber, *Revolution and Reaction*, 219.

50. As the official annual publication of the CDRs subsequently noted: "It was due to the inexistence, in the beginning, of a general plan and unified control of [food] distribution . . . that within the same municipality and the same neighborhood there existed, on the part of the CDRs, different forms and methods of control. This has been resolved by the application of official rationing decreed by the Revolutionary Government." Comités de Defensa de la Revolución, *Memorias 1962*, 220–22.

51. An unnamed former economist who had worked in the Banco Nacional and Hacienda claimed that already by January 1961 some government technicians had proposed rationing some necessary items, but that Fidel Castro had rejected the idea. "Una mirada objetiva al caos económico de Fidel Castro," *FDR* (*Frente Revolucionario Democrático*) *Boletín Informativo Semanal*, June 23, 1961.

52. *Hoy*, March 28, 1961.

53. Ibid.

54. "Al pueblo no le asusta el sacrificio que sea necesario," *Hoy*, April 8, 1961, 7.

55. The rationing of lard was introduced in early July 1961. Generalized food rationing was announced on March 13, 1962.

56. Cited in Pérez, *On Becoming*, 480.

57. "Malanga si, Chiclets no," *Hoy*, August 13, 1960, 1.

58. "Los grandes almacenistas controlaban el comercio en Cuba," *Hoy*, May 30, 1961, 8.

59. Francisco Fernández Rubio, "Los Comités de Defensa de la Revolución," *Bohemia*, May 14, 1961, 42–44, 82.

60. "Primera reunión nacional de producción," *Obra Revolucionaria* 30 (August 1961); 160, cited in Benjamin, *No Free Lunch*, 22.

61. Vilma Espín, "La mujer en la Revolución cubana," *Cuba Socialista*, December 1961, 59–67, quote 66.

62. "He comprendido que alfabetizar es de más utilidad que pelear por un vestido," *Hoy*, June 23, 1961, 6.

63. *Hoy*, December 23, 1961.

64. To say that such expressions were scripted does not imply that they were necessarily false. On the contrary, such a vision did indeed take root among many prorevolutionary Cubans, especially as a result of participation in the literacy campaign. See, for example, the documentary film *Maestra* (directed by Catherine Murphy, 2012). My own interviews corroborated this, especially interviews with Gisela Vásquez, Havana, June 2008, and Hernán Escalante, Havana, June 2008.

65. On early speculation about whether women would be able to withstand the projected shortages in imported cosmetics and other beauty items, see Ana G. Pardo, "Protestará la mujer cubana si escasean sus artículos?," *Carteles*, March 27, 1960, 16–17.

66. Luis Suardíaz, "Testigo de Cargo," cited in Fagen, O'Leary, and Brody, *Cubans in Exile*, 118–19. Suardíaz became an influential cultural authority figure as well as a poet. He occupied the posts of director of literature and publications at the Consejo Nacional de Cultura and director of the national library, and was first vice president of the Union of Artists and Writers. See his biography in *Revista de la Bilbioteca Nacional José Martí* 83, no. 1 (January–June 1992).

67. *Hoy*, April 6, 1961, 1.

68. "Carta del ama de casa al casa-sola," *Hoy*, July 7, 1961.

69. CIA report, subject: "Living Conditions/Anti-Castroist Reaction to Regime's Activities," May 11, 1961, no. 00-B3-156.062, in *CIA Research Reports: Latin America, 1946–76* (microfilm).

70. One of the slogans officially approved for the May 1, 1961, Labor Day parade. A number of other slogans related to consumption were included; see the full list printed in *Hoy* on April 4, 1961.

71. See Herbert Matthews, "Return to Cuba," special issue, *Hispanic American Report* (1964): 1–16.

72. CIA report, "Living Conditions." For similar observations see Matthews, "Return to Cuba."

73. "De fis-minuto en fis-minuto," in "Cartas a Bohemia" section, *Bohemia Libre*, April 22, 1962, 70.

74. "En la misma medida que ellos afecten los intereses de Cuba nosotros afectaremos los intereses de ellos," *Hoy*, June 26, 1960.

75. Cuban-produced canned tropical fruits were cheaper and more widely accessible. Personal communication, Sam Farber, April 2006.

76. Cristobal Zamora, "Los obreros operan por cuesta del estado las grandes tiendas," *Bohemia*, November 6, 1960, 49–50.

77. Ibid. and interview with Belkis Navarro, Havana, July 2005.

78. Zamora, "Los obreros operan por cuesta del estado," 49–50.

79. Letter to Manuel Saco from Oscar, February 3, 1962, *New Leader* Collection of Letters from Cuba, Tamiment Library/Robert F. Wagner Labor Archives, New York University (hereafter NLCLC).

80. CIA report, "Living Conditions."

81. "La Habana, 1962," *Bohemia Libre*, February 25, 1962, 40–41. See also Ana Gus, "Como visten hoy las cubanas," *Bohemia Libre*, September 24, 1961.

82. On the attack on El Flogar, see "Montaner the Terrorist," *Granma International*, August 2, 2005. For the bomb attempt at Sears, see "Condenan trabajadores del Comercio atentados terroristas," *Hoy*, October 1, 1961, 4. The Guantánamo branch of Sears was also attacked by hand grenade; see "Telegramas," *Bohemia Libre*, January 14, 1962, 44.

83. *Hoy*, March 15, 1961.

84. Silvia Pedraza argues that the destruction of El Encanto was meant as "a call . . . a code to let everyone know of the impending landing at Playa Girón." Pedraza, *Political Disaffection*, 103. Phillip Agee has claimed that the attack on El Encanto was a CIA operation. See Agee, "Terrorism and Civil Society as Instruments of US policy in Cuba," Counterpunch.org, August 9, 2003.

85. On Sears's role in disseminating U.S.-style consumer capitalism in Latin America during the Cold War, see Moreno, *Yankee Don't Go Home!*, 177–79.

86. Personal communication, Sam Farber, January 2008.

87. Leonardo Padura, "La Rampa: Asesinato premeditado o muerte natural?," April 7, 2013, http://cafefuerte.com/cuba/noticias-de-cuba/sociedad/2745-la-rampa-muerte -natural-o-asesinato-premeditado.

88. "En Cuba roja," *Bohemia Libre*, April 22, 1962, 57–58.

89. *Carteles*, November 10, 1957.

90. Brunson, "Constructing Afro-Cuban Womanhood."

91. Nadine Fernandez shows that some white Cubans interpreted the shortages of the Special Period of the 1990s as the imposition of a racialized material hardship that made the whole island "blacker," forcing whites to consume things—like sugar water—that they saw as common to poor blacks. Fernandez, *Revolutionizing Romance*, 133, 146.

92. "En Cuba roja," *Bohemia Libre*, April 1, 1962, 52.

93. Séjourné, *La mujer cubana*, 219.

94. Fidel Castro, speech to National Association of Small Farmers (Asociación Nacional de Agricultores Pequeños, ANAP), printed in *Hoy*, May 18, 1961, 6–7.

95. See Cardenal, *En Cuba*, 45–46. Butterfield mentions the higher rations that young research assistants on the Oscar Lewis project received. *People of Buena Ventura*, xviii, xx

96. "Reparto equitativo de los alimentos sin privilegios," *Revolución*, March 13, 1962, 1, 4.

97. Ibid.

98. "Hay que hacer un trabajo adecuado en la distribución de los alimentos," *Bohemia*, March 30, 1962, 42–43.

99. Ibid.

100. Memo from Brigadier General William Craig to Brigadier General Edward G. Lansdale, subject: "Ideas in Support of Project," February 2, 1962, in Chang and Kornbluh, *Cuban Missile Crisis*, 53. See also Craig, "Possible Actions to Provoke, Harass or Disrupt Cuba," February 2, 1962, in Elliston, *Psywar on Cuba*, 90.

101. *No Hay* (pamphlet) (n.p.: n.p., n.d., circa 1965), Angel González Papers, box 26, Cuban Archives, Florida International University Library.

102. "Cartas a *Bohemia Libre*," *Bohemia Libre*, December 24, 1961.

103. Letter to C., March 23, 1962, NLCLC.

104. New legislation prohibited the sale on the street of necessary goods such as razors, soap, and toothpaste. "Prohiben ventas en la calle de objetos de uso necesario," *Hoy*, August 8, 1961, 1. See also Díaz Castañón, *Ideología y revolución*, 169.

105. The revolutionary leadership may have had legitimate reasons to want to restrict private sales of beef, such as reining in the large cattle ranchers in Camagüey Province who actively opposed the revolutionary government and who slaughtered livestock en masse, fearing nationalization. But oral anecdotes suggest that draconian punishments for unauthorized slaughter were occasionally imposed on small farmers, with grievous consequences. Personal communication, Hernán Escalante, Havana, June 2008.

106. "Comprará la ANAP puercos en venta a los campesinos," *Hoy*, December 10, 1961, 3.

107. Associated Press, "Cuba Seeks to Curb Food Speculators," *New York Times*, June 25, 1962, 2. See also *Bohemia*, June 29, 1962.

108. "Beef can't be found," reported a man in Havana, "because they shoot anyone who sells it" (letter to "Comrade" from R.S.O. [Vedado], April 29, 1962, NLCLC).

109. John Bland, "Cuba Handing Back Some Farms," *Chicago Daily Tribune*, June 21, 1962, C1.

110. "En Cuba roja," *Bohemia Libre*, July 30, 1961, 35–39.

111. "CHANG2CC," handbill reproduced in Havana embassy dispatch to Department of State, October 27, 1960, CUSSDCF, *Cuba, 1960–January 1963*.

112. Letter to cousin, May 15, 1962, NLCLC.

113. Letter to son, November 29, 1962, NLCLC.

114. "Del diario de Rufina Moncada," *Hoy*, April 22, 1960, 6.

115. Letter to Ricardo García from Mercedes, July 24, 1961, NLCLC.

116. The "kitchen debate" between Richard Nixon and Nikita Khrushchev in 1959 is the most famous example. See May, *Homeward Bound*, 17-18, 162-64; "Reconversion" in Cohen, *Consumer's Republic*; De Grazia, *Irresistible Empire*; and the essays in Oldenziel and Zachmann, *Cold War Kitchen*. The Soviet trade exhibition that traveled to Havana in early February 1960 had been particularly controversial for sparking these very debates in a context of political polarization.

117. Rosenberg, "Consumer Capitalism and the End of the Cold War."

118. De Grazia, *Irresistible Empire*, 453.

119. Rosenberg, "Consumer Capitalism."

120. See de Grazia, *Irresistible Empire*, and Cohen, *Consumer's Republic*.

121. A CIA memo of spring 1961 mentions that lines comprised both housewives and servants. CIA memo, subject: "Signs of Discontent among the Cuban Populace," distributed April 6, 1961, in *CIA Research Reports: Latin America, 1946-76*.

122. On programs to retrain domestics, see Randall, *Cuban Women Now*, and Guerra, *Visions of Power*.

123. Nazzari, "The 'Woman Question' in Cuba," 112.

124. Letter to Rogelio, March 15, 1961, NLCLC.

125. Letter to Juanita, Varadero, February 14, 1962, NLCLC.

126. Letter to Juanita from illegible (Varadero), February 14, 1962, NLCLC.

127. Letter to Alica from N., March 9, 1962, NLCLC.

128. Letter from Havana, February 10, 1962, NLCLC.

129. See letter to C., March 17, 1962, NLCLC; letter to Don Carlos [Porfirio] from R., April 25, 1962, and letter to Juanita, Varadero, February 14, 1962, NLCLC.

130. "Telegramas," *Bohemia Libre*, August 27, 1961.

131. Letter to C., March 17, 1962, NLCLC; "Cartas a *Bohemia Libre*," *Bohemia Libre*, December 24, 1961.

132. *Hoy*, August 24, 1961.

133. Letter to J. Kingston, March 31, 1961, NLCLC.

134. "En Cuba roja," *Bohemia Libre*, August 27, 1961, 35-39.

135. On the importance of public rallies for displaying and consolidating the new leadership's power, see Guerra, *Visions of Power*.

136. *Bohemia Libre* claimed that as many as several thousand people demonstrated; see July 16, 1961, and August 27, 1961 issues.

137. CIA field report, "Signs of Discontent among the Cuban Populace; Activities of the Government to Strengthen the Regime," March 31, 1961, no. 3/470.587, in *CIA Research Reports: Latin America, 1946-76*.

138. "En Cuba roja," *Bohemia Libre*, July 1962, 51-52.

139. The protest has not been well documented except for several journalistic reports, some of which are in exile periodicals that may make exaggerated claims about government repression. For example, the exile press asserted that security forces

shot down dozens of protesters, although this claim is difficult to corroborate. Sources agree that the protesters were mostly women. James Monahan argues that the women, mostly homemakers, planned a peaceful protest in the town hall, to be followed by prayers in a local church. See Monahan, *Great Deception*, 195–97. On the class background of the protesters, one Cárdenas native argues that they were from all over the city (i.e., of different class backgrounds) but were mostly women. See Pedro Álvarez Peña, "El silencio de los calderos," December 19, 2006, http://www.miscelaneasdecuba .net/web/Article/Index/518100e83a682e0f88c4b9fd#.UYvJNiu4GnY (accessed May 9, 2013).

140. Theodore Draper, "Castro and Communism: A Detailed Account of the Background and Consequence of the Missile Crisis in Cuba," *Reporter: The Magazine of Facts and Ideas* (New York), January 17, 1963, 35–48.

141. " 'El pasado no volverá, el enemigo no hará retroceder la historia,' afirmó Dorticos en el acto de Cárdenas," *Revolución*, June 18, 1962, 2, 4.

142. Domínguez, *Cuba*, 441–44.

143. This is judging from Castro's comment in November 1961 that Matanzas's farmers were "allergic to" and "frightened by" cooperatives. Cited in Thomas, *Cuba*, 1324.

144. Domínguez, *Cuba*, 441–44.

145. Ibid. For this reason Osvaldo Dorticós took the opportunity to reassure peasants even as he denounced urban food protests: he warned that "no one is authorized to persecute, to attack, nor to harm the small agricultural producers or poor *campesinos* of [this] region" (" 'El pasado no volverá,' " 2, 4). Furthermore, later that month some fifty-five small farmers in Matanzas had their lands restored. See John Bland, "Cuba Handing Back Some Farms," *Chicago Daily Tribune*, June 21, 1962, C1; "Enérgica barrida," *Bohemia*, June 29, 1962, 64; "Truth about Cuba Committee," *Bulletin on Cuba*, no. 13 (July 9, 1962).

146. Associated Press, "Display of Force Staged in Cuba in Reply to Food Demonstration," *New York Times*, June 17, 1962, 1, 31. Perico and Jagüey Grande may also have experienced protests; see "En Cuba roja," *Bohemia Libre*, July 1, 1962. On the opening of stores for foreign technicians in Havana, see letter to Rogelio, November 10, 1962, NLCLC.

147. "En Cuba roja," *Bohemia Libre*, July 1, 1962, 51–52; "Los sucesos de Cárdenas," *Bohemia Libre*, July 22, 1962, 64.

148. A personal letter reports the burning of sugarcane and the sabotage of rayon and cordage plants. Those arrested apparently came from the lower strata of the middle sectors—a barber, a mechanic, a photographer, an attorney's clerk, the nephew of a furniture store owner, and an employee of the local market. Letter to "Comrade" from R.S.O., February 19, 1962, NLCLC.

149. According to exile publications, a black market still existed in Havana in 1964 but had been largely weeded out in the rural areas. See "The Lack of Food in Cuba," *Cuban Report* (Miami), January 17, 1964, 3–4, Theodore Draper Papers, box 8, folder 27, Hoover Institution Archives. A 1964 food riot in Santiago de Cuba is mentioned in *Cuban Labor:*

Informative Bulletin of FORDC (Miami, January 1964), Theodore Draper Papers, box 10, folder 26, "FORDC," Hoover Institution Archives. On the everyday problems of distribution, see Jose Matar, "Lucha a fondo contra los defectos del frente de abastecimientos," *Con la Guardia en Alto*, May 1963.

150. As explained by FMC official Consuelo Cazón, who warned about "some lack of understanding [*incomprensiones*] of poor housewives," which was explained by "their occupations and lack of a habit of reading"; "Debemos mejorar cada dia más," *Hoy*, November 13, 1960, 4.

151. "La vigilancia revolucionaria del ama de casa," *Hoy*, September 8, 1960, 8.

152. On official disparagement of housewives, see Smith and Padula, *Sex and Revolution*, 150; and Serra, *New Man*, 117–18. For a contrasting example from the Chinese Revolution, where doing housework was retheorized in the 1950s as a legitimate working-class occupation and identity and an "indirect contribution to socialism," see Shaopeng, "State Discourse on Housewives," 52.

Chapter 6

1. I concur with many of Casavantes Bradford's arguments, but relate the focus on children to fears over changing gender roles, particularly the implications of these changes for teenage girls and adult women as mothers. See Casavantes Bradford, *Revolution*.

2. Historians disagree over the extent to which the revolutionary leadership in the 1960s purposefully set out to subordinate the family to the state and, if so, when this tendency began. Although the leadership did view the family as the incubator of socially conservative values, it seems most likely that the disruption of traditional patterns of family authority in the early 1960s was largely a by-product of other political and structural transformations. See Smith and Padula, *Sex and Revolution*, 144–47; and Hamilton, *Sexual Revolutions in Cuba*, 30–32.

3. Operation Peter Pan began as a visa waiver program through which children could acquire permission to enter the United States. It was officially run in the United States by the Bureau of Security and Consular Affairs and the visa division, but with collaboration from the CIA and the Immigration and Naturalization Service. The State Department collaborated on the Cuban side and worked closely with representatives of the Catholic Church and with the former employees of an English-language private school, the Ruston Academy. Visa waivers often began for children of Cubans engaged in anti-Castro underground activity or youths involved in anti-Castro activities themselves, but were more or less freely given out to families who secretly sought out the Cuban informal networks. See Torres, *Lost Apple*, and Casavantes Bradford, *Revolution*.

4. See Casavantes Bradford for the complex way exile ideas and experience of race intersected with southern American notions as they arrived in Miami. Casavantes Bradford, *Revolution*, 122–37.

5. Benson, *Antiracism in Cuba*.

6. Dubinsky, *Babies without Borders*, 7–8.

7. Ibid., 12; May, *Homeward Bound*.

8. On the importance of childhood in the Soviet Union, see Kelly, *Children's World*; Kirschenbaum, *Small Comrades*.

9. Official accounts on the island point to the loss of property, the grip of the Catholic Church hierarchy, and manipulation by the U.S. government as motivating factors for the anti-Castro groups. See, for example, Arboleya, *La contrarrevolución cubana*, which provides excellent analysis of the emergence of the anti-Castro movement but relies on simplistic assumptions about anti-Castro militants always being motivated by defense of their presumed class interests.

10. On the Florida exile perspective that saw *castrismo* destroying parental authority, unmooring Cuba from the old values of Spanish custom and Catholicism, and fomenting free love among youths, see Smith and Padula, *Sex and Revolution*, 155–56.

11. For an excellent overview, see chapter 1 of Hamilton's 2012 *Sexual Revolutions in Cuba*. For debates over how to interpret the 1975 Family Code especially, see Nazarri, "The 'Woman Question' in Cuba"; Lutjens, "Remaking the Public Sphere"; Larguia and Dumoulin, *Hacia una concepción científica*; Gotkowitz and Turits, "Socialist Morality"; Bengelsdorf, "On the Problem of Studying Women in Cuba"; Bengelsdorf, "[Re]Considering Cuban Women"; Smith and Padula, *Sex and Revolution*; and Murray, "Socialism and Feminism." On single motherhood and state visions of dysfunctional family forms, see Safa, "Hierarchies and Household Change."

12. On how revolutionary openings allow women to challenge and push the Left's limited programs to establish gender equality and ameliorate women's workloads, see Olcott, *Revolutionary Women*, and the essays in Olcott, Vaughan, and Cano, *Sex in Revolution*.

13. Yabur Curí, *Perfil de un comunista*, 41–46, 52.

14. Thomas, *Cuba*, 1252–53.

15. Eloy G. Merino, "Matrimonios y nacimientos," *El Mundo*, August 19, 1959, A4.

16. "Matrimonios colectivos por millares en toda la nación," *Revolución*, September 26, 1960, 5. An August 1960 article in *Hoy* claimed that some 5,000 weddings were set to take place soon, citing a radio announcement. "La revolución une más a la familia cubana," *Hoy*, August 12, 1960, 12.

17. Luis Rolando Cabrera, "La revolución ha legalizado ya miles de matrimonios," *Bohemia*, January 24, 1960, 36–38, 96–97. See also "Matrimonios colectivos por millares en toda la nación," *Revolución*, September 26, 1960, 5; "Operación Matrimonio en Camarioca," *Revolución*, September 9, 1960, 8; and "Menudeo," *Carteles*, February 28, 1960, 24.

18. Torreira Crespo and Buajasán Marrawi, *Operación Peter Pan*, 101. Yabur Maluf's daughter estimated that "within a few months" 100,000 unions had been legalized and 500,000 people were inscribed in the civil registry. Yabur Curí, *Perfil*, 56–57.

19. Hamilton, *Sexual Revolutions in Cuba*, 28.

20. Leandro Blanco, "Logrará la revolución poner fin a las uniones ilegales?," *Bohemia*, February 7, 1960, 30, 99.

21. Luis Rolando Cabrera, "La revolución ha legalizado ya miles de matrimonios," *Bohemia*, January 24, 1960, 36–38, 96–97.

22. See, for example, "Libros en vez de sables," *Bohemia*, September 8, 1960, 55. The use of collective weddings apparently continued throughout the 1960s, although they may have eventually been restricted to certain holidays. Lee Lockwood noted the promotion of such "common weddings" among political prisoners and their partners who had been relocated from the Escambray Mountains to Havana and nearby prison camps. This suggests that the leadership continued to view such weddings as a method of uplift and integration. See Lockwood, *Castro's Cuba*, 279.

23. See the discussion in Hamilton, *Sexual Revolutions in Cuba*. The socialist government later offered various material incentives for marriage, including low-cost food and drink for a reception, a low-cost short honeymoon at a local resort, and some subsidized home items such as sheets and towels. See Heidi Harkonen, "Gender, Kinship and Lifecycle Rituals in Cuba," 65.

24. Interview with Norberta Rivas Viáñez, in Meyer, *El futuro era nuestro*, 230. Yabur's daughter concurs that many low-income couples could not afford the charge of the notary or judge affiliated with the civil registry required for a legal marriage. Yabur Curí, *Perfil*, 56.

25. Interview with Norberta Rivas Viáñez, in Meyer, *El futuro era nuestro*, 230.

26. Ibid., 257.

27. Ibid., 253.

28. Scholars have debated the extent to which the popular classes embraced different standards or values regarding cohabitation, marriage, or sexuality. In his study of relocated urban slum residents, Douglas Butterworth argued that "on the whole . . . there was a general acceptance . . . of premarital sex. This contrasted with the traditional 'middle-class' Cuban values, at least insofar as women were concerned." *People of Buena Ventura*, 53. Carrie Hamilton challenges the notion that "the prevalence of informal unions and illegitimate children among poor and especially black Cubans reflected a fundamentally different set of sexual values from those espoused by wealthy whites." She argues instead that values regarding sexuality and female chastity were often "shared . . . across class and racial divides." *Sexual Revolutions*, 79.

29. Meyer, *El futuro era nuestro*, 256.

30. Ibid., 257.

31. Pérez, *On Becoming Cuban*, 487.

32. Fernández Núñez, *La vivienda en Cuba*.

33. "History Will Absolve Me," full text available at https://www.marxists.org/history /cuba/archive/castro/1953/10/16.htm (accessed October 20, 2014).

34. Printed in *Hoy*, November 13, 1960. Ellipses in original.

35. See *Bohemia*, May 21, 1961, 77.

36. Specifically, he asked them to resign from the popular militias and refrain from changing dollars to pesos on the black market. For an excellent study of relations

among Cuban workers, the Cuban government, and the U.S. authorities at the naval base, see Lipman, *Guantánamo*.

37. Fidel Castro, speech to workers at Caimanera naval base, in *Revolución*, November 16, 1960.

38. Advertisement in *Revolución*, September 1, 1960, 15.

39. On slum clearance and the relocation of slum dwellers in Havana, see Lewis, *Four Men*, and Butterworth, *People of Buena Ventura*. On housing construction during the revolutionary period, see Scarpaci, Segre, and Coyula, *Havana*.

40. See Scarpaci, Segre, and Coyula, *Havana*; Holston, *Modernist City*; and Fraser, *Building the New World*. On plans for the Ciudad de la Construcción, see "Con trabajo voluntario se hace la Ciudad de la Construcción," *Hoy*, November 13, 1960, 3.

41. For drawings of the Ciudad de la Construcción, see *Hoy*, August 21, 1960, 4.

42. Boorstein, *Economic Transformation of Cuba*, 41, cited in Butterworth, *People of Buena Ventura*, 30n6.

43. "Con trabajo voluntario se hace la Ciudad de la Construcción," *Hoy*, November 13, 1960, 3; and "Comedores y lavanderías populares ayudarán a las amas de casa," *Hoy*, August 21, 1960, 8.

44. "Erradican el juego en Marianao," *Hoy*, August 19, 1960, 8. On the abolition of prostitution and the retraining of prostitutes, see Hynson, " 'Count, Capture, and Reeducate' "; see also Lewis, *Four Women*.

45. Speech reprinted in *Hoy*, September 10, 1960, 7.

46. "Lo importante es avanzar sin rastre," *Revolución*, September 10, 1960, 3, 4.

47. Benson, *Antiracism in Cuba*.

48. *Hoy*, November 24, 1960.

49. Guerra, *Visions of Power*, 203.

50. Pedraza, *Political Disaffection*, 88–89; Guerra, *Visions of Power*, 94.

51. See Guerra, "To Condemn the Revolution Is to Condemn Christ."

52. Kirk, *Between God and the Party*, 82–83; and Pedraza, *Political Disaffection*, 87.

53. Kirk, *Between God and the Party*, 83–84; and Pedraza, *Political Disaffection*, especially 87–88 and 107–9.

54. Both citations in Kirk, *Between God and the Party*, 82, 84.

55. Andrés Valdespino, "Lo que el fidelismo no podrá destruir," *Bohemia Libre*, January 15, 1961, 32–34, 78, quote from 33.

56. Arboleya, *La contrarrevolución*; Torreira Crespo and Baujasán Marrawi, *Operación Peter Pan*.

57. See memo from American consulate, Santiago, to Department of State, subject: "First Signs of Open Protest in Oriente Province," dispatch no. 53, November 23, 1960, which notes a daylong strike by Catholic school students; and airgram from American embassy, Havana, to Secretary of State, subject: "Student Opposition to Castro Government in Camagüey" (signed Braddock), November 30, 1960, which notes clashes between Catholic school students and militia, resulting in one student death; CUSS-DCF, *Cuba, 1960–January 1963*.

58. For example, the Catholic publication *La Quincena* published articles in the fall of 1960 asserting that families had the natural and "inalienable" right to raise their children. See Torreira Crespo and Baujasán Marrawi, *Operación Peter Pan*, 95; Torres, *Lost Apple*, 92.

59. See account, and reproduced leaflet, in Casavantes Bradford, *Revolution*, 164–65. The warring leaflets must have had a strong impact on contemporaries, as this incident is recounted multiple times in different sources. See Directorio Revolucionario Estudiantil, *Persecución religiosa en Cuba* (pamphlet) (n.p.: n.p., n.d., circa 1964), Ecuador chapter, CHC, Cuban and Cuban Exile Vertical Files/Associations/Directorio Revolucionario Estudiantil. Also recounted in Andrés Valdespino, "Entre la cruz y la hoz," *Bohemia Libre*, June 4, 1961, 36–39, 82; and in Lewis, *Four Women*.

60. See Justina Álvarez, "Luchemos por los niños desamparados," *Hoy*, May 13, 1959, and "Historia de un matrimonio prohibido," *Hoy*, August 2, 1959, 4.

61. Leiner, *Children Are the Revolution*, 53.

62. "The Children's Circles: Clementina Serra," in Randall, *Cuban Women Now*, 117–36.

63. Ibid., 128. The circles were run by the FMC from 1961 to 1966, then taken over by the Ministry of Industry. See Leiner, *Children Are the Revolution*, 54. As Smith and Padula argue, daycare centers were never sufficient in number, often had inconvenient hours, and were not tied to the expansion of women's paid employment. See Smith and Padula, *Sex and Revolution*, 131–34.

64. Justina Álvarez, "Luchemos por los niños desamparados," *Hoy*, May 13, 1959.

65. "Interesante mesa redonda sobre creación de circulos infantiles," *Hoy*, December 30, 1960, 6. See also "Mil profesoras de corte y costura para las cooperativas," *Hoy*, November 12, 1960, 4.

66. For an example, see the convoluted language and anodyne iconography of the Ministry of Social Welfare advertisement published in *Hoy*, November 27, 1960.

67. See "Está vigente aquello de: 'Estudio, Trabajo y Fusil,'" *Hoy*, January 7, 1961, 18.

68. Enrique Huertas, "Un siniestro plan para arrebatara los padres cubanos la custodia y educación de sus hijos," *Bohemia Libre*, February 5, 1961, 50–53, 59–60.

69. *Rescate*, September 15, 1960, included as enclosure to dispatch no. 964 from American embassy (Havana) to Department of State, subject: "Transmittal of Samples of Clandestine Anti-Castro Publications," October 27, 1960, CUSSDCF, *Cuba, 1960–January 1963*.

70. Cruzada Femenina Cubana, *El comunismo destruye la familia en Cuba* (pamphlet) (n.p.: n.p., 1963).

71. "Defiende a tu hijo y defenderás a Cuba," *Bohemia Libre*, December 4, 1960, 3, 87.

72. Interview with Pilar López, Miami, February 2008; "Mis impresiones sobre la subida al Turquino," *Hoy*, August 30, 1960, 8.

73. Torres, *Lost Apple*, 108.

74. Fagen, "Campaign against Illiteracy," chap. 3 in *Transformation of Political Culture*.

75. See especially ibid., and Herman, "Army of Educators."

76. Guerra, *Visions of Power.*

77. "Children's Crusade," *Newsweek*, April 3, 1961, 51. See also the reservations expressed by the middle-class Havana family of one of the informants in Lewis, *Four Women*, 66.

78. The reference is to the girls brought from the countryside to Havana for sewing classes, meant to serve as technical training. "En Cuba roja," *Bohemia Libre*, June 18, 1961.

79. References to "camps" could indicate, first, the "school-cities," and then a training camp at Varadero beach where *brigadistas* were sent for brief training before being assigned to a rural locale.

80. Letter from B[ertha] to Ricardo García, November 26, 1961, NLCLC. "Paredón!" (To the wall!) refers to the famous phrase shouted during the early days of the revolution, when members of the military were convicted of war crimes and either given prison sentences or executed. On these trials and executions, see Chase, "The Trials."

81. Letter from Abel Mestre, December 22, 1961, NLCLC.

82. Casavantes Bradford, *Revolution*, 97.

83. Ibid., 102.

84. On the way young women negotiated the opposition of their parents, see Harman, "Army of Educators."

85. As Nadine Fernandez shows, even hard-core revolutionary supporters could violently oppose disruptions to traditional patterns of sexuality, especially interracial sexual unions. Fernandez, *Revolutionizing Romance.* Mark Sawyer also found that white parents ostracized children who chose black partners, although he does not discuss these families' political views. See Sawyer, "Unlocking the Official Story."

86. As an educational administrator, she eventually joined the campaign herself in order to accompany them. Interview with Esperanza García Peña conducted by Lyn Smith, Lyn Smith Collection, Library of Congress.

87. "En Cuba roja," *Bohemia Libre*, June 18, 1961.

88. "En Cuba roja," *Bohemia Libre*, August 27, 1961. See also the similar joke that "one goes and two come back"; Lewis, *Four Women*, 66.

89. See Hamilton, *Sexual Revolutions in Cuba*, 28.

90. Departmento de Relaciones Exteriores, Directorio Magisterial Revolucionario, *La destrucción de la escuela privada en Cuba* (pamphlet) (n.p.: n.p., December 1963).

91. Fernandez, *Revolutionizing Romance*, 56. Even among "committed revolutionaries," similar anxieties were expressed around the *escuelas al campo* ("country schools") implemented in 1966, where urban students would be sent for several weeks at a time to work in cultivation. See Casavantes Bradford, *Revolution*, 186. On the *escuelas al campo*, see "El plan las escuelas al campo se renueve," *Juventud Rebelde*, November 5, 2006, consulted at juventudrebelde.cu.

92. James Baker, informal memo dated May 25, 1998, cited in Torres, *Lost Apple*, 120.

93. Campuzano, *Las muchachas de la Habana*, 118–41.

94. "Los brigadistas podrán alfabetizar en el campo acompañándose de sus parientes," *Hoy*, March 22, 1961, 6.

95. Guerra, *Visions of Power*, 165.

96. "Los brigadistas podrán alfabetizar en el campo acompañándose de sus parientes," *Hoy*, March 22, 1961, 6.

97. Campuzano, "Cuba 1961," in *Las muchachas de la Habana*, 127.

98. On contingents of women traveling to Varadero in protest, see interviews with Esperanza García Peña and Osoria Oropesa Herrera conducted by Lyn Smith, both in Lyn Smith Collection, Library of Congress. See also "Escándalo en Varadero," in "En Cuba roja" section, *Bohemia Libre*, July 16, 1961.

99. Directorio Magisterial Cubano, *Cuba: Anécdotas de la enseñanza comunista* (pamphlet) (n.p.: n.p., n.d., circa 1965), CHC, Miami University Library.

100. See Herman, "Army of Educators"; Guerra, *Visions of Power*; and testimonies in the documentary film *Maestra*.

101. As Rebecca Herman argues, the literacy campaign is one example of the way Cuban women acted to transform patriarchy, even if they did not explicitly articulate a challenge to it. Herman, "Army of Educators."

102. Interview with María Teresa Sopeña, in Séjourné, *La mujer cubana*, 287.

103. Recent historiography on the former Eastern bloc suggests that state-led training programs, which often housed youths in separate dormitories and gave them their first opportunity to live away from their parents, provided youths with personal space for sexual exploration. See McLellan, *Love in the Time of Communism*, 38–39. Informal conversations in Cuba suggest that many young people did have their first sexual experiences at the *escuelas al campo*. In his memoir, Reinaldo Arenas depicts the 1960s as a golden era for gay sexual exploration due to the many young men mobilized for military and other duties, housed together far from their families. Arenas, *Antes que anochezca*.

104. "Nuestra portada," *Revista Mella*, February 1961, 15.

105. "Amor y revolución," *Revista Mella*, February 1961, 34–38.

106. Ibid., 34–38, quotes from 38.

107. Indeed, some anti-Castro propaganda featured nightmarish versions of this very scenario. See, for example, Directorio Magisterial Cubano, *Cuba: Anécdotas*. Films produced by the official Cuban film institute have also touched on the issues of relationships between people of different prerevolutionary social classes. For examples, see *De cierta manera* and *Retrato de Teresa*.

108. Fagen, "Campaign against Illiteracy," chap. 3 in *Transformation of Political Culture*.

109. My own interviews and those conducted by others capture the strong impact the literacy campaign had on young *brigadistas*. As one former *brigadista* recounted, "seeing the way of life of those people [i.e., the peasantry], compared with mine, was a shock that has lasted my entire life." Interview with Gisela Vázquez, Havana, June 2008. Another confided that his year as a *brigadista* "was the only year of my life that I would repeat." Interview with Hernán Escalante, Havana, June 2008. See also interview footage in the documentary film *Maestra*. And while the literacy campaign served to politicize many urban youths, the first mass organizations and training programs

shaped the political leanings of many working-class adolescent males from rural areas. See, for example, the first-person account of Reinaldo Arenas, who describes his experience in a new rural school for accountants where they received courses in "Marxist-Leninism." "In reality we, as well as the volunteer teachers in the Sierra Maestra, were the first vanguard [*cuadros*] of the revolution." Arenas, *Antes que anochezca*, 73.

110. Interview with Gisela Vásquez, Havana, June 2008.

111. Interview with Alfonso Jiménez, West Palm Beach, Florida, February 2008. On intergenerational conflict and conflict between siblings over whether to support the revolution, see letter from "cousin," May 15, 1962, and letter from "mother," undated, both in NLCLC.

112. Smith and Padula, *Sex and Revolution*, 151.

113. Quoted in Fagen, O'Leary, and Brody, *Cubans in Exile*, 87.

114. "Puesto que el enemigo se prepara, prepararemos: Alcemos la guardia!," *Hoy*, September 20, 1961, 1. In addition, some months after rumors circulated about Cuban children being sent to the Soviet Union for brainwashing, Fidel Castro had announced a student exchange to be established with Russia, in which 1,000 Cuban students would be sent to the Soviet Union and vice versa. See *Hoy*, January 22, 1961, 1. The initiative seemed to fulfill some parents' worst fears.

115. On state intervention in newspapers, see Thomas, *Cuba*, 1261, 1263.

116. Fox, *Working-Class Émigrés*, 86–87, quote from 87.

117. Ibid., 95.

118. Grandin, *Last Colonial Massacre*, 44; see also 59.

119. Quoted in Kampwirth, *Feminism*, 27.

120. For the full text of the fake law, see "La revolución se ha hecho para los niños," *Hoy*, September 20, 1961, 8–11.

121. "Niños cubanos bajo control de la Rusia Soviética," *Boletín Occidente*, August 1960, 8–9.

122. Enrique Huertas, "Un siniestro plan para arrebatar a los padres cubanos la custodia y educación de sus hijos," *Bohemia Libre*, February 5, 1961, 50–53, 59–60.

123. Torres, *Lost Apple*, 136.

124. Ibid., 90–91, 136.

125. The CIA also subsequently manipulated fear of what had transpired in Cuba to frighten Latin Americans away from leftist leaders, for example during the 1964 elections in Chile by alleging that the Cuban *barbudos* had destroyed families. Power, *Right-Wing Women in Chile*, 81–82, 85–90.

126. Belmonte, *Selling the American Way*, 138.

127. Brennan, *Wives, Mothers, and the Red Menace*, 16.

128. Ibid., 121.

129. Ibid., 94–95.

130. Belmonte, *Selling the American Way*, 146.

131. For example, see Sims, "Cuba," and Sims, "Cuban Labor."

132. Torreira Crespo and Buajasán Marrawi, *Operación Peter Pan*, 95.

133. Letter reproduced in *Bohemia Libre*, September 24, 1961, 73. See also "And Now the Children?," *Time*, October 6, 1961, 41.

134. It was the only such large-scale movement of refugee children in the Western Hemisphere. The best monograph on Operation Peter Pan is Torres, *Lost Apple*. See also Conde, *Operation Pedro Pan*.

135. Interview with Alfonso Jiménez, West Palm Beach, February 2008.

136. Cruzada Femenina Cubana, *El comunismo destruye la familia*.

137. "Esto está pasando en Cuba!" (advertisement placed by group Comité de Vigilancia Democrática), *La República* (San José, Costa Rica), February 20, 1961.

138. *Acción Cubana* (Madrid), January 7, 1960, included in CUSSDCF, *Cuba, 1960–January 1963*. (The place of publication was listed as Luxemburg, but according to State Department officials it was really printed in Madrid.) See American embassy (Madrid) to Department of State (signed William Fraleigh), dispatch no. 388, subject: "Anti-Castro Activities in Spain," January 19, 1961. See similar claims that female militias were "antifeminine" in Ana Gus, "Como visten hoy las cubanas," *Bohemia Libre*, September 24, 1961. For assurances in the prorevolutionary press that carrying a pistol and wearing a uniform did not "diminish that charm of the *criolla* woman," see Santiago Cardosa Arias, "Aquí vienen las mariana grajales," *Revolución*, September 16, 1960, 3, 5.

139. "Cubanita, por qué has caido en esto?," *Bohemia Libre*, January 8, 1961, 3.

140. CIA field report, "Signs of Discontent among the Cuban Populace; Activities of the Government to Strengthen the Regime," March 31, 1961, no. 3/470.587, in *CIA Research Reports: Latin America, 1946–76*.

141. Cited in Torreira Crespo and Baujasán Marrawi, *Operación Peter Pan*, 91.

142. Among many possible examples, see the drawing of an exaggeratedly effeminate Raúl in *Bohemia Libre*, January 22, 1961, 48.

143. Cites in Torreria Crespo and Baujasán Marrawi, *Operación Peter Pan*, 91.

144. "Madre cubana, defiende a tu hijo!," *Bohemia Libre*, October 23, 1960.

145. "And Now the Children?," 41.

146. "Defiende a tu hijo y defenderás a Cuba," *Bohemia Libre*, December 4, 1960, 3, 87.

147. "Niño . . . ahora a tu escuela!," Ministry of Education advertisement, *Bohemia*, September 18, 1960, 39.

148. Interview with Sidiam Campuzano, Union City, New Jersey, March 2008.

149. On the growing rift between the revolutionary leadership and organized labor, see Córdova, *Castro and the Cuban Labor Movement*, and Arboleya, *La contrarevolución*.

150. *Hoy*, December 22, 1959, 1.

151. "La revolución une más a la familia cubana," *Hoy*, August 12, 1960, 12.

152. "Repitamos una y otra vez las palabras de Fidel," *Hoy*, November 10, 1960, 4.

153. Cruzada Femenina Cubana, *El comunismo destruye la familia*.

154. *Bohemia Libre*, January 15, 1961.

155. On the 1950s image of the nuclear, suburban American family as the building block of capitalist democracy and a bulwark against communism, see May, *Homeward Bound*, and Michel, "American Women and the Discourse of the Democratic Family."

156. Interview with Sidiam Campuzano, Union City, New Jersey, March 2008.

157. For a similar denunciation, see the pamphlet published by the opposition group Cuban Freedom Committee, which alleges that Cuban families were being pulled apart by political transformation, changes to property relations, and the scarcity of commodities. Cuban Freedom Committee, *Cuba Today* (pamphlet) (n.p.: n.p., n.d.), appended to Department of State memorandum of conversation, "Views of Exile Group (AREC)," March 23, 1961, CUSSDCF, *Cuba, 1960-January 1963*.

158. Pérez, *On Becoming Cuban*, 479.

159. Cuban Freedom Committee, "Cuba Today."

160. USIA propagandists similarly asserted that access to consumer goods helped American women achieve a high standard of living and bring up their children. See Belmonte, *Selling the American Way*, 138-39. On the concept of "people's capitalism," see ibid., and Rosenberg, "Consumer Capitalism and the End of the Cold War."

161. See, for example, Proclama del Ejército de Liberación Nacional, January 1961, printed in *Bohemia Libre*, which dwells more on the "inalienable" right to raise one's children than on other rights.

162. *FRD Boletín Informativo Semanal*, March 29, 1961.

163. Andrés Valdespino, "El más grave de los crimenes de Fidel Castro," *Bohemia Libre*, November 26, 1960, 4-5.

164. Centro de Juventudes Catolicas de Miami, "Visión cristiana de la mujer," *Mensaje* 1, no. 3 (December 1962): 4-7, Cuban Exile History Archives Project, box 39, folder "Boletines," Florida International University, Special Collections and University Archives.

165. *Hoy*, November 9, 1960, 4.

166. *Hoy*, December 16, 1960. My italics.

167. Fidel Castro, "La revolución se ha hecho para los niños," speech printed in *Hoy*, September 20, 1961, 8-11, quote from 9.

168. On the long historical tradition of viewing Communists as proponents of free love, see Freedman, *No Turning Back*, 59.

169. Castro, "La revolución se ha hecho para niños," 9.

170. Ibid.

171. Gotkowitz and Turits, "Socialist Morality," 9-10. See also Clementina Serra, "Impresiones de un grato recorrido," *Hoy*, October 25, 1961, 9.

Conclusion

1. I heard this sentiment expressed many times during my research in Cuba, especially by elderly men, some of whom went on to warn that Cuba would now have to wrestle with the "consequences" of women's liberation. Similarly, an FMC official commented in the early 1990s that women had "gained more from the revolution than men." Cited in Andaya, *Conceiving Cuba*, 139.

2. Monsiváis, foreword to Olcott, Vaughan, and Cano, *Sex in Revolution*, 5.

3. Westad, *Reviewing the Cold War*, 10-11. Also cited in de Haan, "Continuing Cold War Paradigms," 551.

REFERENCES

Archival Sources

CUBA
  Archivo Nacional
    Fondo Ministerio de Bienestar Social
  Instituto de Historia de Cuba
    Colección Prensa Clandestina
    Fondo Movimiento Femenino
USA
New York City
  Rare Book and Manuscript Library, Columbia University Library
    Herbert L. Matthews Papers
  Tamiment Library/Robert F. Wagner Labor Archives, New York University
    New Leader Collection of Letters from Cuba
Miami, Florida
  Florida International University, Special Collections and University Archives
    Ángel González Papers
    Cuban Pamphlets Collection
  University of Miami Libraries
    Cuban Heritage Collection
      Dysis Guira Papers
      Elena Mederos Papers
      Exile Periodicals Collection
      Tad Szulc Collection of Interview Transcripts
Gainesville, Florida
  George A. Smathers Libraries, University of Florida, Gainesville, Florida
    Ernesto Chávez Collection
Washington, D.C.
  Library of Congress
    Motion Picture, Broadcasting and Recorded Sound Division
      Lyn Smith Collection
  National Archives and Records Administration (NARA)
    Record Groups 59, 84 and Lot Files
Princeton, New Jersey
  Manuscripts Division, Department of Rare Books and Special Collections,
    Princeton University Library
    Carlos Franqui Collection, 1952–81

Palo Alto, California
Hoover Institution, Stanford University
Theodore Draper Papers

Oral History Interviews Conducted by Author

All interviewees have been assigned pseudonyms, except those in italics.
Marisol Álvarez, Havana, January 2006
Rogelio Bárcena, Washington, D.C., September 2011
María Belén, Havana, September 2005
Ramona Betancourt, Havana, September 2005
Sidiam Campuzano, Union City, New Jersey, March 2008.
Dolores Domínguez and Caridad Arango (joint interview), Havana, July 2007.
Hernán Escalante, Havana, June 2008
Valeria Espinoza, Havana, July 2007
Samuel Farber, New York City, April 2006 and January 2008
Gladys Marel García, Miami, December 2011 and Brooklyn, June 2012
Rogelio Gil, Miami, November 2005
Martina Granados, Santo Domingo (conducted by telephone), February 2012
Miguel Guillén, Havana, January 2006 and Havana, June 2007
Eneida Hernández, Havana, September 2005 and Havana, July 2007
Eneida Hernández and Federico Larrazaba (joint interview), Havana, September
    2005
Alfonso Jiménez, West Palm Beach, February 2008
Carmelo Jiménez, Miami, November 2005
María Jiménez, West New York, New Jersey, January 2009.
Pilar López, Miami, February 2008
Ana Losada Prieto, Havana, September 2005
Rosario Marín, Havana, August 2005
Rosario Navarrete, Havana, July 2007
Belkis Navarro, Havana, July 2005
Ariana Núñez, Havana, July 2007
Vicente Robaína, Havana, January 2006
Samuel Rodríguez, Miami, March 2006
Marta Sánchez, Union City, N.J., March 2008
Gisela Vázquez, Havana, June 2008
Lola Zanetti, Havana, July 2007

Periodicals

Unless otherwise noted, all Spanish-language periodicals were published in Cuba.
Bohemia

Bohemia Libre (Caracas; Miami)
Carta Semanal
Carteles
Chicago Daily Tribune
Con la Guardia en Alto
Diario de Cuba (Santiago)
El Mundo
Humanismo (Mexico City)
La Prensa
La República (San José, Costa Rica)
Life
Mujeres
Nation
Newsweek
New York Times
Noticias de Hoy
Prensa Libre
Revista Cuba
Revista Santiago
Revolución
Sierra Maestra
Time
Unidad Femenina
Washington Post

Films

Clandestinos. Directed by Fernando Pérez, ICAIC, 1988.
De Cierta Manera. Directed by Sara Gómez, ICAIC, 1978.
Doctrinas del Corazon. Director Delia Cruz, 2012.
Maestra. Directed by Catherine Murphy, 2012.
Retrato de Teresa. Director Pastor Vega, ICAIC, 1979.

Published Primary Sources

Cairo, Ana, ed. *Viaje a los frutos.* Havana: Ediciones Bachiller, 2006.
Central Intelligence Agency. *CIA Research Reports Latin America: 1946-1976.* Frederick, Md.: University Publications of America, 1982. Microform.
Chang, Lawrence, and Peter Kornbluh. *The Cuban Missile Crisis, 1962: A National Security Archive Documents Reader.* New York: New Press, 1992.
Comités de Defensa de la Revolución. *Memorias 1962.* Havana: Ediciones con la Guardia en Alto, 1963.

Confidential U.S. State Department Central Files. Cuba, 1950–1954: Internal Affairs, *Decimal Numbers 737, 837, and 937 and Foreign Affairs, Decimal Numbers 637* *and 611.37.* Frederick, Md.: University Publications of America, 1986. Microform.

Confidential U.S. State Department Central Files. Cuba, 1955–1959: Internal Affairs, *Decimal Numbers 737, 837, and 937 and Foreign Affairs, Decimal Numbers 637* *and 611.37.* Frederick, Md.: University Publications of America, 1987. Microform.

Confidential U.S. State Department Central Files. Cuba, 1960–January 1963, Foreign *Affairs: Decimal Numbers 637 and 611.37.* Bethesda, Md.: University Publications of America, 1999. Microform.

Department of State. Office of the Historian. *Foreign Relations of the United States,* *1958–60. Cuba.* Vol. 6. Washington, D.C.: U.S. Government Printing Office, 1991.

Elliston, Jon. *Psywar on Cuba: The Declassified History of U.S. Anti-Castro Propaganda.* New York: Ocean Press, 1999.

Guerra López, Dolores, Yolanda González Plasencia, and Amparo Hernández Denis, eds. *Fidel: Mujer, niñez y familia.* Vol. 1. Havana: Instituto de Historia de Cuba, 2010.

Stoner, K. Lynn, ed. *The Women's Movement in Cuba: The Stoner Collection on Cuban* *Feminism.* Wilmington, Del.: Scholarly Resources, Inc, 1990. Microform.

Memoirs, Oral Histories, and Travelers' Accounts

Arenas, Reinaldo. *Antes que anochezca.* Mexico City: Tusquets, 2009.

Belli, Gioconda. *The Country under My Skin.* New York: Anchor Books, 2002.

Blanco, Juan Antonio, and Medea Benjamin. *Cuba: Talking about Revolution.* Melbourne: Ocean Press, 1997.

Canto Bory, Enrique. *Mi vida.* Hato Rey, Puerto Rico: Ramallo Bros., 1997.

Cardenal, Ernesto. *En Cuba.* Mexico, DF: Ediciones Era, 1982.

Castro Porta, Carmen. *La lección del maestro.* Havana: Editorial de Ciencias Sociales, 1990.

Cruz Díaz, Rigoberto. *Chicharrones, la Sierra chiquita.* Santiago de Cuba: Editorial Oriente, 1982.

Cuadras de la Cruz, Gloria, and Marta Cabrales. *El rostro descubierto de la clandestinidad: Memorias de Gloria Cuadras de la Cruz.* Santiago de Cuba: Instituto Cubano del Libro/Editorial Oriente, 2006.

Espín, Vilma, Asela de los Santos, and Yolanda Ferrer. *Women in Cuba: The Making of* *the Revolution within the Revolution.* New York: Pathfinder Press, 2012.

Franqui, Carlos. *Diary of the Cuban Revolution.* New York: Viking Press, 1980.

———. *Family Portrait with Fidel.* New York: Random House, 1984.

Gil, Elena. "Apuntes para mi hijo." Unpublished manuscript, circa 1983. In author's possession.

Guevara, Ernesto Che. *Reminiscences of the Cuban Revolutionary War.* North Melbourne, Australia: Ocean Press, 2006.

Hart Dávalos, Armando. *Aldabonazo: Inside the Cuban Revolutionary Underground,* *1952–58: A Participant's Account.* New York: Pathfinder Press, 2004.

Lewis, Oscar. *Four Men: Living the Revolution; An Oral History of Contemporary Cuba.* Urbana: University of Illinois Press, 1977.

———. *Four Women: Living the Revolution; An Oral History of Contemporary Cuba.* Urbana: University of Illinois Press, 1978.

Leyva Pagán, Georgina. *Historia de una gesta libertadora, 1952–1958.* Havana: Editorial de Ciencias Sociales, 2009.

Lockwood, Lee. *Castro's Cuba, Cuba's Fidel: An American Journalist's Inside Look at Today's Cuba in Text and Picture.* New York: Macmillan, 1967.

Maloof, Judy. *Voices of Resistance: Testimonies of Cuban and Chilean Women.* Lexington: University Press of Kentucky, 1999.

Martínez, Elizabeth Sutherland. *The Youngest Revolution: A Personal Report on Cuba.* New York: Dial Press, 1969.

Meyer, Eugenia. *El futuro era nuestro: Ocho cubanas narran sus historias de vida.* Mexico City: UNAM, Facultad de Filosofia y Letras/Fondo de Cultura Economica, 2007.

Moro, Sonnia. *Nostalgias de una habanera del cerro.* Havana: Ediciones La Memoria, Centro Cultural Pablo de la Torriente Brau, 2006.

Nieves, Dolores, and Alina Feijóo. *Semillas de fuego: Compilación sobre la lucha clandestina en la capital.* 2 vols. Havana: Ciencias Sociales, 1989.

Nieves Rivera, Dolores. *Rogito.* Havana: Editora Política, 1981.

Oltuski, Enrique. *Vida Clandestina: My Life in the Cuban Revolution.* San Francisco: Wiley, 2002.

Oltuski, Enrique, Héctor Rodríguez Llompart, and Eduardo Torres-Cuevas, eds. *Memorias de la revolución.* Havana: Imagen Contemporaneo, 2007.

Randall, Margaret. *Cuban Women Now: Interviews with Cuban Women.* Toronto: Women's Press/Dumont Press Graphix, 1974.

Séjourné, Laurette. *La mujer cubana en el quehacer de la historia.* Mexico, DF: Siglo Veintiuno, 1980.

Suárez Suárez, Reinaldo, and Oscar Puig Corral. *La complejidad de la rebelión.* Havana: Ediciones Memoria, Centro Cultural Pablo de la Torriente Brau, 2010.

Books, Articles, and Dissertations

Álavez Martín, Elena. *Eduardo Chibás en la hora de la Ortodoxia.* Havana: Ciencias Sociales, 1994.

Alexander, Robert J. *Communism in Latin America.* New Brunswick, N.J.: Rutgers University Press, 1957.

Allen, Ann Taylor. "Maternalism in German Feminist Movements." *Journal of Women's History* 5, no. 2 (Fall 1993).

Allen, Jafari. *Venceremos? The Erotics of Black Self-Making in Cuba.* Durham, N.C.: Duke University Press, 2011.

Álvarez Tabío, Pedro. *Celia: Ensayo para una biografía.* Havana: Oficina de Publicaciones del Consejo de Estado, 2003.

Ameringer, Charles. *The Cuban Democratic Experience: The Autentico Years, 1944–1952.* Gainesville: University Press of Florida, 2000.

Andaya, Elise. *Conceiving Cuba: Reproduction, Women, and the State in the Post-Soviet Era.* New Brunswick, N.J.: Rutgers University Press, 2014.

Arboleya, Jesus. *La contrarrevolución cubana.* Havana: Editorial Ciencias Sociales, 2000.

Aretxaga, Begoña. *Los funerales en el nacionalismo radical vasco.* Baroja, 1988.

———. *Shattering Silence: Women, Nationalism, and Political Subjectivity in Northern Ireland.* Princeton, N.J.: Princeton University Press, 1997.

Argote-Freyre, Frank. *Fulgencio Batista: From Revolutionary to Strongman.* New Brunswick, N.J.: Rutgers University Press, 2006.

Bayard de Volo, Lorraine. *Mothers of Heroes and Martyrs: Gender Identity and Politics in Nicaragua, 1979–1999.* Baltimore: Johns Hopkins University Press, 2001.

Becker, Marjorie. *Setting the Virgin on Fire: Lázaro Cárdenas, Michoacán Peasants, and the Redemption of the Mexican Revolution.* Berkeley: University of California Press, 1995.

Bederman, Gail. *Manliness and Civilization: A Cultural History of Gender and Race in the United States, 1880–1917.* Chicago: University of Chicago Press, 1995.

Belmonte, Laura. *Selling the American Way: U.S. Propaganda and the Cold War.* Philadelphia: University of Pennsylvania Press, 2010.

Bengelsdorf, Carollee. "On the Problem of Studying Women in Cuba." In *Cuban Political Economy: Controversies in Cubanology,* edited by Andrew Zimbalist, 119–36. Boulder, Colo.: Westview Press, 1988.

———. "[Re]Considering Cuban Women in a Time of Troubles." In *Daughters of Caliban,* edited by Lopez Springfield, 229–55. Bloomington: Indiana University Press, 1997.

Benjamin, Medea. *No Free Lunch: Food and Revolution in Cuba Today.* San Francisco: Institute for Food and Development Policy, 1984.

Benson, Devyn Spence. *Antiracism in Cuba: The Unfinished Revolution.* Chapel Hill: University of North Carolina Press, 2016.

Bentley, Amy. *Eating for Victory: Food Rationing and the Politics of Domesticity.* Urbana: University of Illinois Press, 1998.

Bethell, Leslie, and Ian Roxborough, eds. *Latin America between the Second World War and the Cold War, 1944–1948.* New York: Cambridge University Press, 1992.

Bonachea, Ramón, and Marta San Martín. *The Cuban Insurrection, 1952–1959.* New Brunswick, N.J.: Transaction Books, 1974.

Bonachea, Rolando E., and Nelson P. Valdés, eds. *Revolutionary Struggle, 1947–1958.* Cambridge, Mass.: MIT Press, 1972.

Boorstein, Edward. *The Economic Transformation of Cuba: A First-Hand Account.* New York: Monthly Review Press, 1968.

Boylan, Kristina. "Gendering the Faith and Altering the Nation: Mexican Catholic Women's Activism, 1917–1940." In *Sex in Revolution: Gender, Politics, and Power in Modern Mexico,* edited by Jocelyn Olcott, Mary K. Vaughan, and Gabriela Cano, 199–222. Durham, N.C.: Duke University Press, 2006.

Brands, Hal. *Latin America's Cold War*. Cambridge, Mass.: Harvard University Press, 2010.

Brennan, Mary C. *Wives, Mothers, and the Red Menace: Conservative Women and the Crusade against Communism*. Boulder: University of Colorado Press, 2008.

Brown, Kathleen. *Good Wives, Nasty Wenches, and Anxious Patriarchs: Gender, Race, and Power in Colonial Virginia*. Chapel Hill: University of North Carolina Press, 1996.

Brunson, Takkara. "Constructing Afro-Cuban Womanhood: Race, Gender and Citizenship in Republican-Era Cuba." Ph.D. diss., University of Texas at Austin, 2011.

Bunck, Julie Marie. *Fidel Castro and the Quest for a Revolutionary Culture in Cuba*. University Park: Pennsylvania State University Press, 1994.

Butterworth, Douglas. *The People of Buena Ventura: Relocation of Slum Dwellers in Postrevolutionary Cuba*. Urbana: University of Illinois Press, 1980.

Campuzano, Luisa. *Las muchachas de la Habana no tienen temor de Dios . . . : Escritoras cubanas (s. XVIII–XXI)*. Havana: Editorial Unión, 2004.

Casavantes Bradford, Anita. *The Revolution Is for the Children: The Politics of Childhood in Havana and Miami, 1959–1962*. Chapel Hill: University of North Carolina Press, 2014.

Castañeda, Jorge. *Compañero: The Life and Death of Che Guevara*. New York: Knopf, 1997.

Chase, Michelle. "The Trials: Violence and Justice in the Aftermath of the Cuban Revolution." In *A Century of Revolution: Insurgent and Counter-Insurgent Violence during Latin America's Long Cold War*, edited by Greg Grandin and Gil Joseph, 163–98. Durham, N.C.: Duke University Press, 2010.

———. "Women's Organizations and the Politics of Gender in Cuba's Urban Insurrection (1952–58)." *Bulletin of Latin American Research* 29, no. 4 (October 2010): 440–58.

Cohen, Lizabeth. *A Consumer's Republic: The Politics of Mass Consumption in Postwar America*. New York: Knopf, 2003.

Conde, Yvonne. *Operation Pedro Pan: The Untold Exodus of 14,048 Cuban Children*. New York: Routledge, 1999.

Córdova, Efrén. *Castro and the Cuban Labor Movement: Statecraft and Society in a Revolutionary Period (1959–1961)*. Lanham, Md.: University Press of America, 1987.

Cowan, Ben. "Why Hasn't This Teacher Been Shot?: Moral-Sexual Panic, the Repressive Right, and Brazil's National Security State." *Hispanic American Historical Review* 92, no. 3 (2012).

Cuesta Braniella, José María. *La resistencia cívica en la guerra de liberación de Cuba*. Havana: Editorial de Ciencias Sociales, 1997.

Cushion, Steve. "The Cold War and Organized Labour in Batista's Cuba." Paper presented at the conference "The Americas and the Cold War," Institute for the Study of the Americas, December 2010.

Davis, Belinda J. *Home Fires Burning: Food, Politics, and Everyday Life in World War I Berlin*. Chapel Hill: University of North Carolina Press, 2000.

De Grazia, Victoria. *Irresistible Empire: America's Advance through Twentieth-Century Europe*. Cambridge, Mass.: Belknap Press of Harvard University Press, 2005.

De Haan, Francisca. "Communist Feminists? The WIDF on Women and Women's Emancipation." Paper presented at the workshop "Communist Feminism(s)," Rice University, March 2012.

———. "Continuing Cold War Paradigms in Western Historiography of Transnational Women's Organisations: The Case of the Women's International Democratic Federation (WIDF)." *Women's History Review* 19, no. 4 (September 2010): 547–73.

De la Fuente, Alejandro. *A Nation for All: Race, Inequality, and Politics in Twentieth-Century Cuba*. Chapel Hill: University of North Carolina Press, 2001.

De la Torre, Miguel A. *La lucha for Cuba: Religion and Politics on the Streets of Miami*. Berkeley: University of California Press, 2003.

De la Torre Mulhare, Mirta. "Sexual Ideology in Pre-Castro Cuba: A Cultural Analysis." Ph.D. diss., University of Pittsburgh, 1969.

Derby, Lauren. *The Dictator's Seduction: Politics and the Popular Imagination in the Era of Trujillo*. Durham, N.C.: Duke University Press, 2009.

Díaz Castañón, Maria del Pilar. *Ideología y revolución: Cuba, 1959–1962*. Havana: Ciencias Sociales, 2001.

Díaz Vallina, Elvira, Olga Dotre Romay, and Caridad Dacosta Pérez. "La mujer revolucionaria en Cuba durante el periodo insurreccional, 1952–58." *Revista de Ciencias Sociales* (Puerto Rico) (June 1997): 24–32.

Domínguez, Jorge. *Cuba: Order and Revolution*. Cambridge, Mass.: Belknap Press of Harvard University Press, 1978.

Draper, Theodore. *Castroism: Theory and Practice*. New York: Praeger, 1965.

———. *Castro's Revolution: Myths and Realities*. New York: Praeger, 1962.

Dubinsky, Karen. *Babies without Borders: Adoption and Migration across the Americas*. New York: New York University Press, 2010.

Ehrlich, Ilan. *Eduardo Chibás: The Incorrigible Man of Cuban Politics*. Lanham, Md.: Rowman and Littlefield, 2015.

Evans, Sara. *Personal Politics: The Roots of Women's Liberation in the Civil Rights Movement and the New Left*. New York: Knopf, 1979.

———. "Sons, Daughters, and Patriarchy: Gender and the 1968 Generation," *American Historical Review*, 114, no. 2 (April 2009): 331–347.

Fagen, Richard. *The Transformation of Political Culture in Cuba*. Stanford: Stanford University Press, 1969.

Fagen, Richard, T. J. O'Leary, and Richard A. Brody. *Cubans in Exile: Disaffection and the Revolution*. Stanford: Stanford University Press, 1968.

Farber, Samuel. "The Cuban Communists in the Early Stage of the Revolution: Revolutionaries or Reformists?" *Latin American Research Review* 18, no. 1 (1983): 59–83.

———. *The Origins of the Cuban Revolution Reconsidered*. Chapel Hill: University of North Carolina Press, 2006.

————. *Revolution and Reaction in Cuba, 1933–1960: A Political Sociology from Machado to Castro*. Middletown, Conn.: Wesleyan University Press, 1976.

Farnsworth-Alvear, Ann. *Dulcinea in the Factory: Myths, Morals, Men, and Women in Colombia's Industrial Experiment, 1905–1960*. Durham, N.C.: Duke University Press, 2000.

Fernandes, Sujatha. "Transnationalism and Feminist Activism: The Case of Magín." *Politics and Gender* 1, no. 3 (September 2005): 431–52.

Fernandez, Nadine. *Revolutionizing Romance: Interracial Couples in Contemporary Cuba*. New Brunswick, N.J.: Rutgers University Press, 2010.

Fernández Núñez, José Manuel. *La vivienda en Cuba*. Havana: Editorial Arte y Literatura, Instituto Cubano del Libro, 1976.

Fernández Soneira, Teresa. *Con la estrella y la cruz: Historia de la Federación de las Juventudes de Acción católica cubana*. Miami: Ediciones Universal, 2002.

Ferrer, Ada. *Insurgent Cuba: Race, Nation, and Revolution, 1868–1898*. Chapel Hill: University of North Carolina Press, 1999.

Fox, Geoffrey E. *Working-Class Émigrés from Cuba*. Palo Alto, Calif.: R and E Research Associates, 1979.

Franco, Jean. *Critical Passions: Selected Essays*. Edited by Mary Louise Pratt and Kathleen Newman. Durham: Duke University Press, 1999.

————. *The Decline and Fall of the Lettered City: Latin America in the Cold War*. Cambridge, Mass.: Harvard University Press, 2002.

Fraser, Valerie. *Building the New World: Studies in the Modern Architecture of Latin America, 1930–1960*. New York: Verso, 2000.

Freedman, Estelle B. *No Turning Back: The History of Feminism and the Future of Women*. New York: Ballantine Books/Random House, 2002.

Friedman, Elisabeth. *Unfinished Transitions: Women and the Gendered Development of Democracy in Venezuela, 1936–1996*. University Park: Pennsylvania State University Press, 2000.

Fusco, Coco. "Hustling for Dollars: Jineterismo in Cuba." In *Global Sex Workers: Rights, Resistance, and Redefinition*, edited by Kamala Kempadoo and Jo Doezma, 151–66. London: Routledge, 1998.

García, Gladys Marel. "Gender: Social Justice in the Revolutionary Period." In *Encyclopedia of Cuba: People, History, Culture*, vol. 1, edited by K. Lynn Stoner et al., 384–87.

————. "Género, historia y sociologia. Cuba, Siglo XX: Mujer y revolución." *Revista Santiago* 86 (1999).

————. *Insurrection and Revolution: Armed Struggle in Cuba, 1952–1959*. Boulder: Lynn Rienner Publishers, 1998.

García Montes, Jorge, and Antonio Alonso Ávila. *Historia del Partido Comunista de Cuba*. Miami: Ediciones Universal, 1970.

García Oliveras, Julio A. *José Antonio Echeverría, la lucha estudiantil contra Batista*. Havana: Editora Política, 1980.

Goldenburg, Boris. "The Rise and Fall of a Party: The Cuban CP (1925–59)." *Problems of Communism* (July/August 1970).

Gonzalez, Mike. "The Culture of the Heroic Guerrilla: The Impact of Cuba in the Sixties." *Bulletin of Latin American Research* 3, no. 2 (1984): 65–75.

González Pagés, Julio César. *En busca de un espacio: Historia de mujeres en Cuba.* Havana: Editorial de Ciencias Sociales, 2003.

Gonzalez-Rivera, Victoria, and Karen Kampwirth. *Radical Women in Latin America: Left and Right.* University Park: Pennsylvania State University Press, 2001.

Gosse, Van. "A Movement of Movements: The Definition and Periodization of the New Left." In *A Companion to Post-1945 America*, edited by Jean-Christophe Agnew and Roy Rosenzweig, 277–302. London: Blackwell, 2002.

———. *Rethinking the New Left: An Interpretative History.* New York: Palgrave/Macmillan, 2005.

———. " 'We Are Highly Adventurous': Fidel Castro and the Romance of the White Guerrilla, 1957–1958." In *Cold War Constructions: The Political Culture of United States Imperialism, 1945–1966*, edited by Christian G. Appy, 238–56. Amherst: University of Massachusetts Press, 2000.

———. *Where the Boys Are: Cuba, Cold War America and the Making of a New Left.* New York: Verso, 1993.

Gotkowitz, Laura, and Richard Turits. "Socialist Morality: Sexual Preference, Family, and State Intervention in Cuba." *Socialism and Democracy* 4, no. 1 (1990): 7–29.

Gott, Richard. *Cuba: A New History.* New Haven, Conn.: Yale University Press, 2004.

Gould, Jeffrey. "Solidarity under Siege: The Latin American Left, 1968." *American Historical Review* (April 2009): 348–75.

———. *To Lead as Equals: Rural Protest and Political Consciousness in Chinandega, Nicaragua, 1912–1979.* Chapel Hill: University of North Carolina Press, 1990.

Grandin, Greg. *The Last Colonial Massacre: Latin America in the Cold War.* Chicago: University of Chicago Press, 2004.

Grau Alsina, Ramon. *Mongo Grau: Cuba desde 1930.* Madrid: Agualarga, 1997.

Green, James N. "Who Is the Macho Who Wants to Kill Me? Male Homosexuality, Revolutionary Masculinity, and the Brazilian Armed Struggle of the 1960s and 1970s." *Hispanic American Historical Review* 92, no. 3 (2012).

Guerra, Lillian. "Gender Policing, Homosexuality, and the New Patriarchy of the Cuban Revolution, 1965–70." *Social History* 35, no. 3 (July 2010): 268–89.

———. "To Condemn the Revolution Is to Condemn Christ: Radicalization, Moral Redemption, and the Sacrifice of Civil Society in Cuba, 1960." *Hispanic American Historical Review* 89, no. 1 (2009): 73–109.

———. *Visions of Power in Cuba: Revolution, Redemption, and Resistance, 1959–1971.* Chapel Hill: University of North Carolina Press, 2012.

Guerrero, Maria Luisa. *Elena Mederos: Una mujer con perfil para la historia.* Washington, D.C.: Of Human Rights/Miami: Ediciones Universal, 1991.

Guzman Bouvard, Marguerite. *Revolutionizing Motherhood: The Mothers of the Plaza de Mayo.* Wilmington, Del.: Scholarly Resources, 1994.

Hamilton, Carrie. *Sexual Revolutions in Cuba: Passion, Politics, and Memory.* Chapel Hill: University of North Carolina Press, 2012.

Harkonen, Heidi. "Gender, Kinship and Lifecycle Rituals in Cuba." *Suomen Antropologi: Journal of the Finnish Anthropological Society* 35, no. 1 (Spring 2010): 60–73.

Harsch, Donna. *Revenge of the Domestic: Women, the Family, and Communism in the German Democratic Republic.* Princeton, N.J.: Princeton University Press, 2007.

Herman, Rebecca. "An Army of Educators: Gender, Revolution, and the Cuban Literacy Campaign of 1961." *Gender and History* 24, no. 1 (April 2012): 93–111.

Holston, James. *The Modernist City: An Anthropological Critique of Brasília.* Chicago: University of Chicago Press, 1989.

Hynson, Rachel. "'Count, Capture, and Reeducate': The Campaign to Rehabilitate Cuba's Female Sex Workers, 1959–1966." *Journal of the History of Sexuality* 24, no. 1 (January 2015).

Ibarra, Jorge. *Prologue to Revolution: Cuba, 1898–1958.* Boulder, Colo.: L. Rienner, 1998.

Ibarra Guitart, Jorge Renato. *El fracaso de los moderados en Cuba: Las alternativas reformistas de 1957 a 1958.* Havana: Editora Política, 2000.

Isserman, Maurice. *If I Had a Hammer: The Death of the Old Left and the Birth of the New Left.* Urbana: University of Illinois Press, 1993.

Jacquette, Jane. "Women in Revolutionary Movements in Latin America." *Journal of Marriage and the Family* 35, no. 2 (1973): 344–54.

James, Daniel. *Resistance and Integration: Peronism and the Argentine Working Class, 1946–1976.* New York: Cambridge University Press, 1988.

Joseph, Gilbert, and Daniela Spenser, eds. *In from the Cold: Latin America's New Encounter with the Cold War.* Durham, N.C.: Duke University Press, 2008.

Judson, C. Fred. *Cuba and the Revolutionary Myth: The Political Education of the Cuban Rebel Army, 1953–1963.* Boulder, Colo.: Westview Press, 1984.

Kampwirth, Karen. *Feminism and the Legacy of Revolution: Nicaragua, El Salvador, Chiapas.* Athens: Ohio University Press, 2004.

Kaplan, Temma. "Female Consciousness and Collective Action: The Case of Barcelona, 1910–1918." *Signs* 7, no. 3 (1982): 545–66.

Karol, K. S. *Guerrillas in Power: The Course of the Cuban Revolution.* New York: Hill and Wang, 1970.

Katsiaficas, George. *The Imagination of the New Left: A Global Analysis of 1968.* Boston: South End Press, 1987.

Kelly, Catriona. *Children's World: Growing Up in Russia, 1890–1991.* New Haven, Conn.: Yale University Press, 2007.

Kirk, John M. *Between God and the Party: Religion and Politics in Revolutionary Cuba.* Gainesville: University Presses of Florida/Tampa: University of South Florida Press, 1989.

Kirschenbaum, Lisa. *Small Comrades: Revolutionizing Childhood in Soviet Russia, 1917–1932.* New York: Routledge, 2000.

Klouzal, Linda A. "Rebellious Affinities: Narratives of Community, Resistance, and Women's Participation in the Cuban Revolution (1952–1959)." Ph.D. diss., University of California, Santa Barbara, 2006.

Klubock, Thomas Miller. *Contested Communities: Class, Gender, and Politics in Chile's El Teniente Copper Mine, 1904–1951*. Durham, N.C.: Duke University Press, 1998.

LaCharité, Norman. *Case Studies in Insurgency and Revolutionary Warfare: Cuba, 1953–59*. Washington, D.C.: Special Operations Research Office, American University, 1963.

Lancaster, Roger N. *Life Is Hard: Machismo, Danger, and the Intimacy of Power in Nicaragua*. Berkeley: University of California Press, 1992.

Langland, Victoria. "Birth Control Pills and Molotov Cocktails: Reading Sex and Revolution in 1968 Brazil." In *In from the Cold: Latin America's New Encounter with the Cold War*, edited by Gilbert Joseph and Daniela Spenser, 308–49. Durham, N.C.: Duke University Press, 2008.

Larguia, Isabel, and John Dumoulin. *Hacia una concepción científica de la emancipación de la mujer*. Havana: Ciencias Sociales, 1983.

Leiner, Marvin. *Children Are the Revolution: Day Care in Cuba*. New York: Viking, 1974.

Lipman, Jana K. *Guantánamo: A Working-Class History between Empire and Revolution*. Berkeley: University of California Press, 2009.

Lobao, Linda. "Women in Revolutionary Movements: Changing Patterns of Latin American Guerrilla Struggle." In *Women and Social Protest*, edited by Guida West and Rhoda Lois Blumberg, 180–204. New York: Oxford University Press, 1990.

Lopez, Ricardo A. "It Is Not Something You Can Be or Come to Be Overnight." In *Latin America's Middle Class: Unsettled Debates and New Histories*, edited by David Parker and Louise Walker, 151–70. Lanham, Md.: Lexington Books, 2013.

López Rivero, Sergio, María Antonia Marqués Dolz, and Zaida Purón Riaño. *Emigración y clandestinidad en el M-26-7: La emisión de bonos*. Havana: Editora Política, 1990.

Luciak, Ilja. *Gender and Democracy in Cuba*. Gainesville: University Press of Florida, 2007.

Lumsden, Ian. *Machos, Maricones, and Gays: Cuba and Homosexuality*. Philadelphia: Temple University Press, 1996.

Lutjens, Sheryl. "Remaking the Public Sphere: Women and Revolution in Cuba." In *Women and Revolution in Africa, Asia, and the New World*, edited by Mary Ann Tetreault, 366–93. Columbia: University of South Carolina Press, 1994.

Luzzatto, Sergio. *The Body of Il Duce: Mussolini's Corpse and the Fortunes of Italy*. New York: Metropolitan Books, 2005.

Mallon, Florencia. "*Barbudos*, Warriors and *Rotos*: The MIR, Masculinity, and Power in the Chilean Agrarian Reform, 1965–1974." In *Changing Men and Masculinities in Latin America*, edited by Matthew C. Gutman. Durham, N.C.: Duke University Press, 2003.

Manley, Elizabeth. "Intimate Violations: Women and the Ajusticiamiento of Dictator Rafael Trujillo, 1944–1961." *The Americas* 69, no. 1 (July 2012): 61–94.

Marchesi, Aldo. "Geographies of Armed Protest: Transnational Cold War, Latin Americanism and the New Left in the Southern Cone (1964–1976)." Ph.D. diss., New York University, January 2013.

———. "Revolution beyond the Sierra Maestra: The Tupamaros and the Development of a Repertoire of Dissent in the Southern Cone." *The Americas* (January 2014): 523–53.

Markarian, Vania. "Sobre viejas y nuevas izquierdas: Los jovenes comunistas uruguayos y el movimiento estudiantil de 1968." *Secuencia*, no. 81 (September–December 2011).

Martínez-Alier (Stolcke), Verena. *Marriage, Class, and Colour in Nineteenth-Century Cuba: A Study of Racial Attitudes and Sexual Values in a Slave Society*. Ann Arbor: University of Michigan Press, 1989 [1972].

May, Elaine Tyler. *Homeward Bound: American Families in the Cold War Era*. New York: Basic Books, 2008.

McLellan, Josie. *Love in the Time of Communism*. Cambridge: Cambridge University Press, 2011.

Michel, Sonya. "American Women and the Discourse of the Democratic Family in World War II." In *Behind the Lines: Gender and the Two World Wars*, edited by Margaret Higonnet et al., 154–67. New Haven, Conn.: Yale University Press, 1987.

Miller, Francesa. *Latin American Women and the Search for Social Justice*. Hanover, N.H.: University Press of New England, 1991.

Molyneux, Maxine. "Mobilization without Emancipation? Women's Interests, the State, and Revolution in Nicaragua." *Feminist Studies* 11, no. 2 (1985): 227–54.

———. "State, Gender, and Institutional Change: The Federacion de Mujeres Cubanas." In *Hidden Histories of Gender and the State in Latin America*, edited by Elizabeth Dore and Maxine Molyneux, 291–321. Durham, N.C.: Duke University Press, 2000.

———. "State Socialism and Women's Emancipation: A Continuing Retrospective." In *Women's Movements in International Perspective: Latin America and Beyond*. New York: Palgrave, 2001.

Monahan, James. *The Great Deception: The Inside Story of How the Kremlin Took Over Cuba*. New York: Farrar, Straus, 1963.

Morán Arce, Lucas. *La Revolución cubana, 1953–1959: Una versión rebelde*. Ponce, Puerto Rico: Imprenta Universitaria, 1980.

Moreno, Julio. *Yankee Don't Go Home! Mexican Nationalism, American Business Culture, and the Shaping of Modern Mexico, 1920–1950*. Chapel Hill: University of North Carolina Press, 2003.

Morley, Morris. *Imperial State and Revolution: The United States and Cuba, 1952–1986*. Cambridge: Cambridge University Press, 1987.

Murray, Nicola. "Socialism and Feminism: Women and the Cuban Revolution, Part I." *Feminist Review* 2 (1979): 57–73.

Nash, Mary. "Milicianas and Homefront Heroines: Images of Women in Revolutionary Spain (1936–1939)." *History of European Ideas* 11, issue 1-6 (January 1989): 235–44.

———. "Women in War: Milicianas and Armed Combat in Revolutionary Spain, 1936–1939." *International History Review* 15, no. 2 (May 1993): 221–440.

Navarro, Marysa. "The Personal Is Political: Las Madres de Plaza de Mayo." In *Power and Popular Protest: Latin American Social Movements*, edited by Susan Eckstein et al., 241–58. Berkeley: University of California Press, 1989.

Nazzari, Muriel. "The 'Woman Question' in Cuba." In *Promissory Notes: Women in the Transition to Socialism*, edited by Sonia Kruks, Rayna Reiter, and Marilyn Young. New York: Monthly Review Press, 1989.

Nelson, Lowry. *Cuba: The Measure of a Revolution*. Minneapolis: University of Minnesota Press, 1972.

O'Connor, James. *The Origins of Socialism in Cuba*. Ithaca, N.Y.: Cornell University Press, 1970.

Olcott, Jocelyn. *Revolutionary Women in Postrevolutionary Mexico*. Durham, N.C.: Duke University Press, 2005.

Olcott, Jocelyn, Mary K. Vaughan, and Gabriela Cano, eds. *Sex in Revolution: Gender, Politics, and Power in Modern Mexico*. Durham, N.C.: Duke University Press, 2006.

Oldenziel, Ruth, and Karin Zachmann. *Cold War Kitchen: Americanization, Technology, and European Users*. Cambridge, Mass.: MIT Press, 2009.

Oltuski, Enrique, Héctor Rodríguez Llompart, and Eduardo Torres-Cuevas. *Memorias de la revolución*. Havana: Imagen Contemporánea, 2007.

Padula, Alfred L. "The Fall of the Bourgeoisie: Cuba, 1959–1961." Ph.D. diss., University of New Mexico, 1974.

Paterson, Thomas G. *Contesting Castro: The United States and the Triumph of the Cuban Revolution*. New York: Oxford University Press, 1994.

Pedraza, Silvia. *Political Disaffection in Cuba's Revolution and Exodus*. New York: Cambridge University Press, 2007.

Pérez, Louis. *Cuba: Between Reform and Revolution*. New York: Oxford University Press, 2006.

———. *Cuba under the Platt Amendment, 1902–1934*. Pittsburgh: University of Pittsburgh Press, 1986.

———. *Essays on Cuban History: Historiography and Research*. Gainesville: University Press of Florida, 1995.

———. *On Becoming Cuban: Identity, Nationality, and Culture*. Chapel Hill: University of North Carolina Press, 1999.

———. *To Die in Cuba: Suicide and Society*. Chapel Hill: University of North Carolina Press, 2005.

Pérez-Stable, Marifeli. *The Cuban Revolution: Origins, Course, and Legacy*. New York: Oxford University Press, 1999.

Perna, Vincenzo. *Timba: The Sound of the Cuban Crisis*. Burlington, Vt.: Ashgate Books, 2005.

Pojmann, Wendy. "For Mothers, Peace and Family: International (Non)-Cooperation among Italian Catholic and Communist Women's Organisations during the Early Cold War." *Gender and History* 23, no. 2 (August 2011): 415–29.

Power, Margaret. *Right-Wing Women in Chile: Feminine Power and the Struggle against Allende, 1964–1973*. University Park: Pennsylvania State University Press, 2002.

Puebla, Teté, and Mary-Alice Waters. *Marianas en combate: Teté Puebla y el pelotón femenino en la guerra revolucionaria cubana, 1956-58*. New York: Pathfinder Press, 2003.

Randall, Margaret. *Gathering Rage: The Failure of Twentieth Century Revolutions to Develop a Feminist Agenda*. New York: Monthly Review Press, 1992.

Ricardo, Yolanda. *La resistencia en las Antillas tiene rostro de mujer: (Transgresiones, Emancipaciones)*. Santo Domingo: Publicaciones de la Academia de Ciencias de la República Dominicana, 2004.

Rodríguez Astiazaraín, Nicolás. *Episodios de la lucha clandestina en la Habana, 1955-1958*. Havana: Editorial de Ciencias Sociales, 2009.

Roig de Leuchsenring, Emilio. *Males y vicios de Cuba republicana*. Havana: Oficina del historiador, 1959.

Rojas, Rafael. *La máquina del olvido: Mito, historia y poder en Cuba*. Mexico, DF: Taurus, 2012.

Rojas Blaquier, Marta. *El primer Partido Comunista de Cuba*. Santiago: Editorial Oriente, 2005.

Rosemblatt, Karin Alejandra. *Gendered Compromises: Political Cultures and the State in Chile, 1920-1950*. Chapel Hill: University of North Carolina Press, 2000.

Rosenberg, Emily S. "Consumer Capitalism and the End of the Cold War." In *Endings*, edited by Melvyn Leffler and Odd Arne Westad, eds. Vol. 3 of *The Cambridge History of the Cold War*, 489-512. Cambridge: Cambridge University Press, 2010.

Rosenthal, Anton. "Spectacle, Fear, and Protest: A Guide to the History of Urban Public Space in Latin America." *Social Science History* 24, no. 1 (Spring 2000): 33-73.

Rubenstein, Anne. "Raised Voices in the Cine Montecarlo: Sex Education, Mass Media, and Oppositional Politics in Mexico." *Journal of Family History* 23 (1998): 312-23.

Ruddick, Sara. *Maternal Thinking: Towards a Politics of Peace*. Boston: Beacon Press, 1989.

Safa, Helen. "Hierarchies and Household Change in Postrevolutionary Cuba." *Latin American Perspectives* 36, no. 1 (2009): 42-52.

Saldaña-Portillo, María Josefina. *The Revolutionary Imagination in the Americas and the Age of Development*. Durham, N.C.: Duke University Press, 2003.

Sawyer, Mark. "Unlocking the Official Story: Comparing the Cuban Revolution's Approach to Race and Gender." *UCLA Journal of International Law and Foreign Affairs* (2000): 403-17.

Scarpaci, Joseph L., Roberto Segre, and Mario Coyula. *Havana: Two Faces of the Antillean Metropolis*. Chapel Hill: University of North Carolina Press, 2002.

Schwartz, Paula. "Redefining Resistance: Women's Activism in Wartime France." In *Behind the Lines: Gender and the Two World Wars*, edited by Margaret Higonnet et al., 141-53. New Haven, Conn.: Yale University Press, 1987.

Schwartz, Rosalie. *Pleasure Island: Tourism and Temptation in Cuba*. Lincoln: University of Nebraska Press, 1997.

Scott, Joan. *Gender and the Politics of History*. New York: Columbia University Press, 1988.

Serra, Ana. *The New Man: Culture and Identity in the Revolution.* Gainesville: University Press of Florida, 2007.

Shaopeng, Song. "The State Discourse on Housewives and Housework in the 1950s in China." In *Rethinking China in the 1950s*, edited by Mechthild Leutner. Piscataway, N.J.: Transaction, 2007.

Shayne, Julie. *The Revolution Question: Feminisms in El Salvador, Chile, and Cuba.* New Brunswick, N.J.: Rutgers University Press, 2004.

Sims, Harold. "Cuba." In *Latin America between the Second World War and the Cold War*, edited by Leslie Bethell and Ian Roxborough, 217–42. Cambridge: Cambridge University Press, 1992.

———. "Cuban Labor and the Communist Party, 1937–1958: An Interpretation," *Cuban Studies* 15, no. 1 (Winter 1985): 43–58.

Smith, Lois M., and Alfred Padula. *Sex and Revolution: Women in Socialist Cuba.* New York: Oxford University Press, 1996.

Sorensen, Diana. *A Turbulent Decade Remembered: Scenes from the Latin American Sixties.* Stanford: Stanford University Press, 2007.

Sosa, Ignacio. *Insurección y democracia en el Circuncaribe.* Mexico, DF: Universidad Nacional Autónoma de México, 1997.

Stoner, K. Lynn. *From the House to the Streets: The Cuban Woman's Movement for Legal Reform, 1898–1940.* Durham, N.C.: Duke University Press, 1991.

———. "Militant Heroines and the Consecration of the Patriarchal State." *Cuban Studies* 34 (February 2004): 71–96.

———. "Ofelia Dominguez Navarro: The Making of a Cuban Socialist Feminist." In *The Human Tradition in Latin America: The Twentieth Century*, edited by William Beezley and Judith Ewell, 181–204. Wilmington, Del.: Scholarly Resources, 1987.

Suchlicki, Jaime. *University Students and Revolution in Cuba, 1920–1968.* Coral Gables, Fla.: University of Miami Press, 1969.

Sweig, Julia. *Inside the Cuban Revolution: Fidel Castro and the Urban Underground.* Cambridge, Mass.: Harvard University Press, 2002.

Tambor, Molly. "Red Saints: Gendering the Cold War, Italy 1943–1953." *Cold War History* 10, no. 3 (2010): 429–56.

Taylor, Diana. *Disappearing Acts: Spectacles of Gender and Nationalism in Argentina's "Dirty War."* Durham, N.C.: Duke University Press, 1997.

Thomas, Hugh. *Cuba, or, The Pursuit of Freedom.* New York: Da Capo Press, 1998.

Thomas-Woodard, Tiffany. " 'Toward the Gates of Eternity': Celia Sanchez Manduley and the Creation of Cuba's New Woman." *Cuban Studies* 34 (2003): 154–80.

Tinsman, Heidi. "A Paradigm of Our Own: Joan Scott in Latin American History." *American Historical Review* 113, no. 5 (December 2008): 1357–74.

———. *Partners in Conflict: The Politics of Gender, Sexuality, and Labor in the Chilean Agrarian Reform, 1950–1973.* Durham, N.C.: Duke University Press, 2002.

Torreira Crespo, Ramón, and José Buajasán Marrawi. *Operación Peter Pan: Un caso de guerra psicológica contra Cuba.* Havana: Editora Política, 2000.

Torres, María de los Angeles. *The Lost Apple: Operation Pedro Pan, Cuban Children in the U.S., and the Promise of a Better Future.* Boston: Beacon Press, 2003.

Tosh, John. *Manliness and Masculinities in Nineteenth-Century Britain.* New York: Pearson, 2005.

Turits, Richard Lee. *Foundations of Despotism: Peasants, the Trujillo Regime, and Modernity in Dominican History.* Stanford: Stanford University Press, 2003.

Verdery, Katherine. *The Political Lives of Dead Bodies: Reburial and Postsocialist Change.* New York: Columbia University Press, 1999.

Weigand, Kate. *Red Feminism: American Communism and the Making of Women's Liberation.* Baltimore: Johns Hopkins University Press, 2001.

Weiner, Lynn. "Maternalism as Paradigm: Defining the Issues." *Journal of Women's History* 5, no. 2 (Fall 1993).

Weinstein, Barbara. "Inventing the 'Mulher Paulista.'" *Journal of Women's History* 18, no. 1 (2006).

Welch, Richard E. *Response to Revolution: The United States and the Cuban Revolution, 1959–1961.* Chapel Hill: University of North Carolina Press, 1985.

Weld, Kirsten. *Paper Cadavers: The Archives of Dictatorship in Guatemala.* Durham, N.C.: Duke University Press, 2014.

Westad, Odd Arne, ed. *Reviewing the Cold War: Approaches, Interpretations, Theory.* London: Frank Cass, 2000.

Whitney, Robert. *State and Revolution in Cuba: Mass Mobilization and Political Change, 1920–1940.* Chapel Hill: University of North Carolina Press, 2001.

Winn, Peter. *Weavers of Revolution: The Yarur Workers and Chile's Road to Socialism.* New York: Oxford University Press, 1986.

Winocur, Marcos. *Las clases olvidadas en la Revolución cubana.* Barcelona: Editorial Crítica, 1979.

Wolf, Eric. *Peasant Wars of the Twentieth Century.* New York: Harper and Row, 1969.

Womack, John. *Zapata and the Mexican Revolution.* New York: Knopf, 1969.

Wood, Elizabeth A. *The Baba and the Comrade: Gender and Politics in Revolutionary Russia.* Bloomington: Indiana University Press, 1997.

Wright, C. Thomas. *Latin America in the Era of the Cuban Revolution.* New York: Praeger, 1991.

Yabur Curí, Roxana. *Perfil de un comunista: Síntesis biográfica de Alfredo Yabur Maluf.* Havana: Editora Política, 1979.

Young, Allen. *Gays under the Cuban Revolution.* San Francisco: Gray Fox Press, 1981.

Zeitlin, Maurice. *Revolutionary Politics and the Cuban Working Class.* New York: Harper and Row, 1970.

Zolov, Eric. "Expanding Our Conceptual Horizons: The Shift from an Old to a New Left in Latin America." *A Contracorriente* 5, no. 2 (Winter 2008): 47–73.

———. "Introduction: Latin America in the Global Sixties." *The Americas* (January 2014): 349–62.

INDEX

Abortion, 113, 187, 188
Abreu, Gerardo ("Fontán"), 51, 52–54
Acción Cívica Cubana, 34
Adolescents. *See* Youth
Afro-Cubans: "backward" consumption
    practices of, 159, 252 (n. 91); Marxist
    Left and, 111, 113; and popular music,
    221 (n. 70); as revolutionary actors,
    54, 67; social clubs and, 180; white
    fears of sexual unions with, 216
    (n. 32). *See also* Race and racism
Agrarian reform, 117, 123, 128, 139, 143–44
Aguirre, Mirta, 90, 247 (n. 122)
Anti-Castro movement, 7, 14, 135, 165, 171,
    202; on literacy campaign, 188–89;
    publications and broadcasts of, 188,
    197, 262 (n. 107); racial imaginary of,
    172, 199, 202–4; spreading of rumors
    by, 194–95; on women, children, and
    family, 79, 172, 173, 197–99, 204–5
Anticolonialism, 26. *See also*
    Anti-imperialism
Anticommunism: and depictions of
    family, 181, 195–96; liberal and
    Catholic strains of, 205, 207–8; moral
    character of, 14; within ranks of
    Twenty-Sixth of July Movement, 66,
    117, 124. *See also* Anti-Castro
    movement; Cold War
Anti-imperialism, 39, 45, 52, 93, 150
Asociación de Ayuda a los Presos, 94
Auténtico Party, 23, 24, 87, 108, 218 (n. 18),
    235 (nn. 66, 75)

Barbudos (guerilla warriors): and displays
    of Catholicism, 75; impact beyond
    Cuba of, 44–47; and other revolutionary

actors, 46–47, 75; rise of icon of, 11, 70–73;
    sexual restraint of, 73–74. *See also* Rebel
    army; Twenty-Sixth of July Movement
Batista, Fulgencio, 1, 22, 23, 24. *See also*
    Protests—against Batista
Bay of Pigs, 3, 147, 160, 186
Belmonte, Laura, 195
Benítez, Conrado, 172
Berman, Máximo, 151
Black market, 161–63
Blacks. *See* Afro-Cubans
Bohemia Libre (magazine), 184, 197, 199, 202
Bonachea, Ramón, 48, 55, 237 (n. 100)
Bonds, 72–73
Boycotts, 11, 20, 27, 28, 35, 43
Brennan, Mary, 195, 196
Buy National campaigns, 34, 138, 140

Campesinos, 44, 64, 112, 160, 166
Campuzano, Luisa, 188
Cardenal, Ernesto, 57
Casal, Lourdes, 52
Casavantes Bradford, Anita, 170, 187, 256
    (nn. 1, 4)
Castro, Fidel: and Catholicism, 75;
    contemporaries' impressions of,
    49–50, 55–56; on family, 206–8; female
    strategists close to, 78; guerrilla
    strategy of, 66; on housing, 177; on
    leisure, 180; Moncada uprising of,
    24–25; on rumors, 193; scholarly and
    popular focus on, 5–6; on shortages,
    138, 151, 159; use of media by, 71, 72; on
    women's militias, 128
Castro, Raúl, 9, 74, 194, 198
Castro Porta, Carmen, 92–93, 235 (n. 76),
    247 (n. 121)

Catholic Action (*Acción Católica*), 111, 223 (n. 86), 233 (n. 33), 240 (n. 24)

Catholic Church and Catholicism, 256 (n. 3), 257 (nn. 9–10); and anticommunism, 205; appeal of maternalism and motherhood within, 89, 91, 173; attacks on (under Batista), 63–64; conflict with revolutionary government, 181–82, 184; and Operation Peter Pan, 256 (n. 3); rebel army and, 75; as sites of protests, 30, 31, 81; and women's activism, 220 (n. 51)

Catholic School Teachers (*Maestras Católicas*), 87

Chibás, Eduardo, 21, 23–24, 93, 101, 217 (n. 4), 218 (n. 11), 237 (n. 107)

Children's Circles, 183–84

Chile, 8, 45, 108, 215 (n. 24)

CIA (Central Intelligence Agency): and anti-Castro movement, 16, 193, 195, 198, 205; and Latin America, 263 (n. 125); and Operation Peter Pan, 256 (n. 3); and women, 198

Cities, role in revolution of, 9–10, 27–28, 36–37, 47–48. *See also* Havana; Santiago de Cuba; Urban underground

Civic Activism. *See* Protests

Civic Resistance Movement (Movimiento de Resistencia Cívica, MRC): handbills printed by, 37, 56, 62, 63; protest actions organized by, 28–29, 32, 35, 84, 218 (n. 9), 233 (n. 36); women's participation within, 22, 77–78, 87

Clandestinos (feature film), 103

Cold War, 3, 14, 22, 24, 70, 87, 124, 126; debates about consumption in, 138, 163–64; definitions of freedom in, 135, 205; gender relations and, 212; symbolism of children and family in, 172, 195–96, 204–5, 207; women's organizations divided over, 106, 124, 127

Colombia, 65

Committees for the Defense of the Revolution (*Comités para la Defensa de la Revolución*, CDRs), 148, 159, 162, 165, 246 (n. 119)

Communist Party (*Partido Socialist Popular*, PSP): and general revolutionary strikes, 66–69; and "Marquitos" Rodríguez, 51; and maternalism, 89–90, 91; newspapers published by, 15, 91, 108; overview of prerevolutionary, 108–10; relations with Twenty-Sixth of July Movement, 12, 48, 67, 115, 123–24, 126–27; stance on revolutionary violence, 90, 114; and the "woman question," 107–11

Consumption: "backwardness" in, 158–59; changes to in revolution, 136, 155–56; as emblematic of modernity, 33–34, 156–58; as engine of national industrialization, 139–40; inequality in, 160–63; intentional disruptions of as protest, 33–39; middle-class identity and, 155–56; political critiques of, 34–35, 37, 150–52, 155; race and, 156–57; revolutionary restraint in, 147, 151–52, 154–55; U.S. influence on, 33–34, 137–38, 150–52; women's prominence within, 20, 32–34, 38–39, 139–43. *See also* Black market; Rationing

Counterrevolution. *See* Anti-Castro movement

Cuadras de la Cruz, Gloria, 21, 30, 217 (n. 7), 243 (n. 68), 247 (n. 121)

Cuban Freedom Committee, 204

Debray, Régis, 48, 223 (n. 2)

Democratic Federation of Cuban Women (*Federación Democrática de Mujeres Cubanas*, FDMC): conception of women's liberation, 111–12, 241 (nn. 35–36), 242 (n. 48); depictions of Soviet Union by, 112–13, 124; formation of, 110–11, 239 (n. 14); and racism, 113–14

Derby, Lauren, 34

Diaspora. *See* Exiles

Domestic labor: anticipated collectivization of, 179, 180, 207; greater burden of after revolution, 13, 163; redistribution of, 122

Domestic servants: Fidel Castro on, 206; government retraining programs for, 142–43, 164; Women's Revolutionary Brigades and, 118

Domínguez, Jorge, 166, 222 (n. 74)

Domínguez, Ofelia, 110

Dominican Republic, 22, 24, 34, 64, 221 (n. 62)

Dubinsky, Karen, 172

Echeverría, José Antonio, 41, 59

Education, revolutionary changes to, 184–90. *See also* Federation of University Students; Literacy campaign; Students; University of Havana

El llano. *See* Urban underground

Embargo against Cuba, 147–48

Espín, Vilma: as FMC head, 132, 133, 247 (n. 121); ridicule of, 194; and Santiago underground, 29, 227 (n. 82), 234 (n. 59); on shortages, 151–52, 248 (n. 20); on women in anti-Batista struggle, 231 (n. 6), 246 (n. 15). *See also* Federation of Cuban Women

Exiles: Cuban, in United States, 16, 160, 172, 173, 192, 205; Spanish, in Cuba, 93, 99. *See also* Immigrants, Spanish, in Cuba; Spanish Civil War

Family: anti-Castro movement and, 205; Cold War propaganda regarding, 195–96; fears of destruction of, 13–14, 181; Fidel Castro statements on, 206; government attempts to bolster, 173–81; political strains upon, 181–94

Family Code of 1975, 3, 257 (n. 11)

Farber, Samuel, 49, 138, 148, 223 (n. 88)

Federation of Cuban Women (*Federación de Mujeres Cubanas*, FMC): centralized power of, 5; congresses of, 121, 250 (n. 47); denunciation of feminism by, 3; formation and activities of, 105–7, 116, 121, 132–34, 183, 245 (n. 98), 246 (nn. 115, 119), 247 (n. 121), 260 (n. 63); and housewives, 168; role of during food shortages, 148, 168, 250 (n. 46); treatment of poor women by, 245 (n. 91); on women's liberation in revolution, 215 (n. 23), 265 (n. 1). *See also* Espín, Vilma

Federation of University Students (*Federación Estudiantil Universitaria*, FEU), 26, 47

Femininity, 5, 197–98

Feminism, 3, 4, 104, 106, 110, 114; Cuban first-wave, 93–94, 110; "revolutionary" forms of, 4, 107; scholarship and, 3–4, 79

Food shortages, 13, 145–46, 164–65; impact on urban women of, 148, 163–67; protests against, 165–67; rise of in urban centers, 145–48; as spurring opposition to revolution, 155–56. *See also* Black market; Rationing

Fox, Geoffrey, 193

Franqui, Carlos, 125

Frayde, Marta, 92, 243 (n. 66), 247 (n. 121)

Freedman, Estelle, 80

Freemasons, 87

Frente Femenino del 26 de Julio, 118

Friedman, Elisabeth, 64, 110

Fuente, Alejandro de la, 111

Funerals: constructions of masculinity and, 56–58, 227 (n. 82); mock, 26, 41, 226 (n. 55); political nature of, 41, 56–59; roles of women in, 26, 59–60, 95, 227 (nn. 74, 77, 82)

García, Gladys Marel, 117, 118, 124, 125, 127

García Bárcena, Rafael, 25

Pelayo, Aida, 92–95, 96–97, 104, 235 (n. 76), 247 (n. 121)

Peña, Lázaro, 207

Pérez, Louis, 33, 34, 57, 115, 137, 177, 204

Pinar del Rio Province, 31, 57, 105, 134, 220 (n. 38)

Porras, Norma, 103

Prado, Pura del, 90–91

Press: exile-produced, 16; government nationalization of, 15, 193; prerevolutionary development in Havana of, 15, 71; as primary source material, 15–16

—clandestine anti-Batista: characteristics of, 49; descriptions of violence in, 55, 56, 58–59; poetry in, 90–91; references to class in, 65; references to fatherhood in, 61–62; women's participation in distribution of, 29 *See also* Radio

Pregnancy, 102, 103, 171

Prison, 55, 94, 95, 96, 103, 118, 236 (n. 89)

Prostitution, 119, 128, 131, 143, 180, 214 (n. 9), 259 (n. 44)

Protests

—against Batista: creativity in, 25–31; funerals as form of, 56–60; role of women in, 25–26, 29–31, 38–39, 41–43, 80–89, 96–97; use of direct action in, 40–43; use of home in, 27–30

—against Castro, 165–67, 188. *See also* Anti-Castro movement

Race and racism: and consumption, 156, 159, 252 (n. 91); expanding revolutionary imaginary toward, 172; FDMC on, 111, 113; and segregation in leisure spaces, 180; and sexuality, 187, 189–90. *See also* Afro-Cubans; Whites and whiteness

Radio, 160; actors, 53, 91; anti-Castro movement's use of, 160, 198; Eduardo Chibás's use of, 217 (n. 4); Radio Rebelde, 30; Radio Swan, 193, 195

Rafael Rodríguez, Carlos, 150

Randall, Margaret, 3

Rape, 74, 103, 188

Rationing, 148, 149; criticisms of, 160, 162; positive depictions of, 159

Ray, Manuel, 177

Rebel army: appeal of, 44; decisions to join, 62; formation of, 23–24, 47–48, 71; sexual restraint in, 73–75; size of, 48. *See also Barbudos*; Twenty-Sixth of July Movement

Rescate, 184

Revolución (newspaper), 129

Revolutionary Democratic Front, 205

Revolutionary Directorate (*Directorio Revolucionario*, DR), 38, 42, 47–48, 50, 59, 66, 77, 90, 174; conflict with "Marquitos" Rodríguez of, 51–52; women's participation in, 77, 78, 92, 98–99, 120, 134, 210

Revolutionary (insurgent) violence: criticisms of, 51, 108; debates over, 40, 46, 47; gendered impact of, 40–43; justifications for, 47, 63, 96–97

"Revolution within the Revolution," 1, 12

Rodríguez, Marcos ("Marquitos"), 51–52, 54

Rodríguez Gómez, Nieves, 90–91

Rosales de Westbrook, Dora, 60, 86

Rumors, 29, 168; Fidel Castro's denunciation of, 202. *See also* Patria Potestad, rumored abolition of

Safe houses, 29, 95, 102

Sánchez Manduley, Celia, 21

San Martín, Marta, 48, 55, 237 (n. 100)

Santiago de Cuba: army and police violence in, 66, 83–84, 238 (n. 118); food protests in, 165, 255–56 (n. 149); student protests in, 219 (n. 31); Twenty-Sixth of July Movement in, 59, 90, 99; women's protests in, 77, 79–84, 86–88, 231–32 (n. 17)

Sarabia, Leida, 87

Serantes, Enrique Pérez, 182

Serra, Clementina, 183, 245 (n. 94), 247 (n. 122)

Service sector growth, 65, 137

Sex and sexuality: and Communist Party, 113; as factor hampering women's political participation, 99–102; and literacy campaign, 187–88, 194; and rebel army, 73–76; and women's militias, 129, 131. See also Homosexuality

Shortages. See Black market; Food shortages; Rationing

Sierra Maestra: formation of rebel army in, 25; journalists' visits to, 71–72; policing of sexuality in, 73–75; transcendent experience of rebels in, 39, 185; women combatants in, 116, 121, 128. See also Mariana Grajales Brigade; Twenty-Sixth of July Movement

Smith, Earl T., 82

Smith, Lois, 132, 192

Socialism: alleviation of household labor in, 163; Cuban nationalist forms of, 123; declaration of revolution as, 189; and first-wave feminism, 93; and gender equity, 3–4; and marriage, 189, 207

Soler, William, 81

Southern Cone, disappearances in, 83

Soviet Union, 123, 124, 147; children, marriage, and family in, 207–8; and Cuban Communist Party, 108–9; as inspiration to FDMC, 112–13

Spanish Civil War, 93, 99, 131. See also Exiles; Immigrants, Spanish, in Cuba

State violence: during funerals, 57; impact of, 40, 59, 84; and production of "martyrs," 55–57; shifts in patterns of, 11, 84–85; against students; 60, 103; use of spectacle in, 84–85; against women activists, 87, 103–4; women's denunciations of, 80–84, 86, 88–92, 96–97. See also Revolutionary violence

Strikes: general revolutionary, plans for, 28, 66–67; in response to death of Frank País, 66, 83–84

Students: anti-Batista protests among, 25–27, 219 (n. 31); anticommunist protests among, 182, 259 (n. 57); sent to Soviet Union, 263 (n. 114). See also Education, revolutionary changes to; Federation of University Students; Literacy campaign; University of Havana

Suardíaz, Luis, 152

Taber, Robert, 71

Taylor, Diana, 85

Telephone, opposition use of, 29, 202

Television, 15, 37, 40, 183

Tiendas del pueblo, 148

Torture by Batista regime, 54–55, 56, 58, 61, 81, 83

Tosh, John, 50

Tourism: criticisms of American, 34, 39; "popular" (revolutionary), 179, 180

Triple A, 47

Twenty-Sixth of July Movement: changing strategies of, 46–47, 66–70; formation of, 47; and organized labor, 66–70; "precursors" to, 19; relations with Communist Party of, 67, 123–24, 126; sexism within, 128; and sexuality, 102; Sierra versus el llano in, 48–49. See also Barbudos; Castro, Fidel; Rebel army

Unión de Muchachas (Venezuela), 110

Unión Laborista de Mujeres, 110

United Nations' Universal Declaration of Human Rights, 87

United States: anticommunism in, 195–96; and Cold War Caribbean, 24; Cuban reliance on trade with, 137, 144, 147, 150, 156; response to revolution, 144, 147–48. See also Anti-imperialism; Bay of Pigs

United States Information Agency (USIA), 196

University of Havana, 25–27, 49, 98. *See also* Federation of University Students; Students

Urban centers. *See* Cities, role in revolution of

Urban reform, 117, 177, 178

Urban underground, 11, 42, 47–48; importance of funerals in, 60; and martyrdom, 55–60; and police repression, 55; politics of, 48–49; psychological stress of, 55; size of, 48, 77; women's participation in, 97–100

Valdespino, Andrés, 182

Venezuela, 24, 64, 110, 233 (n. 38), 243 (n. 65)

Violence. *See* Revolutionary violence; State violence

Verdery, Katherine, 57

Weigand, Kate, 110

Westad, Odd Arne, 212

Westbrook, Joe, 60, 86

Whites and whiteness: anti-Batista movement activists as predominantly, 46, 54, 73, 98, 225 (n. 43), 237 (n. 99); anti-Castro movement activists as predominantly, 172, 199–202, 204; versus "black" forms of consumption, 252 (n. 91); women consumers as, 139, 140, 156. *See also* Afro-Cubans; Race and racism

"Woman Question," rise of: in prerevolutionary Marxist Left, 107–10; in revolutionary moment, 5, 7

Women: all-women's anti-Batista groups, 92–96; as anti-Castro activists, 197–204; and Communist Party, 107–11; as consumers, 20, 32–34, 38–39, 139–43; "defeminization" of, 197–98; demands of in revolution, 121–23, 127–31; difficulties in quantifying, 77–78; as historical

agents, 2; in literacy campaign, 187–88; and martyrdom, 59–61; and maternalist protest, 80–91; and Ortodoxo Party, 21, 30, 87, 93; prevalence of in anti-Batista movement, 20–22, 29, 30, 38–39, 40–43, 78; and shortages, 151–55, 163–69; in urban underground, 97–104. *See also* Consumption; Federation of Cuban Women; Gender relations, changes to; Housewives; "Woman Question," rise of

Women's Congress of 1939, 93, 111

Women's International Democratic Federation (WIDF), 110–12, 239–40 (n. 17)

Women's Revolutionary Brigades (*Brigadas Femeninas Revolucionarias*), 131, 132; formation and activities of, 116–19; and Marxist women, 123–27; and women's militia, 128–29

Women's Revolutionary Unity (*Unidad Femenina Revolucionaria*, UFR), 119–23; and high food prices, 145; on USSR, 124; on women's militia, 129–30

Women's Section of the Twenty-Sixth of July Movement (*Sección Femenina del 26 de Julio*), 116–18

Workers' Social Circles (*Círculos Sociales Obreros*), 179, 180

Working class: criticism of gender reform, 193–94; insurgent disparagement of, 69; response to rationing, 159–60; revolutionary uplift of, 173–80, 206–7; women's demands, 121–23. *See also* Labor, organized

World War II, 127

Yabur Maluf, Alfredo, 174, 176, 177

Youth: Cuban revolution's impact on, 44, 45; frivolity of American, 38. *See also* Students

Zolov, Eric, 47

Envisioning Cuba

Michelle Chase, *Revolution within the Revolution: Women and Gender Politics in Cuba, 1952–1962* (2015).

Aisha K. Finch, *Rethinking Slave Rebellion in Cuba: La Escalera and the Insurgencies of 1841–1844* (2015).

Christina D. Abreu, *Rhythms of Race: Cuban Musicians and the Making of Latino New York City and Miami, 1940–1960* (2015).

Anita Casavantes Bradford, *The Revolution Is for the Children: The Politics of Childhood in Havana and Miami, 1959–1962* (2014).

Tiffany A. Sippial, *Prostitution, Modernity, and the Making of the Cuban Republic, 1840–1920* (2013).

Kathleen López, *Chinese Cubans: A Transnational History* (2013).

Lillian Guerra, *Visions of Power in Cuba: Revolution, Redemption, and Resistance, 1959–1971* (2012).

Carrie Hamilton, *Sexual Revolutions in Cuba: Passion, Politics, and Memory* (2012).

Sherry Johnson, *Climate and Catastrophe in Cuba and the Atlantic World during the Age of Revolution* (2011).

Melina Pappademos, *Black Political Activism and the Cuban Republic* (2011).

Frank Andre Guridy, *Forging Diaspora: Afro-Cubans and African Americans in a World of Empire and Jim Crow* (2010).

Ann Marie Stock, *On Location in Cuba: Street Filmmaking during Times of Transition* (2009).

Alejandro de la Fuente, *Havana and the Atlantic in the Sixteenth Century* (2008).

Reinaldo Funes Monzote, *From Rainforest to Cane Field in Cuba: An Environmental History since 1492* (2008).

Matt D. Childs, *The 1812 Aponte Rebellion in Cuba and the Struggle against Atlantic Slavery* (2006).

Eduardo González, *Cuba and the Tempest: Literature and Cinema in the Time of Diaspora* (2006).

John Lawrence Tone, *War and Genocide in Cuba, 1895–1898* (2006).

Samuel Farber, *The Origins of the Cuban Revolution Reconsidered* (2006).

Lillian Guerra, *The Myth of José Martí: Conflicting Nationalisms in Early Twentieth-Century Cuba* (2005).

Rodrigo Lazo, *Writing to Cuba: Filibustering and Cuban Exiles in the United States* (2005).

Alejandra Bronfman, *Measures of Equality: Social Science, Citizenship, and Race in Cuba, 1902–1940* (2004).

Edna M. Rodríguez-Mangual, *Lydia Cabrera and the Construction of an Afro-Cuban Cultural Identity* (2004).

Gabino La Rosa Corzo, *Runaway Slave Settlements in Cuba: Resistance and Repression* (2003).

Piero Gleijeses, *Conflicting Missions: Havana, Washington, and Africa, 1959–1976* (2002).

Robert Whitney, *State and Revolution in Cuba: Mass Mobilization and Political Change, 1920–1940* (2001).

Alejandro de la Fuente, *A Nation for All: Race, Inequality, and Politics in Twentieth-Century Cuba* (2001).